A Balanced Introduction to Computer Science

A Balanced Introduction to Computer Science

David Reed

Creighton University

PEARSON

Prentice
Hall

Upper Saddle River, NJ 07468

Library of Congress Cataloging-in-Publication Data
CIP DATA AVAILABLE.

Vice President and Editorial Director, ECS: *Marcia J. Horton*
Senior Acquisitions Editor: *Kate Hargett*
Editorial Assistant: *Michael Giacobbe*
Editor in Chief, Development: *Carol Trueheart*
Development Editor: *Lauren Trees*
Vice President and Director of Production and Manufacturing, ESM: *David W. Riccardi*
Executive Managing Editor: *Vince O'Brien*
Managing Editor: *Camille Trentacoste*
Production Editor: *Irwin Zucker*
Director of Creative Services: *Paul Belfanti*
Creative Director: *Carole Anson*
Art Director and Cover Manager: *Jonathan Boylan*
Managing Editor, AV Management and Production: *Patricia Burns*
Art Editor: *Xiaohong Zhu*
Director, Image Resource Center: *Melinda Reo*
Manager, Rights and Permissions: *Zina Arabia*
Manager, Visual Research: *Beth Brenzel*
Manager, Cover Visual Research and Permissions: *Karen Sanatar*
Image Permission Coordinator: *Carolyn Gauntt*
Photo Researcher: *Rachel Lucas*
Manufacturing Manager: *Trudy Pisciotti*
Manufacturing Buyer: *Lisa McDowell*
Marketing Manager: *Pamela Hersperger*

© 2005 Pearson Education, Inc.
Pearson Prentice Hall
Pearson Education, Inc.
Upper Saddle River, NJ 07458

The author and publisher of this book have used their best efforts in preparing this book. These efforts include the development, research, and testing of the theories and programs to determine their effectiveness. The author and publisher make no warranty of any kind, expressed or implied, with regard to these programs or the documentation contained in this book. The author and publisher shall not be liable in any event for incidental or consequential damages in connection with, or arising out of, the furnishing, performance, or use of these programs.

Printed in the United States of America
10   9   8   7   6   5   4   3   2   1

ISBN 0-13-046709-X

Pearson Education Ltd., *London*
Pearson Education Australia Pty. Ltd., *Sydney*
Pearson Education Singapore, Pte. Ltd.
Pearson Education North Asia Ltd., *Hong Kong*
Pearson Education Canada, Inc., *Toronto*
Pearson Educación de Mexico, S.A. de C.V.
Pearson Education—Japan, *Tokyo*
Pearson Education Malaysia, Pte. Ltd.
Pearson Education, Inc., *Upper Saddle River, New Jersey*

Dedicated to Laura, Charlie and Jack —
with all my love and thanks.

Trademark Information

Adobe Photoshop and FrameMaker are registered trademarks of Adobe, Inc.

AMD Athlon is a trademark of Advanced Micro Devices, Inc.

AOL is a registered trademark and AOL Instant Messenger is a trademark of Time Warner, Inc.

Apple Mac OS X is a registered trademark and SimpleText is a trademark of Apple Computers, Inc.

Bose Wave radio is a registered trademark of Bose Corporation.

Corel WordPerfect is a registered trademark of Corel, Inc.

Cray 20-XMP is a trademark of Cray, Inc.

DEC and Hewlett-Packard are registered trademarks of Hewlett-Packard, Inc.

Dell Dimension 4400 and Dell Axim PDA are a trademarks of Dell

Doom is a registered trademark of Id Software, Inc.

Emacs is a trademark of UniPress Software, Inc.

Fairchild Semiconductor is a registered trademark of Fairchild Semiconductor Corporation.

GIF (Graphics Interchange Format) (The Graphics Interchange Format© is the Copyright property of CompuServe Incorporated. GIF$^{(sm)}$ is a Service Mark property of CompuServe Incorporated.)

Google is a registered trademark of Google, Inc.

IBM is a registered trademark of International Business Machines, Inc.

Intel, Celeron, and Intel Pentium 4 are registered trademarks of Intel Corporation.

International Data Corporation (IDC) is a registered trademark of International Data Corporation.

KRAFT Macaroni and Cheese is a registered trademark used with the permission of Kraft Foods.

Linux is a registered trademark of Linus Torvalds.

Macromedia Flash is a trademark of Macromedia, Inc.

Magic 8 Ball is a registered trademark owned by and used with permission from Mattel, Inc. ©2003 Mattel, Inc. All Rights Reserved.

MCI WorldCom is a registered trademark of MCI, Inc.

Microsoft Windows XP, Internet Explorer, Microsoft Works, Microsoft Outlook Microsoft Office XP, NotePad, WordPad, and Word, Visual Studio, PowerPoint, Metrowerks CodeWarrior, Hotmail, and MSN are registered trademarks of Microsoft Corporation.

MITS Altair 8800 is a trademark of Micro Instrumentation Telemetry Systems.

Motorola is a registered trademark of Motorola, Inc.

Motorola PowerPC G4 is a trademark of Motorola

National Semiconductors is a registered trademark of National Semiconductor Corporation.

Netscape Navigator is a registered trademark of Netscape, Inc.

Norton Anti-Virus is a trademark of Symantec Corporation.

Palm m130 and Handspring Treo are trademarks of PalmOne, Inc.

Quicken New User Edition is a registered trademark of Intuit, Inc.

Sprint is a registered trademark of Sprint Communications Company, L.P.

Sun Microsystems is a registered trademark and Java and JavaScript are trademarks of Sun Microsystems, Inc.

TaxCut is a registered trademark of H&R Block.

Texas Instruments is a registered trademark of Texas Instruments Incorporated.

Unified Modeling Language (UML) is a trademark of Object Management Group.

UNIX is a registered trademark of The Open Group.

Yahoo!News, Yahoo!Search, Yahoo!Mail are registered trademarks of Yahoo, Inc.

Contents

≣ 9 Event-Driven Programming 155

▪▪▪ 10 Computer Science as a Discipline 176

17 JavaScript Arrays 304

18 Computers and Society 327

Appendix A: Browser Basics 343

Appendix B: Common Text Editors 350

Preface

Welcome to *A Balanced Introduction to Computer Science*. There are a number of reasons why you might be reading this text. Perhaps you have had limited experience with computers and would like to know more about how they work and how to control them. Or perhaps you recognize the marketability of programming and computer literacy, and would like to expand your skills for the future job market. Or perhaps you are just curious about the World Wide Web and want to know what all the hype is really about. In any case, you are embarking on what I hope will be an exciting, challenging, and rewarding experience.

Balancing Breadth and Depth

This text is different from most introductory computing texts in that it attempts to maintain a balance between computing breadth and programming depth. Traditionally, introductory texts have focused almost exclusively on one approach or the other. Breadth-based texts have emphasized a broad understanding of computers and computer science. By surveying a wide range of topics such as computer organization, graphics, networking, and technology in society, the intent is for students to experience the breadth of the field and develop a perspective to later understand and appreciate the role of technology in their lives. Alternatively, depth-based texts have focused more deeply on the role of programming in computing. The discipline of programming not only develops problem-solving skills, but also is central to many areas of computer science and thus important to appreciating their significance.

While each of these approaches has merit, there are potential weaknesses to either extreme. A breadth-based survey of computing can be too superficial, presenting a broad perspective to students who lack the context or experience to fully comprehend it. And while programming depth can provide experience with many computing concepts, developing proficiency as a programmer and problem-solver requires extensive hands-on experience (especially when learning a complex language such as C++ or Java), and may not be directly relevant to all students.

The approach taken by this text is to balance breadth and depth. Chapters are included on concepts and issues in computing that are most relevant to the beginning student, including computer terminology, the Internet and World Wide Web, the history of computing, the organization and manufacture of computer technology, and technology's impact on society. Mixed among these breadth topics are chapters that introduce fundamental programming concepts and skills in a hands-on, tutorial format. Using the programming language JavaScript, students will develop skills in designing and implementing interactive Web pages. JavaScript's simplicity, natural interfaces, and seamless integration with the Web make it possible for novices to develop interesting and engaging programs quickly. In addition, JavaScript is always available (for free!) for anyone with a Web browser, making it easy to apply programming skills learned from this text to everyday problems.

In striking a balance between breadth and depth, the intent of this text is not to be a complete and exhaustive survey of computing or a reference on JavaScript. Breadth chapters focus on key ideas and concepts that are relevant to beginning students as they attempt to understand computing technology and the field of computer science. Likewise, programming chapters focus on JavaScript features that demonstrate fundamental programming concepts while also allowing for interesting and engaging applications. Links to other sources are provided for the interested reader, including supplemental material and exercises at the end of each programming chapter. This provides a broad perspective on computing as well as enough problem solving and programming depth to appreciate the significance of computer science.

Text Goals

There are three main goals to this text and its accompanying resources. First, it serves to expose the student to the breadth that is the field of computer science. Computer science is more than just the study of computers–it focuses on all facets of computation, from the design and analysis of algorithms (step-by-step sequences of instructions for carrying out tasks), to the engineering and manufacture of computer components, to the development of software systems. Through readings and the use of online resources, the student will study topics such as the history of computer technology, the underlying architecture of modern computers, the translation and execution sequence of programs, and the capabilities and limitations of computation. Using software simulators, the student will build virtual components of a computer and watch the flow of information as a program is translated and executed on the low-level machinery. Through this combination of reading and experimentation, hopefully these concepts will come alive for the student and provide a sense of what computer science is all about.

The second main goal of this text is to teach the student the fundamentals of programming. *Programming is the process of solving problems on the computer*, that is, devising solutions to specific tasks and formalizing those solutions in a language the computer can understand and execute. Programming is the central activity in computer science, providing an inroad to many of the interesting facets and challenges of the field. In learning to program, the student will be learning to analyze problems, think logically, formalize his or her thoughts, and solve problems. It is a discipline, since a systematic approach must be learned, but it is also a creative process, since novel approaches must be found to attack new problems. And since many of the skills developed in programming apply to problem solving in general, experience gained through this text should carry over to other disciplines as well. Finally, the fact that programs are written in the context of interactive Web pages highlights the relevance of programming to applications students use everyday.

The third main goal of this text is to demonstrate the scientific and interdisciplinary nature of computing. Research in various fields of study, most notably the mathematical and natural sciences, is becoming increasingly dependent on computers and programming. By studying and investigating applications in fields such as biology, physics, psychology, and even economics, the student will learn to apply his or her programming skills to a wide range of problems. In addition, the student will develop empirical skills that are common to all scientific endeavors.

Text Features

The balanced approach to computer science and programming taken by this text is evident in the layout of its chapters. There are two types of chapters in the text, those that use narrative to introduce key concepts of computing (i.e., the computer science breadth chapters: 1, 3, 6, 8, 10, 12, 14, 16, and 18) and those that use a tutorial style to develop problem-solving and programming skills (i.e., the programming depth chapters: 2, 4, 5, 7, 9, 11, 13, 15, and 17). The interleaving of these chapters is both intentional and important. It provides variety in the types of activities students will undertake, and thus may be more accommodating to students with different learning styles. Readings and classroom discussions serve as buffers between programming tutorials, allowing the student more time to assimilate programming concepts and skills before beginning the next tutorial. Finally, and perhaps most importantly, the interleaving of chapters supports the student's understanding and appreciation of the content. For example, after developing their own home pages in Chapter 2, students are better prepared to understand what the Web is and how it works in Chapter 3.

Features of the computer science breadth chapters:

- They focus on topics that are most relevant to a beginning student. The goal is not to inundate the student with details, but instead to emphasize the central ideas of that topic.
- Illustrations are used whenever possible to illuminate key points.
- Web-based visualization tools (accessible at the book's Web page: `http://www.prenhall.com/reed`) are provided to complement many of the chapters and support active learning. For example, chapter 14 integrates a suite of simulators that allows the student to explore the internal workings of computers.
- Each chapter ends with a Chapter Summary and Review Questions that encourage reflection and the integration of content from that chapter.

Features of the programming depth chapters:

- They are presented in a tutorial style, recognizing that the only way to learn programming (and, more generally, problemsolving) is to actually do it.
- Exercises follow an incremental approach, allowing students to master programming concepts by first studying existing programs (which are accessible at the book's Web page: `http://www.prenhall.com/reed`) and then making modifications using new tools and constructs. Eventually, students create new programs for solving interesting and hopefully engaging problems.
- Common errors and points of confusion are identified and discussed in special sections called "Common errors to avoid…"
- Problem-solving and program design advice is provided in special sections called "Designer Secrets."
- Each chapter includes a Chapter Summary that presents the key concepts and programming tools in a concise bullet list.
- Supplemental material and exercises are provided at the end of each chapter for further study.

Appendices are provided at the end of this text as references. Appendices A and B provide tutorials on Web browsers and common text editors, which may be useful for students who are not already familiar with computers and the Web. Appendix C is an HTML reference, collecting all of the HTML elements used throughout the text in a table. Appendix D is a JavaScript reference, which similarly collects all of the JavaScript programming constructs. Appendix E provides a full listing of the `random.js` library, which is introduced in Chapter 5 and used in subsequent chapters.

Finally, a collection of nine laboratory assignments, each corresponding to a programming depth chapter, is available to supplement this text. These lab assignments emphasize experimentation, analysis, and the use of programs for solving interdisciplinary problems.

Advice for the Student

This text does not assume any previous experience with computer applications or programming. Certainly, familiarity with computers is a plus (e.g., word processing or email), but is not necessary. Basic computer terminology will be covered in the text as needed, and appendices are provided to assist the novice with simple computer skills, such as using a text editor, saving files to a disk, and browsing the Web. The goal is not to teach you everything you could ever want to know about computers and programming, but instead to provide you with a working set of skills and knowledge. Whenever possible, links to further readings will be provided in case you are interested in a topic and would like to learn more.

Through the use of readings, exercises, and experiments, this text aspires to provide you with a broad sense of what computer science is all about, while simultaneously developing depth as a problem-solver and programmer. The choice of JavaScript as the medium for developing programming skills was specifically made to make this task simpler and also more relevant to students. JavaScript was designed to be a simple scripting language for controlling pages on the World Wide Web. Using JavaScript, you can control actions with the click of the mouse or generate dynamic images on a page. As such, learning JavaScript opens the door for many exciting applications on the Web. Similarities between JavaScript and the programming languages Java and C++ also mean that experience with JavaScript programming can be a stepping-stone to larger-scale programming in these industry-strength languages.

Whether you choose to continue studies in computer science, or merely wish to apply computing skills to your everyday life, the balanced coverage of computing topics as found in this text should prove valuable to you. As always, enjoy and learn.

Advice for the Instructor

The layout of the chapters in this text is designed to provide maximum flexibility for the instructor. Depending on the preferences of the instructor and the goals of the particular course, the right balance and order of the material can be determined for your needs. If you are teaching a traditional non-major course, then a roughly even balance between breadth and depth probably makes sense. If the students are computer knowledgeable and taking this course as part of a computer science sequence, then some breadth topics may be skipped or shortened to allow for greater programming depth.

For example, the materials in this text have been used in a non-majors course at Creighton University. Since the majority of the students in this course are not planning to become computer science majors, the emphasis in the course is in providing a balance between essential topics and fundamental programming concepts. As such, there is a roughly 50/50 division between breadth and depth. Only the first six programming chapters (Chapters 2, 4, 5, 7, 9, and 11) are covered, each taking up one week of class time. While this may seem limiting (no loops?!), the material in these chapters is sufficient to impart the flavor of programming and also to allow the students to do interesting and engaging things. Mixed between these programming chapters are most of the breadth chapters, each taking up one or two 50-minute periods for lecture and/or discussion. Not all of the breadth chapters from the text are covered each semester, and the order may vary as well. For example, in a recent semester I skipped Chapter 8 and moved the content of Chapter 12 later in the course. In addition, I integrated four laboratories into the class periods, which served to apply the students' programming and problem-solving skills to interdisciplinary problems.

By contrast, these materials have been used in a very different course at Dickinson College. This particular course is the first in a two-course sequence that fulfills a laboratory science requirement for the college, and is also considered the first course in the computer science major. As such, greater expectations in terms of time and effort are expected of the students. Weekly two-hour lab periods accompany the class, in which students complete lab assignments. Programming chapters are covered in two to three 50-minute periods each, and select breadth chapters are covered in one or two 50-minute periods.

One of the strengths of this book is the flexibility that it provides the instructor. An instructor might choose one of these extremes, or select a different balance of breadth and depth to best suit his or her students. For example, I envision that many instructors might choose to cover Chapter 13 (loops), perhaps substituting for in-class laboratories or certain breadth topics. The interleaving of breadth and depth chapters throughout the text is specifically designed to support the content and also vary the types of learning activities students engage in. While the relative order in which the programming depth chapters are covered is constrained by their content, it is certainly possible to omit or move some of the computer science breadth chapters. For example, some instructors might prefer covering the history of computers (Chapter 6) earlier in the course, or perhaps covering the chapters on how computers work (Chapter 14) and are built (Chapter 16) together.

As always, enjoy, teach, and learn.

Acknowledgments

This book is the culmination of a long process of thinking, experimenting, implementing, classroom testing, rethinking, reexperimenting, and so on. There are numerous people who have contributed to this book during its development, both tangibly and with moral support. The people at Prentice Hall have been outstanding, including editors Petra Recter and Kate Hargett and production editor Irwin Zucker. I'm eternally grateful to developmental editor Lauren Trees, who helped shape my words my vision – this is certainly a much better book thanks to her contribution. I would also like to thank the following outside reviewers, whose insightful comments were a great help:

Debra Burhans, *Canisius College*
Martin Chetlen, *Moorpark College*
Donald Costello, *University of Nebraska*
Erica Eddy, *University of Wisconsin – Parkside*
Karen Ehrlich, *SUNY College at Fredonia*
Michael Hennessy, *University of Oregon*
Rowan Lindley, *Westchester Community College*

Ronald Marsh, *University of North Dakota*
David Middleton, *Arkansas Tech University*
Arnie Miles, *Georgetown University*
Vince Offenback, *North Seattle Community College*
Roger Priebe, *University of Texas – Austin*
Mary Ann May-Pumphrey *DeAnza College*
Charles Riedesel, *University of Nebraska -- Lincoln*
Patrick Sebrechts, *California State University – San Marcos*
Jim Schmolze, *Tufts University*
Gene Sheppard, *Georgia Perimeter College*
David Valentine, *Slippery Rock University*
Mark Williams, *Lane Community College*

The concepts behind this book were initially formed while I was at Dickinson College, inspired by a hands-on course developed by Nancy Baxter-Hastings. Numerous colleagues at Dickinson taught early versions of the material and contributed new ideas, especially Grant Braught and Craig Miller. In addition to those early colleagues, I would like to thank colleagues at Creighton University, who have also been supportive of the course and its material. ... As a general inspiration and source for great ideas, I gratefully acknowledge my good friend Owen Astrachan, who served as my early role model in teaching as well as embarrassing me in public on numerous occasions.

On a personal note, I would like to thank my parents who raised me to value knowledge and learning, and supported me in my studies. My wife Laura has probably suffered the most during the development of this book–losing me to many late nights of work and having to listen to endless stories about what did and didn't work in class. Her willingness to listen, provide keen insights, and pick up the slack for me at home has made this book possible. Finally, special thanks go to our boys, Charlie and Jack, for their love and patience. Maybe daddy will get some sleep now that the book is done, and he'll be a little perkier in the mornings.

Dave Reed
Creighton University

A Balanced Introduction to Computer Science

Computer Basics

This chapter uses narrative, illustrations, and review questions to introduce computer science and technology concepts.

Computers are incredibly fast, accurate, and stupid: humans are incredibly slow, inaccurate and brilliant; together they are powerful beyond imagination.

Albert Einstein

Computers are to computing as instruments are to music. Software is the score whose interpretations amplifies our reach and lifts our spirits. Leonardo da Vinci called music the shaping of the invisible, and his phrase is even more apt as a description of software.

Alan Kay
Scientific American, 1984

The easiest way to tell the difference between hardware and software is to kick it. If it hurts your toe, it's hardware.

Anonymous

The computer, at least in the form we think of it today, is a relatively new technological development. The first electronic computers were built in the 1940s, and desktop computers accessible to average people date back only to the late 1970s. In a very short time, computers have become integral to nearly every aspect of our society, from business transactions to personal communications. However, while many people use them for work and pleasure every day, few have even a basic understanding of how computers work.

This chapter presents an overview of computer technology, focusing on what computers are, how they are organized, and what they can do. The coverage is not meant to be exhaustive—many of the topics introduced here will be revisited in later chapters. However, this overview should provide a framework for understanding computing concepts as you encounter them throughout the book, as well as making you a wiser consumer of computer technology.

What Is a Computer?

When you think of the word "computer," you probably picture a machine that sits on a desk and is used to create documents, send email, or explore the World Wide Web. This type of computer is often referred to as a ***personal computer*** (***PC***), since it is designed for use by one person at a time, or as a ***desktop computer***, since it is small enough to fit on top of a desk. When people contemplate computers today, many think only of desktop machines; however, a wide variety of computers are used to fulfill different needs. Some, known as ***supercomputers***, are large enough to fill entire rooms and can perform trillions of calculations per second. Researchers involved in complex tasks, such as modeling weather patterns or testing engineering designs, are the primary users of supercomputers. Smaller, less expensive computers include ***laptops***, which can fit in a briefcase, and ***palmtops***, (also called ***personal digital assistants***, or PDAs), which you can hold in your hand. Individuals employ these types of computers for tasks such as word processing and electronic mail. In addition, millions of tiny computers are embedded in (e.g., built into) and used to control everyday devices, such as automobiles, air conditioners, and microwave ovens. Figure 1.1 depicts four diverse types of computers, ranging from a supercomputer that takes up a room to a PDA that fits in a person's hand.

Super Computer
Cray® 20-XMP™

Desktop Computer
Dell Dimension™ 4400

Laptop Computer
Fujistu Amilo M

Palmtop
Palm™ m130

Figure 1.1 Various types of computers.

In general, we will define a ***computer*** as a device that receives, stores, and processes information. While the computers described above may look different and perform diverse functions, they all fit this general definition. For example, a supercomputer is able to receive data on current weather patterns, store that data, and process it to predict when storm conditions will arise. A personal computer is able to recognize characters typed by the user, store these characters in files, and process them to produce a document, spreadsheet, or email message. Likewise, a computer embedded in a car's antilock brake system is able to sense the spin of the wheels, process that data to compute the optimal braking pattern, and bring the car to a safe stop.

Although computers are pervasive in everyday life, few people truly comprehend how they are organized and perform their tasks. Even purchasing a personal computer can be an overwhelming experience involving highly technical information and obscure computer jargon. For example, Figure 1.2 compares the advertised specifications of two desktop computer systems marketed by a major computer manufacturer (June 2003). System 1 is a ***low-end*** computer system, indicating that it is inexpensive but provides limited features and utilizes older technology. System 2 is a ***high-end*** computer, which maximizes performance by incorporating the latest technology, but at a higher cost. Understanding the tradeoffs between these two models requires a significant amount of computer knowledge—and this is a streamlined version of only one table of options for one category of computer system marketed by one company!

The remainder of this chapter will define key terms from Figure 1.2, as well as describing the basic workings of computers. Supplementing the explanations of many of the computing concepts, the chapter provides "Technical Details . . . " relating those concepts to the systems in Figure 1.2. Thus, after completing this chapter, you should be able to appreciate many of the differences between these two systems.

A first step toward understanding the table in Figure 1.2—and, by extension, computers in general—is to distinguish between hardware and software. ***Hardware*** refers to the physical components of the computer, such as the monitor, keyboard, and hard drive. ***Software*** refers to the programs that

	Desktop System 1	Desktop System 2
CPU	2.2 GHz Intel® Celeron® Processor	3.2 GHz Intel® Pentium® 4 Processor
Memory		
Cache	256 K Cache	512 K Cache
RAM	256 MB RAM	1 GB RAM
Hard Drive	40 GB hard drive	500 GB hard drive
Floppy Drive	3.5" 1.44 MB diskette drive	3.5" 1.44 MB diskette drive
CD-ROM/DVD	48x/24x/48x CD-RW/DVD Drive	48x/24x/48x CD-RW/DVD-RW Drive
Input/Output		
Keyboard	Multi-function Keyboard	Multi-function Keyboard
Pointing Device	Optical Wheel Mouse	Optical Wheel Mouse
Screen	17" Color Monitor (15.9" viewable)	18" LCD Flat Panel Display
Speakers	Speakers	5-piece sound system
Modem	56 K Modem	56 K Modem
Network Adapter	10/100 Ethernet Adapter	10/100/1000 Ethernet Adapter
Software		
Operating System	Microsoft Windows XP Home Edition	Microsoft Windows XP Home Edition
Applications	Internet Explorer	Internet Explorer
	Microsoft Works	Microsoft Office XP Small Business
		Quicken® New User Edition
		Norton Anti-Virus™

Figure 1.2 Two different desktop computer systems. (Based on actual advertisements, June 2003.)

execute (i.e., run) on the computer, carrying out tasks such as word processing or accessing the Web. In Figure 1.2, the first three sections (labeled CPU, Memory, and Input/Output) refer to the systems' various hardware components. The last section refers to software components.

Hardware

Given the diversity of modern computers, it is difficult to describe a "typical" computer hardware system. However, certain features are common to most desktop machines, as shown in Figure 1.3.

Although specific components and their appearance may vary from computer to computer, virtually all modern computers have the same underlying structure. This structure is known as the ***von Neumann architecture***, named after computer science pioneer John von Neumann, who formalized his method of computer organization in the early 1950s. The von Neumann architecture identifies three essential components that work together to function as a computer (i.e., a device that receives, stores, and processes information). ***Input/output devices*** allow the user to communicate with the computer by entering commands and then viewing the results. ***Memory*** stores information for the computer to process, as well as ***programs***, or instructions specifying the steps necessary to complete specific tasks. Finally, the ***central processing unit*** (***CPU***) carries out programmatic steps in order to process data. These three components are connected by ***buses***, collections of wires that carry information in the form of electrical signals. (See Chapter 14 for more details about the underlying hardware of computers.)

Computers that use the von Neumann architecture are known as ***stored-program computers***, which means that they can initiate different tasks by retrieving different programs from memory. For example, to complete such actions as creating a text document or performing a computation, the CPU accesses the associated program instructions from memory and executes them in order. If the computer user wishes to perform a new task, he simply loads a new program into memory and instructs the CPU to execute that program. In fact, the von Neumann architecture enables multiple programs to reside in memory at the same time, allowing the CPU to juggle multiple tasks, such as switching back and forth between a Web browser and a text editor.

Figure 1.4 outlines the relationships among the three components of the von Neumann architecture. Additional details regarding how each component works and interacts within the computer are provided in subsequent subsections.

Figure 1.3 A common desktop computer system.

Figure 1.4 The von Neumann architecture.

Central Processing Unit (CPU)

The **central processing unit** (**CPU**) is the brains of the computer, responsible for controlling the internal workings of the machine. You will learn more about how the CPU works in Chapter 14. For now, we note that the CPU is made of **circuitry**, or electronic components wired together to control the flow of electrical signals. The CPU is by far the most complex part of a computer system. The Intel Pentium 4 processor, for example, contains circuitry comprised of more than 42 million individual components. All of this circuitry is packaged onto a small silicon chip encased in plastic, with metal pins for connecting the chip to other hardware components (Figure 1.5). Common CPUs include the Intel Pentium 4, AMD Athlon™, and Motorola PowerPC™ G4.

In controlling the workings of the computer, the CPU has two key tasks: (1) fetching program instructions from memory, and (2) executing those instructions. Since the ultimate behavior of computer programs can be complex, you might expect that the individual instructions executed by the CPU would be complex, but they are not. Even programs with advanced capabilities are broken into sequences of very simple instructions, such as "add two numbers" or "copy a value from one location to another." Of course, it may require thousands or even millions of such low-level instructions to specify

Figure 1.5 Pentium 4 circuitry and packaging.

the behavior of a Web browser or word processor. Fortunately, CPUs can process instruction sequences extremely quickly, which enables the processors to handle these immense programs. CPU speed is generally measured in gigahertz (GHz), which indicates how many *billions* of instructions a CPU can execute *in a second*. For example, a 1.8GHz CPU can execute approximately 1.8 billion simple instructions in a second, thus producing complex behavior at a speed that appears almost instantaneous to the human user.

Technical Details

The first row of the table in Figure 1.2 lists the type of CPU contained in each system. Both System 1 and System 2 utilize CPUs manufactured by Intel, the world's largest manufacturer of processors. However, the particular models used in the two systems differ in cost and performance. These variations are similar to the disparity between two car models manufactured by the same automobile company.

- System 2 contains a Pentium 4 processor, which is Intel's high-end processor. The Pentium 4 provides a broad range of capabilities and is marketed to advanced users who require a high level of performance in processing data and operations. For example, the Pentium 4 has special features that allow it to process images and video very quickly, making it well suited for running graphic-arts applications and interactive games.

- System 1 contains a Celeron processor, which is Intel's economy processor. In the same way that an economy car costs less because features such as weight or horsepower have been diminished, the capabilities of the less expensive Celeron processor are limited in comparison to those of the Pentium 4. The Celeron is marketed to casual users for whom price is the primary concern.

- In terms of processor speed, the 3.2GHz Pentium 4 from System 2 is considerably faster than is the 2.2GHz Celeron from System 1 (3.2 billion instructions per second vs. 2.2 billion instructions per second). These speeds might suggest that the Pentium 4 will complete tasks approximately 50% faster than the Celeron will, but direct comparisons based on CPU speed can be misleading, because different CPUs provide different sets of basic instructions. For example, the Celeron processor, with its more limited set of instructions, might require several steps to carry out a task that could be accomplished in one step using a Pentium 4. Thus, the Pentium 4 might perform certain tasks more than 50% faster than the Celeron does. It is also important to note that a faster CPU does not always translate to a faster application. The speed of many applications is constrained by other factors. For example, a word processing program is limited by the speed at which a person can type characters and the speed at which the monitor can display them—a faster processor will generally not improve its performance.

Memory

The **memory** is the part of a computer that stores programs and data. Modern computers are **digital** devices, which means that they store and process information as **binary digits**, or **bits**—units of data that correspond to one of two potential values. Since bits represent one of only two possibilities, they are referred to as **discrete** values—this is in contrast to **continuous** values (such as those used to store analog audio), which are represented on a scale containing an infinite range of possibilities. Bits are the building blocks of digital memory; usually, the two possible values of a bit are written as 0 and 1, but the values could just as easily be represented as off and on, open and closed, volts and no volts, and so on.

Of course, a single bit is not very useful for storing information, since it can only differentiate between two different values. If you combine two bits, however, there are four different patterns that can be used to represent values: 00, 01, 10, and 11. Similarly, three bits are able to represent eight values using the patterns: 000, 001, 010, 011, 100, 101, 110, and 111. Each additional bit of storage doubles the range of potential values that can be stored, as shown in Figure 1.6. In general, N bits can represent 2^N different values.

```
1 bit    → 2 values      0 1
2 bits   → 4 values      00 01 10 11
3 bits   → 8 values      000 001 010 011 100 101 110 111
4 bits   → 16 values     0000 0001 0010 0011 0100 0101 0110 0111 1000 1001 1010 1011 1100 1101 1111
5 bits   → 32 values     00000 00001 00010 00011 00100 00101 00110 00111 01000 01001 01010 ...
6 bits   → 64 values     000000 000001 000010 000011 000100 000101 000110 000111 001000 ...
7 bits   → 128 values    0000000 0000001 0000010 0000011 0000100 0000101 0000110 0000111 ...
8 bits   → 256 values    00000000 00000001 00000010 00000011 00000100 00000101 00000110 ...
9 bits   → 512 values    000000000 000000001 000000010 000000011 000000100 000000101 ...
10 bits  → 1,024 values  0000000000 0000000001 0000000010 0000000011 0000000100 0000000101 ...
    .
    .
    .
N bits   → 2^N values
```

Figure 1.6   Bit patterns.

Although the bit is the building block of digital memory, memory capacity is usually specified in bytes. A **byte** is a collection of 8 bits, and thus is capable of representing $2^8 = 256$ different values. Since that is sufficient for expressing many ranges of data, including every character on a keyboard, the byte is a more practical unit of measure. Collections of bytes can be identified using prefixes; for example, a **kilobyte** (*KB*) is roughly 1,000 bytes of storage, a **megabyte** (*MB*) is roughly one million bytes of storage, a **gigabyte** (*GB*) is roughly one billion bytes of storage, and a **terabyte** (*TB*) is roughly one trillion bytes of storage (Figure 1.7).

```
byte            → 8 bits
kilobyte (KB)   → 2^10 bytes  = 1,024 bytes (= 8,192 bits)
megabyte (MB)   → 2^20 bytes  = 1,048,576 bytes (= 8,388,608 bits)
gigabyte (GB)   → 2^30 bytes  = 1,073,741,824 bytes (= 8,589,934,592 bits)
terabyte (TB)   → 2^40 bytes  = 1,099,511,627,776 bytes (= 8,796,093,022,208 bits)
```

Figure 1.7   Common data storage units.

Since a byte is sufficient to represent a single character, it may be instructive to think of memory capacity in terms of text. A kilobyte is capable of storing more than 1,000 characters of text (e.g., a few paragraphs), a megabyte more than one million characters of text (e.g., a book), a gigabyte more than one billion characters of text (e.g., a small library), and a terabyte more than one trillion characters of text (e.g., a large book repository). While these capacities may seem large with respect to text, storing other types of data can require extensive memory. For example, a high-resolution photograph might require several megabytes of storage, the audio track of a single song as much as 50 megabytes, and a full-length video perhaps gigabytes.

Although the von Neumann architecture portrays computer memory as a single component, modern computers use a combination of memory types, each with its own performance and cost characteristics. The memory technologies that enable the fastest transfer of bits to and from the CPU are those that use electronic circuitry, where 1 and 0 are represented as the presence or absence of voltage over wires. **Cache** and **RAM** (short for Random Access Memory) are examples of this type of electronic memory. Cache memory, which is usually built into the CPU chip itself, utilizes high-speed circuitry to provide extremely fast access to data. RAM memory, which is packaged on separate chips, communicates with the CPU using lower-speed circuitry; thus, data stored in RAM cannot be accessed as quickly as data in cache, but RAM is significantly less expensive to build. Computer designers balance cost and performance by including a small amount (usually measured in kilobytes) of cache for storing critical data and a larger amount (usually measured in megabytes) of RAM for storing additional data.

Cache and RAM together form a computer's **main memory** (or **primary memory**), holding any and all data that the CPU is actively using. Although main memory is crucial in that its data can be accessed very quickly, it is expensive in comparison to other technologies. In addition, main memory is **volatile**, meaning that it requires a constant flow of electricity to maintain its stored values. When you turn off a computer, the values stored in cache and RAM are lost. Thus, computers require **secondary memory**, which is less expensive and can provide permanent storage. Secondary memory comes in a variety of technologies. A **hard disk** is a metal platter that stores bits as magnetized and nonmagnetized spots. The disk rotates under a sensor, which detects the magnetized spots and interprets them as bits. Although this technology is considerably slower than that of memory built from circuitry, hard-disk storage is much less expensive and can retain data without power. A hard disk is capable of permanently storing vast amounts of information (usually measured in gigabytes), which can be transferred into main memory when needed.

Floppy disks and CDs are examples of inexpensive, portable secondary memory. A **floppy disk** is a smaller, portable version of a hard disk, capable of storing up to 1.44MB of data on a 3.5-inch plastic disk. A **CD** (**Compact Disk**) is a metal disk that stores up to 700MB of data as patterns on its reflective surface. Using **CD-ROM** (**Compact Disk—Read Only Memory**) technology, the patterns are burned onto the surface of the disk with a laser and therefore cannot be overwritten. Using **CD-RW** (**Compact Disk—ReWritable**) technology, patterns are formed in a photosensitive coating on the surface of the disk, allowing data to be overwritten repeatedly.

| RAM chips | Hard disk | Floppy disk | Compact disk (CD) |

Figure 1.8   Various types of memory.

Input/Output devices (I/O)

Clearly, a computer is not very useful if it is not able to communicate with people or other computers. **Input devices** allow the computer to receive data and instructions from an external source, such as a person entering commands at a keyboard. Examples of input devices are keyboards, mice, track pads, microphones, and scanners. Similarly, **output devices** allow the computer to display or broadcast its results. Examples of output devices are monitors, printers, and speakers. Devices that enable the

Technical Details

Each example computer system described in Figure 1.2 contains and/or supports the full range of memory types, from cache and RAM down to floppy disk and CD. The primary differences between the systems are the amount of each memory type they contain and some technical details.

- System 2 contains twice as much cache (512KB vs. 256KB) and four times more RAM (1GB vs. 256MB) than System 1 does. Since main memory is used to store active data, System 2 will provide higher performance for users processing large amounts of information or running multiple programs simultaneously.

- Similarly, System 2 contains more than 12 times the hard-disk space that System 1 does, which means that System 2 can permanently store much larger amounts of information.

- System 1 includes a combination CD-RW/DVD drive, which can both read and write CDs. The numbers 48x/24x/48x specify the speed of the drive in comparison to that of the first CD drives, which had a data transfer rate of 150KB per second. In this case, the CD-RW drive is capable of writing a CD 48x faster (7.2MB/sec), rewriting an existing CD 24x faster (3.6MB/sec), and reading a CD 48x faster (7.2MB/sec). In addition, this drive can play DVDs, which are CDs containing full-length movies or other data stored using a proprietary compression format (see Chapter 12 for more details).

- System 2 includes a combination drive that is capable of reading and writing DVDs as well as CDs.

computer to communicate with other computers are both input and output devices. Examples include modems, Ethernet adapters, and wireless networking adapters. (See Chapter 10 for more details on networking.)

Input and output technology is constantly evolving, making it easier for users to interact with computers and for computers to interact with one another. For example, the introduction of the mouse as an input device was key to the popularization of personal computers in the 1980s. Similarly, improvements in flat-screen technology enabled smaller and lighter laptops computers to become affordable in the 1990s. Today, wireless-networking technology is becoming prevalent, allowing users to access email and the Web through personal digital assistants (PDAs) and cellular phones (Figure 1.9).

Figure 1.9 Dell AXIM™ PDA and Handspring Treo cellular phone/PDA.

Technical Details

Each example computer system in Figure 1.2 includes an assortment of input/output devices, including a keyboard and mouse for input, a screen and speakers for output, and a modem and Ethernet adapter for network communications.

- The term **multifunction keyboard** refers to the fact that, in addition to standard typewriter keys, the keyboard includes special keys (e.g., F1, Print, Home) that provide shortcuts for performing various functions.

- An **optical mouse** uses a laser mechanism—as opposed to a roller—in order to control pointer movements on the screen. Optical mice tend to be easier to use and require less maintenance than mechanical mice.

- The size of a display screen is measured diagonally, which means that the screen for System 1 is 17 inches from top-left corner to bottom-right corner. Measurements can be misleading when comparing different styles of screens, however. When dealing with monitors, part of the screen is obscured by the monitor casing—for this 17-inch monitor, only 15.9-inches are viewable to the user. By contrast, the entire screen on a flat-panel display is visible, so the 18-inch display for System 2 will actually provide 18-inches of usable screen.

- A **modem** (short for **modulator-demodulator**) is a device that allows computers to communicate with other computers over phone lines. Since computers are digital devices (storing data as bits) and most phone lines are analog (transmitting sounds as frequency waves), part of a modem's task is to convert digital data to analog signals for transmission, then convert analog signals back to digital data at the other end. The term "56K" refers to the speed at which the modem can transfer data—in this case, 56K bits per second. This is the fastest speed that can be obtained over phone lines; however, newer technologies (e.g., cable modems, DSL) are able to exceed it.

- **Ethernet** is a popular technology for connecting computers into a small-scale network. Ethernet connections can facilitate very fast communication (as much as 10Mbits, 100Mbits, or 1000Mbits per second, depending on the wiring used), but are limited in range and number of computers (see Chapter 10 for more details).

Software

Whereas **hardware** encompasses the physical components of the computer, **software** refers to the programs that execute on the hardware. A software program is a collection of instructions for the computer (more specifically, the CPU) to carry out in order to complete some task. For example, word processors such as Microsoft Word and Corel® WordPerfect® contain instructions for creating and managing documents; graphics programs such as Adobe® Photoshop® and Macromedia Flash contain instructions for creating and displaying graphical images; and Web browsers such as Microsoft Internet Explorer® and Netscape Navigator® contain instructions for accessing and displaying Web pages. Programs such as these are known as **applications software**, each being designed to carry out tasks within a particular application area, such as word processing, graphical design, or Web access. Since computers are used in many diverse application areas, it is not surprising that a wide variety of applications software is available.

Operating Systems

In contrast to applications software, **systems software** manages the resources and behavior of the computer itself. The largest and most integral systems software stored on a computer is its **operating system**, a collection of programs that controls how the CPU, memory, and I/O devices work together to execute programs. The most fundamental task performed by the operating system is to schedule the CPU's operation, controlling how data and instructions are loaded from memory and accessed by the

CPU. Most modern computers are ***multitasking*** machines, meaning that more than one program can reside in main memory at the same time, sharing the CPU's resources. For example, a personal computer user might perform several tasks simultaneously, such as downloading mail, viewing a Web page, and listening to music. By switching control of the CPU back and forth between active programs at a very fast rate, the operating system can produce the appearance of simultaneous execution.

The operating system also manages the computer's memory, organizing storage into files and directories (or folders). A ***file*** is a document that stores information, such as text (e.g., a term paper), an image (e.g., a picture of your family), sound (e.g., a song), or a program (e.g., a Web browser). The operating system keeps track of where individual files are stored so that they can be accessed when needed. To make storage and retrieval easier for the user, the operating system usually divides the memory into directories (or folders). A ***directory*** is a collection of files that are organized together and labeled with a common name. For example, a student in an English class might place all of her term papers in a single directory and name it "Term Papers," so that she can easily locate any particular paper. Directories are hierarchical in nature, meaning that a directory can store other directories, as well as files. Thus, the student could organize all of her schoolwork in a hierarchical structure by creating a directory for each class and then adding subdirectories for papers and assignments within each class directory.

Finally, the operating system connects the CPU and memory with the computer's other hardware components, allowing software applications to access memory and interact with the input/output devices. This allows a program being executed by the CPU to receive input from a keyboard, fetch data from a hard drive, display results on a screen, and even print the results to a laser printer. To make interacting with the computer easier for the user, most operating systems—including Microsoft Windows, Mac OS, and Linux—provide a ***graphical user interface*** (***GUI***). A GUI (pronounced *gooey*) uses intuitive, visual elements to simplify the process of viewing files and executing programs. Although their organization and appearance may differ, most modern GUIs have similar features and behaviors. Programs, directories, and files are represented as ***icons***—small pictures that convey some aspect of the element they symbolize. By pointing the mouse and clicking on a program or file icon, the user can obtain information about or perform operations on that program or file. For example, the Mac OS X operating system uses a stamp icon (at the bottom left of Figure 1.10) to represent its email application,

Figure 1.10   Example graphical user interface (GUI) from Mac OS X.

whereas Microsoft Windows XP uses an envelope icon (at the left of Figure 1.11). When a user clicks on one of these icons, the operating system opens the associated program, allowing the user to type and view email messages. In both GUIs, directories are represented as icons that look like folders, since a directory organizes files in the same way that a cardboard folder organizes papers.

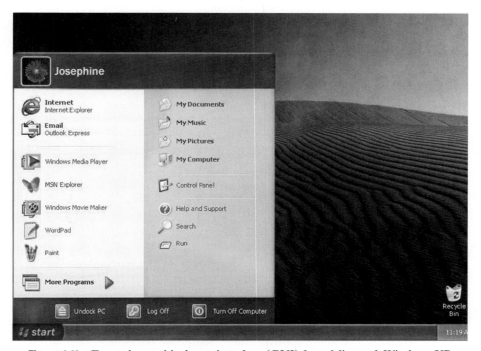

Figure 1.11 Example graphical user interface (GUI) from Microsoft Windows XP.

By clicking the mouse on a folder icon, the user can open that directory and view its contents in a separate window. *Windows* represent separate workspaces that can be active at the same time, displaying files or executing programs. The Mac OS X screen in Figure 1.10 shows three different windows: a program for viewing and sending email (labeled InBox), a listing of files in a directory (labeled Documents), and a window for showing live video (labeled Video Chat with Aki). The Windows XP screen in Figure 1.11 shows only one window: the Start window that contains icons for common programs and directories (labeled by the user name Josephine). Most GUIs also use *pull-down menus* of commands, which allow the user to identify and select common commands easily. For example, Figure 1.10 shows a menu of commands across the top of the screen, with headings such as Finder, File, and Edit. When the user clicks on one of these headings, a list of commands appears from which the user can select. In Figure 1.10, the commands associated with user logins (heading Todd Taylor) are shown.

Internet and the Web

Chapter 3 will describe the history and underlying structure of the Internet and the World Wide Web. However, since you will begin developing Web pages in Chapter 2, a brief overview is worthwhile at this point.

Despite a common misconception, the Internet and the World Wide Web are not the same thing. The Internet is a vast, international network of computers. In the same way that an interstate highway crosses state borders and links cities, the Internet crosses geographic borders and links computers. The physical connections may vary from high-speed dedicated cables (such as cable-modem connections) to slow but inexpensive phone lines, but the effect is that a person sitting at a computer in Omaha, Nebraska (or wherever) is able to share information and communicate with a computer in

Technical Details

Each example computer system in Figure 1.2 is packaged with the Microsoft Windows XP operating system and a suite of applications software.

- Both systems come with Internet Explorer, the Web browser freely distributed by Microsoft. As you will learn in the next section, a Web browser is a program that allows a user to view documents, images, and audio recordings from computers across the world.

- System 1 comes with Microsoft Works, a suite of basic programs for word processing, spreadsheets, and presentations.

- System 2 comes with Microsoft Office XP, a high-powered suite of applications software that includes Word (word processing), Excel (spreadsheets), PowerPoint (presentations), and Access (databases). Quicken (finance management) and Norton Anti-Virus (network security) applications are also provided.

Osaka, Japan (or wherever) (Figure 1.12). The Internet traces its roots back to 1969, when the first long-distance network was established to connect computers at UCLA, UCSB, Stanford Research Institute, and the University of Utah. Throughout the 1970s and 1980s, the network that would eventually be known as the Internet grew steadily; however, its use was limited primarily to government and academic institutions until the development of the World Wide Web in the 1990s.

Whereas the Internet is made up of hardware (computers and the connections that allow them to communicate), the World Wide Web is a collection of software that spans the Internet and enables

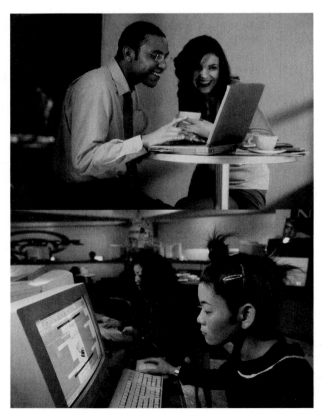

Figure 1.12 Internet users around the world.

THINK:

Internet is *hardware*
- consists of computers around the world and the communications links that connect them

World Wide Web is *software*
- consists of Web pages, images, sound files, etc., and the software that stores and retrieves these files

Figure 1.13 Internet = hardware, Web = software.

the interlinking of documents and resources (Figure 1.13). The basic idea for the Web was proposed in 1989 by Tim Berners-Lee of the European Laboratory for Particle Physics (CERN). In order to allow distant researchers to share information more easily, Berners-Lee designed a system through which documents—even those containing multimedia elements, such as images and sound clips— could be interlinked over the Internet. Through the use of well-defined rules, or **protocols**, that define how pages are formatted, documents could be shared across networks on various types of computers, allowing researchers to disseminate their research broadly. With the introduction of easy-to-use, graphical browsers for viewing documents in the mid 1990s, the Web became accessible to a broader public, resulting in the World Wide Web of today.

Web Browsers and Servers

A **Web page** is nothing more than a text document that contains additional formatting information in a language called **HTML (HyperText Markup Language)**. As you will see in Chapter 2, all you need to create a Web page is a simple text editor and familiarity with the HTML language. To view a Web page in which HTML formatting is properly applied, however, you need a special kind of computer program called a **Web browser**. The job of a Web browser is to access a Web page, interpret the HTML formatting information, and display the formatted page accordingly (see Figure 1.14). The two most popular browsers on the market today are Microsoft Internet Explorer and Netscape Navigator. Most modern computers are sold with one or both of these browsers already installed.

What makes the Web the "World Wide" Web is that, rather than being limited to a single computer, pages instead can be distributed to computers all across the Internet. A **Web server** is an Internet-enabled computer that executes software for providing access to certain Web documents. When you request a Web page, either by typing its name in your browser's Address box or by clicking a link, the browser sends a request over the Internet to the appropriate server. The server locates the specified page and sends it back to your computer.

Web Addresses

Web pages require succinct and specific names so that users can identify them and browsers can locate them. For this purpose, each page is assigned a **Uniform Resource Locator**, or **URL**. For example, the home page for this book has the following address, or URL:

`http://www.prenhall.com/reed/index.html`

| Signifies that the page is to be accessed using the standard means of retrieving Web pages, the HyperText Transfer Protocol (HTTP) | Specifies the name of the Web server that stores the page | Specifies the directory where the page is stored on the server | Specifies the name of the page. Usually, Web pages end with either `.html` or `.htm`, although other extensions are allowed |

A Web page is a text document that contains HTML formatting.

A Web browser is a program that interprets the HTML and displays the page.

Figure 1.14 A Web browser interprets HTML instructions and formats text in a page.

A URL begins with the protocol prefix `http://`, which specifies that the HyperText Transfer Protocol should be used in communications between the browser and server. Additional details on how the HTTP protocol works are provided in Chapter 3. The rest of the URL specifies the location of the desired page. Immediately following `http://` is the server name, identifying the Web server on which the page is stored. Since servers often organize pages in directories, the particular directory where the page is located is specified next, followed by the file name.

Often, a user need not type every portion of a Web page's full URL. When using most browsers, if you omit the protocol prefix, then `http://` is assumed. Also, if the page name is omitted from the end of the URL, then the default name `index.html` is assumed. For this reason, Web designers often name home pages `index.html` so that users need to remember only the file's location, rather than its full name. Thus, the above link to the book's home page can be written as:

`www.prenhall.com/reed`

Similarly, the home page for Prentice Hall's main page can be succinctly written as:

`www.prenhall.com`

which refers to the file named `index.html` in the main directory on the `www.prenhall.com` server.

Accessing Local Pages

As you develop your own Web pages, you will most likely want to store them locally (on a disk or on the hard drive of your computer) while you are working on them. To load a local page into your

Web browser, simply specify the name and directory path for that page, such as `a:\sample.html`, which identifies the file named `sample.html` on the A: drive, which usually is the floppy drive (Figure 1.15).

As the sample page demonstrates, Web pages can contain more than just text. This page includes an image (a picture) and a hyperlink. A *hyperlink* (or *link*, for short) represents a con-

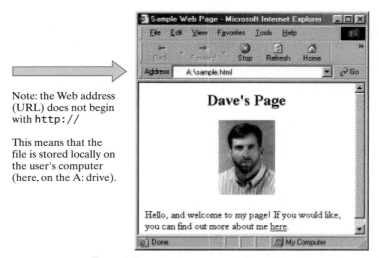

Note: the Web address (URL) does not begin with `http://`

This means that the file is stored locally on the user's computer (here, on the A: drive).

Figure 1.15 The browser Address box.

nection to another page and is usually displayed in a Web page as underlined, colored text. For example, the sample page contains a link labeled <u>here</u>. When a user clicks a link within a Web page, the connected page is retrieved and loaded in the browser. In this instance, clicking the link will load a separate page of personal information. By clicking links, it is possible to navigate, or "surf," the Web from one page to another. The buttons provided by the browser can be useful as you surf from page to page. For example, the Back button will return you to the page you visited most recently.

Looking Ahead...

In this chapter, you were introduced to the basic terminology of computers. Using the specifications of actual computer systems as a reference point, you learned the distinction between hardware and software and gained a basic understanding of how computers are organized. As you expand on this knowledge in subsequent chapters, you will revisit many of these concepts in greater depth. For example, Chapter 6 presents computers from a historical perspective and overviews the evolution of modern computer design. Chapter 8 emphasizes the software aspects of computing, discussing algorithms and their formalization as computer programs. Chapters 14 and 16 delve into the internal workings of computer hardware, focusing on the mechanisms of the CPU and how computer components are designed and manufactured.

The last section of this chapter introduced the World Wide Web, providing a level of understanding sufficient for accessing information on the Web. In the next chapter, you will advance to the next stage by learning how to create your own Web pages using the HTML language. The material in Chapter 2 is presented in a hands-on, tutorial style, so you will be encouraged to apply new concepts to the actual development of a Web page, which you may then display to the world.

Chapter Summary

- A computer is a device that receives, stores, and processes information.

- The term hardware refers to the physical components of the computer, such as the monitor, keyboard, hard drive, etc. Software refers to the programs that execute (i.e., run) on the computer, carrying out tasks such as word processing or accessing the Web.

- Virtually all modern computers have the same underlying structure, known as the von Neumann architecture. The three essential components are input/output devices, memory, and the central processing unit (CPU).

- The CPU is made of circuitry—electronic components wired together to control the flow of electrical signals. It is responsible for fetching program instructions from memory and executing those instructions.

- Memory is the part of the computer that stores programs and data. Memory is commonly divided into (1) main memory (consisting of RAM and cache) which is fast, volatile and expensive, and (2) secondary memory (such as hard disk and CD-ROM) which is slow but permanent and inexpensive.

- A bit (binary digit) is a unit of storage that can differentiate between 2 values, e.g., 0 and 1. A byte is a collection of eight bits and is sufficient for representing 256 different values.

- Input devices allow the computer to receive data and instructions from an external source (e.g., keyboards, mice, track pads, microphones, and scanners). Output devices allow the computer to display or broadcast its results (e.g., monitors, printers, and speakers).

- Programs that carry out tasks within a particular application area, such as word processing, graphical design, or Web access, are known as applications software. Systems software manages the resources and behavior of the computer itself.

- An operating system is a collection of systems software that controls how the CPU, memory, and input/output devices work together.

- The Internet is hardware—a vast, international network of computers that traces its roots back to the 1960s. The World Wide Web is a collection of software that spans the Internet and enables the interlinking of documents and resources.

- A Web page is a text document that contains additional formatting information in a language called HTML (HyperText Markup Language). Web pages are stored on computers known as Web servers, and viewed with programs known as Web browsers.

- A Web address, or Uniform Resource Locator (URL), uniquely identifies the Web server and location of a page so that it can be accessed by a browser.

Review Questions

1. TRUE or FALSE? In order to be classified as a "computer," a device must have a keyboard and display screen.

2. TRUE or FALSE? A bus is a collection of wires that carry information as electrical signals between the hardware components of a computer.

3. TRUE or FALSE? Since computer programs can be complex and difficult to write, they are known as "hardware."

4. TRUE or FALSE? A bit is a unit of data that corresponds to one of two potential values (commonly written as 0 and 1).

5. TRUE or FALSE? A kilobyte of storage is $2^{10} = 1,024$ bytes, where a byte is a collection of 8 bits.

6. TRUE or FALSE? A hard disk is classified as volatile memory, since it requires a constant power supply in order to retain its information.

7. TRUE or FALSE? Keyboards and mice are examples of computer input devices.

8. TRUE or FALSE? A directory is a collection of files that are organized together and labeled with a common name.

9. TRUE or FALSE? The World Wide Web was developed in the early 1970s, shortly after the creation of the Internet.

10. TRUE or FALSE? A Web browser is an example of applications software.

11. Describe the difference between hardware and software and identify two examples of each.

12. Describe the three essential components of a computer that make up the von Neumann architecture. How do these components work together to produce a machine that can be programmed to complete different tasks?

13. Modern computers integrate several different types of memory, such as cache, RAM, hard disk, and floppy disk. Why are different types of memory used, as opposed to the exclusive use of a particular technology? What would be the drawbacks, for example, of using only cache memory, or only hard disk?

14. Computer memory is usually grouped in bytes, which consist of 8 bits each. How many different values can be represented using a byte? How many different values can be represented using two bytes?

15. The Intel Pentium 4 is an example of a processor, or CPU, as are the Celeron and PowerPC. List the two main tasks that the CPU performs in controlling the computer's workings and provide a short explanation of each.

16. In what units are CPU speeds measured, and what does this measurement unit refer to? If one computer has a 1.6GHz Pentium 4 processor and another has a 1.6GHz PowerPC processor, does that imply they will be able to execute the same program in the same amount of time? Explain.

17. Windows XP is an example of an operating system, as are the Mac OS and Linux. List the three main tasks that the operating system performs in controlling the computer's resources and behavior. Provide a short explanation of each.

18. Describe three elements common to a graphical user interface (GUI). How do these elements make it easier for a user to interact with the computer?

19. Suppose you are shopping for a personal computer that you plan to use exclusively for email and Web access. Which would be a better use of your limited funds—a faster CPU or a larger hard drive? Why?

20. It has been said that the Internet could exist without the Web, but the Web couldn't exist without the Internet. Why is this true?

21. What is a Web server, and what role does it play in the World Wide Web?

22. Consider the following fictitious URL: `http://www.acme.com/products/info.html`. What does each part of this URL (separated by slashes) specify?

References

Berners-Lee, Tim, Mark Fischetti, and Michael L. Derouzos. *Weaving the Web: The Original Design and Ultimate Destiny of the World Wide Web*. New York: HarperBusiness, 2000.

Capron, H.L. *Computers: Tools for an Information Age*, 6th ed. Upper Saddle River, NJ: Prentice Hall, 2000.

Comer, Douglas E. *The Internet Book: Everything you need to know about computer networking and how the Internet works*, 3d ed. Upper Saddle River, NJ: Prentice Hall, 2000.

LaMorte, Christopher, and John Lilly. "Computers: History and Development." *Jones Telecommunications and Multimedia Encyclopedia*, 1999. Online at `http://www.digitalcentury.com/encyclo/update/comp_hd.html`.

Malone, Michael. *The Microprocessor: A Biography*. New York: Springer-Verlag, 1995.

Petzold, Charles. *Code: The Hidden Language of Computer Hardware and Software*. Redmond, WA: Microsoft Press, 1999.

HTML and Web Pages

This chapter uses narrative, examples, and hands-on exercises to introduce programming concepts and Web development skills.

HyperText is a way to link and access information of various kinds as a web of nodes in which the user can browse at will.

Tim Berners-Lee
WorldWideWeb: Proposal for a HyperText Project, 1990

The goal of the Web was to be a shared information space through which people (and machines) could communicate. The intent was that this space should span from a private information system to a public information, from high value carefully checked and designed material, to off-the-cuff ideas which make sense only to a few people and may never be read again.

Tim Berners-Lee
The World Wide Web: Past, Present and Future, 1996

If this were a traditional science, Berners-Lee would win a Nobel Prize. What he's done is that significant.

Eric Schmidt, CEO of Novell
Time Magazine, March 29, 1999

The World Wide Web is probably the most pervasive and visible aspect of computing today. Initially designed as a way for researchers to share documents over the Internet, the Web has evolved into a widespread, dynamic medium for communication and commerce. Using a program called a Web browser, people can instantly access documents (commonly referred to as Web pages) stored on computers around the world. With just a few clicks of a mouse, Web users can read newspapers, check sports scores, send email and play interactive games. In addition, the Web provides an easy-to-use interface for advertising and business transactions, as evidenced by the abundance of corporate Web addresses that appear in television and print ads.

In this chapter, we introduce the basics of Web design and its underlying language, HTML. As you read, you will gain hands-on experience by developing your own Web page, adding new features incrementally as you learn. By the end of the chapter, you will be able to join the Web community by making your Web page publicly available. This means that anyone with a Web browser and an Internet connection will be able to access the document you've created.

HTML Basics

A Web page is a text document that contains additional formatting information in a language called **HTML (HyperText Markup Language)**. Using HTML, a Web page creator can identify various features of a page, such as a section heading, a centered table, or an image to be displayed. This information is then interpreted by a Web browser, which formats the page contents appropriately.

HTML Tags

HTML specifies formatting within a page using **tags**. In its simplest form, a tag is a word or symbol surrounded by angular brackets (<>). For example, every Web page must begin with the tag <html> and end with the tag </html>. These tags specify that the enclosed text may contain HTML formatting information and that the browser should interpret the contents accordingly. Two required sections must appear inside every page's HTML tags: a HEAD section, which is delimited by the tags <head> and </head>, and a BODY section, which is delimited by the tags <body> and </body>.

The HEAD section contains information that the browser uses to determine the look of the page. For now, the only information that we will place in the HEAD will be the title of the page, delimited by the tags <title> and </title>. When a browser renders the page, the text occurring between the TITLE tags is displayed in the title bar at the top of the browser window. The BODY section contains the text that will actually appear in the page.

For example, Figure 2.1 shows a simple Web page named demo1.html. In this example, the title of the page is "Title of the Page", which appears in the title bar of the Web browser (Figure 2.2). The text in the body, which is displayed within the browser window, is simply "Text that appears in the page." In this and subsequent figures, HTML tags are highlighted in blue to differentiate them from text that appears in the rendered page.

```
1.  <html>
2.    <!-- demo1.html              Dave Reed    -->
3.    <!-- This is a simple Web page.           -->
4.    <!--------------------------------------->
5.
6.    <head>
7.      <title> Title of the Page </title>
8.    </head>
9.
10.   <body>
11.      Text that appears in the page.
12.   </body>
13. </html>
```

Figure 2.1 A simple Web page.

HTML Elements

You may note that the tags you have seen so far—HTML, HEAD, BODY, and TITLE—all come in pairs. The first tag marks the beginning of a section; the second tag (which is identical to the first except for the slash /) marks the end of the section. For this reason, we will often refer to the first and second tags as **opening** and **closing** tags, respectively. For example, <title> is the opening tag for the TITLE and </title> is the closing tag. **HTML elements**, which form the building blocks of Web pages, are made up of text and the tags that specify the text's role or purpose within the page. For example, <title>Title of the Page</title> can be referred to as a TITLE element, since it represents the piece of the Web page that specifies a title.

Figure 2.2 `demo1.html` rendered in a Web browser.

While most HTML tags come in pairs, some do not. A ***comment*** element, or ***comment*** for short, is defined by a single tag, which begins with `<!--` and ends with `-->`. For example, the Web page in Figure 2.1 contains three comment elements, occurring immediately after the HTML tag (lines 2 through 4). You may think of comments as notes to yourself, or to some future Web developer who might review your HTML text. By placing information such as the file name, last modification date, and general purpose of the page in comments, you ensure proper credit and also simplify the process of updating or modifying the page. As Figure 2.2 shows, comments are ignored by the browser, so this additional text does not clutter up the page when it is rendered. You should always place a sequence of comments at the top of any HTML document you create to identify the file name, author, and purpose of the page.

Numerous software tools on the market allow you to design and create elaborate Web pages. To create simple pages, however, all you really need is a ***text editor***. A text editor is a program in which you can type and edit text, then save that text in a file. Common examples are NotePad and WordPad, which come free with Microsoft Windows, and SimpleText, which comes free on Apple computers. Many software manufacturers also offer free or low-cost text editors that provide special features, such as automatic indentation or color coding of HTML elements. Appendix A includes instructions on using some of these common editors.

To develop a Web page, all you need to do is create a text file containing the desired HTML elements. Then, a browser can be used to render the page. Of course, a Web page rarely looks exactly the way its designer intended the first time it is displayed by a browser. For example, you may make a mistake in entering the contents of the page, or you may simply decide that the page would look better with different formatting. Thus, Web page development usually involves having two windows open at the same time—one running a text editor, which allows the creator to update the page contents, and another running a Web browser, which shows the creator the latest version of the rendered page.

EXERCISE 2.1

Create a simple home page for yourself using some text editor. Your page should have a title, such as "Dave's Home Page," and should contain some basic information about you. Save your page to a disk under the name `index.html`.

Document Formatting

You may have found that, when you displayed your home page, the text didn't appear in the browser window exactly as you typed it. This is inevitable, since the size of the browser window in which the page is rendered may vary. The lines you typed might be too long to fit in the window or might leave wasted white space at the end. To ensure that Web page text looks attractive in various window sizes, the browser automatically adjusts the length of lines to fit the current window, wrapping text to the next line as needed. You may also have noted that, when the browser performs this automatic formatting, it ignores any blank lines, extra spaces, and tabs in your text. When displayed in the browser, any consecutive spaces, tabs, or blank lines will appear as a single space.

Text Spacing

Despite browsers' automatic formatting features, Web designers can control some text spacing by using additional HTML tags. A P element specifies text that is to be treated as a paragraph. Text enclosed within the opening tag <p> and the closing tag </p> will be displayed starting on a new line that is preceded by a blank line. If you wish to break text explicitly without inserting a blank line, you can place a BR element in the text. Unlike the paragraph element, which has opening and closing tags (since there is a logical beginning and end to the paragraph), a BR element is defined by a single tag: <br />. Text that follows a <br /> tag will be displayed starting on a new line. By convention, tags such as <br /> that do not have a corresponding closing tag end with />. In addition, if you don't want to begin a new line but would like to force consecutive spaces in the text, you can do so by inserting the special symbol   in the page. In general, a ***special symbol*** is a word in HTML that has special meaning to the browser when it renders the page. For example, the special symbol   represents a non-breaking space. When a Web page is rendered by a browser, each occurrence of the special symbol   is displayed as a space, no matter where it appears in the text. Figure 2.3 demonstrates the use of tags and the   symbol to control spacing (with the page rendering shown in Figure 2.4).

```
1.  <html>
2.  <!-- demo2.html                   Dave Reed -->
3.  <!-- This page demos text spacing and layout -->
4.  <!------------------------------------------->
5.
6.  <head>
7.    <title> Demo of text layout </title>
8.  </head>
9.
10. <body>
11.   <p>
12.   Here is a paragraph
13.   that is broken across <br />
14.   two lines.
15.   </p>
16.
17.   <p>
18.      Here is another paragraph. <br />
19.   This time, the first line is indented two spaces.
20.   </p>
21. </body>
22. </html>
```

Figure 2.3   A Web page that demonstrates text spacing and layout.

EXERCISE 2.2

Add additional paragraphs to your home page. If you are having trouble thinking of things to write about yourself, consider writing one paragraph that provides biographical data, another that describes your hobbies, and a third listing some favorite books or movies. Use <p></p>, <br />, and   appropriately to make your page readable and attractive.

Figure 2.4 `demo2.html` rendered in a Web browser.

Common errors to avoid...

It is important to note that HTML tags are sequences of characters that are placed in a file along with the text they are intended to format. If you enter a malformed tag, omitting either the opening or closing braces, the tag will not be recognized as HTML and will be displayed as plain text within the page. For example, the text

```
<p>Hello, I'm Dave <br /
My hobbies include hiking and baseball.</p>
```

would be displayed as

```
Hello, I'm Dave <br / My hobbies include hiking and baseball.
```

By contrast, a browser will typically ignore a well-formed tag whose name is misspelled. For example, if you mistakenly type `<bl />` instead of the intended `<br />`, the tag will be ignored, and nothing will appear in its place in the page.

Headings and Alignment

In a large document, it is often useful to divide the text into sections and then provide each with a heading describing the content that follows. HTML includes special tags that enable Web designers to specify headings of various sizes. For example, text enclosed between the tags `<h1>` and `</h1>` is displayed in large, bold letters above the text that follows it. The tags `<h2>` and `</h2>` can be used to display a heading in slightly smaller letters, `<h3>` and `</h3>` are used for even smaller letters, and so on down to `<h6>` and `</h6>`. To divide different parts of a document further, designers can separate sections with a horizontal line using the `<hr />` tag (where HR stands for horizontal rule).

By default, all text in a Web page is displayed left-justified on the page. This means that each heading, paragraph, or line of text begins at the page's left edge. However, it is possible to align text so that it is centered or even right-justified by including a STYLE attribute in the appropriate opening tag. In general, an ***attribute*** is an additional property that can be assigned to an HTML element as part of its tag. The STYLE attribute can be added to an opening tag to specify the alignment of that particular element. For example, the opening tag

```
<h2 style="text-align:center">
```

specifies a heading that will be centered in the page, whereas

```
<p style="text-align:right">
```

specifies a paragraph that will be right-justified in the page.

Figure 2.5 demonstrates the alignment of headings and paragraphs within a page (with the page rendering shown in Figure 2.6). This page also incorporates DIV tags, which can be used to group multiple elements into a single page division. The advantage of arranging multiple elements inside a set of DIV tags is that you can format all enclosed elements at once, as opposed to formatting each individually. In this example, a heading and a paragraph are grouped together and right-justified using DIV tags (lines 25 through 31).

```
1.  <html>
2.  <!- demo3.html                    Dave Reed -->
3.  <!- This page demos headings & alignment.   -->
4.  <!--------------------------------------------->
5.
6.  <head>
7.    <title> Demo of headings </title>
8.  </head>
9.
10. <body>
11.   <h1>Left-Justified Big Heading</h1>
12.   <p>
13.     left-justified text<br />
14.     and more left-justified text
15.   </p>
16.
17.   <hr />
18.   <h2 style="text-align:center">Centered Medium Heading</h2>
19.   <p style="text-align:center">
20.     centered text <br />
21.     and more centered text
22.   </p>
23.
24.   <hr />
25.   <div style="text-align:right">
26.     <h3>Right-Justified Small Heading</h3>
27.     <p>
28.       right-justified text <br />
29.       and more right-justified text
30.     </p>
31.   </div>
32. </body>
33. </html>
```

Figure 2.5 A Web page that demonstrates the alignment of headings and text.

EXERCISE 2.3

Divide your home page into sections. Use a large heading (delimited by H1 tags) to list your name so that it is centered at the top of the page, followed by a horizontal line. For each subsequent text section, use a smaller heading, e.g., H2 or H3. At least one section of your page should contain multiple paragraphs.

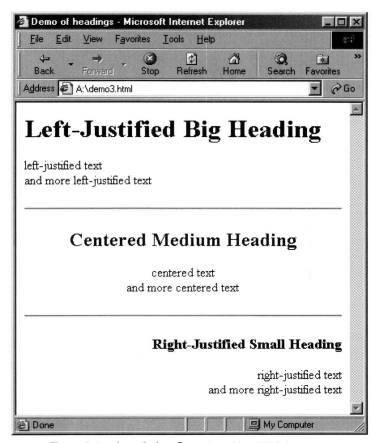

Figure 2.6 demo3.html rendered in a Web browser.

Font Formatting

In printing terminology, a **_font_** defines a particular typeface (such as Times Roman, Courier, or Arial) and size (such as 11 pt. or 12 pt.) used to display characters in a document. In general, Web page creators have limited control over the fonts that are used to display their pages. Browsers allow the user to specify his or her own font preferences by selecting default fonts for viewing pages, so one browser may display a page very differently than another would. There is some font formatting that can be forced in a page, however. For example, text enclosed in the tags `<b></b>` will appear in bold, `<i></i>` indicate text in italics, and `<u></u>` indicate underlined text. In addition, you can change the color of text by enclosing it in SPAN tags of the following form:

```
<span style="color:DESIRED_COLOR"> … </span>
```

SPAN tags serve to group a block of text together for common formatting. The STYLE attribute of the form `style="color:DESIRED_COLOR"` specifies the color of the text within the SPAN tags, where DESIRED_COLOR is a color name such as `red`, `blue`, `darkblue`, or `purple`. A list of the most commonly used color names in HTML is provided in Appendix B. Figure 2.7 demonstrates text formatting within the page (with the page rendering shown in Figure 2.8).

EXERCISE 2.4

Augment your home page by coloring some of the text and using font formatting where appropriate. For example, if you listed favorite books or movies, you could italicize or underline their titles.

```
1. <html>
2. <!- demo4.html                    Dave Reed -->
3. <!- This page demos font formatting.   -->
4. <!------------------------------------->
5.
6. <head>
7.    <title> Demo of font formatting </title>
8. </head>
9.
10. <body>
11.    <p>Here is some <b>bold text</b>.</p>
12.
13.    <p>Here is some <i>italicized text</i>.</p>
14.
15.    <p>Here is some <u>underlined text</u>.</p>
16.
17.    <p>Here is some <span style="color:blue">blue text</span>.</p>
18. </body>
19. </html>
```

Figure 2.7   A Web page that demonstrates text formatting.

Figure 2.8   demo4.html rendered in a Web browser.

Hypertext and Multimedia

Although it is always possible to retrieve a Web page by entering its URL into the browser's Address box, most pages are not accessed this way. The defining feature of the Web is its ability to link pages together through hyperlinks. A ***hyperlink*** is an element on a Web page, usually displayed as underlined text, that connects the page to another page or online resource. When a Web user clicks on a hyperlink, the browser loads the connected page, regardless of its physical location on the Web. Thus, by following a chain of hyperlinks, a user can explore related documents, even if the documents are stored on computers thousands of miles apart. Text that contains embedded hyperlinks is referred to as ***hypertext***.

Common errors to avoid...

When specifying HTML elements with opening and closing tags, it is important to type both tags correctly. If you omit or misspell the opening tag of an element, the browser will ignore the closing tag, and no formatting will occur. On the other hand, if you specify the opening tag but forget or misspell the closing tag, the indicated formatting will continue throughout the document. For example, inexperienced programmers often forget to include the / in closing tags, which in effect specifies two opening tags. If you type <b>oops<b>, any text occurring after this tag set will appear in bold when rendered in a browser.

As previous examples have demonstrated, HTML elements can contain other elements nested inside them. For example, all HTML elements that format text in the page are nested inside the BODY element (<body>...</body>), which is itself nested inside <html>...</html>. When nesting HTML elements, be sure that the order in which you specify the closing tags is exactly opposite to that in which you specified the opening tags. Misordering tags in a nested element, such as <b><i>oops</b></i>, is technically incorrect and may cause the browser to display the text in unintended ways.

In programming terminology, any error related to the format of a statement (such as a misspelled tag name or unmatched opening and closing tags) is known as a **syntax error**. In general, the browser will ignore any HTML syntax error it encounters and continue rendering the page contents as best it can.

Hyperlinks

When inserting a hyperlink into a document, Web designers use the tags <a> and </a> to enclose the text that will represent the link. In this context, A is short for anchor, signifying that the hyperlink anchors (e.g., connects) separate documents together. The designer also must indicate the address of the page to which the link connects; this information is specified within the <a> tag via an attribute named HREF (short for Hypertext REFerence).

The general form of a hyperlink element is:

```
<a href="ADDRESS_OF_PAGE">TEXT LABEL FOR LINK</a>
```

Whatever text you type between <a> and </a> tags will appear as an underlined link when the page is rendered. If the user clicks that text, the browser will replace the current page with the page specified in the opening tag. The address listed in the HREF attribute can be either an **absolute address**, meaning that it specifies the URL of a page on the Web, or a **relative address**, meaning that it specifies a file stored in a location related to that of the Web page itself. For example, the Web page in Figure 2.9 contains two hyperlinks (with the page rendering shown in Figure 2.10). The first (spanning lines 11 and 12) uses an absolute address, specifying the URL (starting with http://) where that page can be found. When a visitor clicks the link labeled "Home Page for *A Balanced Introduction to Computer Science*", the browser will access the linked page and display it in the browser window. The second hyperlink (on line 15) uses a relative address, specifying only the file name of the desired page. Since the http:// prefix is omitted, the browser automatically assumes that this address refers to a file stored in the same directory as the current Web page.

You might note that links within a Web page can appear in different colors. By default, a Web browser displays a link that has been previously visited in one color (usually purple), whereas an unvisited link appears in another color (usually blue).

EXERCISE 2.5

Add a section to your home page containing at least five hyperlinks to sites that you consider useful and/or interesting. To ensure that these hyperlinks work correctly, you should click each one and then view the linked page in your browser.

```
1.  <html>
2.  <!-- demo5.html                    Dave Reed  -->
3.  <!-- This page demos hyperlinks.           -->
4.  <!------------------------------------------->
5.
6.  <head>
7.    <title> Demo of hyperlinks </title>
8.  </head>
9.
10. <body>
11.   <a href="http://www.prenhall.com/reed">
12.     Home Page for <i>A Balanced Introduction to Computer Science</i></a>
13.
14.   <p>
15.   Here is a <a href="local.html">local page</a> you might like.
16.   </p>
17. </body>
18. </html>
```

Figure 2.9 A Web page that demonstrates hyperlinks.

Figure 2.10 demo5.html rendered in a Web browser.

Images

So far, we have discussed ways to format text, font and spacing within a Web page and to create links between your page and other Web resources. However, anyone who has surfed the Web realizes that pages contain much more than text and hyperlinks. The term ***multimedia*** refers to documents that integrate various communication media, such as text, images, movies, and sound clips. In HTML, images are loaded into a page using an <img /> tag. (Note the /> at the end of the tag, signifying that there is no corresponding closing tag.) Standard browsers have built-in capabilities for displaying images in GIF[sm] (Graphics Interchange Format©) and JPEG (Joint Photographic Experts Group) formats, which are the most common methods of storing digital images (The Graphics Interchange Format© is the Copyright property of CompuServe Incorporated. GIF[sm] is a Service Mark property of CompuServe Incorporated.) To render other types of image formats, the browser may require special-purpose extensions called ***plug-ins***. Therefore, if you want an image to be viewable by the majority of Web users, it is advisable to limit yourself to GIF and JPEG formats. (See Chapter 12 for more details on image formats.)

An IMG tag typically has two attributes associated with it. The SRC attribute specifies the location of the image file to be displayed, and the ALT attribute specifies alternate text that appears if the image can't be found or displayed properly. The ALT attribute is particularly crucial when a Web page is rendered by certain types of browsers, such as a text-to-speech browser for the visually impaired. Also, some browsers display the ALT text when the mouse moves over an image, enabling Web designers to provide additional context for images.

The general form of an image element is:

```
<img src="ADDRESS_OF_IMAGE" alt="TEXT_DESCRIPTION" />
```

After encountering an image element when loading a Web page, the browser accesses the source file specified in the tag and displays that image in the page. As was the case with the HREF attribute for hyperlinks, the address assigned to the SRC attribute of an IMG can be either absolute (a complete URL) or relative (a file stored in a location related to that of the page). For example, the image element in Figure 2.11 (line 12) utilizes a relative address, specifying that the browser should display the image file named `reed.gif`, which is stored in the same directory or folder as the Web page (the page rendering is shown in Figure 2.12).

```
1.  <html>
2.  <!-- demo6.html                      Dave Reed -->
3.  <!-- This page demos images.                    -->
4.  <!---------------------------------------------->
5.
6.  <head>
7.     <title> Demo of images </title>
8.  </head>
9.
10.   <body>
11.    <div style="text-align:center">
12.       <img src="reed.gif" alt="Dave Reed" />
13.
14.       <p>This is a picture of the author.</p>
15.    </div>
16.  </body>
17. </html>
```

Figure 2.11 A Web page that demonstrates images.

Figure 2.12 `demo6.html` rendered in a Web browser.

EXERCISE 2.6

Look around the Web, and choose a public-domain image that you would like to include on your Web page. You must be careful not to violate copyrights or otherwise infringe upon the rights of the owner—unless explicitly stated otherwise, you should assume that any image on the Web is private property. Once located, copy the image to your local directory (under Windows, click the right mouse button over the desired image and select Save Image from the resulting menu; under the Mac OS, click on the image while holding down the Control key, then select Download Image to Disk). After saving the image in the directory that contains index.html, incorporate the local image into your home page. Be sure to include alternate text for your image via the ALT attribute.

Lists

When organizing text in a page, it is often convenient to list similar items in sequence. For example, we have mentioned the possibility of listing your hobbies or favorite movies in your home page. HTML provides two different elements for organizing lists. In an ***unordered list***, individual items are preceded by bullets (solid circles), as shown on the left-hand side of Figure 2.13. In an ***ordered list***, the items are numbered in sequence, as shown on the right-hand side of the figure.

In HTML, an unordered list is identified by the tags <ul> and </ul>, whereas an ordered list is identified by the tags <ol> and </ol>. In either type of list, the individual list items are delimited by the tags <li> and </li>. For example, the Web page in Figure 2.14 (rendered in Figure 2.15) contains list elements corresponding to the text lists in Figure 2.13.

Unordered List	Ordered List
• old movies	*1. And Then There Were None*
• Celtic music	*2. Bringing Up Baby*
• baseball	*3. Crouching Tiger, Hidden Dragon*
• hacking around on the computer	*4. Big Trouble in Little China*
	5. The Usual Suspects

Figure 2.13 Examples of unordered and ordered lists.

Formatting Lists

By default, items in an unordered list are preceded by bullets, and items in an ordered list are numbered. However, the page designer can specify alternative formats using the STYLE attribute. Items in an unordered list will be preceded by squares, instead of bullets, if you add the attribute style="list-item-type:square" to the opening UL tag. Likewise, you can specify that an ordered list use letters or roman numerals instead of numbers to identify each list item. The style attributes that correspond to each of these formatting styles are listed in Figure 2.16.

The ability to specify an ordered list's format is especially useful when you wish to nest lists. For example, the Web page in Figure 2.17 (rendered in Figure 2.18) displays an algorithm for finding the oldest person in a room. As you will learn in Chapter 8, an algorithm is a sequence of step-by-step instructions for carrying out some task. In this case, the algorithm has four main steps, which appear in the page as items in an ordered list. The creator of this page has broken the third step into parts "a" and "b" by nesting an ordered list (with appropriate STYLE attribute) inside the third list item.

EXERCISE 2.7

Add a list to your home page. For example, you might list your favorite CDs, your current courses, or the names of your siblings.

```
 1.  <html>
 2.  <!-- demo7.html                                      Dave Reed -->
 3.  <!-- This page demos unordered and ordered lists.           -->
 4.  <!------------------------------------------------------->
 5.
 6.  <head>
 7.    <title> Demo of lists </title>
 8.  </head>
 9.
10.  <body>
11.    <p>My Hobbies
12.    <ul>
13.      <li> old movies </li>
14.      <li> Celtic music </li>
15.      <li> baseball </li>
16.      <li> hacking around on the computer </li>
17.    </ul>
18.    </p>
19.
20.    <p>My Favorite Movies
21.    <ol>
22.      <li> <i>And Then There Were None</i> </li>
23.      <li> <i>Bringing Up Baby</i> </li>
24.      <li> <i>Crouching Tiger, Hidden Dragon</i>  </li>
25.      <li> <i>Big Trouble in Little China</i> </li>
26.      <li> <i>The Usual Suspects</i> </li>
27.    </ol>
28.    </p>
29.  </body>
30.  </html>
```

Figure 2.14 A Web page that demonstrates lists.

Tables

Although it is usually preferable to let the browser determine how text is laid out within a page, there are times when you want things to line up just so. For example, suppose that you want to display a collection of related information about a student. Aligning such data into columns can make a page more attractive and easier to read.

Name:	Chris
Age:	20
Hometown:	Chicago
Major:	Computer Science

In HTML, table elements are used to organize text and other elements into rows and columns. Elements in the same row appear on the same line when rendered by a browser (as is the case with "Name:" and "Chris" above). Elements in the same column are aligned on the left-hand side (as is the case with "Chris", "20", "Chicago", and "Computer Science"). Web designers specify a table element using the tags <table> and </table>. Individual rows in the table are identified by <tr></tr> (short for table row), and the number of columns is determined by the number of data items in the rows, as identified by <td></td> (short for table data). Every time you end one row element and begin another, the browser places the first data item in the first column of that new row. For example, the Web page in Figure 2.19 (rendered in Figure 2.20) contains a table element that displays the aligned text from our sample student information record.

Figure 2.15 `demo7.html` rendered in a Web browser.

`<ul style="list-style-type:square">`	→ Items preceded by squares.
`<ol style="list-style-type:lower-alpha">`	→ Items preceded by lower-case letters (a, b, c, d, ...).
`<ol style="list-style-type:upper-alpha">`	→ Items preceded by upper-case letters (A, B, C, D, ...).
`<ol style="list-style-type:lower-roman">`	→ Items preceded by lower-case roman letters (i, ii, iii, iv, ...).
`<ol style="list-style-type:upper-roman">`	→ Items preceded by upper-case roman letters (I, II, III, ...).

Figure 2.16 Style attributes to format lists.

As this example demonstrates, the browser automatically adjusts the width of each column to accommodate its largest entry. In this case, the width of the first column is determined by the space needed to fit "Hometown:". If the table included a fifth row containing a longer entry in the first column—say "Favorite Movie:"—then the browser would adjust the column size to fit that entry.

Table Borders

If you would like to insert borders between the rows and columns in a table, this is accomplished by assigning a number to the BORDER attribute in the opening TABLE tag. For example, the opening tag `<table border=1>` would begin a table in which a border separated each row and column. The number value assigned to the BORDER attribute refers to the width of the border, as measured in *pixels* (or picture elements, the dots that make up the display on a computer screen). By increasing the number, the page designer can increase the width of the border. For example, the page in Figure 2.21 displays the same table as in Figure 2.19, except that each entry is surrounded by a border 1 pixel wide.

```
 1.  <html>
 2.  <!-demo8.html                            Dave Reed -->
 3.  <!-- This page demos formatted lists.         -->
 4.  <!------------------------------------------->
 5.
 6.  <head>
 7.    <title> Demo of lists </title>
 8.  </head>
 9.
10.  <body>
11.      To find the oldest person in a room:
12.
13.      <ol>
14.        <li> Line up all the people along one wall. </li>
15.        <li> Ask the first person to state his or her name and birthday,
16.             then write this information down on a piece of paper. </li>
17.        <li> For each successive person in line:
18.             <ol style="list-style-type:lower-alpha">
19.               <li> Ask the person his or her name and birthday. </li>
20.               <li> If the stated birthday is earlier than the date
21.                    written on the paper, cross out the old information
22.                    and write down the name and birthday of this person. </li>
23.             </ol> </li>
24.        <li> When you have reached the end of the line, the name and
25.             birthday of the oldest person will be written on the paper. </li>
26.      </ol>
27.  </body>
28.  </html>
```

Figure 2.17   A Web page that demonstrates nested ordered lists.

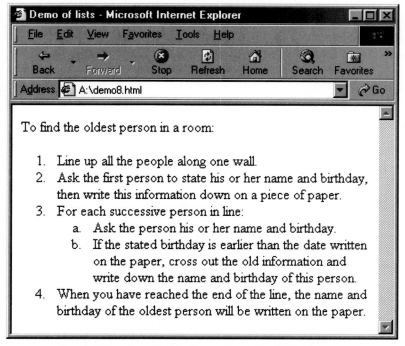

Figure 2.18   `demo8.html` rendered in a Web browser.

```
1.  <html>
2.  <!-- demo9.html                      Dave Reed -->
3.  <!-- This page demos a borderless table.    -->
4.  <!------------------------------------------->
5.
6.  <head>
7.    <title> Demo of tables </title>
8.  </head>
9.
10. <body>
11.   <table>
12.     <tr> <td> Name:     </td> <td> Chris            </td> </tr>
13.     <tr> <td> Age:      </td> <td> 20               </td> </tr>
14.     <tr> <td> Hometown: </td> <td> Chicago          </td> </tr>
15.     <tr> <td> Major:    </td> <td> Computer Science </td> </tr>
16.   </table>
17. </body>
18. </html>
```

Figure 2.19   A Web page that demonstrates a borderless table.

Figure 2.20   demo9.html rendered in a Web browser.

Aligning Images and Text

In addition to organizing text into columns, tables are useful for aligning a variety of HTML elements. For example, a common use of tables is to align an image with text that refers to it. The Web page in Figure 2.23 (rendered in Figure 2.24) contains a table with only one row. An image appears in the first column, and text appears in the second column. The result is that the text appears to the right of the image, centered vertically.

EXERCISE 2.8

Use a table to align text and/or images into rows and columns. For example, you might organize your class schedule into a table, designating a row for each class and columns for listing the course name, room number, and meeting times. Alternatively, you might align the names and email addresses of your friends into columns.

```
1.  <html>
2.  <!-- demo10.html                  Dave Reed -->
3.  <!-- This page demos bordered table.       -->
4.  <!--------------------------------------->
5.
6.  <head>
7.    <title> Demo of tables </title>
8.  </head>
9.
10. <body>
11.   <table border=1>
12.     <tr> <td> Name:     </td> <td> Chris            </td> </tr>
13.     <tr> <td> Age:      </td> <td> 20               </td> </tr>
14.     <tr> <td> Hometown: </td> <td> Chicago          </td> </tr>
15.     <tr> <td> Major:    </td> <td> Computer Science </td> </tr>
16.   </table>
17. </body>
18. </html>
```

Figure 2.21 A Web page that demonstrates a bordered table.

Figure 2.22 demo10.html rendered in a Web browser.

Making Pages Accessible

As you have learned in this chapter, developing Web pages does not require an Internet connection. You have been able to create pages, store them on your computer, and then view the pages in a browser. However, in order for your pages to be retrievable via the Web, you will need access to a Web server connected to the Internet. The easiest way to accomplish this will vary depending on your situation. If you are at a college or university, your school most likely has a Web server available for student use. After obtaining permission to store pages on such a server, you will receive specific instructions on how to copy your pages to the appropriate directories on that server. If your Internet access is supplied through an Internet Service Provider (ISP), such as AOL or MSN, the company will probably offer space on its Web servers for customers to use. You will need to contact the company's customer support in order to determine the steps for uploading your pages.

When you copy a page to a publicly accessible Web server, remember that you must also copy any supporting pages or files needed by the page. For example, in Exercise 2.6, you copied an image onto your disk and incorporated that image into your page. Since you employed a relative address to

```
1.  <html>
2.  <!-- demo11.html                      Dave Reed   -->
3.  <!-- This page demos a table for alignment. -->
4.  <!------------------------------------------------->
5.
6.  <head>
7.    <title> Demo of tables </title>
8.  </head>
9.
10. <body>
11.   <table>
12.     <tr>
13.      <td><img src="seal.gif" alt="Creighton seal" /></td>
14.      <td><a href="http://www.creighton.edu"><b>Creighton University</b></a>
15.            <br />
16.            2500 California Plaza<br />
17.            Omaha, NE   68178</td>
18.     </tr>
19.   </table>
20. </body>
21. </html>
```

Figure 2.23 A Web page that demonstrates a table for image alignment.

Figure 2.24 demo11.html rendered in a Web browser.

identify the image, a browser will assume that the image is stored in the same location as the page, so it is necessary to copy the image along with the page.

EXERCISE 2.9

If you have access to a Web server, copy both your home page and the downloaded image file to the server. After you have done this, anyone should be able to access your page, regardless of his or her location on the Internet.

Common errors to avoid...

Most Web pages refer to supporting documents, such as images or other Web pages, which are stored in the original page's directory or folder. Whenever you move the page from one directory or folder to another, you must be sure to move the supporting documents along with it. If the browser is unable to locate an image file in the expected location, the alternate text specified in the ALT attribute will be displayed (along with box containing an 'X' when using Internet Explorer or older versions of Netscape). If a supporting HTML document (i.e., a linked Web page) cannot be found, then a default screen containing an error message will appear when a user clicks the link.

Looking Ahead...

In this chapter, you learned to create your own Web pages with HTML. By using (1) HTML elements to format and align text, (2) images and links to incorporate visuals and related documents, and (3) lists and tables to organize elements, you created a home page comparable to most found on the Web. In fact, the act of placing your home page on a publicly accessible Web server has effected your transition from Web user to Web contributor. Your home page now serves to introduce you to the world, or at least to anyone in the world with Internet access.

As you have learned via the chapter exercises, creating a Web page involves both artistry (in organizing the layout of elements in the page) and careful, logical thinking (in properly formatting the HTML tags). In practice, most Web designers use a variety of technologies in addition to HTML when developing their pages. These technologies include XML (an extension of HTML in which the Web designer can define his own tags), Macromedia Flash (a program that integrates moving images into a page), and programming languages such as PHP, Java, and JavaScript. While the mastery of all of these technologies is beyond the scope of this book, in subsequent chapters you will learn the fundamentals of JavaScript, the simplest and most popular language for extending HTML. Building upon the skills you have developed in this chapter, you will learn to use JavaScript in the development of dynamic Web pages—pages that not only display text and images, but also interact with the user and react to actions such as mouse clicks and keyboard entries. Before the book continues on to JavaScript, however, Chapter 3 overviews the history and functionality of the Internet and the World Wide Web.

While you may be comfortable using the Internet for email or surfing the Web, chances are you have very little knowledge about how the Internet and the Web were created. Chapter 3 provides a historical context for understanding the evolution of these systems as well as the technical details concerning their workings.

Chapter Summary

- A Web page is a text document that contains additional formatting information in a language called HTML (HyperText Markup Language). A Web browser is a program that displays Web pages by interpreting the HTML and formatting the page accordingly. A Web server is a computer that runs special software for storing and retrieving pages. A Web address (formally known as a Uniform Resource Locator, or URL) specifies the location of a particular Web page.

- HTML specifies formatting within a page using tags. An HTML element, the building block of Web pages, is made up of text enclosed in tags that indicate the text's role or purpose within the page.

- Every HTML document must begin with the tag <html> and end with the tag </html>.

- An HTML document has two main sections, the HEAD and the BODY. The HEAD contains the TITLE of the page, which appears at the top of the browser window when that page is displayed. The BODY contains the text and formatting that you want to appear within the page.

- Comments can be placed at any point in the page and are delimited by `<!--` and `-->`. By placing key information about a page in comments, you ensure proper credit and also simplify the process of updating or modifying the page. The browser ignores comments when the page is loaded.

- Typically, a browser formats text to fit the current window, ignoring blank lines and extra spacing within the HTML document. Designers can control spacing in Web pages by using the `<br />` element, which explicitly breaks a line of text. Similarly, `<p>` and `</p>` tags specify a new paragraph (preceded by a blank line). In addition, the ` ` symbol inserts a space into text.

- The tags `<h1></h1>`, `<h2></h2>`, and `<h3></h3>` can be used to display section headings of decreasing sizes; `<hr />` draws a horizontal line across the page. Designers can add STYLE attributes to headings or paragraphs to control text alignment. For example, `<h2 style="text-align:center">` creates a centered heading.

- Numerous other HTML tags can be used to format text, such as `<b></b>` for bold text, `<i></i>` for italicized text, `<u></u>` for underlined text, and `<span style="color:red"></span>` for red colored text.

- Hyperlinks to other HTML documents can be embedded in a Web page using an anchor element, e.g., `<a href="http://www.prenhall.com">Prentice Hall</a>`. The HREF attribute specifies the address of the linked page.

- GIF and JPEG images can be embedded in a Web page using an image tag, e.g., `<img src="reed.gif" alt="Dave Reed" />`. The SRC attribute specifies the address of the image file to be displayed, and the ALT attribute specifies alternate text to be displayed if the image doesn't load.

- A list can be used to organize items in a page. By default, an unordered list (identified by `<ul></ul>`) displays each item (identified by `<li></li>`) preceded by a bullet. An ordered list (identified by `<ol></ol>`) displays each item (identified by `<li></li>`) preceded by a number.

- A table can be used to organize items into rows and columns. A table is identified by `<table></table>`, with individual rows identified by `<tr></tr>` and entries within that row identified by `<td></td>`.

Supplemental Material and Exercises

Browser Settings

A fundamental idea behind HTML is that, although the creator of a page can use tags to identify various text elements, the browser handles the text's final formatting. This increases the universal accessibility of Web documents—if each specific browser controls a page's formatting, the page can be viewed in different browsers running on different type of machines and operating systems. In addition, this approach allows individual users to customize the way in which pages are displayed in their personal browsers. For example, users can easily increase or decrease the size of text fonts through the "View" menu.

Users can also customize other viewing preferences, such as selecting default fonts and colors and a default home page. If you are using Netscape Navigator, select "Preferences" under the "Edit" menu to see all of the possible options. In Internet Explorer, you can change your preferences by selecting "Internet options" under the "Tools" menu.

EXERCISE 2.10

If you are working on a private computer, customize the browser so that its settings match your personal preferences. If you are working on a publicly accessible computer, you may experiment with the settings, but be sure to reset them to their default values when you are done. It is inconsiderate to impose your preferences on others!

Background Color and Images

By default, most browsers display Web pages with a white background (though individual users can reset this default value via preferences). However, a little color can sometimes make a page more attractive and interesting. To change a page's background color, you must assign a specific color value to the BGCOLOR attribute of the BODY tag. For example, the opening tag

```
<body bgcolor="lightgrey">
```

would cause the background of the page to appear light gray. Appendix B lists the most commonly used color names that are predefined by HTML.

EXERCISE 2.11

Add a background color to your home page. Be careful in your choice of colors, though. Subtle colors, such as lightgrey or lightblue, can be attractive, but bright or dark colors, such as yellow or darkblue, can make reading the page's text extremely difficult. Remember that readability is the primary goal when designing a Web page—if users can't read the contents, it doesn't matter how pretty the page is!

As you surf the Web, you may have noticed that some Web pages have backgrounds comprised of textured patterns or even photographic images. A Web designer can specify an image as the background of a Web page using the BACKGROUND attribute of the BODY tag. For example, the opening tag

```
<body
background="http://wp.netscape.com/assist/net_sites/bg/rock/yellow_rock.gif">
```

would cause the image located at the specified URL to be displayed in the background of the page. In this case, the background would have a yellow, stonelike texture. Note that, if the image is too small to fill the entire browser window (which is usually the case), then the image is repeated to fill the space. This is why simple, repetitive patterns make the best backgrounds.

EXERCISE 2.12

If desired, add a background image to your page (sample images can be found at various Web sites, such as http://wp.netscape.com/assist/net_sites/bg/backgrounds.html and http://www.free-backgrounds.com/). However, be very selective when choosing your image. Plastering your picture in the background of your page might seem like a neat idea, but complex background images almost always detract from the page's readability.

Images as Links

In all the examples you have seen so far, links have been labeled with text—that is, only text appeared between the opening and closing A tags. However, Web designers can anchor a link to any HTML element, including an image. The following example defines an image link, in which an IMG element is placed inside the A tags.

```
<a href="http://www.prenhall.com/reed">
    <img src="http://www.prenhall.com/reed/Images/reed.gif"
        alt="Dave Reed" />
</a>
```

Images that serve as hyperlinks display the same behavior that hypertext does. When a user clicks the image, the browser loads the page specified in the HREF attribute. By default, images enclosed in A tags are surrounded by colored borders to identify the images as links. However, if you do not want the image to appear with a border, you can add attributes to the ANCHOR and IMG tags to remove the border, as in the following:

```
<a href="http://www.prenhall.com/reed"
   style="text-decoration:none">
    <img src="http://www.prenhall.com/reed/Images/reed.gif"
         alt="Dave Reed" border=0 />
</a>
```

EXERCISE 2.13

Add images that serve as links to your home page. The images that you select should have relevance to the link destinations—don't use a picture unless a user could intuitively connect the image to the document represented by the link. Also, do not remove the borders from images unless you have a good reason for doing so. These borders help Web users identify and locate links.

The Internet and the Web

This chapter uses narrative, illustrations, and review questions to introduce computer science and technology concepts.

It shouldn't be too much of a surprise that the Internet has evolved into a force strong enough to reflect the greatest hopes and fears of those who use it. After all, it was designed to withstand nuclear war, not just the puny huffs and puffs of politicians and religious fanatics.

Denise Caruso

There are two ages of the Internet—before Mosaic, and after. The combination of Tim Berners-Lee's Web protocols, which provided connectivity, and Marc Andreesen's browser, which provided a great interface, proved explosive. In twenty-four months, the Web has gone from being unknown to absolutely ubiquitous.

Mark Pesce
A Brief History of Cyberspace, 1995

Looking at the proliferation of personal web pages on the net, it looks like very soon everyone on earth will have 15 megabytes of fame.

M.G. Siriam

The Internet is a vast network of computers that connects people all over the world. Using the Internet, a person in Indiana can communicate freely with a person in India, scientists at different universities can share computing power, and researchers can access libraries of information from the comfort of their own homes or offices. Over the past decade, the World Wide Web has popularized the Internet by providing a simple, intuitive interface through which users can share and access information, thus enabling the Internet to become an essential medium for communication, research, and commerce.

In Chapter 1, we provided an overview of the Internet and the Web from a user's perspective. We emphasized the differences between the Internet and the Web, noting that the Internet encompasses hardware (such as computers, cable, and wires) for facilitating communication, whereas the Web is comprised of software (such as documents, images, and sound clips) stored on and accessed over the Internet. Chapter 2 continued our discussion of the Internet by introducing the basics of Web design and HTML, a language used to format Web documents. In this chapter, we provide additional information about the Internet and Web, including how they were developed, how they work, and their impact on society. The historical contexts that led to the development and growth of the Internet and Web are described, as well as the key technical ideas that shaped their evolution. While not overly technical, this chapter does outline the protocols that define the Internet (TCP/IP) and Web (HTTP/HTML) and make their explosive growth possible.

History of the Internet

One of the most significant advancements in recent computing history is the Internet, the idea for which can be traced back to the early 1960s. While a professor at the Massachusetts Institute of Technology, J.C.R. Licklider (1915–1990) published a series of articles describing a "Galactic Network" of computers that would allow people worldwide to share and access information (Figure 3.1). Licklider was excited by computers' potential to influence scientific and engineering research, but was frustrated by the difficulties involved in accessing computers. Very few computers existed in the early 1960s, and those that were in use tended to be monopolized by a small number of researchers at major universities. Licklider believed that, if computers could be connected over long distances so that a researcher in one state could access a computer in another, then a larger group of researchers would be able to benefit from computers' capabilities. Such a network would also allow institutions to reduce computing costs by sharing resources.

Figure 3.1   J.C.R. Licklider.

In 1962, Licklider was appointed head of the computer research program at the U.S. Department of Defense's Advanced Research Project Agency (ARPA). As part of his job, he was asked to investigate how researchers—especially those working on defense-related projects—could better utilize computers. He immediately saw the opportunity to bring about his Galactic Network and began establishing relationships with the top computer research organizations in the country. Over the next few years, ARPA funded numerous network-related research initiatives, which generated the ideas and technology that would eventually lead to the Internet.

ARPANet

One of those inspired by Licklider's vision of a long-distance network was Larry Roberts (1937–), a computer researcher at MIT (Figure 3.2). In 1967, Roberts was named head of the ARPA project to design a long-distance computer network. Within a year, Roberts and his team had finalized plans for the network, which was to be called the ARPANet. In 1969, the ARPANet became a reality, linking four computers at the University of California at Los Angeles (UCLA), the University of California at Santa Barbara (UCSB), the Stanford Research Institute (SRI), and the University of Utah. The network employed dedicated cables, lines buried in the ground and used solely for communications between the computers. Researchers at the four institutions were able to connect to one another's computers and run programs remotely, meaning that researchers at multiple sites could share both

Figure 3.2 Larry Roberts.

hardware and software costs. In addition, researchers could share information by transferring text and data files from one location to another. It is interesting to note that the transfer rate between the computers—i.e., the speed at which data could be sent and received over the dedicated cables—was 56 Kbits/sec. This is roughly the same rate that today's Internet users can achieve with a modem and standard phone lines. However, at the time, the ARPANet's communication speed represented a dramatic increase over the 160 bits/sec transfer rate obtainable over standard phone lines.

Growth and Privatization

The U.S. Department of Defense originally intended the ARPANet to connect only military installations and universities participating in government projects. Throughout the 1970s and early 1980s, the ARPANet grew at a steady pace, as computers owned by various military contractors and research institutions were added to the network. For example, Figure 3.3 shows a map of the ARPANet in

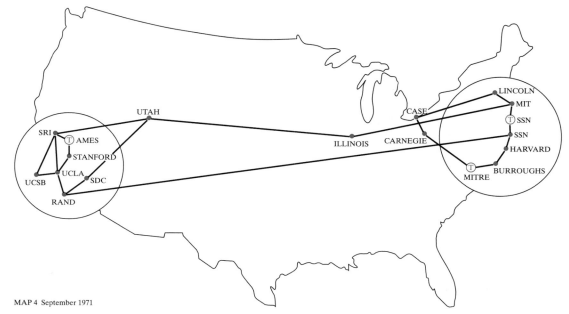

MAP 4 September 1971

Figure 3.3 The ARPANet in 1971. Sites marked with a solid dot utilized Interface Message Processors (IMPs), special-purpose computers that connected up to four terminals to the network. Sites marked with a T utilized Terminal Interface Processors (TIPs), which were introduced in 1971 and allowed up to 64 terminal connections.

ARPANET GEOGRAPHIC MAP, OCTOBER 1980

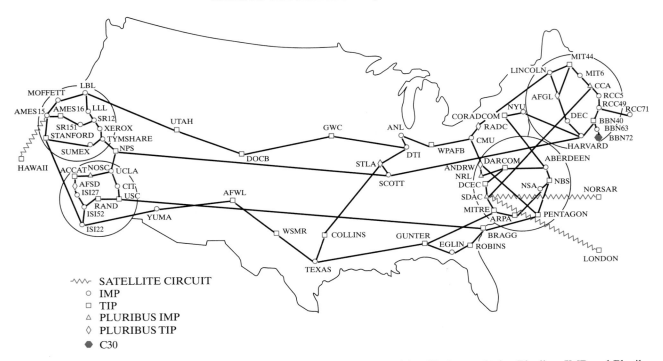

Figure 3.4   The ARPANet in 1980, with the type of networking computer identified at each site. Pluribus IMP and Pluribus TIP were extensions of older IMP and TIP computers that utilized multiple processors to increase capacity. The C30 was a customized, high-speed computer developed by BBN, the original developers of IMP technology.

1971, when the system facilitated communication among 18 computers across the country. By 1980, close to 100 computers were connected to the ARPANet, and satellite connections provided links to select cities outside the continental United States (Figure 3.4).

After more than a decade of slow, steady expansion, the ARPANet experienced an astounding growth spurt in the 1980s. Attracted by network applications such as electronic mail (through which users can send messages and files over the network), newsgroups (through which users can share ideas and results), and remote logins (through which users can share computing power), researchers at virtually every college and university wanted to become a part of the ARPANet. By 1984, the ARPANet encompassed more than 1,000 computers, far exceeding the expectations of its original designers. To accommodate further growth, the National Science Foundation (NSF) became involved with the ARPANet in 1984. The NSF, an independent agency of the U.S. government that promotes the progress of science, funded the construction of high-speed transmission lines that would form the backbone of the expanding network. The term "Internet" was coined in recognition of the similarities between this computer network and the interstate highway system. The backbone connections were analogous to interstate highways, providing fast communications between principal destinations (Figure 3.5). Connected to the backbone were transmission lines, which provided slower, more limited capabilities and linked secondary destinations; these transmission lines could be compared to state highways. Additional connections were required to reach individual computers, in the same way that city and neighborhood roads are used to link individual houses.

Recognizing that continued growth would require an influx of funding and research, the government decided in the mid 1990s to privatize the Internet. Control of the network's hardware was turned over to telecommunications companies and research organizations, which were expected to implement new Internet technologies as they were developed. Today, most of the physical components that make

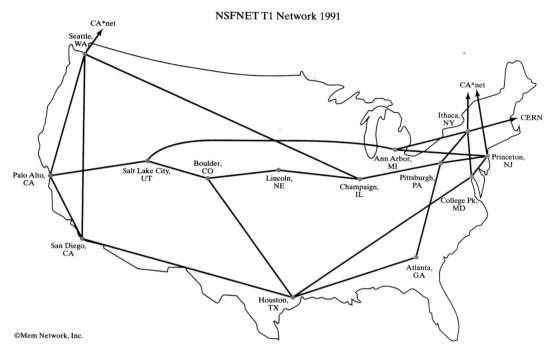

Figure 3.5   The Internet backbone in 1991. The arrows labeled CA*net and CERN are connections to the Canadian and European networks, respectively.

up the Internet, including the high-speed backbone connections, are owned and maintained by commercial firms such as MCI WorldCom, GTE, and Sprint. Other aspects of the Internet are administered by the Internet Society, an international nonprofit organization founded in 1992. The Internet Society maintains and enforces standards, ensuring that all computers on the Internet are able to communicate with each other. (You will learn more about standards in the next section.) It also organizes committees that propose new Internet-related technologies and software and provides a managerial structure for determining when and how technologies are adopted. Key organizations within the Internet Society are identified in Figure 3.6.

Figure 3.7 documents the increasing size of the Internet over the past two decades, as estimated by the Internet Software Consortium (another nonprofit organization involved in developing and disseminating Internet standards). These statistics indicate exponential growth, with the number of Internet-connected computers doubling every one to two years. Of course, this rate of expansion cannot continue indefinitely—the world contains a large but nonetheless limited number of potential network users. To date, however, technological advances have been able to accommodate increasing demand, and no immediate end to growth is foreseen.

How the Internet Works

As we have mentioned, the Internet was novel in that it provided the first efficient computer-to-computer connections over long distances. However, the network's inherent organization was also innovative, representing a significant departure from telephone systems and other communications schemes. The design of the ARPANet—and hence of today's Internet—was strongly influenced by the ideas of Paul Baran (1926–), a researcher at the Rand Corporation in the 1960s.

Distributed Network

The first of Baran's ideas adopted for the ARPANet was that of a ***distributed network***. To fully understand the logic behind the Internet's structure, you must recall that funding for the ARPANet was

Internet Society (ISOC)

Provides leadership in issues relating to the Internet and serves as the organizational home of groups responsible for Internet standards.

Internet Engineering Task Force (IETF)

Develops and disseminates the standards and protocols that define the architecture and software of the Internet.

Internet Architecture Board (IAB)

Defines the overall architecture of the Internet, providing guidance and broad direction to the IETF.

Internet Engineering Steering Group (IESG)

Manages the technical activities of the IETF and oversees the process of standards development.

Internet Research Task Force (IRTF)

Organizes research groups on topics related to Internet protocols, applications, architecture, and technology.

Figure 3.6   The Internet Society and its key organizations.

Year	Computers on the Internet[1]
2002	162,128,493
2000	93,047,785
1998	36,739,000
1996	12,881,000
1994	3,212,000
1992	992,000
1990	313,000
1988	56,000
1986	5,089
1984	1,024
1982	235

Figure 3.7   Internet growth.

provided by the U.S. Department of Defense, which had very specific objectives in mind. Given that the country was in the midst of the Cold War, the military wanted to develop a national communications network that would be resistant to attack. This goal required a design that allowed communication to take place even if parts of the network were damaged or destroyed, either by an enemy action or by normal mechanical failures. Clearly, a centralized network that relied on a small number of master computers to coordinate transmissions would not suffice. For example, the U.S. telephone network of the time relied on central hubs or switches that were responsible for routing service to entire regions. If a hub failed for some reason, entire cities or regions could lose service. Baran proposed a different architecture for a computer network, one in which control was distributed across a large number of machines. His design employed a lattice structure, in which each computer on the network was linked to several others. If a particular computer or connection failed, then communications could be routed around that portion of the network, and the network would continue to transmit data (Figure 3.8).

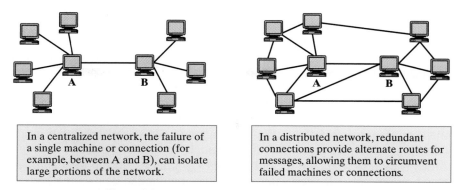

In a centralized network, the failure of a single machine or connection (for example, between A and B), can isolate large portions of the network.

In a distributed network, redundant connections provide alternate routes for messages, allowing them to circumvent failed machines or connections.

Figure 3.8   Centralized vs. distributed networks.

Packet Switching

Baran's other idea central to the ARPANet architecture was that of ***packet switching***. In a packet-switching network, messages to be sent over the network are first broken into small pieces known as ***packets***, and these packets are sent independently to their final destination (Figure 3.9). Transmitting messages in this way offers three key advantages. First, sending information in smaller units increases the efficient use of connections. If a large message were able to monopolize a connection, many smaller messages might be forced to wait. As a real-life example of this effect, think of a line at a busy pay phone. If the person currently on the phone has a long conversation, then everyone else in line must wait, even those who only need to make short calls. However, if phone calls were restricted in length—for example, to a maximum of 3 minutes per call—then each person in line would be guaranteed a turn in a reasonable amount of time. Similarly, limiting the size of network transmissions allows many users to share the connections in a more equitable manner. The second advantage of packet switching is that it allows the network to react to failures or congestion. As each packet works its way toward its destination, routers can recognize failures or network congestion and reroute the packet around trouble areas. The third advantage is that packet switching improves reliability. If a message is broken into packets and the packets are transmitted independently, it is probable that at least part of the message will arrive at its destination, even if some failures occur within the network. If the recipient receives only part of the message, he or she can acknowledge the partial message's receipt and request retransmission from the sender.

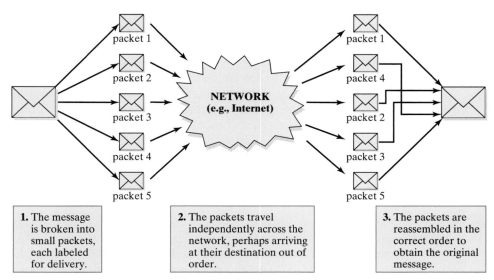

1. The message is broken into small packets, each labeled for delivery.

2. The packets travel independently across the network, perhaps arriving at their destination out of order.

3. The packets are reassembled in the correct order to obtain the original message.

Figure 3.9   A packet-switching network.

Internet Protocols: TCP/IP

Although the terms **distributed** and **packet-switching** can be used to describe the Internet's architecture, these characteristics do not address how computers connected to the Internet are able to communicate with one another. After all, just as people speak different languages and have different customs, computers are built using different technologies, operating systems, and computer languages. If the average American can't speak or understand Russian (and vice versa), how can we expect a computer in Nebraska to exchange data with a computer in Moscow? To solve this problem, the computing community must agree on **protocols**, sets of rules that describe how communication takes place. Internet protocols can be thought of as analogous to the postal service address system, which is used to route letters and packages (jokingly referred to as **snail-mail** by some in the electronic community). If every state or country maintained its own method of labeling mail, sending a letter would be an onerous, if not impossible, task. Fortunately, protocols have been established for uniquely specifying addresses, including zip codes and country codes that allow letters to be sent easily across state and national borders. Similar protocols were established for the Internet to define how sending and receiving computers identify each other, as well as the form in which messages must be labeled for delivery.

Just as houses are assigned addresses that distinguish them from their neighbors, computers on the Internet are assigned unique identifiers known as **IP addresses**. An IP address is a number, usually written as a dotted sequence such as 147.134.2.20. When a new computer is connected to the Internet, the owner's Internet Service Provider (ISP) or equivalent organization must assign the computer an IP address. Once the computer obtains its IP address and is physically linked to the network, the computer can send and receive messages, as well as access other Internet services. The manner in which messages are sent and received over the Internet is defined by a pair of protocols called the **Transmission Control Protocol** (**TCP**) and **Internet Protocol** (**IP**). TCP controls the method by which messages are broken down into packets and then reassembled when they reach their final destination. IP, on the other hand, is concerned with labeling the packets for delivery and controlling the packets' paths from sender to recipient. The combination of these two protocols, written as TCP/IP, is often referred to as the language of the Internet. Any computer that is able to "speak" the language defined by TCP/IP will be able to communicate with any other computer on the Internet.

When a person sends a message over the Internet, specialized software using the rules of TCP breaks that message into packets (no bigger than 1,500 characters each) and labels the packets according to their sequence (for example, packet 2 of 5). Next, software following the rules of IP labels those packets with routing information, including the IP addresses of the source and destination computers. Once labeled, the packets are sent independently over the Internet. Special-purpose machines called **routers** receive the packets, access the routing information, and pass the packets on toward their destination. The routers, which are maintained by the companies and organizations that manage the network connections, use various information sources, including statistics on traffic patterns, to determine the best path for each packet to follow (Figure 3.10). As an analogy, consider driving a car to a familiar destination. You most likely have a standard route that you take, but you might vary that route if you see heavy traffic ahead or know of road closings due to construction. In a similar manner, routers are able to adjust for congestion or machine failures as they direct each individual packet. When the packets arrive at their destination, they may be out of order, due to the various routes by which they traveled. TCP software running on the recipient's computer then reassembles the packets in the correct sequence to recreate the original message.

Domain Names

From an Internet user's perspective, remembering the digits that make up IP addresses would be tedious and error prone. If you mistype only one digit in an IP address, you might mistakenly specify a computer halfway around the world. Fortunately, the Internet supports a **domain-name system** (**DNS**) where

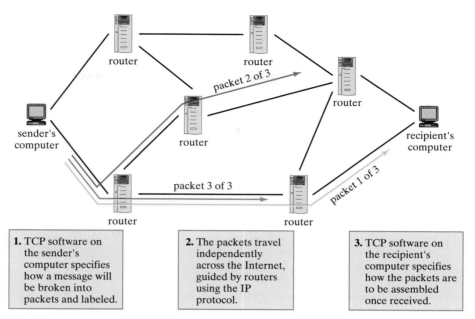

1. TCP software on the sender's computer specifies how a message will be broken into packets and labeled.

2. The packets travel independently across the Internet, guided by routers using the IP protocol.

3. TCP software on the recipient's computer specifies how the packets are to be assembled once received.

Figure 3.10 Transmitting a message over the Internet.

each individual machine is assigned a name that can be used in place of its IP address. For example, the computer with IP address 147.134.2.20 can be referred to by the name `bluejay.creighton.edu`. Such names, commonly referred to as ***domain names***, are hierarchical in nature, which makes them easier to remember. The leftmost part of a domain name specifies the name of the machine, whereas the subsequent parts indicate the organization (and possibly sub-organizations) to which the computer belongs. The rightmost part of the domain name is known as the ***top-level domain*** and identifies the type of organization with which the computer is associated. For example, the computer `bluejay.creighton.edu` is named `bluejay` and belongs to Creighton University, which is an educational institution. Similarly, `www.sales.acme.com` is a computer named `www` (a common name given to Web servers) belonging to the sales department of a fictitious Acme Corporation, which is a commercial business. Since 1998, the assignment of domain names and IP addresses has been coordinated by the Internet Corporation for Assigned Names and Numbers (ICANN), a nonprofit coalition of businesses, academic institutions, and individuals. ICANN accredits companies, known as ***domain-name registrars***, which sell domain-name rights directly to consumers.

Figure 3.11 lists examples of common top-level domains. However, Internet users should be aware that these top-level domains are used primarily by American companies and organizations. Computers located in other countries are often identified by country-specific top-level domains, such as `ca` (Canada), `uk` (United Kingdom), `br` (Brazil), and `in` (India).

Top Level Domain	Primary Use
edu	U.S. educational institutions
com	Commercial organizations
org	Nonprofit organizations
mil	U.S. military
gov	U.S. government
net	Network providers and busnesses

Figure 3.11 Top-level domain names.

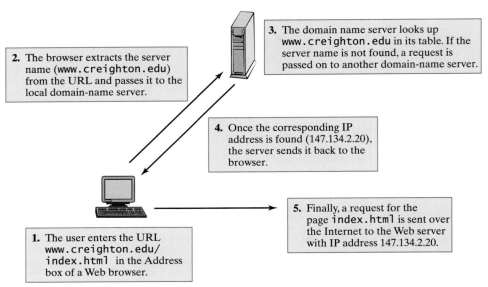

2. The browser extracts the server name (`www.creighton.edu`) from the URL and passes it to the local domain-name server.

3. The domain name server looks up `www.creighton.edu` in its table. If the server name is not found, a request is passed on to another domain-name server.

4. Once the corresponding IP address is found (147.134.2.20), the server sends it back to the browser.

1. The user enters the URL `www.creighton.edu/index.html` in the Address box of a Web browser.

5. Finally, a request for the page `index.html` is sent over the Internet to the Web server with IP address 147.134.2.20.

Figure 3.12 Domain-name servers translate domain names into IP addresses.

Domain names help Internet users identify specific computers efficiently, because these names are much easier to remember than numeric IP addresses are. However, any communication that takes place over the Internet requires the IP addresses of the source and destination computers. Special-purpose computers called **domain-name servers** are used to store mappings between domain names and their corresponding IP addresses. When a computer sends a message to a destination such as `bluejay.creighton.edu`, the sending computer first transmits a request to a domain-name server, which matches the recipient's domain name to an IP address. After looking up the domain name in a table, the domain-name server returns the associated IP address (here, 147.134.2.20) to the sender's computer. This enables the sender to transmit the message to the correct destination. If a particular domain-name server does not have the requested domain name stored locally, it forwards the request to another domain-name server on the Internet; this process continues until the corresponding IP address is found (see Figure 3.12).

History of the Web

Although Internet communications among universities and government organizations were common in the 1980s, the Internet did not achieve mainstream popularity until the early 1990s, when the World Wide Web was developed. The Web, a multimedia environment in which documents can be seamlessly linked over the Internet, was the brainchild of Tim Berners-Lee (1955–), pictured in Figure 3.13. During the 1980s, Berners-Lee was a researcher at the European Laboratory for Particle Physics (CERN). Since CERN researchers were located all across Europe and used different types of computers and software, they found it difficult to share information effectively. To address this problem, Berners-Lee envisioned a system in which researchers could freely exchange data, regardless of their locations and the types of computers they used. In 1989, he proposed the basic idea for the Web, suggesting that documents could be stored on Internet-linked computers such that an authorized individual on one computer could have access to files stored on another.

Hypertext and the Web

Although Berners-Lee's vision for the Web was revolutionary, his idea was built upon a long-standing practice of linking related documents to enable easy access. Books containing **hypertext**, or documents with interlinked text and media, have existed for millennia. This hypertext might tie a portion of a document to related annotations, as in the Jewish Talmud (first century B.C.), or might provide

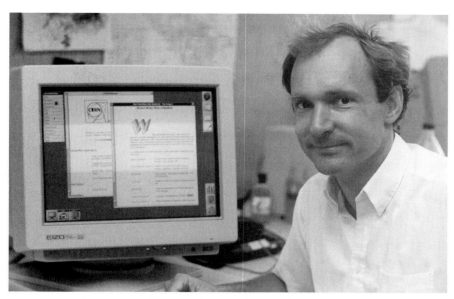

Figure 3.13　Tim Berners-Lee.

links to nonsequential alternate story lines, as in the Indian epic Ramayana (third century B.C.). The concept of an electronic hypertext system was first conceived in 1945, when Presidential science advisor Vannevar Bush (1890–1974) outlined designs for a machine that would store textual and graphical information in such a way that any piece of information could be arbitrarily linked to any other piece. The first small-scale computer hypertext systems were developed in the 1960s and culminated in the popular HyperCard system that shipped with Apple Macintosh computers in the late 1980s.

Berners-Lee was innovative, however, in that he combined the key ideas of hypertext with the distributed nature of the Internet. His design for the Web relied on two different types of software running on Internet-enabled computers. The first kind of software executes on a ***Web server***, a computer that stores documents and "serves" them to other computers that want access. The second kind, called a ***Web browser***, allows users to request and view the documents stored on servers. Using Berners-Lee's system, a person running a Web browser could quickly access and jump between documents, even if the servers storing those documents were thousands of miles apart.

Mainstream Adoption of the Web

In 1990, Berners-Lee produced working prototypes of a Web server and browser. His browser was limited by today's standards, in that it was text based and offered only limited support for images and other media. This early version of the Web acquired a small but enthusiastic following when Berners-Lee made it available over the Internet in 1991. However, the Web might have remained an obscure research tool if others had not expanded on Berners-Lee's creation, developing browsers designed to accommodate the average computer user. In 1993, Marc Andreesen (1971–) and Eric Bina (1964–), of the University of Illinois' National Center for Supercomputing Association (NCSA), wrote the first graphical browser, which they called Mosaic (Figure 3.14). Mosaic employed buttons and clickable links as navigational aids, making the Web easier to traverse. The browser also supported the integration of images and media within pages, which enabled developers to create more visually appealing Web documents. The response to Mosaic's release in 1993 was overwhelming. As more and more people learned how easy it was to store and access information using the Web, the number of Web servers on the Internet grew from 50 in 1992 to 3,000 in 1994.[2] In 1994, Andreesen left NCSA to found the Netscape Communications Corporation, which marketed an extension of the Mosaic browser called Netscape Navigator. Originally, Netscape charged a small fee for its browser, although students and educators were exempt from this cost. However, when Microsoft introduced its Internet Explorer browser as free software in 1995, Netscape was eventually forced to

Figure 3.14 Marc Andreesen

follow suit. The availability of free, easy-to-use browsers certainly contributed to the astounding growth of the Web in the mid 1990s.

The late 1990s were a dynamic time for the Web, during which Netscape and Microsoft released enhanced versions of their browsers and battled for market share. Initially, Netscape was successful in capitalizing on its first-mover advantage—in 1996, approximately 75% of all operational browsers were Netscape products. By 1999, however, Internet Explorer had surpassed Navigator as the most commonly used browser.[3] Finding it difficult to compete with Microsoft, Andreesen relinquished control of Netscape in 1999, selling the company to AOL for $10 billion in stock. By 2002, it was estimated that more than 90% of all browsers in use were versions of Internet Explorer.[4]

The reasons behind Internet Explorer's ultimate dominance of the browser market are a topic of some debate. Certainly, Microsoft's financial position was much stronger than Netscape's. Owing to its success with other software products, Microsoft possessed vast resources with which to develop and market its browsers. Netscape's income, on the other hand, was derived solely from browser-based technology, and the company suffered financially when Microsoft's marketing strategy forced it to release its browser for free. More significantly, though, Microsoft was able to leverage its dominance in operating systems by packaging Internet Explorer as part of Windows. Any customer who purchased a computer with a Windows operating system automatically received a copy of Internet Explorer. While this strategy proved highly successful, it also led to legal problems for Microsoft, which was found guilty of several antitrust charges in the late 1990s.

Although Internet Explorer and Netscape Navigator are still the most popular browsers on the market, the software industry also offers numerous others to satisfy niche markets. These include text-based browsers for environments that don't support graphics, text-to-speech browsers for vision-impaired users, and browsers designed to run on new technologies such as cell phones and personal digital assistants (PDAs).

Web Growth

Figure 3.15 documents the growth of the World Wide Web over the past decade, as estimated by the 2002 Netcraft Web Server Survey. It is interesting to note the dramatic increases in the Web's size after advances in browser technology: the release of Mosaic in 1993, Netscape in 1995, and Internet Explorer in 1996. The number of active Web servers has also grown considerably during the past ten years—according to the latest estimates, roughly one out of every five computers on the Internet (20.4%) acts as a server. Of course, each Web server can store a large number of pages, so the size of the Web in terms of pages is even more impressive. In 2002, the Google search engine (google.com) claimed to have

Year	Computers on the Internet[5]	Web Servers on on the Internet[6]
2002	162,128,493	33,082,657
2000	93,047,785	18,169,498
1998	36,739,000	4,279,000
1996	12,881,000	300,000
1994	3,212,000	3,000
1992	992,000	50

Figure 3.15   Internet and Web growth.

more than 3 billion Web pages indexed, and other sources estimate that the Web encompasses as many as 5 billion pages.

The Web's development is now guided by a nonprofit organization called the World Wide Web Consortium (W3C), which was founded by Berners-Lee in 1994. The W3C maintains and regulates Web-related standards and oversees the design of Web-based technologies. Similar to the Internet Society, the W3C relies mainly on volunteer labor from technically qualified and interested individuals.

How the Web Works

Like Internet communications, the World Wide Web relies on protocols to ensure that Web pages are accessible to any computer, regardless of the machine's hardware, operating system, browser, or location. The standards most central to the Web interactions are HTML and the HyperText Transfer Protocol (HTTP), which work in combination with TCP/IP to enable the exchange of Web pages over the Internet.

HTML

As we saw in Chapters 1 and 2, authors define the content of Web pages using HTML, the HyperText Markup Language. By placing tags and special symbols within text documents, designers can create pages; format the included text; and incorporate links, images, and other media. Part of a Web browser's job is to read HTML tags and render pages accordingly. For example, when a browser encounters text enclosed in <b></b> tags, it interprets those tags as specifying bold text and displays the characters in a heavier font.

HTML is an evolving standard, which means that new features are added to the language in response to changes in technology and user needs. The current standard for HTML, as defined by the World Wide Web Consortium, is known as XHTML 1.0, recognizing the language's connections to the more general hypertext language XML. In particular, HTML has incorporated many features from XML, including the ability to define new, customized tags (although these advanced features are beyond the scope of this book). Web browsers work because they all know and follow the HTML standard. Although there are subtle differences among browsers, all Web browsers understand the same basic set of tags and display text and formatting similarly. Thus, when an author places an HTML document on a Web server, all users who view the page will see the same formatting, regardless of their machines or browser software.

Web Protocol: HTTP

To a person "surfing" the Web, the process of locating, accessing, and displaying Web pages is transparent. When the person requests a particular page, either by entering its location into the browser's Address box or by clicking a link, the new page is displayed in the browser window as if by magic. In reality, complex communications are taking place between the computer running the browser and the Web server that stores the desired page. When the person requests the page, the browser must first identify the Web server on which that page resides. Recall from Chapter 1 that the Web address, or URL, for a

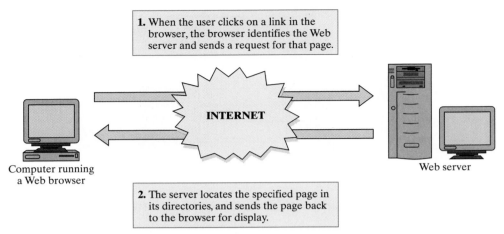

1. When the user clicks on a link in the browser, the browser identifies the Web server and sends a request for that page.

INTERNET

Computer running
a Web browser

Web server

2. The server locates the specified page in its directories, and sends the page back to the browser for display.

Figure 3.16   Web browser and server communications.

page includes the name of the server, as well as the document name. Once the server name has been extracted from the URL, the browser sends a message to that server over the Internet and requests the page (following the steps depicted in Figure 3.10). The Web server receives the request, locates the page within its directories, and sends the page's text back in a message. When the message is received, the browser interprets the HTML formatting information embedded in the page and displays the page accordingly in the browser window (Figure 3.16). The protocol that determines how messages exchanged between browsers and servers are formatted is known as the ***HyperText Transfer Protocol (HTTP)***.

Caching

It is interesting to note that accessing a single page might involve several rounds of communication between the browser and server. If the Web page contains embedded elements, such as images or sound clips, the browser will not recognize this until it begins displaying the page. When the browser encounters an HTML tag that specifies an embedded element, the browser must then send a separate message to the server requesting the item. Thus, loading a page that contains 10 images will require 11 interactions between the browser and server—one for the page itself and one for each of the 10 images. To avoid redundant and excessive downloading, most browsers utilize a technique called ***caching***. When a page or image is first downloaded, it is stored in a temporary directory on the user's computer. The next time the page or image is requested, the browser first checks to see if it has a copy stored locally in the cache, and, if so, whether the copy is up to date (this is accomplished by contacting the server and asking how recently the page was changed). If an up-to-date copy is stored locally, then the browser can display this copy, instead of downloading the original. Note that it is still necessary for the browser to contact the Web server, since the document on the server might have been modified since it was last cached. However, caching can still save time, because the browser avoids downloading redundant copies.

Looking Ahead...

In the short time since their inception, the Internet and World Wide Web have revolutionized the way in which people use computers. As recently as 20 years ago, most computers were stand-alone devices, not connected to any other computers. With the popularization of the Internet, however, computers have progressed from computation devices into sophisticated communications vehicles. Through electronic mail, instant messaging, and online chat rooms, people from around the world can communicate, sharing ideas and computing resources. The World Wide Web, an even more recent invention, has also greatly affected the role of computers in our society. By offering instant access to massive amounts of data, the Web has changed the way in which we communicate, learn, research, shop, and entertain ourselves. Furthermore, because almost anyone can create a Web page, the Web allows us to share information about ourselves and our work—from family photos to unpublished novels—with the world.

In Chapter 2, you were introduced to the basics of Web design and created your own Web page using HTML. Now that you are familiar with the history and architecture of the Internet and Web, the next chapter will teach you how to extend your pages to make them interactive. In this chapter, we will present the fundamentals of the JavaScript programming language, which you will be working with throughout the programming portion of this book. Instead of just displaying text and images, JavaScript-enabled pages prompt the user for information and incorporate that information within the page. Once you become skilled at developing pages that respond and react to user input, you will be able to contribute even more engaging and useful documents to the Web.

Chapter Summary

- The Internet traces its roots back to the ARPANet, which was funded by the U.S. Department of Defense's Advanced Research Project Agency (ARPA). In 1969, the ARPANet linked four computers at UCLA, UCSB, SRI, and Utah

- The growth of the ARPANet in the 1970s greatly exceeded expectations, prompting the National Science Foundation (NSF) to become involved in the upgrading and maintenance of the ARPANet in 1984.

- In the mid 1980s, the ARPANet became known as the Internet, acknowledging its structural similarities with the nation's interstate highway system.

- Recognizing that continued growth would require an influx of funding and research, the government decided in the mid 1990s to privatize the Internet.

- In 2002, there were an estimated 162 million computers connected to the Internet.

- The design of the ARPANet—and hence of today's Internet—was strongly influenced by the ideas of Paul Baran, who proposed that it be distributed and packet-switching.

- In a distributed network, control is distributed across a large number of machines, allowing for messages to be rerouted along alternate connections when a particular computer or connection fails.

- In a packet-switching network, messages are broken into smaller packets and sent independently. Advantages of this approach include a more efficient use of the connections, the ability to react to failures and congestion, and improved reliability.

- The Internet Society maintains and enforces standards and protocols concerning the Internet, and also organizes committees that propose new Internet-related technologies and software.

- The Transmission Control Protocol (TCP) controls the method by which messages are broken down into packets and then reassembled when they reach their final destination. The Internet Protocol (IP) is concerned with labeling the packets for delivery and controlling the packets' paths from sender to recipient.

- Each computer on the Internet is assigned an IP address (e.g., 147.134.2.20) that uniquely identifies it. Domain names (e.g., bluejay.creighton.edu) can alternatively be used and then mapped to IP addresses by domain name servers.

- First proposed by Tim Berners-Lee in 1989, the World Wide Web is a multimedia environment in which documents can be seamlessly linked over the Internet.

- The Web relies on two different types of software running on Internet-enabled computers: a Web server stores documents and "serves" them to computers that want access; a Web browser, allows users to request and view the documents stored on servers.

- While working prototypes of the Web were available in 1990, the growth of the Web was slow until the introduction of graphical browsers (NCSA Mosaic in 1993, Netscape Navigator in 1995, and Microsoft Internet Explorer in 1996), which better integrated multimedia elements and made navigation simpler.

- In 2002, there were an estimated 33 million Web servers worldwide, providing access to 3-5 billion Web pages.

- The Web's development is now guided by a non-profit organization called the World Wide Web consortium (W3C), which was founded by Berners-Lee in 1994.

- The standards most central to the Web interations are HTML and HTTP. The Hypertext Markup Language (HTML) defines the content of Web pages, whereas the HyperText Transfer Protocol (HTTP) determines how messages exchanged between browsers and servers are formatted.

Review Questions

1. TRUE or FALSE? The ARPANet, the precursor to today's Internet, was funded primarily by the U.S. Department of Defense.
2. TRUE or FALSE? Since the ARPANet used ordinary phone lines to connect computers over large distances, it was slow compared to existing technologies of the time.
3. TRUE or FALSE? In a centralized computer network, the failure of a single machine or connection can isolate large portions of the network.
4. TRUE or FALSE? A router is a special-purpose computer on the Internet that receives message packets, accesses routing information, and passes the packets on toward their destination.
5. TRUE or FALSE? When a message is broken into packets for transmission over the Internet, it is guaranteed that all packets will take the same route from source to destination.
6. TRUE or FALSE? 147.134.2.20 is an example of an IP address.
7. The Internet Society, an international nonprofit organization, maintains and enforces standards for the hardware and software of the Internet.
8. TRUE or FALSE? The World Wide Web was developed in the early 1970s, shortly after the development of the Internet.
9. TRUE or FALSE? Microsoft marketed the first commercial Web browser.
10. TRUE or FALSE? In the URL http://www.prenhall.com/reed/index.html, the part www.prenhall.com identifies the Web server where the page is stored.
11. The Internet of today evolved from the ARPANet of the 1960s and 70s. In what ways is the Internet similar to the old ARPANet? In what ways is it different?
12. The Internet is often described as the "Information Superhighway." Describe how the analogy of a highway system fits the structure of the Internet.
13. Paul Baran proposed two ground-breaking design ideas for the structure and behavior of the ARPANet. Describe these design ideas and the benefits they provide.
14. Describe how packet switching can increase the reliability of a network.
15. Internet communications are defined by a set of protocols called TCP/IP. What do TCP and IP stand for, and what is the role of each protocol in transmitting and receiving information?
16. What is an IP address? What steps are involved in mapping a computer's domain name (e.g., bluejay.creighton.edu) to its IP address?
17. Which has grown at a faster rate, the Internet or the Web? Justify your answer.
18. What is hypertext? How are the key ideas of hypertext incorporated into the Web?

19. What specific features did the Mosaic browser include that were not available in earlier browsers? How did these features help make the Web accessible to a larger audience?

20. Describe two factors that contributed to Microsoft's dominance of the browser market.

21. What does HTTP stand for, and what is its role in facilitating Web communications?

22. The World Wide Web Consortium maintains and regulates Web-related standards and oversees the design of Web-based technologies. Visit its Web site (`www.w3.org`) to review the organization's goals and list of technologies under active development. Describe three technologies (other than HTML, HTTP, and XML) whose development is managed by the World Wide Web Consortium.

23. How does caching improve the performance of a Web browser? Does caching reduce the number of interactions that take place between the browser and the Web server?

References

"All About the Internet Society." *Internet Society*, May 2003. Online at `http://www.isoc.org/isoc/`.

Berners-Lee, Tim, Mark Fischetti, and Michael L. Derouzos. *Weaving the Web: The Original Design and Ultimate Destiny of the World Wide Web.* New York: HarperBusiness, 2000.

Bush, Vannevar. "As We May Think." *Atlantic Monthly*, July 1945. Online at `http://www.theatlantic.com/unbound/flashbks/computer/bushf.htm`.

Comer, Douglas E. *The Internet Book: Everything you need to know about computer networking and how the Internet works*, 3rd ed. Upper Saddle River, NJ: Prentice Hall, 2000.

Deitel, H.M., P.J. Deitel, and T.R. Nieto. *Internet and World Wide Web: How to Program.* Upper Saddle River, NJ: Prentice Hall, 2000.

Griffin, Scott. "Internet Pioneers." December 2000. Online at `http://www.ibiblio.org/pioneers/index.html`.

Hafner, Katie, and Matthew Lyon. *Where Wizards Stay Up Late: The Origins of the Internet.* New York: Touchstone Books, 1998.

Leiner, Barry M., et al. "A Brief History of the Internet, Version 3.31." *Internet Society*, August 2000. Online at `http://www.isoc.org/internet/history/brief.shtml`.

Endnotes

1. "Internet Domain Survey." *Internet Software Consortium*, July 2002. Online at `http://www.isc.org/ds/`.

2. "Netcraft Web Server Survey." *Netcraft*, January 2003. Online at `http://www.netcraft.com/survey/`.

3. Borland, John. "Browser Wars: High Price, Huge Rewards." *CNETNews.com*, April 2003. Online at `http://zdnet.com.com/2100-1104-996866.html`.

4. Borland, John. "Browser Wars: High Price, Huge Rewards." *CNETNews.com*, April 2003. Online at `http://zdnet.com.com/2100-1104-996866.html`.

5. "Internet Domain Survey." *Internet Software Consortium*, July 2002. Online at `http://www.isc.org/ds/`.

6. "Netcraft Web Server Survey." *Netcraft*, January 2003. Online at `http://www.netcraft.com/survey/`.

Chapter

JavaScript and Dynamic Web Pages

This chapter uses narrative, examples, and hands-on exercises to introduce programming concepts and Web development skills.

Calling JavaScript 'the glue that holds Web pages together' is short and easy to use, but doesn't do justice to what's going on. Glue sets and hardens, but JavaScript is more dynamic than glue. It can create a reaction and make things keep going, like a catalyst.

Brendan Eich
Innovators of the Net: Brendan Eich and JavaScript, 1998

Kids are taking PCs and the Internet to new heights. They're the ones that are designing the cutting-edge web sites. They're the ones that are pushing forth things like digital music, digital photos, instant messaging; and they will take this tool in directions that we don't even expect.

Bill Gates
Washington2Washington Educational Partnership, 2000

As you learned in Chapters 2 and 3, the World Wide Web is a vast, interconnected network of documents that effectively integrates text and media such as images, movies, and sounds. The HyperText Markup Language (HTML) consists of tags that identify the contents of a page and provide formatting information for the Web browser. Using HTML tags, it is possible to develop attractive, information-rich pages that can be displayed on the Web. However, when used alone, HTML can produce only *static pages*. This means that HTML pages look the same and behave in the same manner each time they are loaded into a browser.

In 1995, Brendan Eich and his research team at Netscape Communications Corporation developed a simple programming language, JavaScript, for augmenting Web pages and making them *dynamic*—that is, capable of changing their appearance over time or in response to a user's actions (such as typing, mouse clicks, and other input methods). JavaScript statements are commands that instruct the browser to perform some action within the page, such as prompting the user for his name or displaying that name in a customized message. In this chapter, you will begin augmenting your own Web pages with JavaScript, focusing on simple techniques for enabling user interaction. You will learn to write JavaScript statements that prompt the user for information, store that information in memory, and display text in the page that incorporates the user's input. In subsequent chapters, you will build upon these basic skills, mastering the fundamentals of programming through the development of dynamic Web pages.

Dynamic Web Pages

If you have spent any time surfing the Web, you have no doubt encountered pages that change while you are looking at them, varying their contents and responding to your actions. At commercial sites, banner ads may cycle as you view the site or may react when you place the mouse pointer over them. Similarly, search engines prompt you to enter specific topics on which you want information and then retrieve lists of Web pages related to those topics. These are examples of *dynamic* pages, in that their behavior changes each time they are loaded or as events occur. As you have learned in previous chapters, HTML is a text-formatting language that allows the page designer to stipulate the structure and layout of a page. It is known as a "markup language," since it lets the user specify page formatting and layout by marking up the text with tags and special symbols. Although HTML is sufficient for creating *static* pages—pages in which the content doesn't change—it does not provide capabilities for specifying dynamic behavior. In order for page designers to indicate actions that are to occur within the page, a programming language is needed.

A ***programming language*** is a language for specifying instructions that a computer can execute. Each ***statement*** in a programming language specifies a particular action that the computer is to carry out, such as changing an image or opening a new window when the user clicks a button. As you will see in Chapters 6 and 8, general-purpose programming languages such as C++ and Java allow the programmer to write applications that solve a variety of problems. JavaScript, which was derived from Java, is a simple programming language designed for a very specific task: adding dynamic features to Web pages. The simplest way to add dynamic content to a Web page is to embed JavaScript statements directly within the page using SCRIPT tags. When a designer embeds statements between the tags `<script type="text/javascript">` and `</script>`, the Web browser recognizes the statements as JavaScript code and automatically executes them when the page is loaded. This means that the actions specified by the statements are carried out in order.

Interaction via Assignments and Write Statements

Since JavaScript was designed to be simple, creating a basic dynamic Web page does not require extensive programming skills. For example, Figure 4.1 shows a Web page that demonstrates dynamic behavior, interacting with the user and displaying a message based on that interaction. The page performs these tasks via two JavaScript statements, embedded within SCRIPT tags. The first statement instructs the browser to prompt the user for his or her name, and the second statement displays a greeting in the page that includes that name. In this and subsequent figures, JavaScript statements are highlighted in gray to differentiate them from HTML elements and text within the page. The remainder of this section discusses the details of each JavaScript statement from Figure 4.1.

- The first JavaScript statement (line 12) within the SCRIPT tags performs the task of asking the user to enter a name and remembering the name for future reference. The text to the right of the '=' instructs the browser to prompt the user for his or her name. The browser accomplishes this by opening a ***prompt window***, a separate window in which the user can enter values (Figure 4.2). In this example, the user can enter a name in the input box (the white rectangle inside the prompt window) and then click the OK button to submit the name.

  The text to the left of the '=' is known as a ***variable***. In programming terminology, a variable is a name used to symbolize a dynamic value, i.e., one that might change each time the page is loaded. In other words, a variable stores a value in memory, making that value accessible via the variable's name. In this example, the name entered by the user in the prompt window is assigned to the variable `firstName`. Thus, the user's name is stored under the variable name `firstName`, and each subsequent reference to `firstName` in the page accesses the user's name.

```
1.  <html>
2.  <!-- greet.html                                    Dave Reed -->
3.  <!-- Web page that displays a personalized greeting.     -->
4.  <!------------------------------------------------------->
5.
6.  <head>
7.     <title> Greetings </title>
8.  </head>
9.
10. <body>
11.   <script type="text/javascript">
12.     firstName = prompt("Please enter your name", "");
13.
14.     document.write("Hello " + firstName + ", welcome to my Web page.");
15.   </script>
16.
17.   <p>
18.   Whatever else you want to appear in your Web page...
19.   </p>
20. </body>
21. </html>
```

Figure 4.1 JavaScript statements embedded in a Web page.

Figure 4.2 Prompt window that appears when `greet.html` is loaded.

A JavaScript statement of this form, with a variable on the left side of '=' and some value on the right, is known as an ***assignment statement***. In general, the user can be prompted for any value and that value remembered using a JavaScript assignment statement of the form:

```
VARIABLE = prompt("PROMPT_MESSAGE", "");
```

Of course, the actual variable name will depend on the value being stored. Likewise, the page designer can vary the message that appears in the prompt window so that it requests any desired user input. In the place of "PROMPT_MESSAGE", any sequence of characters enclosed in quotes can be inserted. Such a sequence is known as a ***string literal***, or just a ***string***. In JavaScript statements, strings represent literal text that is displayed exactly as it is written (but without the quotes).

- The second JavaScript statement in Figure 4.1 (Line 14) displays a message in the page that incorporates the user's name. This type of JavaScript statement is known as a ***write statement***, since its purpose is to write a message in the Web page. The message displayed by a write statement can be text (a string) or a combination of text and variables connected with +. The + operator connects the pieces of the message together, substituting the value of a variable whenever a variable is encountered. For example, if "Dave" had been entered and stored in the variable `firstName`, then the above write statement would substitute "Dave" in place of the variable, producing the following message at the appropriate location in the page (Figure 4.3):

```
Hello Dave, welcome to my Web page.
```

In general, any message can be displayed in a Web page using a JavaScript write statement of the form:

```
document.write("MESSAGE TO BE DISPLAYED" + VARIABLE + "MORE MESSAGE" + …);
```

Of course, the literal text in the message will depend on the particular page, as will the names of variables that the message should include. If the message to be displayed is long, it can be broken into different sections, with pieces appearing on separate lines. For example,

```
document.write("MESSAGE TO BE DISPLAYED" + VARIABLE +
               "MORE MESSAGE" + …);
```

Figure 4.3   Final rendering of `greet.html` in a Web browser.

Common errors to avoid...

You may note that each JavaScript statement in Figure 4.1 ends with a semicolon. Technically, every basic JavaScript statement must end with a semicolon, though browsers tend to be forgiving if you occasionally omit the semicolons. Since there are instances in which missing semicolons can cause confusion or even errors, you should always include semicolons at the end of your statements.

Also, when breaking a long message into pieces and displaying it with a write statement, you must be very careful that each line contains only complete pieces (i.e., variables and/or character sequences enclosed in quotes). In particular, you cannot start a string on one line and continue it on the next. The starting quote and ending quote of each piece of text must be on the same line.

EXERCISE 4.1

Enter the `greet.html` text from Figure 4.1 into a new Web page and verify that the code behaves as described. Try entering different values in the input box and viewing the results. What is displayed if the user clicks OK without entering a value in the input area?

Formatting Output

The output produced by a write statement is embedded in the Web page, and the browser displays this output just as it does any other text. In particular, if a string in a write statement includes HTML tags, the browser will interpret those tags and format the text accordingly. For example, suppose that the write statement from Figure 4.1 (line 14) were modified to include HTML tags within the text:

```
document.write("Hello <i>" + firstName + "</i>, welcome to my Web page.");
```

Assuming that the variable firstName stores the value "Dave", this modified statement would write the text

```
Hello <i>Dave</i>, welcome to my Web page.
```

into the Web page, which the browser would display as

```
Hello Dave, welcome to my Web page.
```

In general, JavaScript treats any sequence of characters enclosed in quotes as literal text. Since the <i> </i> tags appear inside the quotes, they are written to the page just as any other text would be, and the browser interprets them as HTML formatting information. By contrast, anything not enclosed in quotes is interpreted less literally. In this example, the browser recognizes firstName as a variable whose value must be substituted into the message. If you had mistakenly enclosed the variable name in quotes, the browser would treat the name as literal text; this means that "firstName", rather firstName's value, would be displayed in the message.

EXERCISE 4.2

Modify your greet.html page so that the user's name appears in bold and the output is broken across two lines. For example:

```
Hello Dave,
welcome to my Web page.
```

⚠ Common errors to avoid...

While you were working on Exercise 4.2 (i.e., adding new JavaScript code to the greet.html page), perhaps you made a mistake at some point. For example, you might have forgotten the closing quotes on the message, or you might have misspelled document.write. Such errors in the format of HTML or JavaScript statements are known as *syntax errors*. For the most part, HTML syntax errors are easy to spot and correct; usually, the browser ignores malformed tags and continues on with the page. By contrast, when a syntax error occurs in JavaScript code, the page may fail to load. Since the designer cannot look at the rendered page to determine the exact nature and location of the problem, JavaScript syntax errors are more difficult to handle.

Fortunately, modern Web browsers provide features that help programmers identify and correct JavaScript syntax errors. Using Internet Explorer, you can set your preferences so that, which the browser encounters a JavaScript syntax error, a window appears to provide an error message specifying the cause of the error. To change your settings, select Internet Options under the Tools menu and click the Advanced tab. Then, make sure the box labeled Display a notification about every script error is checked.

Using Netscape Navigator, an error message will not automatically appear. Instead, messages can be seen in a separate window called the JavaScript Console. To open the JavaScript Console and view the error messages, select Web Development and then JavaScript Console from under the Tools menu, or simply type javascript: in the Address box.

JavaScript Variables

As the `greet.html` page from Figure 4.1 demonstrates, a variable can be used to represent a value, such as a name entered by the user. With a few exceptions, you can choose any name you wish to represent a value. Technically, a variable name can be any sequence of letters, digits, and underscores, as long as the sequence starts with a letter. Neither spaces nor special characters can be used in variable names. For example, all of the following are valid JavaScript variable names:

```
tempInFahr      SUM      current_age      Sum2Date      x
```

By contrast, the following are not valid JavaScript variable names:

```
2hotforU      salary$      two words      "sum_to_date"
```

The first name, `2hotforU`, is invalid, because it starts with a digit. The remaining names are invalid, because they contain characters other than letters, digits, and underscores.

JavaScript is case sensitive, meaning that capitalization matters. Consequently, variable names such as `sum,` `Sum`, and `SUM` all represent different variables. Also, JavaScript and Web browsers reserve certain words for other purposes, and these words should not be used to represent variables (Figure 4.5).

Reserved Words That Shouldn't Be Used as Variable Names				
abstract	delete	function	null	throw
boolean	do	goto	package	throws
break	double	if	private	transient
byte	else	implements	protected	true
case	enum	import	public	try
catch	export	in	return	typeof
char	extends	instanceof	short	var
class	false	int	static	void
const	final	interface	super	volatile
continue	finally	long	switch	while
debugger	float	native	synchronized	with
default	for	new	this	

Figure 4.4 JavaScript reserved words.

EXERCISE 4.3

Modify your `greet.html` page so that it prompts the user twice, once for his or her first name and again for last name. You will need to use a second variable to store the last name. To increase the readability of your code and thus make it easier to understand and modify in the future, choose a name that suggests the variable's purpose, such as `lastName` or `surname`. Once the user has submitted both names, the page should display the following message (with the appropriate names substituted, of course).

```
Hello Dave Reed,
or may I just call you Dave?
```

Variables and Memory Cells

In the abstract, a variable is a name that represents some dynamic value. If you are familiar with algebra, this concept is not new to you. For example, the equation $y = x^2 + 1$ refers to an abstract relationship between variables x and y. By substituting the desired value of x into the equation, we

Common errors to avoid...

The case sensitivity of variables in JavaScript can lead to subtle errors. For example, suppose that you assign a value to a variable called lastName, then later attempt to refer to that value with the name lastname.

```
lastName = prompt("Enter your last name", "");
    .
    .
    .
document.write(lastname);
```

An error will occur when this code is executed, since the variable lastname has not been assigned a value (despite the fact that lastName has). The error message would identify the write statement as the source of the error and would report that "lastname is not defined."

can determine the corresponding value of y. Within a computer program, variables refer to values that might change over time.

In practice, computers keep track of the values that variables represent by associating each variable with a specific piece of memory, known as a ***memory cell***. Each memory cell inside the computer stores the value of its corresponding variable. In JavaScript, a programmer assigns a value to a variable (thus storing the value in the variable's associated memory cell) via an assignment statement. For example, in the greet.html page (Figure 4.1), the variable firstName is assigned the value obtained by the prompt (i.e., the name entered by the user).

```
firstName = prompt("Please enter your name", "");
```

You can visualize assignments to variables by drawing a box to symbolize the memory cell and labeling the box with the variable name. When an assignment is made, the assigned value is written in the box to represent its storage in the corresponding memory cell.

firstName

After you assign a value to a particular variable, any reference to the variable name evaluates to the value stored in its associated memory cell. This means that the value stored in the memory cell is substituted for the variable name wherever that name appears. For example, after assignment of the value "Dave" to the variable firstName, the following two write statements are equivalent:

```
document.write("Hello " + firstName + ", welcome to my Web page.");
document.write("Hello Dave, welcome to my Web page.");
```

Once you create a variable, you can repeatedly assign values to that variable, but only the most recent value is retained in memory. Each new assignment overwrites the old contents of the memory cell with the new value being assigned. For example, the JavaScript code in Figure 4.5 prompts the user to enter a favorite food (Figure 4.6), stores the response in the variable food, and displays a message containing the specified food (Figure 4.7). The page then prompts the user to enter a least favorite food

```
1.   <html>
2.   <!-- food.html                                           Dave Reed -->
3.   <!-- Web page that prompts for and displays food preferences. -->
4.   <!------------------------------------------------------------------>
5.
6.   <head>
7.     <title> Who's Hungry? </title>
8.   </head>
9.
10.  <body>
11.    <script type="text/javascript">
12.      food = prompt("What is your favorite food?", "");
13.      document.write("Your favorite food is " + food + "<br />");
14.
15.      food = prompt("What is your least favorite food?", "");
16.      document.write("Your least favorite food is " + food);
17.    </script>
18.  </body>
19.  </html>
```

Figure 4.5   Web page that prompts the user for and then displays favorite/least favorite foods.

Figure 4.6   Prompt window for inputting a favorite food (`food.html`).

Figure 4.7   Message containing the favorite food is displayed (`food.html`).

(Figure 4.8) and displays this input in a similar manner (Figure 4.9). Since the favorite food is no longer needed, the same variable food can be reused to store the least favorite food, overwriting the old value.

Figure 4.8 Prompt window for inputting a least favorite food (food.html).

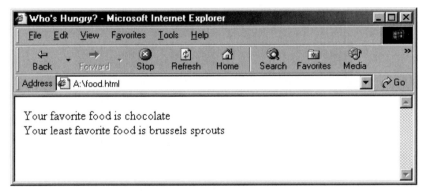

Figure 4.9 Final rendering of food.html in a Web browser.

EXERCISE 4.4

Enter the food.html text from Figure 4.5 into a new Web page and verify that the code behaves as described.

As you create Web pages, you will undoubtedly make typing errors. Mistyping the name of a variable can lead to unexpected results and may even cause an error message to appear in the browser. For example, imagine that the programmer unintentionally mistyped the variable name food in the second assignment statement of food.html (line 15), resulting in the following JavaScript code:

```
food = prompt("What is your favorite food?", "");
document.write("Your favorite food is " + food + "<br />");
foud = prompt("What is your least favorite food?", "");
document.write("Your least favorite food is " + food);
```

How would the browser react to this error? Modify the code in food.html to verify your prediction.

Now, consider a mistyped variable name at a different location, as part of the write statement at line 16:

```
document.write("Your least favorite food is " + foood);
```

How would the browser react to this error? Modify the code in food.html to verify your prediction.

EXERCISE 4.5

What would happen if the second and third statements (lines 13 and 15) in food.html (Figure 4.5) were swapped? That is, what if the programmer typed the following JavaScript code between the SCRIPT tags:

```
food = prompt("What is your favorite food?", "");
food = prompt("What is your least favorite food?", "");

document.write("Your favorite food is " + food + "<br />");
document.write("Your least favorite food is " + food);
```

Modify the code in food.html to verify your prediction.

Designer Secrets

You may have noticed that the JavaScript code you have written tends to follow a certain pattern. This should not be surprising, since the tasks you have performed in this chapter have been comparable in nature. In the case of greet.html (Figure 4.1), the page's purpose was to prompt the user for his or her name(s) and incorporate the name(s) in the text of the page. Similarly, the food.html page (Figure 4.5) prompted the user for a favorite and least favorite food and then incorporated them in the text of the page.

Whenever you are writing a page that asks the user to enter information and then incorporates that information in the page, you will need to include a particular sequence of JavaScript statements. Initially, one or more assignment statements will prompt the user for input values and store them in variables. Then, one or more write statements will display messages that involve the input values. Thus, the following general pattern holds:

```
<script type="text/javascript">
    input1 = prompt("PROMPT FOR 1ST VALUE", "");
    input2 = prompt("PROMPT FOR 2ND VALUE", "");
        .
        .
        .
    inputN = prompt("PROMPT FOR NTH VALUE", "");
    document.write("MESSAGE INVOLVING input1, …, inputN");
</script>
```

Interactive Pages

Figure 4.10 presents another example of an interactive Web page, this time using JavaScript code to display a verse of the children's song "Old MacDonald Had a Farm." The user is prompted to enter the name of an animal and the sound it makes; the words that the user provides are then incorporated into the write statements that display the verse.

This page differs from our previous examples in that each prompt contains a default value. Up to this point, all the prompts we have used in Web pages have been of the following form:

```
VARIABLE = prompt("PROMPT_MESSAGE", "");
```

The first string that appears inside the parentheses specifies the message that is to appear in the prompt window. Although so far we have ignored the second string, it in fact specifies a ***default*** value—a value that appears in the input box before the user types anything. When the second string is empty (i.e., it is a pair of quotes with no text in between), the prompt window will initially contain an empty input box. However, if the programmer specifies a default value within the quotes, then that value will appear in the input box, and the user can click OK to accept it. In Figure 4.10, the default values of "cow" and "moo" are provided for the animal name and sound, respectively (lines 14 and 15). If the user is happy with these choices, she simply clicks OK in each prompt window, and the cow verse will be displayed (Figures 4.11 – 4.13). If she wishes to see a different verse, she can always type over the default values and provide her own animal and sound.

```
1.   <html>
2.   <!-- oldmac.html                              Dave Reed -->
3.   <!-- Web page that displays a verse of Old MacDonald. -->
4.   <!------------------------------------------------------->
5.
6.   <head>
7.     <title> Old MacDonald </title>
8.   </head>
9.
10.  <body>
11.    <h3 style="text-align:center">Old MacDonald Had a Farm</h3>
12.
13.    <script type="text/javascript">
14.      animal = prompt("Enter a kind of animal:", "cow");
15.      sound = prompt("What kind of sound does it make?", "moo");
16.
17.      document.write("<p>Old MacDonald had a farm, E-I-E-I-O.<br />");
18.      document.write("And on that farm he had a " + animal + ", E-I-E-I-O.<br />");
19.      document.write("With a " + sound + "-" + sound + " here, and a " +
20.                     sound + "-" + sound + " there,<br />");
21.      document.write("  here a " + sound + ", there a " + sound +
22.                     ", everywhere a " + sound + "-" + sound + ".<br />");
23.      document.write("Old MacDonald had a farm, E-I-E-I-O.</p>");
24.    </script>
25.  </body>
26.  </html>
```

Figure 4.10 Web page that displays a verse of the song "Old MacDonald."

EXERCISE 4.6

Enter the oldmac.html text from Figure 4.10 into a new Web page and verify that it behaves as described. Once you have done this, modify the page so that it displays three verses of the song, prompting the user for an animal and a sound between each verse. You can create a three-verse version by cutting and pasting three copies of the code on lines 14 through 23, all within the same pair of SCRIPT tags. The same variables can be used for each verse, since each assignment to a variable overwrites the previous value. To make it easy for the user to display different verses, the calls to prompt should use different default values for each verse.

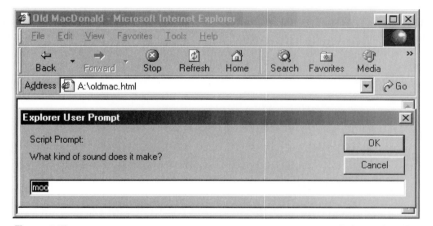

Figure 4.11   Prompt window for inputting the animal name (`oldmac.html`).

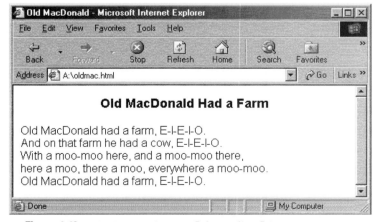

Figure 4.12   Prompt window for inputting the animal sound (`oldmac.html`).

Figure 4.13   Final rendering of `oldmac.html` in a Web browser.

Localizing Changes with Variables

In addition to storing values entered by the user, variables can also store values to which a programmer refers over and over. When a value is used repeatedly throughout a page, consistency problems can arise if the programmer wishes to change that value. Altering the value would require finding every occurrence in the page and making the exact same modification to each. To simplify such changes, the programmer could utilize a variable, assigning the value to that variable once and then using the variable throughout the code. Then, if she wanted to change the value, the programmer would only need to revise the one assignment.

For example, you may note that the refrain "E-I-E-I-O" appears several times in the "Old MacDonald" verse. Depending on the source, this refrain may be spelled differently, such as "Eeyigh-Eeyigh-Oh". If you wanted to be able to modify the refrain more easily, you could use a variable to store the desired string:

```
refrain = "E-I-E-I-O";
```

Once the value "E-I-E-I-O" is stored in the variable `refrain`, each occurrence of the string in the write statements can be replaced by the variable name. For example,

```
document.write("<p>Old MacDonald had a farm, " + refrain + ".<br />");
```

Since the browser substitutes the variable's value for every occurrence of the variable when rendering write statements, the displayed message is unchanged. However, using a variable allows you to change the spelling of the refrain throughout the page by making a single adjustment to the assignment, such as:

```
refrain = "Eeyigh-Eeyigh-Oh";
```

EXERCISE 4.7

Modify your `oldmac.html` page so that the song refrain is stored in a variable. For example,

```
refrain = "E-I-E-I-O";
```

Then, replace each occurrence of the string "E-I-E-I-O" with the refrain variable, as shown in the write statement that appears earlier in this section. If you complete the exercise correctly, the page's behavior should not change. This is because the value assigned to `refrain` is exactly the same as the text you are replacing.

EXERCISE 4.8

Modify your `oldmac.html` page so that the alternate spelling "Eeyigh-Eeyigh-Oh" is used in all the verses. [*Hint:* Since you have replaced the refrain text with a variable, this modification should require only a minimal change to your code.]

Example: Interactive Stories

A popular children's party activity is fill-in-the-blank stories, where a potentially humorous story is written down with blanks inserted in place of some of the key words. Before reading the story, the storyteller asks others present to fill in the blanks. Those selecting the words are told only the type of word required and have no other knowledge of the story. This lack of context in selecting words can result in an entertaining story when the words are plugged into the appropriate places. For example, consider the following beginning to a story:

```
It was a adjective kind of day when person's name walked out into the street.
The sky was a deep color, and same name was walking his new pet animal ...
```

Common errors to avoid...

When students begin to write JavaScript statements involving strings and variables, two error types occur particularly often. Learning to recognize and understand each type of error can save you considerable amounts of time and frustration.

Error: unterminated string literal

This error message appears when the browser encounters the beginning of a string but fails to find the closing quote on the same line. If necessary, a programmer can break a write statement across multiple lines, but each individual string must start and terminate on a single line. Thus, when text is too long to fit on one line, you must separate it into two strings, which are connected using '+'. For example,

```
document.write("This example is illegal since the
                string is broken across lines");

document.write("This example is OK, since the message " +
               "is broken into two distinct strings");
```

Error: missing) after argument list

This error message appears when the components of a message are not connected correctly, such as when the '+' is missing between two pieces of a message. When a string or variable is not followed by a '+', the browser expects to encounter a right parenthesis, which would signify the end of the write statement. For example, the write statement:

```
document.write("The value of x is " x);
```

would produce this error, since there is no '+' connecting the string and the variable. The correct form of the statement is:

```
document.write("The value of x is " + x);
```

Then, imagine that the participants make the following substitutions:

```
adjective = smarmy
person's name = Chris
color = mauve
animal = gnu
```

If the blanks are replaced with these words, then the story will read,

It was a <u>smarmy</u> kind of day when <u>Chris</u> walked out into the street. The sky was a deep <u>mauve,</u> and <u>Chris</u> was walking his new pet <u>gnu</u> ...

Now that you know how to create interactive Web pages using HTML and JavaScript, you can design and write a simple page that generates fill-in-the-blank stories.

 ### EXERCISE 4.9

Create a Web page named `story.html` that serves as an interactive fill-in-the-blank story program. Your page should contain JavaScript code that prompts the user for words to fill in the blanks in a story and then stores the entered words in variables. After reading in the user's word choices, your code should display the story in the Web page, using the values of the variables where appropriate.

The content of the story can be anything that you like—be creative! However, your story must meet the following conditions.

- It must be at least two paragraphs long.
- It must have at least six missing words.
- At least one of the missing words must be used multiple times in the story. For example, the person's name was used twice in the sample story above.
- The page should have a title, centered at the top, which includes your name.

Looking Ahead ...

In this chapter, you learned to create interactive Web pages using the JavaScript programming language. By including JavaScript statements between SCRIPT tags in a page, you were able to instruct the browser to prompt the user for information, store that information in variables, and then display text in the page that incorporated the user's input. In subsequent chapters, you will learn to add other dynamic features to Web pages using JavaScript.

Whereas all the interactive pages in this chapter involved text (such as a person's name, a favorite food, or fill-in-the-blank words), many tasks involve storing and manipulating numbers. For example, you might want to create a Web page for computing your course average, given your homework and test grades. Similarly, you might require a page for converting measurements from English to metric. Chapter 5 will focus on tasks such as these, which involve prompting for numbers, storing them, and processing them using various mathematical operations. Through tracing the behavior of sequences of assignment statements, you will not only learn about number representation and mathematical functions but also reinforce your understanding of variables and how they work. In addition, the differences between strings and numbers, both in their form and usage, will be highlighted.

Chapter Summary

- JavaScript is a simple programming language for making dynamic Web pages. Using JavaScript, Web designers can create pages that interact with the user and vary their contents each time they are loaded.

- A JavaScript statement is an instruction that tells the browser to perform some specific action, such as prompting the user for a value or displaying text within the page.

- JavaScript statements can be embedded between the tags `<script type="text/javascript">` and `</script>` inside the BODY of a Web page. When the Web page is loaded, the browser executes the statements inside the SCRIPT tags (i.e., the browser carries out in order the actions specified by those statements).

- An assignment statement is used to assign a name to a dynamic value, such as a name entered by the user at a prompt.

- When prompting the user for a value, the programmer can specify a string (a sequence of characters enclosed in quotes) that serves as the prompt message, followed by another string that specifies a default value for the prompt.

- A write statement is used to display a message within the Web page. A write statement can display text (a string) or a combination of text and variables connected with '+'.

- Since a message displayed by a write statement is embedded directly into the Web page, text within the message can be formatted using HTML tags.

- A variable is a name that is given to a dynamic value so that the value can be remembered and referred to later.

- In JavaScript, a variable name can be any sequence of letters, digits, and underscores that starts with a letter. Since JavaScript is case sensitive, capitalization matters.

- Each JavaScript variable is associated with a corresponding memory cell that stores the variable's value. A value is assigned to a variable (and thus stored in the corresponding memory cell) via an assignment statement (using '=').

- To simply the modification of a value used repeatedly throughout a page, a programmer can utilize a variable to represent the value. Then, if the value must be altered, the change can be accomplished with only one modification (to the assignment).

Supplemental Material and Exercises

Mixing Dynamic and Static Text

In all the examples you have seen so far, we have used write statements to display entire messages, even though only part of each message involved dynamic content. For example, the following write statement (from Figure 4.1) displays a message in which the user's name might change each time the page is loaded. However, the rest of the message (the two strings) will always be the same.

```
document.write("Hello " + firstName + ", welcome to my Web page.");
```

Since parts of this message are static (the same every time the page is loaded), it is possible to include those parts in the HTML text, leaving only the dynamic text (here, the user's name) in the JavaScript write statement. For example, consider the greet1.html page in Figure 4.14. The JavaScript assignment (line 12) that prompts the user for his name and stores that name in a variable is enclosed in its own pair of SCRIPT tags. Then, each time that name is needed within the page, we have included a separate write statement containing the firstName variable (enclosed in SCRIPT tags).

```
1.  <html>
2.  <!-- greet1.html                              Dave Reed -->
3.  <!-- Web page that displays a personalized greeting.   -->
4.  <!------------------------------------------------------------->
5.
6.  <head>
7.    <title> Greetings </title>
8.  </head>
9.
10. <body>
11.   <script type="text/javascript">
12.     firstName = prompt("Enter your name", "");
13.   </script>
14.
15.   <p>
16.   Hello <script type="text/javascript">document.write(firstName);</script>,
17.   how are you?
18.   </p>
19.
20.   <p>
21.   Would you believe that
22.   <script type="text/javascript">document.write(firstName);</script>
23.   is my name too?
24.   </p>
25. </body>
26. </html>
```

Figure 4.14   Web page that mixes dynamic and static content.

Figure 4.15 Prompt window for inputting the user's name (`greet1.html`).

Figure 4.16 Final rendering of `greet1.html` in a Web browser.

The advantage of this particular approach is that you can cleanly separate the static, unchanging content of the page from the dynamic content produced by JavaScript code. If you want the user's name to appear several times within your page, you can write the static content of the page and then insert the name using a write statement at each occurrence.

EXERCISE 4.10

Modify your home page so that it first prompts the user to enter a name, then inserts that name at several places within the page. You should use SCRIPT tags at the top of the BODY to read in the user's name and then add separate SCRIPT tags for each occurrence of the name within the page.

Nesting Quotes

As we have seen, JavaScript write statements can be used to display messages within a Web page. When creating a write statement, a Web designer must enclose the message text within quote marks to differentiate this text from variables and other code elements. The text and surrounding quote marks together are called a *string*, and programmers can delimit strings with either single quotes (') or double quotes ("). Thus, either of the following JavaScript write statements could be used to display the simple message: `Hello world!`

```
document.write("Hello world!");
document.write('Hello world!');
```

The ability to use either type of quotation mark is particularly useful when a programmer wants to display a message that incorporates quotes. For example, if you wish to display a message containing a single quote (or apostrophe), you can enclose the message in double quotes—this prevents the browser from misinterpreting a quote mark that is part of the message as indicating the end of the string. Similarly, if your message contains double quotation marks, you should delimit the message with single quotes. In the case of deeply nested quotation marks (e.g., quotes within quotes within quotes), a single quote can be represented as \' and a double quote as \". Using this backslash notation, it doesn't matter what type of quotation marks enclose the string, since the backslash properly identifies the nested character as part of the message.

For example, the following write statements would produce the same output:

```
document.write('The page said "Hello world" at the top.');
document.write("The page said \"Hello world\" at the top.");
```

EXERCISE 4.11

What error(s) occur when a JavaScript string contains incorrectly nested quotation marks? For example, enter the following write statement in a Web page and describe what happens when the statement is executed.

```
document.write("The page said "Hello world." at the top");
```

EXERCISE 4.12

On paper, specify JavaScript write statements that would produce the following lines of text. Then, verify that your write statements work by adding them to the BODY of a Web page (enclosed in SCRIPT tags).

```
The announcer screamed "Cubs win! Cubs win!"
The oath began as "I, 'state your name' swear to uphold..."
The oath began as "I, "state your name" swear to uphold..."
```

Alert Windows

In this chapter, you learned how to prompt the user for values by inserting JavaScript prompt statements into a page. When prompt("PROMPT MESSAGE", " ") appears on the right side of an assignment statement, the browser opens a prompt window in which the user can enter a value, such as a name. A similar type of JavaScript statement, alert, can be used when the programmer wants to alert the user to a message or piece of information, but no input is required. An alert statement has the following general form:

```
alert("ALERT MESSAGE");
```

where the alert message to be displayed is a string. Similar to prompt statements, alert statements cause a new window to appear and display a specified message. Unlike a prompt window, however, an alert window does not include a dialog box. After reading the message, the user simply clicks the OK button to close the alert window.

For example, the code below, when embedded in the body of a Web page, would cause the alert window in Figure 4.17 to appear.

```
<script type="text/javascript">
  alert("Welcome to my page");
</script>
```

Figure 4.17   Alert window.

Although alert windows are easy to create, many users find them annoying. Using a write statement, the programmer could have embedded the message directly into the page, rather than including it in a separate window that users must click to close. Later in the text, we will employ alert windows to warn the user when something has gone wrong (for example, if an input value has been entered in the wrong format). For now, however, there is one particular application for which alert windows can be useful.

In the `bye.html` page (Figure 4.18), the BODY tag (line 9) includes a new attribute, named ONUNLOAD. This attribute specifies code that is executed when the user leaves the page, either by hitting the back button, clicking a link, or entering a new address in the Address box. In this case, the ONUNLOAD attribute specifies an `alert` statement, causing the browser to display the message "Thanks for visiting!" when the user leaves the page.

```
1   <html>
2   <!-- bye.html                                    Dave Reed -->
3   <!-- Demonstrates call to alert when page unloads.    -->
4   <!------------------------------------------------------------>
5   <head>
6     <title> Bye Bye Page </title>
7   </head>
8
9   <body onUnload="alert('Thanks for visiting!');">
10     Whatever is supposed to appear in the page...
11   </body>
12  </html>
```

Figure 4.18   Web page that pops up an alert window when the page unloads.

Figure 4.19   Alert window appears when the user leaves the page (`bye.html`).

EXERCISE 4.13

Add an ONUNLOAD attribute containing an alert statement to your home page, causing users to receive a farewell message when they leave. Be warned that many users find such farewells annoying, since they require the user to perform an additional action (closing the alert window) in order to leave your page.

EXERCISE 4.14

Modify your home page to incorporate features of the greet.html page (Figure 4.1) and the bye.html page (Figure 4.18). When you have completed this exercise, your home page should prompt the user to enter a name and then display a customized farewell when the user leaves the page. For example, if the user entered the name "Dave" when the page was loaded, then a message such as "So long, Dave, thanks for visiting" should be displayed in an alert window when the page is unloaded.

5 Chapter

JavaScript Numbers and Expressions

This chapter uses narrative, examples, and hands-on exercises to introduce programming concepts and Web development skills.

It is a capital mistake to theorize before one has data. Insensibly one begins to twist facts to suit theories, instead of theories to suit facts.

Sir Arthur Conan Doyle
A Scandal in Bohemia

Every creator painfully experiences the chasm between his inner vision and its ultimate expression.

Cleveland Amory

In Chapter 4, you began using JavaScript to develop interactive Web pages. Using prompt, assignment statements, and write statements, you were able to write pages that ask the user to provide certain information (such as words for a fill-in-the-blank story) and then display messages that incorporate those words. All of the examples we considered, however, involved reading in and storing text. In addition to strings—text enclosed in quotes—you can use JavaScript to read and store other types of data. In this chapter, you will learn to prompt for, store, and manipulate numbers with JavaScript code. The pages that you write will be able to perform computations on numbers using the standard mathematical operators (addition, subtraction, multiplication, and division). In addition, you will be introduced to functions as units of computational abstraction, and you will become familiar with some of JavaScript's predefined mathematical functions.

Data Types and Operators

Each unit of information processed by a computer belongs to a general category, or **data type**, which defines the ways in which the information can be handled within a program. So far, you have used JavaScript variables to store strings. However, strings represent only one JavaScript data type—values can also be **numbers** and **Booleans** (true/false values that will be explored in Chapter 11). Each JavaScript data type is associated with a specific set of predefined operators, which are part of the JavaScript language and may be used by programmers to manipulate values of that type. For example, you have already seen that strings can be concatenated (joined end to end) using the + operator. Similarly, JavaScript predefines the standard arithmetic operators + (addition), − (subtraction), * (multiplication), and / (division) for use with numbers.

JavaScript variables can be assigned various kinds of numerical values, including numbers and mathematical expressions formed by applying operators to numbers and/or other variables. When an expression appears on the right-hand side of an assignment statement, that expression is evaluated and then the resulting value is assigned to the variable on the left-hand side. For example, Figure 5.1 traces a sequence of assignments, in which the result of each assignment is represented by the memory cell(s) to the right. In the first assignment, the variable x is assigned the number 24, which is then stored in the memory cell corresponding to x. In the second assignment, the expression on the right-hand side evaluates to 1024, resulting in 1024 being assigned to y's memory cell while x remains unchanged. In the third assignment, the expression on the right-hand side evaluates to 1023 (this computation is performed using the current value of y). Therefore, 1023 is assigned to x's memory cell, overwriting the cell's previous contents.

Figure 5.1 Tracing a sequence of assignment statements.

So far, we have established that JavaScript variables can store various data types. Similarly, JavaScript write statements can be used to display values of any type, including numbers and mathematical expressions. When an expression appears in a write statement, the expression is evaluated, and the resulting value is displayed as part of the message. It is important to recall that, when any portion of an expression is enclosed in parentheses, that subexpression must be evaluated before other operators are applied. For example, the write statement:

```
document.write("The sum of 3 and 7 is " + (3 + 7));
```

would produce the output:

```
The sum of 3 and 7 is 10.
```

and the write statement:

```
x = 18;

document.write("Twice " + x + " is " + (2*x));
```

would produce the output: `Twice 18 is 36.`

EXERCISE 5.1

Trace the execution of the following JavaScript code and try to predict its behavior. For each assignment, fill in the values of the variables in their corresponding boxes—even those values that aren't changed. For each write statement, list the output that would be displayed.

```
num1 = 14;
```
num1

```
num2 = 8 - (3 + 2);
```
num1   num2

```
document.write("num1 = " + num1 + ", num2 = " + num2 + "<br />");
```

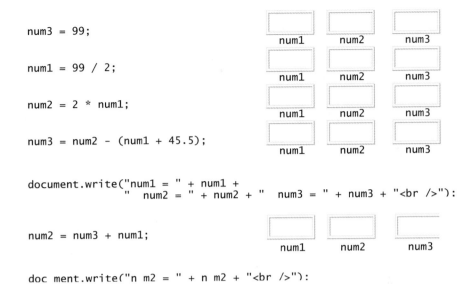

```
num3 = 99;

num1 = 99 / 2;

num2 = 2 * num1;

num3 = num2 - (num1 + 45.5);

document.write("num1 = " + num1 +
        "   num2 = " + num2 + "   num3 = " + num3 + "<br />"):

num2 = num3 + num1;

doc ment.write("n m2 = " + n m2 + "<br />"):
```

Verify your predictions by entering the above code into a Web page (within SCRIPT tags) and loading that page in the browser. Do the write statements produce the messages you expected?

Variables and Expressions

In mathematics, the symbol '=' is used to indicate equality—thus, a statement such as x = x + 1; wouldn't make much sense in an algebraic context. However, you must remind yourself that JavaScript uses '=' to assign values to variables, rather than to test equality. As we saw in Chapter 4, the expression on the right-hand side of an assignment is evaluated using the current values of variables. Then, the value of that expression is assigned to the variable on the left-hand side of the assignment. In the example x = x + 1;, the current value of x is increased by 1, and the result is assigned back to x.

Common errors to avoid...

Try to refrain from using the word "equals" when referring to the = operator. Instead, say "gets" to emphasize the fact that an assignment statement gives the variable on the left-hand side a value. Thus, you should refer to the assignment "x = x + 1;" as "x *gets* x + 1;". This reading will reinforce your knowledge of the operator's purpose and will prevent confusion later, when the equality operator (==) is introduced.

EXERCISE 5.2

Trace the execution of the following JavaScript code and try to predict its behavior. For each assignment, fill in the values of the variables in their corresponding boxes—even those values that aren't changed. For each write statement, list the output that would be displayed.

```
q = 0;

q = q + 1;

doc ment.write("a = " + a + "<br />"):
```

```
q = q + 1;
```
q

```
t = q * q;
```
q   t

```
document.write("q = " + q + "   t = " + t + "<br />"):
```

Verify your predictions by entering the above code into a Web page (within SCRIPT tags) and loading that page in the browser. Do the write statements produce the messages that you expected?

Number Representation

As we have seen in this chapter's examples, JavaScript can store numbers in variables and use numbers to perform computations. The following list provides several useful facts regarding how JavaScript stores and manipulates numbers:

- To improve readability, JavaScript automatically displays very large or very small values using *scientific notation*. In this format, values are written as numbers between 1 and 10 multiplied by 10 to a particular power. For example, if you attempted to display the number 1000000000000000000000000 using a JavaScript write statement, the number would be displayed as 1e24, symbolizing 1 times 10 to the 24th power. In general, JavaScript displays a value (X * 10Y) as XeY, where the e stands for *exponent*, the power to which 10 is raised.

- Like most programming languages, JavaScript stores all numbers in memory cells of a fixed size (64 bits, to be exact). As a result, only a finite range of numbers can be represented in JavaScript. For example, 1e308 (which represents a one followed by 308 zeros!) can be represented in JavaScript, but 1e309 cannot. If you try to evaluate 1e309, the value will be treated as "Infinity". Similarly, 1e-323 is representable, but 1e-324 is rounded down to 0.

- Even within this range of numbers, JavaScript cannot represent all possible values. Between any two numbers lie infinitely more numbers, so representing all of them on a computer is impossible. Instead, JavaScript can represent approximately 17 significant digits (ignoring leading and trailing zeros). For example, JavaScript represents the number 0.9999999999999999 (with 16 9s to the right of the decimal) exactly, but 0.99999999999999999 (with 17 9s) is rounded up to the value 1.

Common errors to avoid...

According to mathematical convention, multiplication and division have "higher precedence" in expressions than addition and subtraction do. This means that, in an expression containing both a multiplication/division and an addition/subtraction operation, the multiplication/division operator is applied first. Thus, the expression (2 + 4 * 5) will evaluate to (2 + (4 * 5)) = 22. If more than one operator of the same precedence appears in an expression (such as a series of divisions), the operators are applied from left to right. Thus, (8 / 4 / 2) will evaluate to ((8 / 4) / 2) = 1.

Although JavaScript adheres strictly to these precedence rules, it can be risky to rely on your own knowledge of the rules when creating complex mathematical expressions. For example, a programmer might write (x+1 * z), intending that the value of x be increased by one before the multiplication occurs. To avoid this kind of mistake, we recommend always using parentheses to group subexpressions—this will make your expressions easier to read and will ensure that the operators are evaluated in the correct order. Using this technique, the expression above would be written as ((x+1) * z).

Evaluating Mixed Expressions

In JavaScript, the + operator serves two purposes. When applied to numeric values, + represents addition, as demonstrated above. When applied to string values, however, the + operator indicates concatenation. Chapter 4 demonstrated this behavior repeatedly in cases where a write statement's output message is broken into pieces and then joined using +. The following examples, similar to those from Chapter 4, use the + operator to concatenate string values.

```
document.write("This is a really long message that " +
               "is broken into pieces across lines.");
color = prompt("What is your favorite color?", "");
document.write("I like " + color + " too!");
```

When the + operator is applied to *mixed values*—values of different data types, such as a string and a number—the browser automatically converts the number into a string and then concatenates the two values. (Note that, when a digit or series of digits is enclosed in quotes, it is treated as a string, rather than as a number.) The steps involved in evaluating a mixed expression are shown in the example below:

```
"We're number " + 1   →   "We're number " + "1"
                      →   "We're number 1"
```

If programmers do not take proper care, mixed expressions involving strings and numbers can produce unexpected results. Since expressions involving only the + operator are evaluated from left to right, the two expressions below appear similar but generate substantially different results. In the first example, the leftmost + is applied to the numbers 3 and 2, yielding the number 5. The subsequent + is then applied to 5 and " is the sum", producing the string "5 is the sum". In the second example, the leftmost + is applied to "the sum is " and 3, yielding the string "the sum is 3". The subsequent + is then applied to "the sum is 3" and 2, resulting in the string "the sum is 32".

```
3 + 2 + " is the sum"   →   (3 + 2) + " is the sum"
                        →   5 + " is the sum"
                        →   "5" + " is the sum"
                        →   "5 is the sum"
"the sum is " + 3 + 2   →   ("the sum is " + 3) + 2
                        →   ("the sum is " + "3") + 2
                        →   "the sum is 3" + 2
                        →   "the sum is 3" + "2"
                        →   "the sum is 32"
```

EXERCISE 5.3

What strings do each of the following expressions yield? Use the notation from the examples to show the steps involved in each evaluation.

```
"My favorite number is " + 10 + 24
"My favorite number is " + (10 + 24)
"My favorite number is " + 10 + "" + 24
```

Verify your predictions by displaying the value of each expression in a Web page (using write statements within SCRIPT tags). Do the write statements produce the messages you expected?

Common errors to avoid...

Programmers must be particularly careful when using write statements to display messages that contain embedded mathematical expressions. As Exercise 5.3 illustrated, the left-to-right evaluation of write statement messages can cause values to be concatenated when the programmer intended them to be added. For example, consider the following statement:

```
document.write("Double that number is " + x + x);
```

The programmer probably wanted to add the value of x to itself and then concatenate the resulting value to the string "Double that number is". However, because evaluation moves from left to right, the first x would be concatenated with the string to its left and then the result would be concatenated with the second x. To avoid errors such as this, always surround mathematical expressions with parentheses when mixing with strings.

Prompting for Numbers

Special care must be taken when prompting the user for number values. This is because prompt always returns the user's input in the form of a string, even when the user enters a number. For example, if a user enters 500, prompt would return the input value as "500". Usually, this is not a problem, because JavaScript automatically converts a string of digits into a number when a numeric operation (such as * or −) is applied. However, confusion and errors can occur when the addition operator is applied to such a value, since + can be interpreted as string concatenation. Consider the following sequence of JavaScript statements:

```
myNumber = prompt("Enter a number", "");
document.write("One more is " + (myNumber + 1));
```

If the user enters the number 12, the write statement would display the message "One more is 121". This occurs because myNumber has been assigned the string value "12"; thus, (myNumber + 1) is a mixed expression, and JavaScript employs concatenation to evaluate it.

Fortunately, JavaScript provides a method of explicitly converting strings to numeric values: the predefined parseFloat function. In mathematical terms, a *function* is a mapping from some number of inputs to a single output. In this case, the parseFloat function takes a single input, a string that represents a number (such as "500"), and produces as output the corresponding number value (here, 500).

From a programming point of view, a function can be seen as a unit of computational abstraction. In order to convert a string into its corresponding number, you do not need to know the steps involved in the conversion. You simply apply the predefined parseFloat function and obtain the desired value. With this computational perspective in mind, we will often refer to applying a function to inputs as *calling that function*, and we will refer to the output of the function as its *return value*. When calling a function in JavaScript, you write the function name first, followed by the inputs in parentheses. For example, the call parseFloat("12") would return the value 12, whereas parseFloat("3.14159") would return 3.14159. Similarly, prompt is a JavaScript function that takes two strings as inputs (the prompt message and default value) and returns the text entered by the user in the input box. Other JavaScript commands you have used—including write and alert statements—are also considered JavaScript functions. For functions that require more than one input, JavaScript specifies the order in which the inputs are listed within the parentheses.

A function call can appear anywhere in a JavaScript expression. When an expression containing a function call is evaluated, the return value for that call is substituted into the expression. For example, the following code uses `parseFloat` to read in and store a number from the user. The first assignment prompts the user for a number and stores that value as a string. If the user enters 12 at the prompt, the second assignment would call `parseFloat` with "12" as input, which would return the number 12. This numeric value is then assigned back to the variable myNumber. Finally, the expression (myNumber + 1) adds the two numbers, yielding the message "One more is 13".

```
myNumber = prompt("Enter a number", "");
myNumber = parseFloat(myNumber);

document.write("One more is " + (myNumber + 1));
```

The `ftoc.html` page uses the `prompt` and `parseFloat` functions (shown in Figure 5.2) to convert temperatures from Fahrenheit to Celsius. When first loaded, the page prompts the user to enter a temperature in degrees Fahrenheit (line 15). After the Fahrenheit temperature has been read in and stored as a number (line 16), the temperature is converted to Celsius using the formula: `(5/9) * (tempInFahr − 32)`. The converted temperature is stored in the variable `tempInCelsius` (line 18); then, write statements display both the original Fahrenheit temperature and the newly converted Celsius temperature (lines 20 through 22). Figure 5.4 shows the final rendering of the conversion from Fahrenheit to Celsius after inputting the temperatures in Figure 5.3.

```
1.  <html>
2.  <!-- ftoc.html                                       Dave Reed -->
3.  <!--                                                            -->
4.  <!-- Converts a temperature from Fahrenheit to Celsius.  -->
5.  <!----------------------------------------------------------->
6.
7.  <head>
8.    <title>Fahrenheit to Celsius</title>
9.  </head>
10.
11. <body>
12.   <h3 style="text-align:center">Temperature Conversion Page</h3>
13.
14.   <script type="text/javascript">
15.     tempInFahr = prompt("Enter the temperature (in Fahrenheit):", "32");
16.     tempInFahr = parseFloat(tempInFahr);
17.
18.     tempInCelsius = (5/9) * (tempInFahr - 32);
19.
20.     document.write("You entered " + tempInFahr + " degrees Fahrenheit.<br />");
21.     document.write("That's equivalent to " + tempInCelsius +
22.                    " degrees Celsius.");
23.   </script>
24. </body>
25. </html>
```

Figure 5.2 Web page that converts a temperature from Fahrenheit to Celsius.

EXERCISE 5.4

Enter the `ftoc.html` text from Figure 5.3 into a new Web page and verify that the code behaves as described. Then, use your page to convert each of the following temperatures from Fahrenheit to Celsius and report the corresponding temperatures.

```
98.6 Fahrenheit

100 Fahrenheit

212 Fahrenheit

0 Fahrenheit
```

Figure 5.3 Prompt window for inputting the temperature (`ftoc.html`).

Figure 5.4 Final rendering of `ftoc.html` in a Web browser.

EXERCISE 5.5

Define a page named `ctof.html` that is similar to your `ftoc.html` page but performs the opposite conversion. This means that the page should prompt the user for a temperature in degrees Celsius and then convert that temperature to Fahrenheit using the formula:

```
tempInFahr = ((9/5) * tempInCelsius) + 32;
```

Once you have completed the page, use it to convert the following temperatures:

```
0 Celsius
20 Celsius
-10 Celsius
88 Celsius
```

EXERCISE 5.6

Create a Web page named `grades.html` that can be used to compute a student's overall average for a course. Your page should prompt the user to enter his or her homework average, lab average, midterm score, and final exam score. The page should store each value as a number in a separate variable and then use the four numbers to compute the overall course average. Assume the following grade weightings:

Homework	25%
Labs	20%
Midterm	25%
Final exam	30%

To compute the overall course average, scale each individual grade by the appropriate factor and then add the four values. The following expression demonstrates the necessary calculation.

```
average = homework*0.25 + labs*0.20 + midterm*0.25 + exam*0.30;
```

The page should display the grades entered by the student, as well as the overall average. Your page should appear similar to the sample in Figure 5.5.

Figure 5.5 Sample appearance of `grades.html` page.

Designer Secrets

In Chapter 4, when we examined Web pages that performed related tasks, we looked for general patterns that we could extrapolate from the pages' code. In particular, the examples in Chapter 4 involved prompting the user for inputs (words or phrases) and then displaying those inputs in messages. The patterns we discerned in these pages' JavaScript code consisted of a sequence of statements to read in and store the inputs (using prompts and assignments to variables), followed by write statements.

The pages in this chapter perform tasks similar to those in Chapter 4, but involving numerical computations. The pages' JavaScript statements read in and store numbers, perform some computation on those numbers, and then display the result. Thus, the pattern for these types of tasks includes the conversion of input values to numbers (using parseFloat) and the additional step(s) necessary to perform the desired computation.

```
<script type="text/javascript">
    number1 = prompt("PROMPT MESSAGE", "");
    number1 = parseFloat(number1);
    number2 = prompt("PROMPT MESSAGE", "");
    number2 = parseFloat(number2);
    . . .
    numberN = prompt("PROMPT MESSAGE", "");
    numberN = parseFloat(numberN);

    answer = SOME EXPRESSION INVOLVING number1, …, numberN;

    document.write("MESSAGE INVOLVING answer");
</script>
```

Predefined JavaScript Functions

In addition to the standard arithmetic operations, JavaScript provides an extensive library of predefined mathematical functions, including a function that calculates the square root of an input (Math.sqrt) and a function that returns the larger of two inputs (Math.max). These functions have names beginning with the prefix "Math.", signifying that they are part of a library of mathematical routines. (Technically speaking, Math is the name of a JavaScript *object* that contains these functions—objects are introduced in Chapter 15.)

For example, the mathtest.html page in Figure 5.6 demonstrates the use of the Math.sqrt function. The page prompts the user for a number (line 15) (Figure 5.7) and then calls Math.sqrt with that number as input (line 18). The function call is part of an expression that concatenates text with the return value from the function. This expression is in turn incorporated into a write statement, causing the page to display a message containing the text and return value. Figure 5.8 shows the final rendering of the square root calculation after inputting the number in Figure 5.7.

EXERCISE 5.7

Modify the mathtest.html page from Figure 5.6 and use it to determine the purpose of each of the following mathematical functions. Be sure to test each function using a variety of numerical inputs, including negative numbers and fractions. Descriptions of the Math.sqrt and Math.max functions are already provided for you.

Function	Inputs	Description
Math.sqrt	one number	*returns the square root of the input*
Math.max	two number	*returns the greater of the two inputs*
Math.min	two number	
Math.abs	one number	
Math.floor	one number	
Math.ceil	one number	
Math.round	one number	

```
1.  <html>
2.  <!-- mathtest.html                    Dave Reed -->
3.  <!--                                              -->
4.  <!-- This page tests the Math.sqrt function.  -->
5.  <!----------------------------------------------->
6.
7.  <head>
8.    <title>Function Tester</title>
9.  </head>
10.
11. <body>
12.   <h3 style="text-align:center">Math Function Tester</h3>
13.
14.   <script type="text/javascript">
15.     number = prompt("Enter a number", 0);
16.     number = parseFloat(number);
17.
18.     document.write("Math.sqrt(" + number + ") = " + Math.sqrt(number));
19.   </script>
20. </body>
21. </html>
```

Figure 5.6   Web page that prompts the user for a number and displays its square root.

Figure 5.7   Prompt window for inputting a number (mathtest.html).

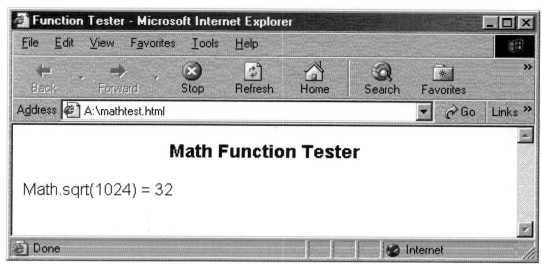

Figure 5.8 Final rendering of `mathtest.html` in a Web browser.

Common errors to avoid...

Inexperienced programmers commonly make two types of errors when attempting to call functions. The ability to recognize and correct these errors will save you a lot of time as you start incorporating functions in your pages.

1. If you mistype the name of a function, then an error will occur when the browser attempts to execute the function call. The browser will attempt to identify the error by displaying a descriptive error message in a separate window. If you are using Netscape Navigator, the error message will read, "Error: XXX is not a function" or "Error: XXX is not defined", where XXX represents the mistyped name. If you are using Internet Explorer, the error message is more cryptic—it states, "Error: Object Expected". This message refers to the fact that the browser expected to locate an object with that name (i.e., the function), but could not find its definition.

2. If you specify a function call with the wrong number of inputs, the browser does not generate an error, but the call might produce unexpected results. Inputs are automatically matched with function parameters in left-to-right order. If too many inputs are provided in the function call, the extra input values are simply ignored. If too few inputs are provided, the remaining parameters are assigned the special symbol `undefined`.

3. Similarly, unexpected results may be produced if you specify a function call with the wrong type of inputs. Whenever possible, the browser automatically converts between numbers and strings so that inputs match the specified type. Thus, the call `Math.sqrt("9")` will return the value 3. However, imagine that a function requires a number, but the specified input is a string that cannot be converted to a number. In such a case, the function would return the value NaN (a special symbol that stands for "Not a Number"). Any mathematical operations performed on NaN will likewise yield NaN. Thus, the call `Math.sqrt("xyz")` will produce NaN, as will `Math.sqrt("xyz")+1`.

Raising Numbers to a Power

The predefined function `Math.pow` can be called to raise a number to a power. For example, the call `Math.pow(2, 3)` returns 2^3 = 8. The inputs to `Math.pow` can be any number values, including negative numbers and fractions. For example, `Math.pow(2, −1)` returns 0.5, and `Math.pow(9, 0.5)` returns 3.

EXERCISE 5.8

Recall from Chapter 1 that computer memory is comprised of individual bits of data. A *bit* (short for *binary digit*) can store one of only two values, commonly referred to as 0 and 1. However, using two bits, you can represent four different values through the bit patterns 00, 01, 10, and 11. With three bits, you can represent eight different values—via 000, 001, 010, 011, 100, 101, 110, and 111. In general, N bits of memory enable you to represent 2N different values.

Create a Web page named `bits.html` that prompts the user to enter a number of bits and stores that number in a variable named N. Your page should then compute and display 2^N, the number of values that can be represented using the specified quantity of bits. For example, if the user entered 10 at the prompt, the page would display the message:

```
With 10 bits, you can represent 1024 different values.
```

Once you have created your page, use it to determine the number of values that each of the following can represent:

```
8 bits (1 byte)
16 bits (2 byte)
32 bits (4 bytes)
64 bits (8 bytes)
```

Generating Random Numbers

Recall that a function is a mapping from some number of inputs to a single output. According to this definition, a function can require zero inputs. At first, you might not see the purpose of a function without inputs; however, there is a predefined function named `Math.random` that takes no inputs and returns a useful result. Every time `Math.random()` is called, a different pseudorandom number between 0 (inclusive) and 1 (exclusive) is returned. That is, the smallest value that may be returned is 0, and the largest value is very close to but not quite 1. We use the term "pseudorandom" to describe the results of `Math.random`, because the function actually uses a complex algorithm to generate random-seeming values from within that range. As you will see throughout this book, `Math.random` is useful whenever random chance is involved in the behavior of a page, such as selecting a random image each time the page is loaded or simulating the rolls of dice.

EXERCISE 5.9

Evaluate each of the following expressions 10 times, and report the results.

```
Math.random()
2*Math.random()
2*Math.random() + 1
Math.floor(2*Math.random()+1)
```

EXERCISE 5.10

Most lotteries work by selecting a random sequence of balls, each labeled with an integer in some specified range. For example, Pick-4 lotteries typically utilize four bins, each containing 10 balls labeled 0 through 9. If there are 10 balls to choose from in each of four bins, then $10^4 = 10,000$ different number sequences can potentially be picked. Increasing the number of balls significantly increases the number of possible sequences, which significantly decreases a person's odds of winning. For example, if there are 20 balls to choose from in each bin, $20^4 = 160,000$ different number sequences could be selected.

Common errors to avoid...

Since the `Math.random` function does not require any inputs, you might be tempted to leave off the parentheses when attempting to call it. Although such an omission does not generate an error, the resulting behavior is far from that of the intended call. Like variable names, function names represent values. However, instead of representing a number or string, a function name represents a collection of JavaScript statements that define a computation. If you specify the name of a function and do not include parentheses, you are accessing the value associated with that function name. Thus, `document.write(Math.random);` would actually display the value (underlying code) of the `Math.random` function, not the result of a call. In this case, the browser would identify the random function as predefined, displaying:

```
function random() { [native code] }
```

Create a Web page named `pick4.html` that prompts the user for the highest ball number and then generates a random Pick-4 sequence. That is, if the user enters 9 as the highest ball number, then the page should generate and display four numbers in the range 0 to 9, such as 5-0-8-2.

Note: You can generate a random integer in the range 0 to N using the expression:

```
Math.floor((N+1)*Math.random())
```

Since the call `Math.random()` returns a number in the range 0 (inclusive) to 1 (exclusive), multiplying that number by $N+1$ yields a number in the range 0 (inclusive) to $N+1$ (exclusive). Rounding that number down using `Math.floor` yields an integer in the desired range: 0 to N.

Programming Errors and Debugging

In computer jargon, the term **bug** refers to an error in a program. Although computer historians debate the origin of this word, we know that it was used as early as 1945, when an error generated by the Harvard Mark II computer was eventually traced to a moth that had flown into the machine and shorted out one of its relays. In any case, **debugging** is the process of systematically locating and fixing errors in a program.

Although rarely fun, debugging is a fact of life for programmers. It is uncommon for a program of any complexity to work perfectly the first time it is executed. Instead, programming is a continual cycle of designing, testing, debugging, redesigning, testing, debugging, and so on. Errors that you find when testing and debugging your program often lead you to other errors and can even force you to redesign entire sections of code.

Three types of errors can occur in a program:

1. **Syntax** errors are simply typographic errors, such as omitting a quote or misspelling a function name. Because the browser catches these types of errors, they are usually easy to identify and fix.
2. **Run-time** errors occur when operations are applied to illegal values; for example, dividing by zero or attempting to multiply a string would generate a run-time error. These errors are also caught by the browser, which either produces an error message or—in the case of number values—continues execution using the NaN value.
3. **Logic** errors represent flaws in the design or implementation of a program. If your program runs but produces the wrong answer, the problem can be traced to a logic error (or, more often, to numerous logic errors). Unlike syntax and run-time errors, logic errors are not caught by the browser. The code is legal—it's just not what you intended! Logic errors are the most difficult type to address, because it is your responsibility to determine where the program went wrong.

Since the programs you've written so far have been relatively short and uncomplicated, errors have probably been easy to spot and correct. However, debugging more complex programs—such as those you will implement in future chapters—can be a daunting task. A simple but effective way of identifying logic errors is to place diagnostic write statements at various intervals throughout a program. These are nothing more than write statements that display the values of variables at certain points in the program's execution. Alternatively, you can call the predefined `alert` function (introduced in Chapter 4's supplemental material), causing a separate alert window to appear and display variable values. Diagnostic write statements or `alert` calls allow you to discern the exact location of an error. For example, if you see that a certain variable has the correct value at one point in the code, but an incorrect value at a later point, then you know that an error occurred somewhere in between. Once you have identified and fixed the logic errors in your code, you can remove the diagnostic write statements or `alert` calls.

In practice, it is much more efficient to avoid bugs than to waste effort fixing them. This might seem obvious, but it is a profound lesson to learn. A little extra time spent reviewing your program design at the beginning of a project can save you lots of debugging time later on. As a rule, students tend to rush into coding without thinking through their ideas and then become frustrated when they spend the majority of their time trying to debug ill-conceived code. As the noted computer science professor and software developer Henry Ledgard once quipped, "The sooner you start coding your program, the longer it's going to take." We discuss the tenets of effective program design in Chapter 8, once your programming skills have advanced further.

Another important fact to recognize is that bugs are rarely unique. As you program, you will likely make the same mistakes over and over until you learn from them. Be sure to approach debugging as an instructive exercise. When you identify a bug, make a mental note of the error and how it manifested itself, so that you can locate (or avoid) similar bugs more easily in the future.

Looking Ahead...

In this chapter, you were introduced to numbers as a JavaScript data type—including how numbers are represented, stored, displayed, and processed using mathematical operators. After mastering these basics, you learned to create interactive Web pages that manipulate numbers. These pages worked by prompting the user to enter values, employing the specified values in some computation involving mathematic operators and/or functions and then displaying the results in the page. Also, since your pages are becoming increasingly more complex, the final section of this chapter considered the types of errors that can occur when programming and approaches to avoiding and responding to errors.

Now that you have been exposed to many basic programming concepts—such as how various data types are stored, manipulated, and displayed—the next chapter will provide perspective on how the machines that run programs were developed and evolved over time. Chapter 6 traces the history of computer technology, emphasizing the technological advances that led to modern computers and the impact of those advances on our society. This information should help you understand computers in a broader context as you continue to develop your programming skills.

Chapter Summary

- JavaScript has three basic data types: strings, numbers, and Booleans.
- The basic arithmetic operators + (addition), − (subtraction), * (multiplication), and / (division) are provided for numbers.
- JavaScript variables can be assigned values of any type, including numbers and mathematical expressions formed by applying operators to numbers and/or other variables.

- When an assignment statement is executed, the expression on the right-hand side is evaluated first, and then the resulting value is assigned to the variable on the left-hand side.

- For readability, JavaScript uses scientific notation to display very small and very large numbers.

- Since numbers are stored in memory cells of fixed size, JavaScript can represent only a limited range of numbers. If numbers exceed a certain number of significant digits, the numbers may be rounded off.

- In JavaScript, multiplication and division have higher precedence than addition and subtraction do. When an expression contains operators of equal precedence, the expression is evaluated in left-to-right order.

- When the + operator is applied to a string and a number, the number is automatically converted to a string, and the two values are concatenated.

- The `prompt` function always returns a string value, even when the user enters a number. A string can be converted to its corresponding numeric value using the predefined `parseFloat` function.

- Mathematically speaking, a function is a mapping from some number of inputs to a single output. From a programming perspective, a function is a unit of computational abstraction. When calling a function, you do not need to understand the steps the function uses; you simply apply the desired function and obtain the result.

- JavaScript provides an extensive library of predefined mathematical functions, including square root (`Math.sqrt`), absolute value (`Math.abs`), maximum (`Math.max`), minimum (`Math.min`), round down (`Math.floor`), round up (`Math.ceil`), round to the nearest integer (`Math.round`), and raise to a power (`Math.pow`).

- The random number function (`Math.random`) is an example of a function requiring no inputs. Each call to `Math.random` returns a random number between 0 (inclusive) and 1 (exclusive).

- Debugging is the process of systematically locating and fixing errors (also known as bugs) in a program. Three types of errors can occur in a program: (1) syntax errors are typographic errors, such as omitting a quote; (2) run-time errors occur when operations are applied to illegal values such as multiplying string values; and (3) logic errors occur when the program runs but produces unintended results.

Supplemental Material and Exercises

More on Expressions and Assignments

This chapter contains several exercises that ask you to trace the execution of assignment statements. Tracing code is an excellent way to make sure that you understand exactly what is going on as expressions are evaluated and values are assigned to variables. Although the exercises in this chapter emphasized numbers and numeric expressions, you can also trace code execution to make sure that you understand string concatenation and the evaluation of mixed expressions.

EXERCISE 5.11

Trace the execution of the following JavaScript code and try to predict its behavior. For each assignment, fill in the values of the variables in their corresponding boxes—even those values that aren't changed. For each write statement, list the output that would be displayed.

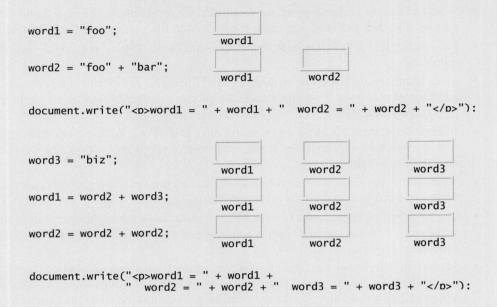

```
word1 = "foo";
```

word1

```
word2 = "foo" + "bar";
```

word1   word2

```
document.write("<p>word1 = " + word1 + "   word2 = " + word2 + "</p>"):
```

```
word3 = "biz";
```

word1   word2   word3

```
word1 = word2 + word3;
```

word1   word2   word3

```
word2 = word2 + word2;
```

word1   word2   word3

```
document.write("<p>word1 = " + word1 +
               "   word2 = " + word2 + "   word3 = " + word3 + "</p>"):
```

Verify your predictions by entering the above code into a Web page (within SCRIPT tags) and loading that page in the browser. Do the write statements produce the messages you expected?

EXERCISE 5.12

Trace the execution of the following JavaScript code and try to predict its behavior. For each assignment, fill in the values of the variables in their corresponding boxes—even those values that aren't changed. For each write statement, list the output that would be displayed.

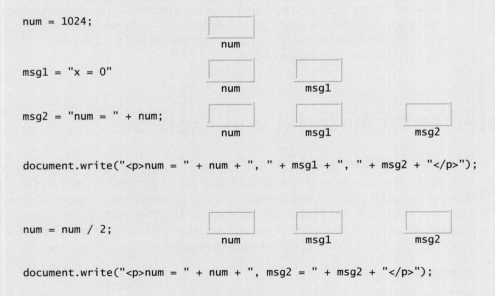

```
num = 1024;
```

num

```
msg1 = "x = 0"
```

num   msg1

```
msg2 = "num = " + num;
```

num   msg1   msg2

```
document.write("<p>num = " + num + ", " + msg1 + ", " + msg2 + "</p>");
```

```
num = num / 2;
```

num   msg1   msg2

```
document.write("<p>num = " + num + ", msg2 = " + msg2 + "</p>");
```

Verify your predictions by entering the above code into a Web page (within SCRIPT tags) and loading that page in the browser. Do the write statements produce the messages you expected?

EXERCISE 5.13

Imagine that you wanted to swap the values of two variables. How would you accomplish the switch? Consider the following example, in which num1 is assigned the value 12 and num2 is assigned −9.3:

```
  12      -9.3

  num1    num2
```

After executing some JavaScript statements, we would like to swap the two values, so that num1 is −9.3 and num2 is 12:

```
  -9.3     12

  num1    num2
```

Do the following two statements accomplish the desired switch? If not, would reversing the two statements facilitate the swap? Explain your answer.

```
num1 = num2;
num2 = num1;
```

Write several JavaScript statements that correctly swap the values of num1 and num2. [*Hint:* You might need to use a third variable.]

More Practice with parseFloat

Several exercises in this chapter demonstrated the use of the predefined parseFloat function to convert a string of digits into its corresponding number. In particular, programmers employ the parseFloat function whenever a numeric value is read in from the user, because the prompt function always returns a string value. To read in a numeric value, two lines in the following form are required:

```
variableName = prompt("Enter a value...", "");
variableName = parseFloat(variableName);
```

The first line reads in the user's input as a string value and stores it in the variable variableName. The second line calls the parseFloat function to convert the string to a numeric value and reassign that number back to the variable.

Programmers can combine these two statements into one by sending the output of the prompt function directly as input to the parseFloat function:

```
variableName = parseFloat(prompt(""Enter a value...", ""));
```

If you prefer, you may use this abbreviated notation when reading in and storing number values.

EXERCISE 5.14

Owing to dogs' shorter life span, one year in a dog's life can be considered equivalent to approximately seven human years. Create a Web page named dogage.html that prompts the user to enter the age of a dog and then displays that age in human years. Your program's output should resemble the following example:

```
Your dog is 10 years old – that's 70 to you and me!
```

EXERCISE 5.15

Trace the execution of the following JavaScript code and try to predict its behavior. Be sure to differentiate between string values and numeric values in the memory cells by enclosing all string values in quotes. Assume that the user enters the value 1024 at the prompt.

```
x = prompt("Enter a number:", "");
```
```
                                        ┌──────────┐
                                        │          │
                                        └──────────┘
                                             x
```
```
document.write("Double " + x + " is " + (2 * x) + "<br />")
```

```
document.write("Double " + x + " is " + (x + x) + "<br />")
```

```
x = parseFloat(x);
```
```
                                        ┌──────────┐
                                        │          │
                                        └──────────┘
                                             x
```
```
document.write("Double " + x + " is " + (x + x) + "<br />")
```

Verify your predictions by entering the above code into a Web page (within SCRIPT tags) and loading that page in the browser. Do the write statements produce the messages you expected?

The Remainder Operator

In addition to the traditional mathematical operators, JavaScript provides an additional operator, '%', known as the remainder operator. When applied to two numbers, the remainder operator computes the number that would remain after dividing the first number by the second. For example, (7 % 2) would evaluate to 1, since 2 divides 7 three times with a remainder of 1. Likewise, (15 % 3) would evaluate to 0, since 3 divides 15 five times with a remainder of 0.

The remainder operator is especially applicable to problems in which a value must be broken down into pieces of varying sizes. For example, some computer applications allow you to determine how many seconds have elapsed between two events. While this is useful for timing short intervals, it can be difficult to comprehend larger time periods when they are represented in seconds. For example, most people cannot immediately calculate the length of 12345 seconds. When broken into hours and minutes, however, this interval is easy to understand: 3 hours, 25 minutes, and 45 seconds.

Assuming that the number of seconds is stored in a variable named `seconds`, the following JavaScript code can convert a specific number of seconds into hours, minutes, and seconds.

```
hours = Math.floor(seconds / (60*60));
seconds = seconds % (60*60);

minutes = Math.floor(seconds / 60);
seconds = seconds % 60;
```

The first assignment computes the number of hours in the specified interval—seconds is divided by the number of seconds in an hour, yielding the length of `seconds` measured in hours. Then `Math.floor` is called to round down the value, eliminating any partial hours. In the second assignment, the remainder operator is used to reset `seconds` to the number of seconds remaining after the full hours are subtracted. For example, dividing 12345 by (60*60) yields 3.42916667, which is rounded down to 3 full hours by the `Math.floor` function. The remainder after dividing 12345 by (60*60) is 1545, which is the number of seconds remaining after the three hours have been removed.

Similarly, the next two assignments compute the number of minutes and then the remaining seconds after the minutes have been taken away. Continuing with our example, dividing 1545 by 60 yields 25.75, which is rounded down to 25 full minutes. The remainder after dividing 1545 by 60 is 45, the number of seconds remaining after the 25 minutes have been removed.

EXERCISE 5.16

Create a Web page named `times.html` that prompts the user to enter a number of seconds and stores that number in a variable. Your page should use the method outlined in this section to break that number of seconds into hours, minutes, and seconds. You should also include a write statement that displays the time in hours, minutes, and seconds. For example, if the user enters 12345 at the prompt, the page should display:

```
That's equivalent to 3 hours, 25 minutes, and 45 seconds.
```

Use your page to convert each of the following time intervals:

20 seconds

500 seconds

86400 seconds

123456 seconds

EXERCISE 5.17

Add code to your `times.html` page so that the page also calculates the number of days when breaking up intervals. That is, the number of seconds should first be broken into a number of days (using the same technique as in Exercise 5.16). Then, divide the interval into hours, minutes, and seconds as before.

Use your page to convert each of the following time intervals:

86399 seconds

86400 seconds

123456 seconds

1000000 seconds

Chapter

The History of Computers

This chapter uses narrative, illustrations, and review questions to introduce computer science and technology concepts.

Where a calculator on the ENIAC is equipped with 18,000 vacuum tubes and weighs 30 tons, computers in the future may have only 1,000 vacuum tubes and weigh only $1\frac{1}{2}$ tons.

Popular Mechanics, 1949

Never trust a computer you can't lift.

Stan Mazor, 1970

If the automobile had followed the same development cycle as the computer, a Rolls Royce would today cost $100, get one million miles to the gallon, and explode once a year, killing everyone inside.

Robert X. Cringely

Computers are such an integral part of our society that it is sometimes difficult to imagine life without them. However, computers as we know them are relatively new devices—the first electronic computers date back only to the 1940s. Over the past 60 years, technology has advanced at an astounding rate, with the capacity and speed of computers doubling every 12 to 18 months. Today, pocket calculators contain many times more memory capacity and processing power than did the mammoth computers of the 1950s and 1960s.

This chapter provides an overview of the history of computers and computer technology, tracing the progression from primitive mechanical calculators to modern PCs. As you will see, the development of computers has been rapid, but far from steady. Several key inventions have completely revolutionized computing technology, prompting drastic improvements in computer design, efficiency, and ease of use. Owing to this punctuated evolution, the history of computers is commonly divided into generations, each with its own defining technology (Figure 6.1). Although later chapters will revisit some of the more technical material, this chapter explores history's most significant computer-related inventions, why and how they came about, and their eventual impact on society.

	Time Period	Defining Technology
Generation 0	1642–1945	Mechanical devices (e.g., gears, relays)
Generation 1	1945–1954	Vacuum tubes
Generation 2	1954–1963	Transistors
Generation 3	1963–1973	Integrated circuits
Generation 4	1973–1985	Very large scale integration (VLSI)
Generation 5	1985–????	Parallel processing and networking

Figure 6.1 Generations of computer technology.

Generation 0: Mechanical Computers (1642–1945)

The 17th century was a period of great scientific achievement, sometimes referred to as "the century of genius."[1] Scientific pioneers such as astronomers Galileo (1564–1642) and Kepler (1570–1630), mathematicians Fermat (1601–1665) and Leibniz (1646–1716), and physicists Boyle (1627–1691) and Newton (1643–1727) laid the foundation for modern science by defining a rigorous, methodical approach to technical investigation based on a belief in unalterable natural laws. The universe, it was believed, was a complex machine that could be understood through careful observation and experimentation. Owing to this increased interest in complex science and mathematics, as well as contemporary advancements in mechanics, the first computing devices were invented during this period.

The German inventor Wilhelm Schickard (1592–1635) is credited with building the first working calculator in 1623. However, the details of Schickard's design were lost in a fire soon after the calculator's construction, and historians know little about the workings of this machine. The earliest prototype that has survived is that of the French scientist Blaise Pascal (1623–1662), who built a mechanical calculator in 1642, when he was only 19. His machine used mechanical gears and was powered by hand—a person could enter numbers up to eight digits long using dials and then turn a crank to either add or subtract (Figure 6.2). Thirty years later, the German mathematician Gottfried Wilhelm von Leibniz (1646–1716) expanded on Pascal's designs to build a mechanical calculator that could also multiply and divide.

While inventors such as Pascal and Leibniz were able to demonstrate the design principles of mechanical calculators, constructing working models was difficult, owing to the precision required in making and assembling all the interlocking pieces. It wasn't until the early 1800s, when manufacturing methods improved to the point where mass production was possible, that mechanical calculators

Figure 6.2 Pascal's calculator. A person entered digits by turning the wheels along the bottom, turned a crank, and viewed the results of calculations in the windows along the top.

became commonplace in businesses and laboratories. A variation of Leibniz's calculator, built by Thomas de Colmar (1785–1870) in 1820, was widely used throughout the 19th century.

Programmable Devices

Although mechanical calculators grew in popularity during the 1800s, the first programmable machine was not a calculator at all, but a loom. Around 1801, Frenchman Joseph-Marie Jacquard (1752–1834) invented a programmable loom in which removable punch cards were used to represent patterns (Figure 6.3). Before Jacquard designed this loom, producing tapestries and patterned fabric was complex and tedious work. To generate a pattern, loom operators had to manually weave different colored threads (called wefts) over and under the cross-threads (called warps), producing the desired effect. Jacquard devised a way of encoding the thread patterns using metal cards with holes punched in them. When a card was fed through the machine, hooks passed through the holes to raise selected warp threads and create a specific over-and-under pattern. Using Jacquard's invention, complex brocades could be symbolized on the cards and reproduced exactly. Furthermore, weavers could program the same loom to generate different patterns simply by switching the cards. In addition to laying the foundation for later programmable devices, Jacquard's loom had a significant impact on the economy and culture of 19th-century Europe. Elaborate fabrics, which were once considered a symbol of wealth and prestige, could now be mass produced, and therefore became affordable to the masses.

Approximately twenty years later, Jacquard's idea of storing information as holes punched into cards resurfaced in the work of English mathematician Charles Babbage (1791–1871). Babbage incorporated

Figure 6.3 Jacquard's loom. A string of punch cards for controlling the weave pattern is shown to the left, feeding into the top of the loom.

punch cards in the 1821 design of his Difference Engine, a steam-powered mechanical calculator for solving mathematical equations (Figure 6.4). Due to limitations in manufacturing technology, Babbage was never able to construct a fully functional model of the Difference Engine. However, a prototype that punched output onto copper plates was built and used to compute data for naval navigation. In 1833, Babbage expanded on his plans for the Difference Engine to design a more powerful machine that included many of the features of modern computers. Babbage envisioned this machine, which he called the Analytical Engine, as a general-purpose, programmable computer that accepted input via punched cards and printed output on paper. Like modern computers, the Analytical Engine was to encompass various integrated components, including a readable/writable memory (which Babbage called the **store**) for holding data and programs and a control unit (which he called the **mill**) for fetching and executing instructions. Although a working model of the Analytical Engine was never completed, its innovative and visionary design was popularized by the writings and patronage of Augusta Ada Byron, Countess of Lovelace (1815–1852). Ada Byron's extensive notes on the Analytical Engine included step-by-step instructions to be carried out by the machine; this contribution has since led the computing industry to recognize her as the world's first programmer.

During the late 19th century, the use of punch cards resurfaced yet again in a tabulating machine invented by Herman Hollerith (1860–1929). Hollerith's machine (Figure 6.5) was designed to sort and tabulate data for the 1890 U.S. census, employing punch cards to encode census data. Each hole on a card represented a specific piece of information, such as a census respondent's gender, age, or home state. The tabulating machine interpreted the patterns on the cards in much the same way that Jacquard's loom read the thread patterns encoded on its cards. In Hollerith's tabulating machine, metal pegs passed through holes in the cards and made an electrical connection with a metal plate below. The machine sensed these electrical connections and used them to sort and calculate data. For

Figure 6.4 Babbage's Difference Engine, with interlocking gears and numbered wheels visible.

Figure 6.5 Hollerith's tabulating machine. The operator could select desired characteristics (e.g., age, gender, income) by turning the dials on the console and feeding punch cards through the mechanism on the desktop. Cards were then sorted based on those characteristics into slots on the right.

example, when the machine's operators specified a desired pattern of holes, the machine could sort or count all the cards corresponding to people with a given set of characteristics (such as all men, aged 30–40, from Maryland). Using Hollerith's tabulating machine, the U.S. government processed the 1890 census in six weeks—which represented a vast improvement over the seven years required to calculate the 1880 census! In 1896, Hollerith founded the Tabulating Machine Company to market his machine. Eventually, under the leadership of Thomas J. Watson, Sr. (1874–1956), Hollerith's company would become known as International Business Machines (IBM).

Electromagnetic Relays

Despite the progression of mechanical calculators and programmable machines, computer technology as we think of it today did not really begin to develop until the 1930s, when electromagnetic relays were utilized. An ***electromagnetic relay***, a mechanical switch that can be used to control the flow of electricity through a wire, consists of a magnet attached to a metal arm (Figure 6.6). By default, the metal arm is in an open position, disconnected from the other metal components of the relay and thus interrupting the flow of electricity. However, if current is applied to a control wire, the magnetic field generated by the magnet pulls the arm so that it closes, allowing electricity to flow through the relay. By combining these simple electrical switches, researchers were first able to define the complex logic that controls a computer. The German engineer Konrad Zuse (1910–1995) is credited with building the first relay-powered computer in the late 1930s. However, his work was classified by the German government and eventually destroyed during World War II; thus, it did not influence other researchers. During the same time period, John Atanasoff (1903–1995) at Iowa State and George Stibitz (1904–1995) at Bell Labs independently designed and built computers using electromagnetic relays. In the early 1940s, Harvard University's Howard Aiken (1900–1973) rediscovered Babbage's designs and applied some of Babbage's ideas to modern technology; Aiken's work culminated in the construction of the Mark I computer in 1944.

Figure 6.6 Electromagnetic relay. When an electrical current is applied to the wire at the bottom, the metal coil to the left generates a magnetic field. The magnetic attraction pulls the armature on the right, closing the switch and allowing electricity to flow through the relay. (Photograph by Grant Braught, 2003.)

When compared to that of modern computers, the speed and computational power of these early machines might seem primitive. For example, the Mark I computer could perform a series of mathematical operations, but its computational capabilities were limited to addition, subtraction, multiplication, division, and various trigonometric functions. It could store only 72 numbers in memory and required roughly 1/10 of a second to perform an addition, 6 seconds to perform a multiplication, and 12 seconds to perform a division. Nevertheless, the Mark I represented a major advance in that it could complete complex calculations approximately 100 times faster than could existing technology of the time.

Generation 1: Vacuum Tubes (1945–1954)

Although electromagnetic relays certainly function much faster than wheels and gears can, relay-based computing still required the opening and closing of mechanical switches. Thus, maximum computing speeds were limited by the inertia of moving parts. Relays also posed reliability problems, since they had a tendency to jam. A classic example is an incident involving the Harvard Mark II (1947), in which a computer failure was eventually traced to a moth that had become wedged between relay contacts. Grace Murray Hopper (1906–1992), who was on Aiken's staff at the time, taped the moth into the computer logbook and facetiously noted the "First actual case of bug being found."[2]

During the mid 1940s, computer designers began to replace electromagnetic relays with *vacuum tubes*, small glass tubes from which all or most of the gas has been removed, permitting electrons to move with minimal interference from gas molecules (Figure 6.7). Although vacuum tubes had been invented in 1906 by Lee de Forest (1873–1961), they did not represent an affordable alternative to relays until the 1940s, when improvements in manufacturing reduced their cost significantly. Vacuum tubes are similar in function to electromagnetic relays, in that they are capable of controlling the flow

Figure 6.7 Vacuum tube. A filament inside the tube controls the flow of electricity—when a current is applied to the filament, electrons are released to bridge the vacuum and allow electrical current to flow through the tube.

of electricity, dependent on whether they are "on" or "off". However, since vacuum tubes have no moving parts (only the electrons move), they enable the switching of electrical signals at speeds far exceeding those of relays. The ability to modify electrical signals up to 1,000 times faster allowed vacuum tube powered machines to perform complex calculations more quickly, thus drastically enhancing the capabilities of computers.

Computing and World War II

The development of the electronic (vacuum tube) computer, like many other technological inventions, was hastened by World War II. Building upon the ideas of computer pioneer Alan Turing (1912–1954), the British government built the first electronic computer, COLOSSUS, to decode encrypted Nazi communications (Figure 6.8). COLOSSUS contained more than 2,300 vacuum tubes and was uniquely adapted to its intended purpose as a code breaker. It included five different processing units, each of which could read in and interpret 5,000 characters of code per second. Using COLOSSUS, British Intelligence was able to decode many Nazi military communications, providing invaluable support to Allied operations during the war. Although COLOSSUS became operational in 1943, its design did not significantly influence other researchers, because its existence remained classified for over 30 years.

At roughly the same time in the United States, John Mauchly (1907–1980) and J. Presper Eckert (1919–1995) were building an electronic computer called ENIAC (Electronic Numerical Integrator And Computer) at the University of Pennsylvania (Figure 6.9). The ENIAC was designed to compute ballistics tables for the U.S. Army, but it was not completed until 1946. The machine consisted of 18,000 vacuum tubes and 1,500 relays, weighed 30 tons, and required 140 kilowatts of power. In some respects, the ENIAC was less advanced than its predecessors—it could store only 20 numbers in memory, whereas the Mark I could store 72. On the other hand, the ENIAC could perform more complex calculations than the Mark I could and operated up to 500 times faster (the ENIAC could complete 5,000 additions per second). Another advantage of the ENIAC was that it was programmable, meaning that it could be reconfigured to perform different computations. However, reprogramming the machine involved manually setting as many as 6,000 multiposition switches and reconnecting cables. In essence, the ENIAC's operators "reprogrammed" the computer by rewiring it to carry out each new task.

Figure 6.8 The COLOSSUS at Bletchley Park, England. The messages to be decoded were fed into the machine on paper tape, as shown on the right. The panels show some of the more than 2,300 vacuum tubes that comprised the logic for breaking German codes. *Courtesy of the Computer History Museum.*

Figure 6.9 ENIAC, with some of its 18,000 vacuum tubes visible (U.S. Army photo).

The von Neumann Architecture

Among the scientists involved in the ENIAC project was John von Neumann (1903–1957), who, along with Turing, is considered to be one of computer science's founding fathers (Figure 6.10). Von Neumann recognized that programming via switches and cables was tedious and error prone. To address this problem, he designed an alternative computer architecture in which programs could be stored in memory along with data. Although Babbage initially proposed this idea in his plans for the Analytical Engine, von Neumann is credited with formalizing it in accordance with modern designs (see Chapter 1 for more details on the von Neumann architecture). Von Neumann also introduced the use of binary (base 2) representation in memory, which provided many advantages over decimal (base 10) representation, which had been employed previously (see Chapter 12 for more on binary numbers). The von Neumann architecture was first used in vacuum tube computers such as EDVAC (Eckert and Mauchly at Penn, 1952) and IAS (von Neumann at Princeton, 1952), and it continues to form the basis for nearly all modern computers.

Figure 6.10 John von Neumann with the IAS computer (Princeton University).

Once computer designers adopted von Neumann's "stored-program" architecture, the process of programming computers became even more important than designing them. Before von Neumann, computers were not so much programmed as they were wired to perform a particular task. However, through the von Neumann architecture, a program could be read in (via cards or tapes) and stored in the computer's memory. At first, programs were written in *machine language*, sequences of 0s and 1s that corresponded to instructions executed by the hardware. This was an improvement over rewiring, but it still required programmers to write and manipulate pages of binary numbers—a formidable and error-prone task. In the early 1950s, computer designers introduced *assembly languages*, which simplified the act of programming somewhat by substituting mnemonic names for binary numbers. (See Chapter 8 for more details regarding machine and assembly languages.)

The early 1950s also marked the emergence of the commercial computer industry. Eckert and Mauchly left the University of Pennsylvania to form their own company and, in 1951, the Eckert-Mauchly Computer Corporation (later a part of Remington-Rand, then Sperry-Rand) began selling the UNIVAC I computer. The first UNIVAC I was purchased by the U.S. Census Bureau, and a subsequent UNIVAC I captured the public imagination when CBS used it to predict the 1952 presidential election. Several other companies soon joined Eckert-Mauchly and began to market computers commercially. It is interesting to note that, at this time, International Business Machines (IBM) was a small company producing card punches and mechanical card-sorting machines. IBM entered the computer industry in 1953 but did not begin its rise to prominence until the early 1960s.

Generation 2: Transistors (1954–1963)

As computing technology evolved throughout the early 1950s, the disadvantages of vacuum tubes became more apparent. In addition to being relatively large (several inches long), vacuum tubes dissipated an enormous amount of heat, which meant that they required lots of space for cooling and tended to burn out frequently. The next major advance in computer technology was the replacement of vacuum tubes with *transistors* (Figure 6.11). Invented by John Bardeen (1908–1991), Walter Brattain (1902–1987), and William Shockley (1910–1989) in 1948, a transistor is a piece of silicon whose conductivity can be turned on and off using an electric current (see Chapter 16 for more details). Transistors were much smaller, cheaper, more reliable, and more energy efficient than vacuum tubes were. Thus, transistors' introduction allowed computer designers to produce smaller, faster machines at a drastically lower cost.

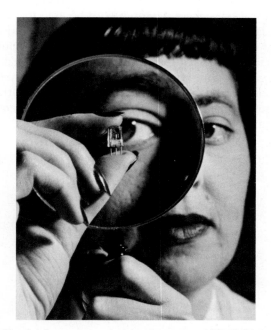

Figure 6.11   A laboratory technician inspects a 1952 RCA transistor.

Many experts consider transistors to be the most important technological development of the 20th century. Transistors spurred the proliferation of countless small and affordable electronic devices—including radios, televisions, phones, and computers—as well as the information-based, media-reliant economy that accompanied these inventions. The scientific community recognized the potential impact of transistors almost immediately, awarding Bardeen, Brattain, and Shockley the 1956 Nobel Prize in Physics. The first transistorized computers, Sperry-Rand's LARC and IBM's STRETCH, were supercomputers commissioned in 1956 by the Atomic Energy Commission to assist in nuclear research. By the early 1960s, companies such as IBM, Sperry-Rand, and Digital Equipment Corporation (DEC) began marketing transistor-based computers to private businesses.

High-Level Programming Languages

As transistors enabled the creation of more affordable computers, even more emphasis was placed on programming. If people other than engineering experts were going to use computers, interacting with the computer would have to become simpler. In 1957, John Backus (1924–) and his group at IBM introduced the first *high-level programming language*, FORTRAN (FORmula TRANslator). This language allowed programmers to work at a higher level of abstraction, specifying computer tasks via mathematical formulas instead of assembly-level instructions. High-level languages like FORTRAN greatly simplified the task of programming, though IBM's original claims that FORTRAN would "eliminate coding errors and the debugging process"[3] were overly optimistic. FORTRAN was soon followed by other high-level languages, including LISP (John McCarthy at MIT, 1959), BASIC (John Kemeny at Dartmouth, 1959), and COBOL (Grace Murray Hopper at the Department of Defense, 1960). (Again, see Chapter 8 for more details.)

Generation 3: Integrated Circuits (1963–1973)

Transistors represented a major improvement over the vacuum tubes they replaced: they were smaller, cheaper to mass produce, and more energy efficient. By wiring transistors together, a computer designer could build circuits to perform particular computations. However, even simple calculations, such as adding two numbers, could require complex circuitry involving hundreds or even thousands of transistors. Linking transistors together via wires was tedious and limited the reduction of transistor size (since a person had to be able to physically connect wires between transistors). In 1958, Jack Kilby (1923–) at Texas Instruments and Robert Noyce (1927–1990) at Fairchild Semiconductor Corporation independently developed techniques for mass producing much smaller, interconnected transistors. Instead of building individual transistors and connecting wires, Kilby and Noyce proposed manufacturing the transistors and their connections together as metallic patterns on a silicon disc. As both researchers demonstrated, transistors could be formed out of layers of conductive and nonconductive metals, while their connections could be made as lines of conductive metal (Figure 6.12).

Figure 6.12 Microscopic photograph of electronic circuitry. Transistors (seen as small rectangles) and connecting wires (seen as lines) are constructed out of layers of metal on a silicon chip.

Since building this type of circuitry involved layering the transistors and their connections together during a circuit's construction, the transistors could be made much smaller and also placed closer together than before. Initially, tens or even hundreds of transistors could be layered onto the same disc and connected to form simple circuits. This type of disc, known as an ***integrated circuit*** or ***IC chip***, is packaged in metal or plastic and accompanied by external pins that connect to other components (Figure 6.13). The ability to package transistors and related circuitry on mass-produced ICs made it possible to build computers that were smaller, faster, and cheaper. Instead of starting with transistors, an engineer could build computers out of prepackaged IC chips, which simplified design and construction tasks. In recognition of his work in developing the integrated circuit, Jack Kilby was awarded the 2000 Nobel Prize in Physics.

Figure 6.13　Early integrated circuits, packaged in plastic with metal pins as connectors.

Large Scale Integration

As manufacturing technology improved, the number of transistors that could be mounted on a single chip increased. In 1965, Gordon Moore (1929–) of Intel Corporation noticed that the number of transistors that could fit on a chip doubled every 12 to 18 months. This trend, which became known as Moore's Law, has continued to be an accurate predictor of technological advancements. By the 1970s, the ***large scale integration*** (*LSI*) of thousands of transistors on a single IC chip became possible. In 1971, Intel took the logical step of combining all the control circuitry for a calculator into a single chip called a ***microprocessor***. This first microprocessor, the Intel 4004, contained more than 2,300 transistors (Figure 6.14). Three years later, Intel released the 8080, which contained 6,000 transistors and could be programmed to perform a wide variety of computational task. The Intel 8080 and its successors, the 8086 and 8088 chips, served as central processing units for numerous personal computers in the 1970s. Other chip vendors, including Texas Instruments, National Semiconductors, Fairchild Semiconductors, and Motorola, also began producing microprocessors during this period.

Computing for Businesses

The development of integrated circuits facilitated the construction of even faster and cheaper computers. Whereas only large corporations could afford computers in the early 1960s, IC technology allowed manufacturers to lower computer prices significantly, enabling small businesses to purchase their own machines. This meant that more and more people needed to be able to interact with computers. A key to making computers accessible to nontechnical users was the development of operating systems, master control programs that oversee the computer's operation, manage peripheral devices (such as keyboards, monitors, and printers), and schedule the execution of tasks. Specialized programming languages were also developed to fill the needs of computers' new, broader base of

Figure 6.14 Microscopic image of the Intel 4044 microprocessor, with the connections between transistors dyed to appear white. The rectangles around the outside represent the pins, which connected the circuitry of the chip to the other computer components.

users. In 1971, Niklaus Wirth (1934–) developed Pascal, a simple language designed primarily for teaching programming skills, but which has dedicated users to this day. In 1972, Dennis Ritchie (1941–) developed C, a programming language used in the development of UNIX and numerous other operating systems in the 1970s and 80s.

Generation 4: VLSI (1973–1985)

So far, each computer generation we have discussed was defined by the introduction of a new technology. By contrast, the jump from generation 3 to generation 4 is based largely upon scale. By the mid 1970s, advances in manufacturing technology led to the ***very large scale integration*** (VLSI) of hundreds of thousands and eventually millions of transistors on an IC chip. To understand the speed of this evolution, consider Figure 6.15, which lists chips in the Intel family, the year they were released, and the number of transistors they contained. It is interesting to note that the first microprocessor, the 4004, had approximately the same number of switching devices (transistors) as did the 1943 COLOSSUS, which used vacuum tubes. Throughout the 1970s and 80s, successive generations of IC chips held more and more transistors, thus providing more complex functionality in the same amount of space. It is astounding to consider that the Pentium 4, which was released in 2000, contains more than 42 million transistors, with individual transistors as small as 0.18 microns (0.00000000018 meters).

The Personal Computer Revolution

Once VSLI enabled the mass production of microprocessors (entire processing units on individual chips), the cost of computers dropped to the point where individuals could afford them. The first personal computer (PC), the MITS Altair 8800, was marketed in 1975 for less than $500. In reality, the Altair was a computer kit consisting of all the necessary electronic components, including the Intel 8080 microprocessor that served as the machine's central processing unit. Customers were responsible for wiring and soldering these components together to assemble the computer. Once constructed, the Altair had no keyboard, no monitor, and no permanent storage—the user entered instructions directly

Year	Intel Processor	Number of Transistors[4]
2000	Pentium 4	42,000,000
1999	Pentium III	9,500,000
1997	Pentium II	7,500,000
1993	Pentium	3,100,000
1989	80486	1,200,000
1985	80386	275,000
1982	80286	134,000
1978	8088	29,000
1974	8080	6,000
1972	8008	3,500
1971	4004	2,300

Figure 6.15   Numbers of transistors in Intel processors.

by flipping switches on the console and viewed output as blinking lights. However, despite these limitations, demand for the Altair was overwhelming.

Although the company that sold the Altair, MITS, folded within a few years, other small computer companies were able to successfully navigate the PC market during the late 1970s. In 1976, Steven Jobs (1955–) and Stephen Wozniak (1950–) started selling a computer kit similar to the Altair, which they called the Apple. In 1977, the two men founded Apple Computers and began marketing the Apple II, the first preassembled personal computer that included a keyboard, color monitor, sound, and graphics (Figure 6.16). By 1980, Apple's annual sales of personal computers reached nearly $200 million.[5] Other companies such as Tandy, Amiga, and Commodore soon began promoting their own versions of the personal computer. IBM, which was a dominant force in the world of business computing but had been slow to enter the personal computer market, introduced the IBM PC in 1980 and immediately became a key player. In 1984, Apple countered with the Macintosh, which introduced the now familiar graphical user interface of windows, icons, pull-down menus, and a mouse pointer.

Figure 6.16   Steven Jobs, John Sculley, and Stephen Wozniak introduce the Apple IIc (1984).

Throughout the early years of computing, the software industry was dominated by a few large companies, such as IBM and Hewlett-Packard, which developed specialized programs and marketed them in combination with hardware systems. As more and more people began using computers for business and pleasure, the software industry grew and adapted. Bill Gates (1955–) and Paul Allen (1955–) are credited with writing the first commercial software for personal computers, an interpreter for the BASIC programming language that ran on the Altair (Figure 6.17). The two founded Microsoft in 1975, while Gates was a freshman at Harvard, and have built the company into the software giant it is today. Much of Microsoft's initial success can be attributed to its marketing of the MS-DOS operating system for PCs, as well as popular applications programs such as word processors and spreadsheets. By the mid 1990s, Microsoft Windows (the successor to MS-DOS) had become the dominant operating system for desktop computers, and Bill Gates had become the richest person in the world.

Figure 6.17 Paul Allen and Bill Gates (1981).

Object-Oriented Programming

The past twenty years have also produced a proliferation of new programming languages, including those with an emphasis on object-oriented programming methodologies. Object orientation is an approach to software development in which the programmer models software components after real-world objects. In 1980, Alan Kay (1940–) developed Smalltalk, the first object-oriented language. Ada, a programming language developed for the Department of Defense to be used in government contracts, was also introduced in 1980. In 1985, Bjarne Stroustrup (1950–) developed C++, an object-oriented extension of the C language. C++ and its offshoot Java (developed in 1995 at Sun Microsystems) have become the dominant languages in commercial software development today. Modern high-level programming languages are discussed in Chapter 8, and Chapter 15 covers object-oriented programming techniques in greater detail.

Generation 5: Parallel Processing & Networking (1985–????)

The scope of computer technology's fifth generation remains a debated issue among computer science historians. Unlike previous generations, which were punctuated by monolithic shifts in technology or scale, modern computer history has been defined by advances in ***parallel processing*** and ***networking***. Parallel processing refers to the integration of multiple (sometimes hundreds or thousands of) processors in a single computer. By sharing the computational load across multiple processors, a parallel computer is able to execute programs in a fraction of the time required by a single-processor computer. For example, high-end Web servers commonly utilize multiple processors. Recall that a Web server receives requests for Web pages, looks up those pages in its own local storage, and then sends the pages back to the requesting computers. Since each request is independent, multiple processors can be used to service requests simultaneously, thus improving overall performance. More details on parallel processing are provided in Chapter 10.

Networking advancements have had an even more significant impact on recent computing history. Until the 1990s, most computers were ***stand-alone*** devices, not connected to other computers. Small-scale networks of computers were common in large businesses, but communication between networks was rare. The first large-scale computer network, the ARPAnet, was created in 1969, but its use was initially limited to government and academic researchers. The ARPAnet—or Internet, as it would later be called—grew at a slow but steady pace during the 1970s and 80s. However, the Internet's scope and popularity increased dramatically in the 1990s with the development of the World Wide Web, a multimedia environment in which documents can be seamlessly linked together and accessed remotely. As of 2002, it is estimated that more than 160 million computers are connected to the Internet,[6] of which more than 33 million are Web servers storing up to 5 billion individual Web pages.[7] For more details on the development of the Internet and Web, refer back to Chapter 3.

Looking Ahead ...

The evolutionary pace of computing technology has been nothing short of astounding. Fueled by key inventions (vacuum tubes, transistors, integrated circuits, VSLI and networking), each generation of computers represented a dramatic improvement over its predecessors, both in computational power and affordability. It is interesting to note, however, that progress has not been without its price. Modern computer systems, both hardware and software, often exceed our capacity to fully understand them. When the number of components reaches into the thousands or even millions, it becomes infeasible to predict all possible interactions and, by extension, all potential problems. Therefore, users of computer technology have become accustomed to occasional errors or system failures. Although the industry has devised techniques for developing more robust systems, consumer demands have tended to place a higher priority on improving performance, rather than providing greater reliability.

Now that you are equipped with a better understanding of computer technology and its history, you are prepared to tackle more complex programming tasks. In the next chapter, you will learn to design and implement your own functions. As you have already seen in your interactions with predefined functions such as `Math.sqrt` and `Math.random`, functions allow programmers to solve complex problems by using abstraction to simplify design and implementation. The skills covered in Chapter 7 will enable you to move beyond assembling programs from preexisting functions to building your own, customized computational abstractions.

Chapter Summary

- The history of computers is commonly divided into generations, each with its own defining technology that prompted drastic improvements in computer design, efficiency, and ease of use.

- Generation 0 (1642–1945) is defined by mechanical computing devices, such as Pascal's calculator (1642), Babbage's Difference Engine (1821), and Aiken's Mark I (1944).

- The first programmable device was Jacquard's loom (1801), which used metal cards with holes punched into them to specify the pattern to be woven into a tapestry. Punch cards were subsequently used in Babbage's Analytical Engine (1833) and Hollerith's tabulating machine (1890).

- An electromagnetic relay is a mechanical switch that can be used to control the flow of electricity through a wire. Relays were used to construct mechanical computers in the 1930s and 40s.

- Generation 1 (1945–1954) is defined by vacuum tubes–small glass tubes from which all or most of the gas has been removed. Since vacuum tubes have no moving parts, they enable the switching of electrical signals at speeds far exceeding those of relays.

- The first electronic (vacuum tube) computer was COLOSSUS (1943), built by the British government to decode encrypted Nazi communications. Since COLOSSUS was classified, the first publicly known electronic computer was ENIAC (1946), developed at the University of Pennsylvania.

- In the early 1950s, John von Neumann introduced the design of a stored-program computer–one in which programs could be stored in memory along with data. The von Neumann architecture continues to form the basis for nearly all modern computers.

- Generation 2 (1954–1963) is defined by transistors–pieces of silicon whose conductivity can be turned on and off using an electric current. Since transistors were smaller, cheaper, more reliable, and more energy-efficient than vacuum tubes, they allowed for the production of more powerful yet inexpensive computers.

- As computers became more affordable, high-level programming languages such as FORTRAN (1957), LISP (1959) and COBOL (1960) made it easier for non-technical users to program and interact with computers.

- Generation 3 (1963–1973) is defined by integrated circuits (ICs)–electronic circuitry that is layered onto silicon chips and packaged in metal or plastic. The ability to package transistors and related circuitry on mass-produced ICs made it possible to build computers that were smaller, faster, and cheaper.

- Moore's Law predicts that the number of transistors that can fit on a chip will double every 12 to 18 months.

- A microprocessor is a single chip that contains all of the circuitry for a computing device, such as a calculator or computer. The first microprocessor was the Intel 4004 (1971).

- Generation 4 (1973–1985) is defined by very large scale integration (VLSI)–the ability to manufacture hundreds of thousands or even millions of transistors on an IC chip.

- The personal computer revolution occurred when technological advances allowed for the production of affordable, desktop computers, such as the MITS Altair 8800 (1975), Apple II (1977), and IBM PC (1980). The development of graphical user interfaces (GUIs) and the growth of the software industry, led by Microsoft, also made computers more accessible to non-technical users.

- The scope of Generation 5 (1985-????) remains a debated issue, but advances in parallel processing and networking have had significant impacts on modern computing.

Review Questions

1. TRUE or FALSE? The first programmable machine was a mechanical calculator designed by Charles Babbage.

2. TRUE or FALSE? Ada Byron is generally acknowledged as the world's first programmer, due to her work on Babbage's Analytical Engine.

3. TRUE or FALSE? An electromagnetic relay is a mechanical switch that can be used to control the flow of electricity through a wire.

4. TRUE or FALSE? Vacuum tubes, since they have no moving parts, enable the switching of electrical signals at speeds far exceeding those of relays.

5. TRUE or FALSE? Although they were large and expensive by today's standards, early computers such as the MARK I and ENIAC were comparable in performance (memory capacity and processing speed) to modern desktop computers.

6. TRUE or FALSE? Since transistors were smaller and produced less heat than vacuum tubes, they allowed for the design of smaller and faster computers.

7. TRUE or FALSE? A microprocessor is a special-purpose computer that is used to control scientific machinery.

8. TRUE or FALSE? Moore's Law states that the number of transistors that can be manufactured on a computer chip doubles every 12 to 18 months.

9. TRUE or FALSE? The first personal computer was the IBM PC, which first hit the market in 1980.

10. TRUE or FALSE? Many Web servers improve performance by utilizing parallel processing, in which multiple processors run simultaneously to handle page requests.

11. Mechanical calculators, such as those designed by Pascal and Leibniz, were first developed in the 1600s. However, they were not widely used in businesses and laboratories until the 1800s. Why was this the case?

12. Jacquard's loom, although unrelated to computing, influenced the development of modern computing devices. What design features of that machine are relevant to modern computer architectures?

13. What advantages did vacuum tubes provide over electromagnetic relays? What were the disadvantages of vacuum tubes?

14. As it did with many technologies, World War II greatly influenced the development of computers. In what ways did the war effort contribute to the evolution of computer technology? In what ways did the need for secrecy during the war hinder computer development?

15. What features of Babbage's Analytical Engine did von Neumann incorporate into his architecture? Why did it take over a century for Babbage's vision of a general purpose, programmable computer to be realized?

16. While it was claimed that the ENIAC was programmable, programming it to perform a different task required rewiring and reconfiguring the physical components of the machine. Describe how the adoption of the von Neumann architecture allowed subsequent machines to be more easily programmed to perform different tasks.

17. What is a transistor, and how did the introduction of transistors lead to faster and cheaper computers? What other effects did transistors have on modern technology and society?

18. What does the acronym VLSI stand for? How did the development of VLSI technology contribute to the personal computer revolution of the late 1970s?

19. What was the first personal computer and when was it first marketed? How was this product different from today's PCs?

20. Describe two innovations introduced by Apple Computer in the late 1970s and early 1980s.

21. Each generation of computers resulted in machines that were cheaper, faster, and thus accessible to more people. How did this trend affect the development of programming languages?

22. Two of the technological advances described in this chapter were so influential that they earned their inventors a Nobel Prize in Physics. Identify the inventions and inventors.

Endnotes

1. Huggins, James A. "The 17th Century: The Coming of Science." October 2002. Online at `http://www.uu.edu/centers/science/voice/`.

2. U.S. Naval Historical Center Photograph #: NH 96566-KN, Department of the Navy—Navy Historical Center. September 1999. Online at `http://www.history.navy.mil/photos/pers-us/uspers-h/g-hoppr.htm`.

3. IBM Programming Research Group. `Preliminary Report, Specifications for the IBM Mathematical FORmula TRANslating System, FORTRAN`. New York: IBM Corp., 1954.

4. Intel Research. "Silicon—Moore's Law." August 2003. Online at `http://www.uu.edu/centers/science/voice/`.

5. Robert Metz. "I.B.M. Threat to Apple." *New York Times,* September 2, 1981.

6. "Internet Domain Survey." `Internet Software Consortium`, July 2002. Online at `http://www.isc.org/ds/`.

7. "Netcraft Web Server Survey." `Netcraft`, January 2003. Online at `http://www.netcraft.com/survey/`.

References

Computer History Museum. "Timeline of Computer History." January 2003. Online at `http://www.computerhistory.org/timeline/`.

Goldstine, Herman H. *The Computer from Pascal to von Neumann*. Princeton, NJ: Princeton University Press, 1972.

Intel Museum. "A History of the Microprocessor." January 2003. Online at `http://www.intel.com/intel/intelis/museum/exhibit/hist_micro/index.htm`.

LaMorte, Christopher, and John Lilly. "Computers: History and Development." *Jones Telecommunications and Multimedia Encyclopedia*, 1999. Online at `http://www.digitalcentury.com/encyclo/update/comp_hd.html`.

Levy, Steven. *Hackers: Heroes of the Computer Revolution*. New York: Penguin Putnam, 1994.

Long, Larry, and Nancy Long. *Computers*, 5th ed. Upper Saddle River, NJ: Prentice Hall, 1998.

Malone, Michael. *The Microprocessor: A Biography*. New York: Springer-Verlag, 1995.

Stern, Nancy. *From ENIAC to UNIVAC: An Appraisal of the Eckert-Mauchly Computers*. Burlington, MA: Digital Press, 1981.

Stranahan, Paul. "Personal Computers: History and Development." *Jones Telecommunications and Multimedia Encyclopedia*, 1999. Online at `http://www.digitalcentury.com/encyclo/update/pc_hd.html`.

Winegrad, Dilys, and Atsushi Akera. "A Short History of the Second American Revolution." *Penn Almanac*, 42(18), 1996. Online at `http://www.upenn.edu/almanac/v42/n18/eniac.html`.

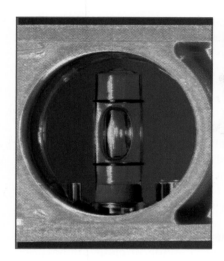

Abstraction and User-Defined Functions

This chapter uses narrative, examples, and hands-on exercises to introduce programming concepts and Web development skills.

> *In the development of the understanding of complex phenomena, the most powerful tool available to the human intellect is abstraction. Abstraction arises from the recognition of similarities between certain objects, situations, or processes in the real world and the decision to concentrate on these similarities and to ignore, for the time being, their differences.*
>
> C.A.R. Hoare
> *Structured Programming*
>
> *Civilization advances by extending the number of important operations which we can perform without thinking.*
>
> Alfred Lord Whitehead
> *An Introduction to Mathematics*

*A*bstraction is the process of ignoring minutiae and focusing on the big picture. In modern life, we are constantly confronted with objects much too complex to be understood by the average person. For example, to really grasp how a television works, one must have extensive knowledge of electrical engineering, electronics, and physics. However, most of us watch and operate television sets every day. This is possible because we abstract away unnecessary details and focus on the features relevant to our needs. At the level of abstraction through which most people view a television, it is a box with several inputs (power cord, on/off button, channel selector, and volume control) and two outputs (picture and sound). This degree of understanding enables us to watch and have control over the television set without knowing the specifics of television's functionality.

You have already been introduced to the idea of abstraction in programming through JavaScript's predefined functions, such as the mathematical functions introduced in Chapter 5. In a programming language, a function represents a unit of computation from which the details are abstracted away. For example, the computation involved in finding the square root of a number is certainly not trivial, but the `Math.sqrt` function encapsulates this multistep process in a single function call. Without worrying about how this function computes the square root, the programmer is able to call the function and use it to obtain a result. In this chapter, you will learn how to introduce your own abstractions into JavaScript by defining your own functions. After exploring the various components of a function—including parameters, return statements, and local variables—the chapter describes when it is appropriate to define new functions and how to implement them.

User-Defined Functions

Functions simplify the programmer's task in two important ways. First, functions help minimize the amount of detail that programmers must keep track of. Since the `Math.sqrt` function is available, the programmer does not need to remember the sequence of steps involved in computing a square root. Instead, he or she only needs to remember how to call the `Math.sqrt` function. Second, functions help minimize the length and complexity of code. Given that the `Math.sqrt` function has been defined, the square root of a value can be obtained via a single call to this function. This can significantly reduce code complexity, because the number of steps otherwise required to compute the square root would be considerable.

JavaScript's predefined functions represent a collection of useful, general-purpose abstractions. Since computations such as square root and absolute value are common in many applications, JavaScript's designers provided these abstractions for you in the form of predefined functions. Individual programmers can construct new abstractions by defining functions of their own design. Such functions are typically referred to as ***user-defined functions***. You can encapsulate any computation that you find especially useful as a user-defined function. Once you write a function definition and include it in a Web page, your function can be called just like any predefined function. In this way, user-defined functions can be viewed as extending the capabilities of the JavaScript language.

As an example, recall the formula for converting a temperature in degrees Fahrenheit to degrees Celsius:

    (5/9) * (tempInFahr - 32)

In Chapter 5, you wrote a page that evaluated this expression for various values of `tempInFahr`. However, if temperature conversion were a task that you needed to perform relatively often, you might waste a lot of time remembering and retyping this formula. To increase efficiency, you could encapsulate the computation in a function and save it. Then, you could simply copy your function definition into the page and call the function any time you wanted to convert temperatures. Rather than rewriting the formula for each conversion, you would need to remember only the function name and required inputs.

Figure 7.1 shows a JavaScript function that converts Fahrenheit temperatures to equivalent Celsius ones. We describe the key parts of this definition below:

```
function FahrToCelsius(tempInFahr)
// Assumes: tempInFahr is a temperature in Fahrenheit
// Returns: the equivalent temperature in Celsius
{
    return (5/9) * (tempInFahr - 32);
}
```

Figure 7.1   User-defined function to convert from Fahrenheit to Celsius.

- The first line specifies that you are defining a function named `FahrToCelsius` that takes one input. The variable name in parentheses, known as a *parameter* (because it is part of the function definition), represents the function's necessary input. When the function is called, the input value specified in the function call is assigned to the parameter for use in the function's computation. For example, in the call `FahrToCelsius(212)`, the parameter `tempInFahr` would be assigned the value 212. Thus, the function would evaluate the expression (5/9) * (212- 32), resulting in the value 100.
- The second and third lines are ***comments*** that describe the function's input and output. In JavaScript, the browser ignores anything that appears to the right of a double slash (the purpose

and treatment of JavaScript comments are similar to those of HTML comments, which are delimited by <!-- and -->). The first comment line describes assumptions made about the inputs. Here, we assume that `tempInFahr` represents a temperature in degrees Fahrenheit. The second comment line describes the value that is computed and returned by the function. Although JavaScript does not require programmers to insert comments, you should always include them in your functions to improve the readability of your code. Code that is easier to read and understand is also easier to modify and reuse, which can help you avoid writing entirely new code to perform similar tasks.

- The actual code that carries out the function's computation is enclosed in curly braces (`{}`). In this example, the function definition contains only one line of JavaScript code, but functions can encompass any sequence of statements. A ***return statement***, a special JavaScript statement included within the curly braces, specifies the value that should be returned by the function (i.e., its output value). A return statement consists of the word `return`, followed by an expression. When a return statement is executed, the expression is evaluated, and the result is returned as the value of the function call. Although not required, we suggest that you indent the code inside the curly braces to improve readability, making it easier to spot where the function definition begins and ends.

The Structure of Functions

The general form of a simple, user-defined function is shown in Figure 7.2. The portions of this abstract definition that appear in all capitals represent values that will vary from function to function. When creating function names, you must follow the same rules used for variable names—each must start with a letter and consist only of letters, digits, and underscores. As with variables, the name chosen for a function should suggest the function's purpose, such as the `FahrToCelsius` name above. The number of parameters, as well as their names, will be determined by the details of your particular function. Since the `FahrToCelsius` function takes a single input, the function has one parameter, named `tempInFahr` to indicate that it represents a temperature in degrees Fahrenheit. The statements that appear inside the curly braces stipulate whatever computations are to be carried out, usually ending in a return statement that specifies the output of the function.

```
function FUNCTION_NAME(PARAMETER_1, PARAMETER_2,..., PARAMETER_n)
// Assumes: DESCRIPTION OF ASSUMPTIONS MADE ABOUT PARAMETERS
// Returns: DESCRIPTION OF VALUE RETURNED BY FUNCTION
{
    STATEMENTS_TO_PERFORM_(AND_RETURN)_THE DESIRED_COMPUTATION;
}
```

Figure 7.2   General form of a simple, user-defined function.

In order to make a user-defined function accessible in a Web page, you must include the function definition in that page. The simplest way to do this is to place the definition directly in the HEAD of the page, enclosed in SCRIPT tags. For example, the `convert.html` page in Figure 7.3 defines the `FahrToCelsius` function in the HEAD (lines 9 through 14), then calls it from the BODY to convert a temperature from Fahrenheit to Celsius (line 23). In fact, the behavior of this page is equivalent to that of the `ftoc.html` page you wrote in Chapter 5 (Exercise 5.4). The rendered page is shown in Figure 7.4.

EXERCISE 7.1

Enter the `convert.html` text from Figure 7.2 into a new Web page. Then, load this page in the browser and verify that the code behaves as described.

Once you have done this, modify the page so that it prompts the user for two values, the low and high temperatures for a given day. Your new page should display both temperatures as they were entered, as well as their Celsius equivalents.

```
1.  <html>
2.  <!-- convert.html                                     Dave Reed -->
3.  <!-- This page converts a temperature from Fahrenheit to Celsius. -->
4.  <!------------------------------------------------------------------>
5.
6.  <head>
7.    <title> New Improved Temperature Conversion </title>
8.    <script type="text/javascript">
9.      function FahrToCelsius(tempInFahr)
10.     // Assumes: tempInFahr is a temperature in Fahrenheit
11.     // Returns: the equivalent temperature in Celsius
12.     {
13.         return (5/9) * (tempInFahr - 32);
14.     }
15.   </script>
16. </head>
17.
18. <body>
19.   <script type="text/javascript">
20.     tempF = prompt("Enter the temperature (in Fahrenheit):", "32");
21.     tempF = parseFloat(tempF);
22.
23.     tempC = FahrToCelsius(tempF);
24.
25.     document.write("You entered " + tempF + " degrees Fahrenheit.<br />");
26.     document.write("That's equivalent to " + tempC +
27.                    " degrees Celsius.");
28.   </script>
29. </body>
30. </html>
```

Figure 7.3   Web page that uses a function to convert temperatures.

Figure 7.4   `convert.html` rendered in a Web browser.

Multiple Functions in a Page

When the browser encounters a function definition within SCRIPT tags in the HEAD of a page, it associates the code in that function definition with the function name. The result is that the function is defined and subsequently can be called from the BODY of the page. If you wish to incorporate more than one user-defined function in a page, all their definitions can be placed within the same SCRIPT tags in the HEAD. For example, suppose you wanted to define a function that performed the opposite temperature conversion to the one in Figure 7.3, taking a temperature in degrees

Celsius and returning the equivalent temperature in degrees Fahrenheit. This function definition could be placed within the SCRIPT tags, along with FahrToCelsius, and then both user-defined functions would be available for use in the page.

EXERCISE 7.2

Define a function named CelsiusToFahr for converting Celsius temperatures to Fahrenheit. The formula used to convert from Celsius to Fahrenheit is as follows:

```
tempInFahr = ((9/5) * tempInCelsius) + 32;
```

Insert the definition of your CelsiusToFahr function inside the SCRIPT tags in the HEAD of the convert.html page. Modify the body of the page so that it performs the opposite conversion, prompting users to enter the low and high temperatures in Celsius and then displaying them in Fahrenheit.

Common errors to avoid...

In Chapter 4, we described the rules for creating valid variable names. Function names must adhere to these same rules—the name must begin with a letter and consist of letters, digits, and/or underscores. Sometimes, beginning programmers accidentally give a variable the same name as a function. For example, in the convert.html page above, you might inadvertently reuse the name FahrToCelsius to represent a variable in the body of the page. This would not generate an immediate error, but any subsequent attempt to call the function would cause the browser to display the error message, "Error: function expected" (using Internet Explorer) or "Error: FahrToCelsius is not a function" (using Netscape). To prevent this problem, take care to select unique function and variable names, thus avoiding conflicts.

Functions with No Return Statement

Recall that, mathematically speaking, a function is a mapping from some number of inputs to an output. In general, the programmer specifies the output of a function by placing a return statement at the end of the function code. When the browser encounters the return statement, it returns the designated value as the output of the function. Knowing this, it might surprise you to learn that the return statement in a function is optional. If the programmer does not specify a return statement, a special value, undefined, is automatically returned when the end of the function is reached. In fact, you may think of such a function as having the statement "return undefined;" implicitly added at the end. However, any attempt to use the undefined value in an expression will result in a run-time error.

The ability to define a function without a return statement is useful when defining functions for producing output. For example, in Chapter 4, you wrote a Web page that rendered verses of the children's song "Old MacDonald." In Exercise 4.7, you modified the oldmac.html page to display several verses of the song. Completing this task was somewhat tedious, however, since it involved copying entire sequences of write statements to display each verse in succession. Figure 7.5 presents an alternate implementation of oldmac.html, which produces the same output via a function. By encapsulating all the write statements needed to display a single verse, the OldMacVerse function (lines 9 through 23) greatly simplifies the necessary code. Now, adding verses to the song simply involves inserting function calls into the BODY of the page, with the appropriate animal name and sound specified as inputs (lines 29 through 32). Note that, in the case of the OldMacVerse function, the purpose of each call is to display a song verse, rather than to compute a value. As such, there is no need for an explicit return value. The rendered page is shown in Figure 7.6.

```
1.  <html>
2.  <!-- newmac.html                                          Dave Reed -->
3.  <!-- This page uses a function to display verses from Old MacDonald. -->
4.  <!------------------------------------------------------------------->
5.
6.  <head>
7.    <title> New Improved Old MacDonald </title>
8.    <script type="text/javascript">
9.      function OldMacVerse(animal, sound)
10.     // Assumes: animal and sound are strings
11.     // Results: displays corresponding Old MacDonald verse
12.     {
13.       document.write("<p>Old MacDonald had a farm, E-I-E-I-O.<br />");
14.       document.write("And on that farm he had a " + animal +
15.                      ", E-I-E-I-O.<br />");
16.       document.write("With a " + sound + "-" + sound +
17.                      " here, and a " + sound + "-" + sound +
18.                      " there,<br />");
19.       document.write("   here a " + sound + ", there a " +
20.                      sound + ", everywhere a " + sound + "-" +
21.                      sound + ".<br />");
22.       document.write("Old MacDonald had a farm, E-I-E-I-O.</p>");
23.     }
24.   </script>
25. </head>
26.
27. <body>
28.   <script type="text/javascript">
29.     OldMacVerse("cow", "moo");
30.     OldMacVerse("pig", "oink");
31.     OldMacVerse("duck", "quack");
32.     OldMacVerse("horse", "neigh");
33.   </script>
34. </body>
35. </html>
```

Figure 7.5 Web page that displays "Old MacDonald" verses using a function.

EXERCISE 7.3

Enter the newmac.html text into a new Web page, load the page in the browser, and verify that the code displays four verses as described. Then, modify the page so that it prints a fifth verse. You can include any animal you wish in the verse's song text.

Multiple Inputs

When calling a function with multiple inputs, the inputs must be specified in the order in which the parameters appear in the function definition. This is because the first input in the function call is assigned to the first parameter in the function, the second input is assigned to the second parameter, and so on. For example, in the function call OldMacVerse("cow", "moo"), the input value "cow" is assigned to the parameter animal, whereas "moo" is assigned to sound.

EXERCISE 7.4

What would you expect to happen as a result of the following call?

```
OldMacVerse("baa", "sheep");
```

Modify your newmac.html page to include the function call above, then load the page and verify your prediction.

Figure 7.6 `newmac.html` rendered in a Web browser.

Designer Secrets

In this chapter, you have learned how to define your own functions. Since it merely involves encapsulating other statements under a single name, this skill does not directly enable us to solve new types of problems. We are currently limited to writing programs that read and store values (using prompts and assignments), perform computations on those values (using expressions and math functions), and display the results (using write statements). However, the capacity to define and use functions is key to solving complex problems, as well as to developing reusable code. As the Old MacDonald example demonstrated, defining a function and calling it repeatedly can greatly simplify and shorten code. Likewise, the ability to place user-defined functions in libraries enables programmers to reuse previously written JavaScript sequences easily. We introduce the use of code libraries later in this chapter.

To successfully define a function, you must know the necessary inputs, the computation to be performed using those inputs, and the output you wish the function to return. For beginners, knowing *how* to define a function is generally not as difficult as knowing *when* to define a function. For now, the following design guidelines apply:

- If a particular computation is complex—meaning that it requires extra variables and/or multiple lines to define—place the code for that computation in a separate function.
- If you have to perform a particular computation repeatedly within a page, place the code for that computation in a separate function and call the function as needed.

Parameters and Local Variables

We can view functions as units of computational abstraction, in that a function encapsulates a computation or output sequence, allowing the programmer to incorporate that computation or output simply by calling the function. Parameters play an important role in functions, since they facilitate the creation of generalized computations (i.e., the function defines a formula, but certain values within the formula can differ each time the function is called). For example, the `FahrToCelsius` function isn't limited to converting a single temperature from Fahrenheit to Celsius—it works for any temperature value passed to the `tempInFahr` parameter. Similarly, a programmer can employ the `OldMacVerse` function to print any verse of the song simply by providing the desired animal name and sound as inputs.

Technically, a parameter is a ***local variable***, meaning it exists only inside its particular function. When the function is called, the program allocates memory cells for the parameters and then assigns each input from the call to its corresponding parameter. For example, the call `FahrToCelsius(100)` from Figure 7.3 would allocate a memory cell for the parameter `tempInFahr` and store the input value 100 in that cell. Likewise, the call `OldMacVerse("duck", "quack")` from Figure 7.5 would allocate memory cells for the parameters `animal` and `sound` and store the values `"duck"` and `"quack"` in those cells, respectively. Once a parameter has been assigned a value, you can refer to that parameter within the function just as you would any other variable. However, when the function terminates, the parameters "go away," and their associated memory cells are freed.

By default, variables other than parameters are ***global variables***, meaning that they exist and can be accessed by JavaScript code anywhere in the page (both in the HEAD and the BODY). It is possible to use the same name to refer to a global variable (e.g., a variable in the BODY) and a local variable (e.g., a parameter in a function). Within the function that defines the local variable, any reference to that name will denote the local variable. However, if you refer to the same name outside the function, the global variable will be accessed.

For example, suppose the code in the BODY of the `newmac.html` page was modified, as shown in Figure 7.7. In this program, the variable names `animal` and `sound` appear in two different places: they are employed to store the user's input in the BODY, but they also act as parameters in the `OldMacVerse` function. To the browser, these are completely different sets of variables, since they appear in different environments (much the same way that Paris, France, and Paris, Texas, are recognizable as different cities). If it helps, you can think of each variable as including a subscript that identifies its environment, such as $animal_{BODY}$, $sound_{BODY}$, $animal_{OldMacVerse}$, and $sound_{OldMacVerse}$. When `OldMacVerse` is called the first time (line 32), the corresponding variables in the BODY and in the function will have the same values, since $animal_{BODY}$ and $sound_{BODY}$ are passed in as inputs and assigned to the parameters $animal_{OldMacVerse}$ and $sound_{OldMacVerse}$. During the second call (line 33), however, the parameters will be assigned `"duck"` and `"quack"`, but these values will not affect the variables in the BODY. This means that, when you define a function, you do not need to worry whether your parameter names coincide with those of existing global variables in the page's BODY. You can choose whatever names you wish without fear that conflicts will occur.

EXERCISE 7.5

Enter the `testmac.html` text into a new Web page. Then, load this page in the browser and verify that the code behaves as described. If you reversed the inputs in the first function call—i.e., `OldMacVerse(sound, animal)`—would the browser be able to recognize the mismatch? Why or why not?

Declaring Local Variables

In previous chapters, we have seen that variables are useful for storing intermediate values in a complex computation, as well as generalizing code to make subsequent modifications easier. Within a user-defined function, the programmer is free to create new variables and use them in specifying the function's computation. However, unlike function parameters, variables that are created within a

```
1.  <html>
2.  <!-- testmac.html                           Dave Reed -->
3.  <!-- This page displays two verses of OldMacDonald. -->
4.  <!------------------------------------------------------>
5.
6.  <head>
7.    <title> Old MacDonald Test </title>
8.    <script type="text/javascript">
9.      function OldMacVerse(animal, sound)
10.     // Assumes: animal and sound are strings
11.     // Results: displays corresponding Old MacDonald verse
12.     {
13.       document.write("<p>Old MacDonald had a farm, E-I-E-I-O.<br />");
14.       document.write("And on that farm he had a " + animal +
15.                      ", E-I-E-I-O.<br />");
16.       document.write("With a " + sound + "-" + sound +
17.                      " here, and a " + sound + "-" + sound +
18.                      " there,<br />");
19.       document.write("   here a " + sound + ", there a " +
20.                      sound + ", everywhere a " + sound + "-" +
21.                      sound + ".<br />");
22.       document.write("Old MacDonald had a farm, E-I-E-I-O.</p>");
23.     }
24.   </script>
25. </head>
26.
27. <body>
28.   <script type="text/javascript">
29.     animal = prompt("Enter the name of an animal:", "");
30.     sound = prompt("What sound does it make?", "");
31.
32.     OldMacVerse(animal, sound);
33.     OldMacVerse("duck", "quack");
34.   </script>
35. </body>
36. </html>
```

Figure 7.7 Modified page that distinguishes global v. local variables.

function by assigning a value to a new variable name are global to the entire page. This means that naming conflicts with already existing variables might occur. In order to make such variables local, the programmer must identify them in a ***variable declaration*** at the beginning of the function. A variable declaration, which is usually included directly after the curly braces, consists of the word var, followed by the names of the variables to be localized.

```
var LOCAL_1, LOCAL_2, …, LOCAL_n;
```

For example, consider the IncomeTax function in Figure 7.8, which computes a person's income tax payment according to the following system:

- The taxpayer's deduction is the larger of two numbers: the standard deduction ($4,150) or the itemized deduction (computed using some complicated form).
- Taxable income is determined by subtracting the deduction from the taxpayer's gross income (or 0, whichever is larger).
- Total tax owed is determined by multiplying the taxable income by the tax rate (13%).

The IncomeTax function computes a taxpayer's total income tax payment, using the inputs income (representing the individual's gross income) and itemized (representing the individual's

```
function IncomeTax(income, itemized)
// Assumes: income >= 0, itemized >= 0
// Returns: flat tax (13%) due after deductions
{
    var deduction, taxableIncome, totalTax;

    deduction = Math.max(itemized, 4150);
    taxableIncome = Math.max(income - deduction, 0);
    totalTax = 0.13*taxableIncome

    return totalTax;
}
```

Figure 7.8 Function that uses local variables in computing income tax.

itemized deduction). The first line in this function is a variable declaration, which specifies that the new variables `deduction`, `taxableIncome`, and `totalTax` will be used in the function. Since these variables are declared to be local, they exist only inside the function and will go away when the function terminates.

EXERCISE 7.6

Create a Web page named `taxes.html` and enter the `IncomeTax` function into the HEAD (enclosed in SCRIPT tags). In the BODY of the page, prompt the user to enter values representing his or her income and itemized deduction. The page should call the `IncomeTax` function and then display the amount of tax owed.

Use your page to determine the amount a person would owe with:

```
income = 100000.00  itemized = 12017.50

income =  42500.00  itemized =  8900.99

income =  13267.45  itemized = 14000.00
```

Whenever you want to use variables exclusively within a function, you should declare those variables, preceded by the keyword `var`, at the beginning of the function. Otherwise, the variables will persist after the function returns its value and might accidentally overwrite existing variables. For example, the variable declaration in the `IncomeTax` function ensures that the included variables are local to the function (i.e., $deduction_{IncomeTax}$, $taxableIncome_{IncomeTax}$, and $totalTax_{IncomeTax}$). Without the declaration, the variables would be treated as global to the entire page (i.e., $deduction_{BODY}$, $taxableIncome_{BODY}$, and $totalTax_{BODY}$). If the BODY of the page already contained variables with the same names, those variables would be affected by assignments in the function.

Common errors to avoid...

Forgetting to declare a variable used within a function as local will not cause an error, but may lead to confusion if another variable with the same name appears elsewhere in the page. For this reason, we STRONGLY recommend that you double-check each function you write, making sure that all variables used to store temporary values are declared.

Since parameters are automatically treated as local to a function, they do not need to be declared. In fact, some browser versions will report an error if you accidentally declare a parameter.

EXERCISE 7.7

Computer science often deals with extremes when it comes to time. Even though modern computers can perform billions of operations per second, some tasks—such as decoding an encrypted message—still might require decades of computation.

Create a Web page named `years.html` that prompts the user to enter a specific number of years and then displays the corresponding time in seconds. To simplify this task, ignore leap years and assume that all years consist of exactly 365 days. For example, given an input value of 2.5, your page might display the following output:

```
You entered 2.5 years.  That's 78840000 seconds!
```

Your page should include the definition of a function named `YearsToSeconds` that requires one input, a value corresponding to a number of years, and returns the equivalent time in seconds. Feel free to use local variables to store temporary values during the computation. For example, you might first convert the number of years to days and store that value in a variable named `numDays`, then convert the value to hours, minutes, and finally seconds. Be sure to declare any variables that you use within the function.

Once you complete your page, use it to approximate the number of seconds that are left in the current school semester. How many seconds remain in your college career? Report your results.

The `random.js` Library

All the functions we have written so far have been fairly specialized. For example, it is difficult to imagine other applications in which the `OldMacVerse` function would be useful. When you are unlikely to reuse a function, placing its definition directly in the HEAD of the page from which it is called is a natural approach.

For more general-purpose functions—ones that you might employ in a variety of applications—we use a different technique. Instead of placing definitions directly in Web pages, you can define general-purpose functions in separate files, or *libraries*, and then load the files into pages as needed. Programmers can load a library file into a page using SCRIPT tags with the SRC attribute assigned to the file name:

```
<script type="text/javascript" src="LIBRARY_FILENAME"></script>
```

Note that we do not include any code between the two SCRIPT tags—instead, the code is contained in the library file and inserted into the page when the browser encounters the SCRIPT tags. By convention, SCRIPT tags that load library files are included in the HEAD of a page, to ensure that the browser loads all functions definitions first before executing JavaScript code in the BODY.

As an example, the author has provided the library file `random.js` (accessible at `http://www.prenhall.com/reed`) for your use. This library contains several general-purpose functions used to produce random values. Recall from Chapter 5 that the `Math.random` function can be called to generate a random number from the range 0 (inclusive) to 1 (exclusive). The functions in the `random.js` library build upon `Math.random`, offering additional flexibility and power. The functions defined in the library are listed in Figure 7.9.

To access any of these functions, you must include the `random.js` library in your Web page by incorporating SCRIPT tags with the SRC attribute assigned to the URL of the library. For example, the `picknum.html` page (Figure 7.10) loads the `random.js` library and displays a number generated by the `RandomInt` function. The rendered page is shown in Figure 7.11.

EXERCISE 7.8

The traditional test for determining whether someone has ESP (extrasensory perception) involves asking the person to guess randomly selected values. For example, you might generate random integers in some range—such as one to four—and then have the person try to guess each number. Given four possible values, you would expect random guessing to be correct approximately one-fourth of the time. If a person were correct significantly more often, you might be tempted to say that he or she has ESP (rather than being just lucky).

Enter the `pickem.html` text from Figure 7.10 into a new Web page and modify the page so that it serves as an ESP test. Your code should generate a random integer between one and four, store that number in a variable, and then prompt the user to guess a value in that range. After the user enters a guess, your page should display that guess, along with the random number that was generated. For example,

```
You guessed 2.  My number was 3.
```

After implementing this page, test your ESP potential by repeatedly loading the page and trying to guess the number. Out of 20 tests, how many times did you guess correctly? Do you think you have ESP?

Function	Inputs	Output
RandomNum	Two numbers (low and high limits of a range) e.g., RandomNum (2, 4.5)	A random number from the range low (inclusive) to high (exclusive)
RandomInt	Two integers (low and high limits of a range) e.g., RandomInt(1, 10)	A random integer from the range low to high (both inclusive)
RandomChar	A nonempty string e.g., RandomChar("abcd")	A random character taken from the string
RandomOneOf	A list of options (in brackets, separated by commas) e.g., RandomOneOf(["yes", "no"])	A random value taken from the list of options

Figure 7.9 Functions defined in the `random.js` library.

```
1.  <html>
2.  <!-- picknum.html                                          Dave Reed -->
3.  <!-- This page uses RandomInt to pick and display a random number. -->
4.  <!---------------------------------------------------------------->
5.
6.  <head>
7.    <title> Random Number Test </title>
8.    <script type="text/javascript"
9.            src="http://www.prenhall.com/reed/random.js">
10.   </script>
11. </head>
12.
13. <body>
14.   <script type="text/javascript">
15.     x = RandomInt(1, 3);
16.     document.write("The number is " + x + ".");
17.   </script>
18. </body>
19. </html>
```

Figure 7.10 Web page that uses a function from the `random.js` library to pick a random number.

EXERCISE 7.9

A popular children's toy is the Magic 8 Ball®, an oversized billiard ball that yields answers to simple questions. (Magic 8 Ball is a trademark owned by and used with permission from Mattel, Inc. © 2003 Mattel, Inc. All Rights Reserved.) To receive its wisdom, you ask the Magic 8 Ball a question, shake it vigorously, and then read the response that appears in a window on its side. Functionally speaking, the Magic 8 Ball determines its answer by randomly selecting from a list of predetermined responses, such as "yes", "no", and "reply hazy—try again".

Create a Web page named `magic.html` that simulates the functionality of a Magic 8 Ball. The page should prompt the user to enter a yes-or-no question, then call the `RandomOneOf` function to randomly select from a list of at least five possible responses. Both the question and response should be displayed on the page. For example,

```
QUESTION: Will the Cubs win the World Series in my lifetime?
```

```
ANSWER: highly unlikely
```

Test your page to make sure that it operates correctly, providing a (potentially) different answer each time it is loaded.

Figure 7.11 `picknum.html` rendered in a Web browser.

Common errors to avoid...

When beginning programmers attempt to load a JavaScript code library, errors of two types commonly occur.

1. If the SCRIPT tags are malformed or the name/address of the library is incorrect, the library will fail to load. This will not cause an error in itself, but any subsequent attempt to call a function from the library will produce "Error: Object Expected" (using Internet Explorer) or "Error: XXX is not a function" (using Netscape Navigator), where XXX represents the typed function name.

2. When you use the SRC attribute in a pair of SCRIPT tags to load a code library, you cannot place additional JavaScript code between the tags. You can think of the SRC attribute as causing the contents of the library to be inserted between the tags, overwriting any other code that was erroneously placed there. Thus, if a given page incorporates both a function loaded from a library and a function defined directly in the HEAD, two pairs of SCRIPT tags are required. Similarly, if a page utilizes functions from multiple library files, each library requires its own pair of SCRIPT tags.

Looking Ahead...

In this chapter, you learned to extend the expressive power of JavaScript by defining your own functions. A user-defined function introduces a unit of computational abstraction, since it encapsulates a computation or sequence of write statements under a single name. Once a function has been defined, the programmer no longer needs to know the details of how it works—she simply needs to know how to call that function. As you saw in this chapter, JavaScript functions can be defined in the HEAD of a Web page, or they can be collected in a library file and loaded into pages when needed.

At this point in the text, you have developed an impressive set of programming skills, including the ability to use variables, assignments, expressions, functions, and libraries. The next chapter, Chapter 8, attempts to generalize some of these skills, focusing on the concept of an algorithm and its connection to programming. As you will learn, an algorithm is a step-by-step sequence of instructions for carrying out some task. A program is a special kind of algorithm, in which the instructions specify actions to be carried out by the computer (such as prompting the user for his name or displaying a message in a page). In Chapter 8, several examples of complex algorithms are studied, as well as techniques for implementing and executing algorithms as programs.

Chapter Summary

- Functions simplify the programmer's task by (1) minimizing the amount of detail that the programmer must keep track of, and (2) minimizing the size and complexity of code.

- A parameter is a function-specific variable. When a function is called, its parameters are automatically assigned values corresponding to the input values in the call. If a function has multiple parameters, they are matched with the input values in sequential order: the first parameter is assigned the first input value, the second parameter is assigned the second input value, and so on.

- Programmers insert comments in JavaScript programs by placing a double slash (//) at the beginning of a line.

- In a function definition, a return statement specifies the value that should be returned by a function. Return statements are optional, since some functions are designed to display text in the page, rather than to compute a value.

- The general form in which programmers define functions is as follows:

```
function FUNCTION_NAME(PARAMETER_1, PARAMETER_2,..., PARAMETER_n)
// Assumes: DESCRIPTION OF ASSUMPTIONS MADE ABOUT PARAMETERS
// Returns: DESCRIPTION OF VALUE RETURNED BY FUNCTION
{
    STATEMENTS_TO_PERFORM_(AND_RETURN)_THE DESIRED_COMPUTATION;

}
```

- Parameters are considered local variables, meaning they exist and can be accessed only from within the function. By default, variables other than parameters are global variables, meaning that they exist and can be accessed by JavaScript code anywhere in the page (in both the HEAD and the BODY).

- Variables that are used to provide temporary storage within a function should be declared as local using the keyword var. When a function definition declares certain variables as local, the variables exist only while the function executes (similar to parameters), and their values will not alter other variables that might share their names.

- Special-purpose functions can be defined directly in the HEAD of a Web page, enclosed in SCRIPT tags. General-purpose function definitions should be placed in separate library files and then loaded into Web pages as needed. To load a library file, use SCRIPT tags of the form:

```
<script type="text/javascript" src="LIBRARY_FILENAME"></script>
```

- The random.js library defines functions for generating random numbers in a specified range (RandomNum), random integers in a specified range (RandomInt), random characters from a string (RandomChar), and random items from a list of options (RandomOneOf).

Supplemental Material and Exercises

Function Names vs. Function Calls

When beginning programmers attempt to call a function, they often make the mistake of writing only the function name, rather than the complete call. For example, imagine that you wanted to create a write statement that displays the result of the FahrToCelcius function, and you typed the following code:

```
document.write(FahrToCelsius);
```

Although the programmer writing this might intend to call the function FahrToCelsius, the statement is not recognized as a function call, because it lacks parentheses after the function name—e.g., FahrToCelsius(212). Even if a function has no inputs, you must include an empty set of parentheses, as in the call Math.random().

Omitting the parentheses in a function call will not necessarily produce an error message. Technically speaking, the name of a function is a variable just like any other: the value represented by a function name is a string containing the function's full definition. As with any variable, a function name's value can be displayed or compared with another value. For example, assuming that the FahrToCelsius function were defined as it is in this chapter, the write statement above would actually display the definition of that function:

```
function FahrToCelsius(tempInFahr) { return (5 / 9) * (tempInFahr - 32); }
```

EXERCISE 7.10

If you list only a function name instead of a call to that function, will this type of mistake ever produce an error in JavaScript code? If so, give an example. If not, explain why.

EXERCISE 7.11

When employing a user-defined function, you can always review the function definition by placing the function name in a write statement (as demonstrated above). Does this same option exist for predefined JavaScript functions? For example, could you review the source code for Math.sqrt by displaying the function name? Try it and report the results.

More Practice with Parameters and Local Variables

In addition to shortening pages by consolidating redundant code, using functions can produce code that is simpler to modify. For example, consider our most recent version of the Old MacDonald page (Figure 7.5). Since the program now displays every verse of the song using the same function, any changes made to that function would automatically affect all verses. By writing a function to encapsulate the general task of displaying a verse, you are able to make modifications once and ensure consistency across all verses.

EXERCISE 7.12

In Chapter 4 (Exercise 4.9), you modified the code in your Old MacDonald page so that you could alter the spelling of the song refrain. This exercise asks you to add similar functionality to your newmac.html page by incorporating a variable that defines the refrain's spelling (e.g., "E-I-E-I-O" or "Eeyigh-Eeyigh-Oh"). The program should employ this variable when displaying the verse so that the value assigned to the variable determines which variation of the refrain is displayed.

Note: Be sure to declare the variable at the top of the function to make it local to the function.

EXERCISE 7.13

Consider the IncomeTax function from Figure 7.8. Most workers have part of their paychecks withheld every month and directly applied toward their income tax payment. When such workers file their taxes at the end of the year, the total amount withheld during the year is subtracted from their computed tax to determine the amount owed. Modify the IncomeTax function so that it takes a third input, the amount withheld. The function should compute the amount owed by the taxpayer (stored in a variable named taxOwed) and return that value. Be sure to add taxOwed to the variable declarations, limiting the variable's existence to inside the function. Then, modify your page so that it prompts the user for the amount withheld and calls the function accordingly.

Once your page is complete, use it to determine the amount a person would owe with:

```
income = 100000.00  itemized = 12017.50  withheld = 10000.00

income =  42500.00  itemized =  8900.99  withheld =  6250.75

income =  13267.45  itemized = 14000.00  withheld =     0.00
```

More Practice with Libraries

As we demonstrated via the random.js library, useful function definitions can be grouped together in a library file and then loaded into any page where those functions might be needed. You may find that, as you write more programs, you employ certain functions over and over. If this is the case, you might consider defining your own library file to make function reuse easier.

EXERCISE 7.14

Imagine that you are working for a weather service and you need to convert temperatures between Fahrenheit and Celsius on a regular basis. Define a library file named convert.js that contains your definitions of the functions FahrToCelsius and CelsiusToFahr. Store your convert.js library in the same directory as your other Web pages, then modify your convert.html page so that the functions are accessed from the library.

EXERCISE 7.15

Extend your convert.js library by adding functions for converting measurements between the Imperial and metric systems. First, define functions for converting from inches to centimeters, and vice versa (1 in. = 2.54 cm). Once you have defined these functions, you can use them to define functions that convert from feet to meters, and vice versa (1 ft = 12 in. 1 m = 100 cm). Finally, use those functions to help convert from miles to kilometers, and vice versa (1 mi = 5,280 ft, 1 km = 1,000 m).

Add code to your convert.html page so that it tests your new conversion functions.

For the next exercise, you will need to replicate the process of rolling two six-sided dice. As we learned in Chapter 5, programmers can generate a random number within a range by evaluating expressions involving calls to Math.random and Math.floor. However, the RandomInt function from the random.js library provides a much simpler method of accomplishing this task. To obtain the sum of two dice rolls, you can simply call the RandomInt function twice and then combine the returned values:

```
roll = RandomInt(1,6) + RandomInt(1,6);
```

EXERCISE 7.16

Evaluate and display the value of the above expression at least 30 times, then report your results. Each time you evaluate the expression, you should obtain an integer between 2 and 12, but there is a greater likelihood of obtaining numbers in the middle of the range. Do your experiments meet these expectations?

Layers of Abstraction

In the real world, problems are often too complex to be solved from scratch every time. Instead, solutions to simple tasks are encapsulated in abstractions, which then can be used to solve slightly more complex tasks. These solutions are similarly encapsulated in abstractions and used to solve even more complex problems. In this manner, abstractions are built on top of one another, and complex problems can be solved in small, incremental steps.

Programming techniques employ a similar incremental approach. For example, the RandomInt function incorporates the Math.random and Math.floor functions that are predefined in JavaScript. Once you had access to the new RandomInt function, you were able to use it to simulate the roll of two six-sided dice by evaluating the expression RandomInt(1,6) + RandomInt(1,6). Since dice rolls are useful in many applications, you will be performing numerous dice simulations throughout this course. Thus, you may find it helpful to build upon the RandomInt function in order to define yet another level of abstraction.

EXERCISE 7.17

Define a function named DiceRoll that simulates the act of rolling two dice. The function should have one parameter, representing the number of sides on the dice. To simulate the dice rolls, your function should call RandomInt twice and then return the sum of the two rolls.

Test this function in a Web page that generates and displays random dice rolls.

EXERCISE 7.18

Reimplement your pick4.html page from Chapter 5 (Exercise 5.10) using the RandomInt function from random.js. The program should obtain values for each of four lottery balls by allowing the user to specify the range of integers on the balls and then calling the RandomInt function four times.

Function-Calling Sequence

Whenever a function is called, a specific sequence of events takes place. If you understand this sequence, you should be able to trace the execution of any function and ascertain its behavior. For example, consider the page in Figure 7.12, which computes the distance between two points (x_1, y_1) and (x_2, y_2) using the distance formula:

$$\sqrt{(x_1 - x_2)^2 + (y_1 - y_2)^2}$$

In Figure 7.12, the points are specified in the code: $(3, 4)$ and $(0, 0)$. However, the code could easily be generalized to prompt the user for the points and then compute the distance between them.

When the Distance function is called in the BODY of the page (line 24), the following events occur:

1. The inputs to the function are evaluated first, with the variables x and y evaluating to 3 and 4, respectively.
2. Next, execution jumps to the Distance function to perform the actual computation.
3. Within the function, new memory cells are allocated for the parameters and local variables. In the case of the parameters, their associated memory cells are assigned the values of the corresponding inputs from the call. This means that the parameters x1, y1, x2, and y2 are assigned 0, 0, 3 and 4, respectively.
4. The statements in the function are executed in order, assigning temp1 the value 9 and temp2 the value 16.
5. When execution reaches the return statement, the expression in the statement is evaluated, yielding 5.

```
1.  <html>
2.  <!-- dist.html                                    Dave Reed -->
3.  <!------------------------------------------------------------>
4.  <head>
5.    <title>Point Distance</title>
6.    <script type="text/javascript">
7.      function Distance(x1, y1, x2, y2)
8.      // Assumes: (x1,y1) and (x2,y2) are coordinates
9.      // Returns: the distance between the two points
10.     {
11.       var temp1, temp2;
12.
13.       temp1 = Math.pow(x1 - x2, 2);
14.       temp2 = Math.pow(y1 - y2, 2);
15.       return Math.sqrt(temp1 + temp2);
16.     }
17.   </script>
18.  </head>
19.
20.  <body>
21.    <script type="text/javascript">
22.        x = 3;
23.        y = 4;
24.        d = Distance(0, 0, x, y);
25.
26.        document.write("The distance is between (0,0) and " +
27.                        "(" + x + ", " + y + ") is " + d);
28.    </script>
29.  </body>
30.  </html>
```

Figure 7.12 Web page that computes the distance between $(0, 0)$ and $(3, 4)$.

6. After the return value is computed, the function's execution is complete. Since the parameters and local variables exist only inside the function, the memory cells associated with these variables are *deallocated*—i.e., they are made available for other uses.

7. Once the memory cells have been freed, 5 can be returned as the result of the function call. In this case, the function call appears on the right-hand side of an assignment, so d is assigned 5.

In general, the calling sequence for functions is as follows:

1. The inputs in the function call are evaluated.

2. Execution jumps to the function that is being called.

3. Memory cells are allocated for each parameter and local variable in the function, and, in the case of parameters, the values of the corresponding inputs are assigned to the memory cells.

4. The statements in the body of the function are executed in order.

5. When a return statement is encountered, the expression is evaluated.

6. Memory cells associated with the parameters and local variables are deallocated (destroyed).

7. Upon return, the value yielded by the return statement replaces the function call in the expression in which the call appears.

Using the list above as a template, trace the sequence of events that would result from the call to `Distance` in the following write statement:

```
document.write( Distance(2, 1+1, 3+2, 6) );
```

After you evaluate the function on paper, enter the `dist.html` text into a new Web page and modify the page to verify your final answer.

EXERCISE 7.20

What would happen if you placed a statement after the return statement in a function? For example, what if you inserted another return statement immediately following the existing one in `Distance`? Would a second additional statement affect the behavior of the function? Why or why not? Verify your answer by adding a second return statement to the `Distance` function and then calling the function as before.

Since each function in a page can have its own local variables, it is possible to have the same variable name refer to separate memory cells. For example, suppose that `Distance`'s local variables `temp1` and `temp2` were instead named `x` and `y` (so that they shared their names with the global variables in the BODY). Although readers might find this confusing, the browser is not confused at all. The global variables named `x` and `y` are separate from the local variables `x` and `y`, and the local variables are accessible only from within the `distance` function. Using the subscript notation introduced in this chapter, we can think of the local variables as $x_{Distance}$ and $y_{Distance}$, and the global variables as x_{BODY} and y_{BODY}. Assignments made to `x` and `y` within the function would affect only the local variables ($x_{Distance}$ and $y_{Distance}$), leaving the global variables (x_{BODY} and y_{BODY}) unchanged.

EXERCISE 7.21

Test whether global and local variables behave as described by modifying the `dist.html` page. Rename the local variables in the function `x` and `y`, then verify that the output of the page is unchanged.

Once again, the purpose of defining functions is to build independent units of abstraction. The ultimate goal is to call a function without worrying about how it works. Declaring variables inside a function to be local is instrumental in achieving this level of abstraction. If all variables used inside a function are declared to be local, then the execution of that function does not affect and is not affected by any external variables. However, if functions access and change global variables, the results may be difficult to predict or control. For example, suppose that the variables in the `Distance` function were named `x` and `y`, but were not declared to be local. If this were the case, then assignments to those variables would affect the global variables that appear in the BODY.

EXERCISE 7.22

To demonstrate this undesirable effect, modify your `dist.html` page further by "commenting out" the variable declarations in the `Distance` function. That is, place double slashes (//) at the front of the variable declaration, which will cause the browser to ignore the declaration and treat the function's variables as global. Assuming that the variables in the function are still named `x` and `y`, what output is produced by this modified page? Why does the output differ from that in the last exercise?

8 Chapter

Algorithms and Programming Languages

This chapter uses narrative, illustrations, hands-on experimentation, and review questions to introduce computer science and technology concepts.

> *When I am working on a problem, I never think about beauty. I think only of how to solve the problem. But when I have finished, if the solution is not beautiful, I know it is wrong.*
>
> R. Buckminster Fuller
>
> *If you cannot describe what you are doing as a process, you don't know what you're doing.*
>
> W. Edwards Deming
>
> *A programming language is a system of notation for describing computations. A useful programming language must therefore be suited for both description (i.e., for human writers and readers of programs) and for computation (i.e., for efficient implementation on computers). But human beings and computers are so different that it is difficult to find notational devices that are well suited to the capabilities of both.*
>
> R.D. Tennant
> *Principles of Programming Languages*

The central concept underlying all computation is that of the **algorithm**, a step-by-step sequence of instructions for carrying out some task. When you interact with a computer, you provide instructions in the form of mouse clicks, menu selections, or command sequences. These instructions tell the computer to execute particular tasks, such as copying a piece of text or saving an image. At a more detailed level, when you write JavaScript statements, you are specifying instructions that the browser must follow in order to perform actions, such as prompting the user for input or displaying a message in the page.

This chapter presents an overview of algorithms, their design and analysis, and their connection to computer science. After introducing techniques for solving problems, we provide several example algorithms for you to study, accompanying each with an interactive Web page that will help you visualize and experiment with the algorithms. We also discuss the evolution of programming languages and the advantage of using advanced languages to write computer algorithms at a high level of abstraction. After completing this chapter, you will be familiar with the steps involved in designing an algorithm, coding it in a programming language, and executing the resulting program.

Algorithms

Programming may be viewed as the process of designing and implementing algorithms that a computer (or a program executing on that computer) can carry out. The programmer's job is to create an algorithm for accomplishing a given objective and then to translate the individual steps of the algorithm into a programming language that the computer understands. For example, the JavaScript programs you have written have contained statements that instruct the browser to carry out particular tasks, such as displaying a message or updating an image in the page. The browser understands these statements and is therefore able to carry them out, producing the desired results.

Algorithms in the Real World

The use of algorithms is not limited to the domain of computing. For example, a recipe for baking chocolate chip cookies is an algorithm. By following the instructions carefully, anyone familiar with cooking should be able to bake a perfect batch of cookies. Similarly, when you give someone directions to your house, you are defining an algorithm that the person can follow to reach that specific destination. Algorithms are prevalent in modern society, because we are constantly faced with unfamiliar tasks that we could not complete without instructions. You probably don't know exactly how long to cook macaroni or how to assemble a bicycle, so algorithms are provided (e.g., cooking instructions on the macaroni box, or printed assembly instructions accompanying the bike) to guide you through these activities.

Of course, we have all had experiences with vague or misleading instructions, such as recipes that assume the knowledge of a master chef or directions to a house that rely on obscure landmarks. In order for an algorithm to be effective, it must be stated in a manner that its intended executor can understand. If you buy an expensive cookbook, it will probably assume that you are experienced in the kitchen. Instructions such as "create a white sauce" or "fold in egg whites until desired consistency" are probably clear to a chef. On the other hand, the instructions on the side of a typical macaroni-and-cheese box do not assume much culinary expertise. They tend to be simple and precise, like those in Figure 8.1. As you have no doubt experienced in developing interactive Web pages, computers are more demanding with regard to algorithm specificity than any human audience could be. Computers require that the steps in an algorithm be stated in an extremely precise form. Even simple mistakes in a program, such as misspelling a variable name or forgetting a comma, can confuse the computer and render it unable to execute the program.

Specifying the solution to a problem in precise steps can be difficult, and the process often requires experience, creativity, and deep thought. However, once the problem's solution is designed and written down in the form of an algorithm, that particular problem can be solved by anyone capable of following the algorithm steps. The earliest surviving examples of written algorithms date back some four thousand years to the Babylonian civilization that inhabited present-day Iraq. Archeologists have discovered numerous examples of Babylonian clay tablets containing step-by-step instructions for solving mathematical and geometric problems (Figure 8.2).

Designing and Analyzing Algorithms

Life is full of problems whose solutions require a careful, step-by-step approach. Designing solutions to those problems involves both logical reasoning and creativity. In his classic book, *How to Solve It*, the mathematician George Polya (1887–1985) outlined four steps that can be applied to solving most problems:

1. Understand the problem.
2. Devise a plan.
3. Carry out your plan.
4. Examine the solution.

EASY COOK DIRECTIONS:

TOP OF STOVE

- **BOIL 6 cups of water.** Stir in Macaroni. Boil 11 to 14 minutes, stirring occasionally.
- **DRAIN. DO NOT RINSE.** Return to pan.
- **ADD** 3 Tbsp. margarine, 3 Tbsp. milk and Cheese Sauce Mix; mix well. Makes about 2 cups.

NO DRAIN MICROWAVE

- **POUR** Macaroni into 1 or 2 quart microwavable bowl. Add 1 cups hot water.
- **MICROWAVE** uncovered, on HIGH 12 to 14 minutes or until water is absorbed, stirring every 5 minutes. Continue as directed above.

Figure 8.1   Cooking instructions on a box of KRAFT® Macaroni and Cheese. (KRAFT is a registered trademark used with the permission of Kraft Foods.)

Figure 8.2   Ancient Babylonians used cuneiform writing to record mathematical formulas and then carved them into clay tablets. Such tablets represent the first historical examples of written algorithms. *British Museum, London, UK/Bridgeman Art Library*

Polya's first step, understanding the problem, involves identifying exactly what is required (What are the initial conditions? What is the overall goal?) and what constraints are involved (What properties must the solution have?). For example, suppose that you are presented with the following task:

Problem Statement: Find the oldest person in a room full of people.

At first glance, this problem seems relatively straightforward to comprehend. The initial condition is a room full of people. The goal is to identify the oldest person. However, deeper issues have to be explored before a solution can be proposed. For example, how do you determine how old a person is? Can you tell someone's age just by looking at her? If you ask someone his age, will he tell the truth? What if there is more than one oldest person (i.e., if two individuals were born on the same day at the same time)?

For simplicity, let us assume that, when asked, a person will give his or her real birthday. Also, let us further assume that we don't care about the time of day at which a person was born—if two people were born on the same day, they are considered the same age. If there is more than one oldest person, finding any one of them is acceptable.

Equipped with our new understanding of the problem, we are prepared to devise a solution:

Finding the oldest person in a room (Algorithm 1):

1. Line up all the people along one wall.
2. Ask the first person to state his or her name and birthday, then write this information down on a piece of paper.
3. For each successive person in line:
   a. Ask the person his or her name and birthday.
   b. If the stated birthday is earlier than the date written on the paper, cross out the old information and write down the name and birthday of this person.
4. When you have reached the end of the line, the name and birthday of the oldest person will be written on the paper.

To see how this algorithm works, we can carry out the steps on a fictitious group of people (Figure 8.3). Initially, you write down the name and birthday of the first person (Chris, 8/4/82). Working your way down the line, you ask each person's birthday and update the page when an earlier birthday is encountered (first Pat, 10/7/80; then Joan, 2/6/80). When you reach the end of the line, the name and birthday of the oldest person (Joan, 2/6/80) is written on the paper.

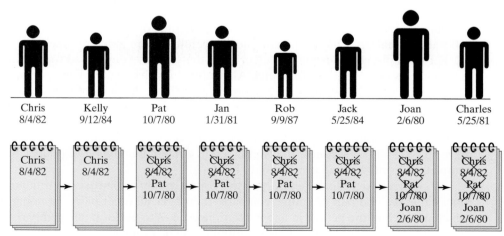

Figure 8.3 Algorithm 1 for finding the oldest person.

This algorithm is simple, and it's easy to see that it would work on any group of people. Since you go through the entire line, every person is eventually asked his or her birthday. When you reach the oldest person, his or her birthday will be earlier than the birthday currently on the paper. And once you write the oldest person's information down, that name will stay on the paper, since no one older will be found.

An Alternative Algorithm

Algorithm 1, as demonstrated in Figure 8.3, effectively locates the oldest person in a room. However, this problem—like most—can be solved many different ways. Once alternative algorithms for the same task have been proposed, you can analyze each option to determine which is simpler, more efficient, or better serves your particular objectives. As an example, consider the following alternative algorithm for finding the oldest person:

Finding the oldest person in a room (Algorithm 2):

1. Line up all the people along one wall.
2. As long as there is more than one person in the line, repeatedly:
   a. Have the people pair up (1st and 2nd in line, 3rd and 4th in line, and so on). If there are an odd number of people, the last person will remain without a partner.
   b. Ask each pair of people to compare their birthdays.
   c. Request that the younger of the two leave the line.
3. When there is only one person left in the line, that person is the oldest.

Algorithm 2 is slightly more complex than Algorithm 1, but has the same end result—the oldest person in the room is located. In the first round, each pair compare their birthdays, and the younger of the two partners subsequently leaves the line. Thus, the number of people in line is cut roughly in half (if there are an odd number of people, the extra person will remain). The older members of the original pairs then repeat this process, reducing the size of the line each time. Eventually, the number of people in line drops to one. Clearly, the oldest person cannot have left, since he or she would have been older than any potential partner in the line. Therefore, the last person remaining is the oldest. Figure 8.4 demonstrates performing this algorithm on the same eight people used in Figure 8.3. In three rounds, the line of people shrinks until it contains only the oldest person.

Algorithm Analysis

When more than one algorithm has been established to solve a problem, it is necessary to determine which is better. Often, there is not a single correct answer: your choice for the "better" algorithm depends upon what features matter to you. If you don't care how long it takes to solve a problem but want to be sure of the answer, it makes sense for you to favor the simplest, most easily understood algorithm. However, if you are concerned about the time or effort required to solve the problem, you will want to analyze your alternatives more carefully before making a decision.

For example, consider the two algorithms that we have developed for finding the oldest person in a room. As Figure 8.3 demonstrates, Algorithm 1 involves asking each person's birthday and then comparing it with the birthday written on the page. Thus, the amount of time needed to find the oldest person using Algorithm 1 will be directly proportional to the number of people. If there are 100 people in line and it takes 5 seconds to compare birthdays, then executing Algorithm 1 will require $5*100 = 500$ seconds. Likewise, if there are 200 people in line, then executing Algorithm 1 will require $5*200 = 1,000$ seconds. In general, if you double the number of people, the time necessary to complete Algorithm 1 will also double.

By contrast, Algorithm 2 allows you to perform multiple comparisons simultaneously, which saves time. While the first pair of people compares their ages, all other pairs are doing the same. Thus, you can eliminate half the people in line in the time it takes to perform one comparison. This implies that the total time involved in executing Algorithm 2 will be proportional to the number of rounds needed to shrink the line down to one person. In Figure 8.4, we reduced a group of eight people to the single oldest person in three rounds: $8 \rightarrow 4 \rightarrow 2 \rightarrow 1$. If there were twice as many people in the room, it

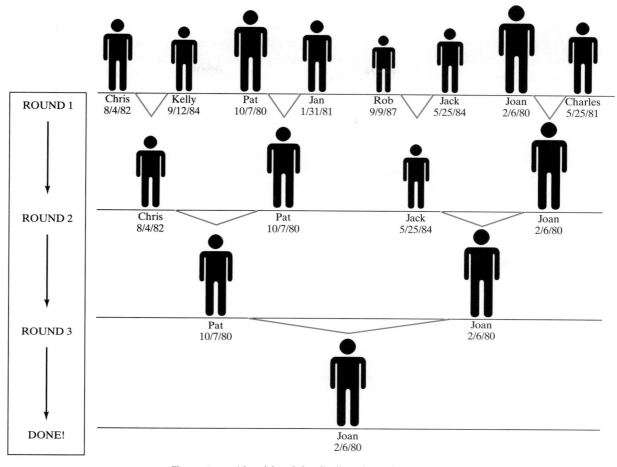

ROUND 1

Chris
8/4/82

Kelly
9/12/84

Pat
10/7/80

Jan
1/31/81

Rob
9/9/87

Jack
5/25/84

Joan
2/6/80

Charles
5/25/81

ROUND 2

Chris
8/4/82

Pat
10/7/80

Jack
5/25/84

Joan
2/6/80

ROUND 3

Pat
10/7/80

Joan
2/6/80

DONE!

Joan
2/6/80

Figure 8.4　Algorithm 2 for finding the oldest person.

would still require only four rounds to eliminate all but the single oldest person: $16 \rightarrow 8 \rightarrow 4 \rightarrow 2 \rightarrow 1$. In mathematics, the notion of a logarithm captures this halving effect: $\lceil \log_2(N) \rceil$ represents the number of times a value N can be halved before it reaches 1, where $\lceil\ \rceil$ denotes rounding up to the next integer if necessary (Figure 8.5). Therefore, Algorithm 2 will find the oldest person in an amount

N	$\lceil \log_2(N) \rceil$
100	7
200	8
400	9
800	10
1,600	11
. . .	. . .
10,000	14
20,000	15
40,000	16
. . .	. . .
1,000,000	20

Figure 8.5　Table of logarithms (where $\lceil\ \rceil$ denotes rounding up to the next integer).

of time proportional to the logarithm of the number of people. For example, if there are 100 people in line and it takes 5 seconds to compare birthdays, completing Algorithm 2 will require $5 * \lceil \log_2(100) \rceil = 5 * 7 = 35$ seconds. If there are 200 people in line, then completing Algorithm 2 will require $5 * \lceil \log_2(200) \rceil = 5 * 8 = 40$ seconds. In general, if you double the number of people, the time required to execute Algorithm 2 will increase by the duration of one additional comparison.

An algorithm's performance can be measured by the speed at which the algorithm (or program designed to carry out that algorithm) accomplishes its task. It should be noted that the relative performance of these algorithms remains the same, regardless of how long it takes to complete an individual comparison. In the timings we have considered so far, we assumed that birthdays could be compared in 5 seconds. If a comparison instead took 10 seconds, you would still find that doubling the number of people doubles the time needed to perform Algorithm 1: 100 people would require $10 * 100 = 1,000$ seconds, and 200 people would require $10 * 200 = 2,000$ seconds. Likewise, doubling the number of people increases Algorithm 2's execution time by the duration of one additional comparison: 100 people would require $10 * \lceil \log_2(100) \rceil = 10 * 7 = 70$ seconds, and 200 people would require $10 * \lceil \log_2(200) \rceil = 10 * 8 = 80$ seconds.

Big-Oh Notation

To represent an algorithm's performance in relation to the size of the problem, computer scientists use what is known as the *Big-Oh* notation. Executing an $O(N)$ algorithm requires time proportional to the size of the problem. That is, if the problem size doubles, the time needed to solve that problem using the algorithm will also double. By contrast, executing an $O(\log N)$ algorithm requires time proportional to the logarithm of the problem size. That is, if the problem size doubles, the time needed to solve that problem increases by a constant amount. Based on our previous analysis, we can classify Algorithm 1 for finding the oldest person as an $O(N)$ algorithm, where problem size N is defined as the number of people in the room. Algorithm 2, on the other hand, is classified as an $O(\log N)$ algorithm. The performance difference between an $O(N)$ algorithm and an $O(\log N)$ algorithm can be quite dramatic, especially when you are contemplating extremely large problems. As we demonstrated above, Algorithm 1 would need 1,000 seconds to handle 200 people (assuming 5 seconds per comparison), whereas Algorithm 2 would need only 40. As the number of people increases, the performance benefit offered by Algorithm 2 increases as well. If the room in question contained 1,000 people, completing Algorithm 1 would require 5,000 seconds, whereas Algorithm 2 could be executed in only 50 seconds.

Algorithm Example: Searching a List

The problem of finding the oldest person in a room is similar to a more general problem that occurs frequently in computer science. Computers are often required to store and maintain large amounts of information and then search through data for particular values. For example, commercial databases typically contain large numbers of records, such as product inventories or payroll receipts, and allow the user to search for information on particular entries. Similarly, a Web browser that executes a JavaScript program must keep track of all the variables used throughout the program, as well as their corresponding values. Each time a variable appears in an expression, the browser must access the list of variables to obtain the associated value.

If a computer attempted to locate information in an arbitrary manner, pinpointing a particular entry in a list would be time consuming and tedious. For example, consider the task of searching a large payroll database for a particular record. If the computer simply selected entries at random and compared them with the desired record, there would be no guarantee that the computer would eventually find the correct entry. A systematic approach (i.e., an algorithm) is needed to ensure that the desired entry is found, no matter where it appears in the database.

Sequential Search

The simplest algorithm for searching a list is *sequential search,* an approach that involves examining each list item in sequential order until the desired item is found.

Sequential search for finding an item in a list:

1. Start at the beginning of the list.
2. For each item in the list:
    a. Examine the item. If that item is the one you are seeking, then you are done.
    b. If it is not the item you are seeking, then go on to the next item in the list.

If you reach the end of the list and have not found the item, then it was not in the list. This algorithm is simple and guaranteed to find the item if it is in the list, but its execution can take a very long time. If the desired item is at the end of the list or not in the list at all, then the algorithm will have to look at every entry before returning a result. Although sequentially searching a list of 10 or 100 items might be feasible, this approach becomes impractical when a list contains thousands or tens of thousands of entries. Just imagine how tedious searching a phone book in this manner would be!

Binary Search

Fortunately, there is a more efficient algorithm for searching a list, as long as the list adheres to some organizational structure. For example, entries in the phone book are alphabetized to help people find numbers quickly. If you were looking for "Dave Reed" in the phone book, you might guess that it would appear toward the back of the book, since 'R' is late in the alphabet. However, if you opened the book to a page near the end and found "Joan Smith" at the top, you would know that you had gone too far and would back up some number of pages. In most cases, your knowledge of the alphabet and the phone book's alphabetical ordering system should enable you to hone in on an entry after a few page flips.

By generalizing this approach, we can create an algorithm for searching any ordered list. The first step is to inspect the entry at the middle position of the list (rounding down this position number if the list contains an even number of items). If this middle entry is the one you are looking for, then you are done. If, in the list's ordering scheme, the middle entry comes after the item you are seeking (e.g., "Joan Smith" comes after "Dave Reed" alphabetically), then you know that the desired item appears in the first half of the list (unless the item is not in the list at all). However, if the middle entry comes before the desired item in sequence (e.g., "Adam Miller" comes before "Dave Reed"), then the desired item must appear in the second half of the list. Once you have determined the half in which the item must appear, you can search that half via the same technique. Because each check cuts the list that must be searched in half, this algorithm is known as *binary search*.

Binary search for finding an item in an ordered list:

1. Initially, the potential range in which the item could occur is the entire list.
2. As long as items remain in the potential range and the desired item has not been found, repeatedly:
    a. Examine at the middle entry in the potential range.
    b. If the middle entry is the item you are looking for, then you are done.
    c. If the middle entry is greater than the desired item, then reduce the potential range to those entries left of the middle.
    d. If the middle entry is less than the desired item, then reduce the potential range to those entries right of the middle.

Since step 2 consistently reduces the range in which the item could occur, repeating this step will eventually converge on the item (or reduce the potential range down to nothing, indicating that the item is not in the list). Figure 8.6 depicts a binary search that locates "Illinois" in an alphabetical list of state names. Since "Illinois" could conceivably appear anywhere in the list, the initial range that must be searched is the entire list (positions 1 through 15). Thus, you begin by checking the midpoint of this range, which is located by averaging the left and right boundaries of the range: position $(1 + 15)/2 = 8$. Since the entry at position 8, "Missouri", comes after "Illinois" in the alphabet, you know that "Illinois" must appear in the left half of the list. Note that, in the second step, we have crossed out the entries at position 8 and beyond to highlight the fact that they are no longer under

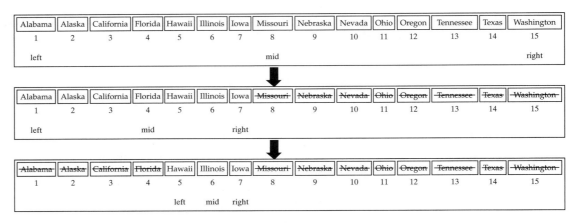

Figure 8.6 Steps in a binary search for "Illinois". The labels "left" and "right" denote the range in which the desired item can appear. With each step, the middle item in the range is checked and half the range is eliminated.

consideration. After eliminating part of the list, you repeat the process, checking the midpoint of the new potential range, position (1 + 7)/2 = 4. Since the entry at position 4, "Florida", comes before "Illinois" in the alphabet, you know that "Illinois" must occupy a position to the right of position 4. The potential range in which "Illinois" can appear is now limited to positions 5 through 7. As before, you check the midpoint of the new potential range, position (5 + 7)/2 = 6. Since the entry at that position is indeed "Illinois", the search concludes successfully.

The Web page `search.html` (accessible at `http://www.prenhall.com/reed`) provides an interactive tool for studying the behavior of the binary search algorithm. Included with the page is a list of state names similar to the one used in Figure 8.6. The user can enter a desired state name in a text box, then click a button to see the steps required to locate that name in the list.

Algorithm Analysis

Recall that, in the worst case, sequential search involves checking every single entry in a list. This implies that the time required to locate a list item using sequential search is proportional to the size of the list. Thus, sequential search is an $O(N)$ algorithm, where problem size N is defined as the number of items in the list.

By contrast, when you perform a binary search, each examination of an entry enables you to rule out an entire range of entries. For example, in Figure 8.6, checking the midpoint of the list and finding that "Missouri" comes after "Illinois" allowed for the elimination of eight entries (positions 8–15). Subsequently checking the midpoint of the list's first half and finding that "Florida" comes before "Illinois" eliminated an additional four entries (positions 1–4). In general, each time you look at an entry, you can rule out roughly half the remaining entries. This halving effect yields the same logarithmic behavior that we noted in Algorithm 2 for finding the oldest person in a room. Thus, the time required to find a list item using binary search is proportional to the logarithm of the size of the list, making binary search an $O(\log N)$ algorithm. This makes binary search a much more efficient technique for traversing large amounts of information. Using binary search, a phone book for a small town (10,000 people) could be searched in at most $\lceil \log_2(10,000) \rceil = 14$ checks, a large city (1 million people) in at most $\lceil \log_2(1,000,000) \rceil = 20$ checks, and the entire United States (280 million people) in at most $\lceil \log_2(280,000,000) \rceil = 29$ checks.

Algorithm Example: Approximating a Square Root

Recall that, in Chapter 7, we introduced the `Math.sqrt` function as an example of computational abstraction. Since JavaScript predefines this function, it was not necessary for you to understand how the function works—you just needed to know how to use it. In this section, however, we are going to examine the actual steps required to calculate the square root of a number. Several different algorithms can be used to perform this computation; one in particular, devised by Sir Isaac Newton (1643–1727) in the late 17th century (Figure 8.7), is simple to describe and is discussed below.

Figure 8.7   Sir Isaac Newton.

Newton's algorithm for finding the square root of N:

1. Start with the initial approximation 1.
2. As long as the approximation isn't close enough, repeatedly:
   a. Refine the approximation using the formula
      newApproximation = (oldApproximation + N/oldApproximation)/2.

While reading Newton's algorithm, you might have noticed that the stopping condition is somewhat vague. Since some numbers' square roots (such as the square root of 2) cannot be represented as finite fractions, Newton's algorithm will not always be able to find the exact square root. However, each successive approximation is guaranteed to be closer to the square root. Thus, the person using the algorithm can determine exactly how close the approximation needs to be in order to suffice.

For example, suppose that we wanted to find the square root of 1,024. Newton's algorithm starts with the initial approximation 1. The next approximation is obtained by plugging 1 into Newton's formula; we therefore evaluate the expression $(1 + 1{,}024/1)/2$, which yields 512.5. The next approximation is $(512.5 + 1{,}024/512.5)/2 = 257.2$, followed by $(257.2 + 1{,}024/257.2)/2 = 130.6$, and so on. After only 10 refinements, the approximation is so close to the actual square root, 32, that a computer will round the value to 32 (see Figure 8.8).

The Web page Newton.html (accessible at http://www.prenhall.com/reed) provides an interactive tool for studying the behavior of Newton's algorithm. The user can enter a desired number N in a text box, then click a button to see the first approximation of N's square root as calculated using Newton's algorithm. Each time the user clicks the button, the program displays a successive approximation. Users can continue clicking until the desired level of accuracy is reached.

Algorithm Analysis

Analyzing the performance of Newton's algorithm is trickier than in previous examples, and a detailed investigation of this topic is beyond the scope of this book. The algorithm does converge on the square root in the sense that each successive approximation is closer to the square root than the

```
Initial approximation = 1
Next approximation = 512.5
Next approximation = 257.2490243902439
Next approximation = 130.16480157022683
Next approximation = 69.22732405448894
Next approximation = 42.00958563100827
Next approximation = 33.19248741685438
Next approximation = 32.02142090500024
Next approximation = 32.0000071648159
Next approximation = 32.0000000000008
Next approximation = 32
```

Figure 8.8   Using Newton's algorithm to calculate the square root of 1,024.

previous one was. However, the fact that the square root might be a nonterminating fraction makes it difficult to define the exact number of steps required for convergence. In general, the algorithm does tend to demonstrate logarithmic behavior, since the difference between a given approximation and the actual square root is cut roughly in half by each successive refinement.

Algorithms and Programming

Programming is all about designing and coding algorithms for solving problems. The intended executor of those algorithms is the computer or a program executing on that computer, which must be able to understand the instructions and then carry them out in order. Since computers are not very intelligent, the instructions they receive must be extraordinarily specific. Unfortunately, human languages such as English are notoriously ambiguous, and the technology for programming computers in a human language is still many years away. Instead, we write computer instructions in programming languages, which are more constrained and exact than human languages are.

The level of precision necessary to write a successful program often frustrates beginning programmers. However, it is much easier to program today's computers than those of fifty years ago. As we explained in Chapter 6, the first electronic computers were not programmable at all—machines such as the ENIAC were wired to perform a certain computation. Although users could enter inputs via switches, the computational steps that the computer performed could be changed only by rewiring the physical components into a different configuration. Clearly, this arrangement made specifying an algorithm tedious and time consuming. With the advent of von Neumann's stored-program architecture, computers could be programmed instead of rewired. For the first time, computing engineers were able to write algorithms as sequences of instructions in a language understood by the computer, and these instructions could be loaded into memory and executed.

Machine Languages

Programming languages introduce a level of abstraction that insulates the programmer from the computer's low-level, mechanical details. Instead of having to worry about which wires should connect which components, the programmer must instead learn to speak the language that controls the machinery. However, the first programming languages, which were developed in the late 1940s, provided a very low level of abstraction. Instructions written in these languages correspond directly to the hardware operations of a particular machine. As such, these languages are called ***machine languages***. Machine-language instructions deal directly with the computer's physical components, including main memory locations and registers, memory cells located inside the CPU and used for storing values as computations take place. (Chapter 14 discusses the role of registers in greater detail.) Examples of these primitive instructions might include:

- Move the value at main memory address 100 to register 3.
- Add 1 to the value in register 3.
- Jump to the instruction at main memory address 1024.

Of course, machine-language instructions aren't represented as statements in English. As we learned in Chapter 1, computers store and manipulate data in the form of binary values (i.e., patterns of 0s and 1s). It is not surprising, then, that machine-language instructions are also represented in binary. For example, the above instructions might be written as:

- 0110011001000011
- 1100000000010011
- 0101010000000000

Thus, machine-language programs are comprised of binary-number sequences corresponding to primitive machine operations. Although writing such a program and storing it in memory is certainly preferable to rewiring the machine, machine languages do not facilitate easy, intuitive programming. Programmers have to memorize the binary codes that correspond to machine instructions, which is extremely tedious. Entering in long sequences of zeros and ones is error prone, to say the least. And, if errors do occur, trying to debug a sheet full of zeros and ones is next to impossible. To make matters worse, each type of computer has its own machine language that correlates directly to the machine's underlying hardware. Machine-language programs written for one type of computer can be executed only on identical machines.

To provide a taste of what these earlier programmers went through, Figure 8.9 depicts an excerpt from an actual machine-language program. How easy do you think it would be to look at this program and determine what it does? If you ran this program and it did not behave as desired, how easy would it be to work through the code and determine where it went wrong?

```
0000000000000011010000110010101101100011011000110111100101110011000110111000 00
1110000000000000110011101100011011000110011001001011111011000110110111101101 10
1011100000110100101101100011000110101011001000001011100000000001011111011010 001000101011
1110111000101110100011011101100100000000000010111110101111011011000110011101 010
1111101011111001101101101101111101100110111010001110010011001010110000101101 1010
1010000010001100101001000100011011101101011110111001101110100011100100110010 10110000
1011011010101111101010010001101101101011110111001101110100011100100110010101 100
0010110101000000000001011111010111111011011000111000110101011111010111111001 10111011
0111101110011011101100100110010011001001100011001101110100001000000110011011 1000110
0000000110010101101110011001000110110001011111010111110100011001010010001101 1
1011011110111001101110100011100100110010101100001011011010000000000110110101 1100
00101101001011011100000000000110001101101111011101010101110100000000000000000 0000000
```

Figure 8.9 Excerpt from a machine-language program.

High-Level Languages

Although machine languages enable computers to be reprogrammed without being rewired, these languages introduce only a low level of abstraction. Since each binary instruction corresponds to a physical operation, programmers must still specify algorithms at the level of the machinery. Furthermore, the programmer has to represent all instructions and data as binary-number sequences.

In the early 1950s, programming capabilities evolved through the introduction of *assembly languages*. Assembly languages provide a slightly higher level of abstraction by allowing programmers to specify instructions using words, rather than binary-number sequences. However, these words still correspond to operations performed by the computer's physical components, so assembly-language programming still involves thinking at a low level of abstraction.

In order to solve complex problems quickly and reliably, programmers must be able to write instructions at a higher level of abstraction that more closely relates to the way humans think. When we solve problems, we make use of high-level abstractions and constructs, such as variables, conditional choices, repetition, and functions. A language that includes such abstractions provides a more natural framework through which to solve problems. Starting in the late 1950s, computer scientists began developing *high-level languages* to address this need. The first such language was FORTRAN, written by John Backus (1924–) at IBM in 1957. Two years later, John McCarthy (1927–) invented LISP at

MIT, and a multitude of high-level languages soon followed. JavaScript, the high-level language that you have been using throughout this text, was invented in 1995 by Brendan Eich (1964–) and his research team at Netscape Communications Corporation.

Figure 8.10 depicts two different high-level language programs that perform the same task: each asks the user to enter a name and then displays a customized greeting. The program on the left is written in JavaScript, and the one on the right is written in C++. As you can see, high-level programming languages are much closer to human languages than machine languages are. With only a little knowledge of each language, anyone could detect and fix errors in these programs.

```
<html>
<!-- hello.html            Dave Reed   -->
<!-- This page displays a greeting.    -->
<!------------------------------------->

<head>
  <title>Greetings</title>
<head>

<body>
  <script type="text/javascript">
    username = prompt("Enter your name", "");

    document.write("Hello " + username + "!");
  </script>
</body>
</html>
```

```
// hello.cpp              Dave Reed
// This program displays a greeting.
//////////////////////////////////////

#include <iostream>
#include <string>
using namespace std;

int main()
{
   string userName;
   cout << "Enter your name" << endl;
   cin >> userName;

   cout << "Hello " << userName << "!";

   return 0;
}
```

Figure 8.10 High-level language programs (JavaScript and C++).

Another advantage of high-level languages is that the resulting programs are machine independent. Because high-level instructions are not specific to the underlying computer's hardware configuration, programs written in high-level languages are theoretically portable across computers. Such portability is essential, because it enables programmers to market their software to a wide variety of users. If a different version of the same program were required for each brand of computer, software development would be both inefficient and prohibitively expensive.

Not surprisingly, almost all software development today utilizes high-level programming languages, such as C++ and Java. However, it should be noted that low-level languages have not gone away. As you will see in the next section, programs written in a high-level language must still be translated into the machine language of a particular computer before they can be executed. And in application areas where execution time is critical, say in controllers for jet stabilizers, modern programmers may still utilize assembly and machine languages in order to optimize the use of memory and the sequencing of instructions.

Program Translation

While it is desirable for programmers to be able to reason at a high level of abstraction, we cannot forget that programs are written to be executed. At some point, a high-level program must be translated to machine instructions that computer hardware can implement. Two basic techniques, known as interpretation and compilation, are employed to perform these translations. However, before we formally define these approaches, let us examine the following analogies.

Consider the task of translating a speech from one language to another. Usually, this is accomplished by having an interpreter listen to the speech as it is being given, translating it a phrase or sentence at a time (Figure 8.11). In effect, the interpreter becomes a substitute for the original speaker, repeating the speaker's words in a different language after a slight delay to perform the translation (Figure 8.12). One advantage of this approach is that it provides a real-time translation: an observer

1. A speech is delivered in Chinese. → 2. An interpreter listens, translates each sentence, and speaks in English. → 3. The listener hears each sentence in English (with some delay).

Figure 8.11 Using an interpreter to translate a speech.

Figure 8.12 Chinese Premier Deng Xiaoping with interpreter (1975).

can see the speaker and hear the translated words in the same approximate time frame. The immediacy of the translation also enables the observer to give feedback to the interpreter. For example, if the interpreter were using the wrong dialect of a language, the observer could correct this early in the speech.

If there is no need for the translation to be provided in real time, the interpreter could instead translate the speech in its entirety after the fact. Given a recording (or transcript), a translator could take the time to convert the entire speech to the desired language and then produce a recording (or transcript) of the translation (Figure 8.13). Although this approach is less immediate and more time consuming than real-time interpretation is, there are several advantages. A key benefit is that, once

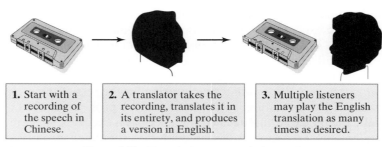

1. Start with a recording of the speech in Chinese. → 2. A translator takes the recording, translates it in its entirety, and produces a version in English. → 3. Multiple listeners may play the English translation as many times as desired.

Figure 8.13 Translating a recorded speech.

the speech has been translated, multiple people can listen to it as many times as desired, without the need for retranslation. Furthermore, after the initial translation process, listeners do not have to suffer through additional delays when hearing the content of the speech. This approach is clearly required for translating books, since it is impractical to translate the book phrase by phrase every time someone wants to read it.

Interpreters and Compilers

Translating a high-level language program into machine language is not unlike translating spoken languages. The two techniques we have described are analogous to the two approaches used in programming-language translation: *interpretation* and *compilation*. The interpretation approach relies on a program known as an *interpreter* to translate and execute the statements in a high-level language program. An interpreter reads the statements one at a time, immediately translating and executing each statement before processing the next one. This is, in fact, what happens when JavaScript programs are executed. A JavaScript interpreter is embedded in every modern Web browser; when the browser loads a page containing JavaScript code, the interpreter executes the code one statement at a time, displaying the corresponding output in the page (Figure 8.14).

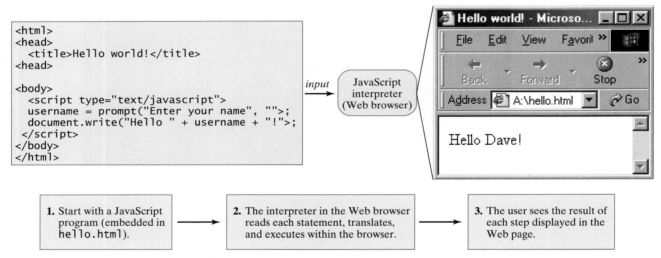

Figure 8.14 Interpreting a JavaScript program.

By contrast, the compilation approach relies on a program known as a *compiler* to translate the entire high-level language program into its equivalent machine-language instructions. The resulting machine-language program can then be executed directly on the computer (Figure 8.15). Most programming languages used in the development of commercial software, such as C and C++, employ the compilation technique.

As with the human-language translation options, there are tradeoffs between the interpretation and compilation approaches. An interpreter starts producing results almost immediately, since it reads in and executes each instruction before moving on to the next. This immediacy is particularly desirable for languages used in highly interactive applications. For example, JavaScript was designed specifically for adding dynamic, interactive features to Web pages. If the first statement in a JavaScript program involves prompting the user for a value, then you would like this to happen as soon as the page loads, rather than waiting for the rest of the program to be translated. The disadvantage of interpretation, however, is that the program executes more slowly. The interpreter must take the time to translate each statement as it executes, so there will be a slight delay between each statement's execution. A compiler, on the other hand, produces a machine-language program that can be run directly on the underlying hardware. Once compiled, the program will run very

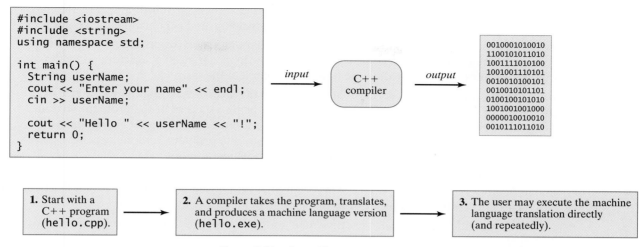

```
#include <iostream>
#include <string>
using namespace std;

int main() {
  String userName;
  cout << "Enter your name" << endl;
  cin >> userName;

  cout << "Hello " << userName << "!";
  return 0;
}
```

input → C++ compiler → output

```
0010001010010
1100101011010
1001111010100
1001001110101
0010010100101
0010010101101
0100100101010
1001001001000
0000010010010
0010111011010
```

1. Start with a C++ program (hello.cpp). → **2.** A compiler takes the program, translates, and produces a machine language version (hello.exe). → **3.** The user may execute the machine language translation directly (and repeatedly).

Figure 8.15 Compiling a C++ program.

quickly. If a language is intended for developing large software applications, execution speed is of the utmost importance; thus, languages such as C++ are translated using compilers. The drawback to compilation, however, is that the programmer must take the time to compile the entire program before executing it.

Looking Ahead...

In this chapter, you looked at programming from an algorithmic perspective. You learned that programming, in essence, is the process of designing algorithms for solving problems and then implementing those algorithms so that a computer can understand them. After introducing the basics of algorithm design, we explored several example problems: finding the oldest person in a room, finding a particular entry in a list, and computing the square root of a number. In addition, we described methods for translating programs from a high-level language such as JavaScript to the underlying, low-level language of the computer.

Now that you are equipped with a more general understanding of algorithms, you are can move on to solving more complex programmatic problems. The next chapter, Chapter 9, introduces a new method of facilitating user interaction within Web pages—instead of communicating with the user through prompt boxes and write statements, your pages will utilize buttons and text boxes. The underlying algorithms that you define and implement will remain the same, so the programming skills you have developed so far will still be used. However, you will be able to use these new interactive elements to significantly improve your pages' appearance and ease of use.

Chapter Summary

- The central concept underlying all computation is that of the algorithm, a step-by-step sequence of instructions for carrying out some task.
- Programming may be viewed as the process of designing and implementing algorithms that a computer (or a program executing on that computer) can carry out.
- Algorithms are prevalent in modern society (e.g., cooking instructions, directions for assembling a bike), because we are constantly faced with unfamiliar tasks that we could not complete without instructions.

- George Polya outlined four steps that can be applied to solving most problems: (1) understand the problem, (2) devise a plan, (3) carry out your plan, and (4) examine the solution.
- Performance measures the speed at which a particular algorithm (or program designed to carry out that algorithm) accomplishes its task. Performance may be characterized by the number of steps involved or the time it takes to complete the task.
- Big-Oh notation is used to represent an algorithm's performance in relation to the size of the problem. An $O(N)$ algorithm requires time proportional to the size of the problem, so doubling the problem size will roughly double the time required. An $O(\log N)$ algorithm requires time proportional to the logarithm of the size of the problem, so doubling the problem size only increases the time required by a constant amount.
- The sequential search algorithm, which can be used to find a particular item in a list, is an example of an $O(N)$ algorithm, where N is the number of items in the list. Binary search, which can be used when the list is ordered, is an example of an $O(\log N)$ algorithm.
- Newton's algorithm is a simple, yet efficient, algorithm for approximating the square root of a number.
- Machine languages are low-level programming languages in which each instruction is a binary number sequence that corresponds directly to a hardware operation of the machine. Assembly languages provide a slightly higher level of abstraction by allowing programmers to specify instructions using words, rather than binary-number sequences.
- High-level programming languages provide abstractions and problem-solving constructs that make problem-solving simpler and more intuitive for the programmer.
- Before it can be executed on a computer, a program written in a high-level language must be translated into the machine language for that particular computer. This can be accomplished via an interpreter (which translates and executes each statement in the program in sequence) or a compiler (which translates the entire program into an equivalent machine-language program).

Review Questions

1. TRUE or FALSE? An algorithm is a step-by-step sequence of instructions for carrying out some task.
2. TRUE or FALSE? A sequence of instructions for assembling a bookcase does not qualify as an "algorithm," since the instructions are not written in formal, mathematical notation.
3. TRUE or FALSE? For a precise, clearly stated problem, there can be only one algorithm that provides a solution.
4. TRUE or FALSE? Big-Oh notation is used to measure the exact number of seconds required by a particular algorithm when executing on a particular computer.
5. TRUE or FALSE? Suppose you have been given a sorted list of 100 names and need to find a particular name in that list. Using sequential search, it is possible that you might have to look at every location in the list before finding the desired name.
6. TRUE or FALSE? Suppose you have been given a sorted list of 100 names and need to find a particular name in that list. Using binary search, it is possible that you might have to look at every location in the list before finding the desired name.
7. TRUE or FALSE? Binary search is an example of an $O(\log N)$ algorithm, where the number of items in the list to be searched is N.
8. TRUE or FALSE? One advantage of assembly languages over machine languages is that they enable the programmer to use words to identify instructions instead of using binary-number sequences.

9. TRUE or FALSE? JavaScript, C++, and Java are all examples of high-level programming languages.

10. TRUE or FALSE? When a Web page is loaded into a Web browser, JavaScript code in that page is executed by a JavaScript interpreter that is embedded in the browser.

11. An algorithm must be clear to its intended executor in order to be effective. Give an example of a real-world algorithm that you have encountered and felt was *not* clear. Do you think that the algorithm writer did a poor job, or do you think that the algorithm was formalized with a different audience in mind? Explain your answer. Then, give an example of a real-world algorithm that you felt was clearly stated. What features of this algorithm allow you to understand it more easily?

12. Write an algorithm for directing a person to your house, apartment, or dorm from a central location. For example, if you live on campus, the directions might originate at a campus landmark. Assume that the person following the directions is familiar with the neighborhood or campus.

13. Write an alternative algorithm for directing a person to your residence, but this time, assume that the person is unfamiliar with the area. How does this condition affect the way you describe the algorithm?

14. Suppose that you were asked to arrange a group of people in sequence from oldest to youngest. You must organize a line that begins with the oldest person and continues in descending order according to age. Describe an algorithm for completing this task.

15. Suppose that you have been given an $O(N)$ algorithm that averages student grades, where N is the number of grades. If it takes 1 minute to average 100 grades using the algorithm, how long would you expect it to take to average 200 grades? 400 grades? Justify your answer.

16. Suppose you needed to look up a number in your local phone book. Roughly, what is the population of your city? How many checks would be required, in the worst case, to find the phone number using sequential search? How many checks would be required, in the worst case, to find the phone number using binary search?

17. Consider the list of states from Figure 8.5. Which state in the list is the "easiest" to find using binary search? That is, which state could be located in the fewest number of checks? Generalize your answer so that it applies to any sorted list of items.

18. Again, consider the list of states from Figure 8.5. Which state in the list is the "hardest" to find using binary search? That is, which state would require the largest number of checks to be located? Generalize your answer so that it applies to any sorted list of items.

19. Refer to the `Newton.html` page. How many refinements does Newton's algorithm require to compute the square root of 900? 10,000? 152,399,025?

20. Imagine that, while you are using Newton's algorithm, the approximations converge on the actual square root of the number. What would happen if you tried to further refine the square root? Would the value change? Why or why not?

21. A disadvantage of machine languages is that they are machine dependent. That is, each machine language is specific to a particular computer, and different computers require different machine languages. Describe why this is the case.

22. Describe two advantages of high-level language programming over machine-language programming.

23. What is the difference between a compiler and an interpreter? What characteristics of an interpreter make it better suited for executing JavaScript programs?

References

Brassard, Gilles, and Paul Bratley. *Fundamentals of Algorithmics.* Upper Saddle River, NJ: Prentice Hall, 1996.

Knuth, Donald E. "Algorithms in Modern Mathematics and Computer Science." *Lecture Notes in Computer Science 122*, 1981. Also appears in *Selected Papers in Computer Science.* Cambridge, MA: Cambridge University Press, 1996.

Knuth, Donald E. "Ancient Babylonian Algorithms." *Communications of the ACM*, 15(7), 1972. Also appears in *Selected Papers in Computer Science.* Cambridge, MA: Cambridge University Press, 1996.

Knuth, Donald E. *The Art of Computer Programming*, Vol. 3, *Sorting and Searching*, 2d ed. Reading, MA: Addison-Wesley, 1998.

Polya, George. *How to Solve It: A New Aspect of Mathematical Method*, 2d ed. Princeton, NJ: Princeton University Press, 1945.

Sedgewick, Robert. *Algorithms in* C++, Parts 1–4, *Fundamentals, Data Structures, Sorting, Searching*, 3d ed. Reading, MA: Addison-Wesley, 1998.

Skiena, Steven S. *The Algorithm Design Manual.* New York: Springer-Verlag, 1997.

Event-Driven Programming

Chapter 9

This chapter uses narrative, examples, and hands-on exercises to introduce programming concepts and Web development skills.

The Internet already has too many static pages. Why add yours to the list? To get noticed, your page must be live, it must do something, or offer some service. What better way is there to liven pages up yourself than to use JavaScript, writing a short script that runs in the browser, right in front of the user? JavaScript puts all the elements in a web page—and the web page itself!—under your control.

Steven Holzner
Essential JavaScript

When I can't handle events, I let them handle themselves.

Henry Ford

One feature that makes the World Wide Web so popular is its interactive nature. When you access a Web page, you don't just view it—you interact with it. You click links and buttons to access other pages or to make new windows appear, or you enter information and view responses based on your input. In these and many other ways, Web pages respond to your actions. We refer to such Web pages as "event-driven," in that they react to user-initiated events such as mouse clicks or keyboard entries.

Programmers can use JavaScript code to specify the way in which Web pages handle various events. Thus, you can now apply your JavaScript programming skills to writing event-driven Web pages. For example, instead of prompting users to enter a list of grades, you can design a page in which users type grades in boxes and then click a button to compute their course average. Although the same JavaScript code can compute the average in either case, the event-driven page offers the user a more attractive and easy-to-use interface.

In this chapter, you will begin using JavaScript as a tool for controlling event-driven Web pages. The first section demonstrates the use of buttons to initiate actions. We then introduce text boxes and text areas, HTML elements used to read in user input and display output. At the end of the chapter, you will learn how to define events that cause different images to appear in a page. It is important to note that the event-driven features introduced in this chapter are far from exhaustive. In fact, HTML provides numerous additional elements (such as radio buttons, check boxes, and selections lists) and JavaScript provides additional methods for controlling those elements. However, buttons, text boxes, and text areas are the most commonly used tools for building event-driven pages and in many situations are sufficient. This book will focus exclusively on these page elements.

Initiating Actions via Buttons

An *event handler* is an HTML element that can be programmed (using JavaScript) to respond to a user's actions. The simplest type of event handler that can appear in Web pages is a button. If you have spent any time surfing the Web, you have no doubt run across buttons like the one shown in Figure 9.1.

Figure 9.1 An HTML button.

A button is an HTML element that you can embed in a Web page, just as you would an image or a table. Unlike these static elements, however, buttons can be associated with JavaScript code that will run only when the buttons are clicked. For example, the button in Figure 9.1 might be assigned JavaScript statements that cause a new page or window to open. When a user clicks this button, the associated code will execute, redirecting the user's browser to the specified page. The following represents a generalized button element:

```
<input type="button" value="BUTTON_LABEL" onClick="JAVASCRIPT_CODE" />
```

A button's VALUE specifies the text label that appears on the button. For example, the button in Figure 9.1 has the following attribute assignment: value="Click here for free money!". The ONCLICK attribute specifies the action that occurs when a user clicks the button. This attribute can be assigned any JavaScript statement or sequence of statements, enclosed in quotes.

Buttons and Forms

Unlike HTML elements that can appear anywhere in a page, button elements must always be placed inside form elements. A *form* is a grouping of buttons and other event-driven elements within a page, delimited by the tags <form name="FORM_NAME"> and </form>. Commercial Web developers often employ forms to collect user input that must be transmitted over the Internet, such as an online purchaser's credit-card details and mailing address. However, since this text will not utilize forms for this purpose, we can think of them simply as necessary wrapping for buttons and other event handlers.

In the Web page in Figure 9.2, a form named LuckyForm contains a button with the label "Click Here for Lucky Number". Once this page has been loaded, clicking the button will call the DisplayNumber function to pick a lucky number—specified as a random integer between 1 and 100—and display it in an alert window (Figure 9.3).

EXERCISE 9.1

Enter the contents of lucky.html from Figure 9.2 into a new Web page, then load the page in the browser to verify that it behaves as described.

Once you have done this, save a copy of the page under the name lotto.html and modify it so that it predicts the winning combination for a PICK-4 lottery. You should update the page's text appropriately and modify the button so that its label reads "Click for Today's PICK-4 Winner". The DisplayNumber function, instead of displaying a single number, should select four random numbers from the range 0 to 9 and then display them in an alert window, separated by dashes. Figure 9.4 depicts an example of an alert window that contains a PICK-4 winning number.

```
1.  <html>
2.  <!-- lucky.html                                        Dave Reed -->
3.  <!-- This page displays a lucky number at the click of a button. -->
4.  <!------------------------------------------------------------------>
5.
6.  <head>
7.    <title> Dave's Lucky Number </title>
8.    <script type="text/javascript"
9.            src="http://www.prenhall.com/reed/random.js">
10.   </script>
11.   <script type="text/javascript">
12.     function DisplayNumber()
13.     // Results: displays random number in an alert window
14.     {
15.       var luckyNum;
16.
17.       luckyNum = RandomInt(1, 100);
18.
19.       alert("Your lucky number is: " + luckyNum);
20.     }
21.   </script>
22.  </head>
23.
24.  <body>
25.    <div style="text-align:center">
26.      <h2>Lucky Dave's Gift To You</h2>
27.
28.      <p>Numbers rule our lives.  If you would like the benefit of Lucky Dave's
29.      amazing powers of prognostication, click on the button below to receive
30.      your guaranteed lucky number for the day!</p>
31.
32.      <form name="LuckyForm">
33.        <input type="button" value="Click Here for Lucky Number"
34.               onClick="DisplayNumber();" />
35.      </form>
36.    </div>
37.  </body>
38.  </html>
```

Figure 9.2 Simple Web page containing a button.

Input/Output via Text Boxes

A button provides a simple mechanism through which users can interact with a Web page. By clicking the button, the user initiates some action. Although an alert window is sufficient for displaying a simple message, most tasks require more elaborate types of user interaction, such as where the user enters several inputs and then views the results of a computation. Fortunately, HTML provides another form element, called a text box, that can be used to implement these more complex interactions. A ***text box***, as its name suggests, is a box that can contain text (words or phrases). Unlike an alert window or prompt window, however, a text box is displayed within the page itself. When the user enters characters in a text box, that input is directly accessible via JavaScript code; similarly, JavaScript statements can assign text to text boxes. Thus, a text box can be used both to receive user input and to display the results of computations within the page.

The following represents a generalized text box element:

```
<input type="text" name="TEXTBOX_NAME" size=NUM_CHARS value="INITIAL_TEXT" />
```

Figure 9.3 `lucky.html` rendered in a Web browser.

Figure 9.4 Sample of a PICK-4 alert window.

A text box's NAME attribute specifies the name used to identify that box. The SIZE attribute defines the size of the box, which is measured by the number of characters it can contain. The VALUE attribute (if present) specifies the text that the text box initially contains. Like buttons, text boxes are form elements and therefore must appear inside form tags.

As you contemplate the functionality of text boxes, it may help you to think of memory cells as an analogy. Recall that every JavaScript variable is associated with a specific memory cell—each reference to a variable accesses the value in its memory cell, and each assignment to the variable stores a value in that same memory cell (overwriting any value that was previously saved there). As you will see in the following sections, a text box stores a value that can be accessed and assigned in a similar manner. The main difference between a variable and a text box is that the contents of a text box are visible in the page, whereas the values of a variable are hidden.

Text Boxes for Displaying Output

Using JavaScript code, programmers can display a message in a text box by encapsulating the message as a string and assigning the string to the box's VALUE attribute. When you assign a value to a text box, you must specify the ***absolute name*** of the box; this is accomplished by typing the word "document", followed by the name of the form containing the box, then the text-box name (all separated by periods). JavaScript requires the use of full, absolute names as a way of avoiding confusion, since a page might contain multiple forms with text boxes of the same name. The following represents a generalized assignment to a text box:

```
document.FORM_NAME.TEXTBOX_NAME.value = STRING_TO_BE_DISPLAYED;
```

For example, Figure 9.5 depicts a modified version of the lucky.html page, which uses a text box, rather than a separate alert window, to display the lucky number. The text box, named number, is four characters wide and initially appears blank (i.e., its initial contents consist of an empty string ""). When the user clicks the button labeled "Click Here for Lucky Number", the DisplayNumber function is called to pick a random number between 1 and 100, as in Figure 9.3. However, instead of

```
 1.  <html>
 2.  <!-- lucky1.html                                  Dave Reed -->
 3.  <!-- This page displays a lucky number in a text box. -->
 4.  <!------------------------------------------------------>
 5.
 6.  <head>
 7.    <title> Fun with Forms </title>
 8.    <script type="text/javascript"
 9.            src="http://www.prenhall.com/reed/random.js">
10.    </script>
11.    <script type="text/javascript">
12.      function DisplayNumber()
13.      // Assumes: document.LuckyForm.number exists in the page
14.      // Results: displays random number in the text box
15.      {
16.        var luckyNum;
17.
18.        luckyNum = RandomInt(1, 100);
19.
20.        document.LuckyForm.number.value = luckyNum;
21.      }
22.    </script>
23.  </head>
24.
25.  <body>
26.    <div style="text-align:center">
27.      <h2>Lucky Dave's Gift To You</h2>
28.
29.      <p>Numbers rule our lives.  If you would like the benefit of Lucky Dave's
30.      amazing powers of prognostication, click on the button below to receive
31.      your guaranteed lucky number for the day!</p>
32.
33.      <form name="LuckyForm">
34.        <input type="button" value="Click Here for Lucky Number"
35.               onClick="DisplayNumber();" />
36.        <br /><br />
37.        <hr /><br />
38.        Your lucky number is: <input type="text" name="number" size=4 value="" />
39.      </form>
40.    </div>
41.  </body>
42.  </html>
```

Figure 9.5 Web page that displays a number in a text box.

displaying the number in an alert window, the function displays the number in the text box via the assignment: document.LuckyForm.number.value = luckyNum. The rendered page is shown in Figure 9.6.

Figure 9.6 lucky1.html rendered in a Web browser.

EXERCISE 9.2

Enter the revised lucky.html text from Figure 9.5 into a Web page, then load the page in the browser to verify that it behaves as described.

Make similar modifications to your lotto.html page, causing it to display the winning PICK-4 lottery numbers in a text box. This means that your DisplayWinner function must generate the four random numbers, concatenate them so that they are separated by hyphens, and assign the resulting string to a text box.

Common errors to avoid...

Although form elements such as buttons and text boxes must appear within form tags, it is not necessary to separate each form element in its own form. In most cases, you can enclose every form element in a page within a single set of form tags. It is not an error to include multiple forms in a page, but this practice can lead to unnecessary confusion, since you must be sure to associate each element with its correct form name.

Like variables, form elements must have unique names so that they can be identified. If you mistakenly use the same name to represent multiple form elements, no error will occur. However, the name will be associated with the last element that you defined, and all subsequent access statements will refer to that element.

Text Boxes for Accessing Input

Whereas some text boxes are used to display output, others are employed to handle user input. When a text box is intended to accept input, users can enter data by clicking the mouse pointer inside the box and typing. JavaScript code then accesses the text box's contents using the absolute name of the text box (where FORM_NAME and TEXTBOX_NAME will vary for each text box):

```
document.FORM_NAME.TEXTBOX_NAME.value
```

For example, the Web page in Figure 9.7 is an event-driven version of the temperature conversion page convert.html from Chapter 7. The page contains a text box named fahrBox, which accepts user input. The user enters a Fahrenheit temperature in fahrBox and then clicks the button labeled "Convert to Celsius". When the button is clicked, the Convert function accesses the value that the

```
1.  <html>
2.  <!-- convert1.html                                         Dave Reed -->
3.  <!-- This page converts temperatures from Fahrenheit to Celsius. -->
4.  <!------------------------------------------------------------------>
5.  <head>
6.    <title>Temperature Conversion Page</title>
7.
8.    <script type="text/javascript">
9.      function FahrToCelsius(tempInFahr)
10.     // Assumes: tempInFahr is a temperature in Fahrenheit
11.     // Returns: the equivalent temperature in Celsius
12.     {
13.       return (5/9) * (tempInFahr - 32);
14.     }
15.
16.     function Convert()
17.     // Assumes: document.TempForm.fahrBox contains degrees Fahrenheit
18.     // Results: assigns document.TempForm.celsiusBox the equiv. temperature
19.     {
20.       var tempF, tempC;
21.
22.       tempF = parseFloat(document.TempForm.fahrBox.value);
23.       tempC = FahrToCelsius(tempF);
24.
25.       document.TempForm.celsiusBox.value = tempC;
26.     }
27.   </script>
28. </head>
29.
30. <body>
31.   <h2>Temperature Conversion Page</h2>
32.   <hr /><br />
33.   <form name="TempForm">
34.     Enter a temperature in degrees Fahrenheit:
35.       <input type="text" name="fahrBox" size=10 value="" />
36.     <br /><br />
37.     <input type="button" value="Convert to Celsius" onClick="Convert();" />
38.     <br /><br />
39.     Equivalent temperature in degrees Celsius:
40.       <input type="text" name="celsiusBox" size=10 value="" />
41.   </form>
42. </body>
43. </html>
```

Figure 9.7   Web page that uses text boxes for input and output.

user entered and computes the corresponding Celsius temperature. The result of the computation is then assigned to a text box named `celsiusBox`, which displays the converted temperature on the page, as shown in Figure 9.8.

Figure 9.8 `convert1.html` rendered in a Web browser.

Common errors to avoid...

Note that, in the example from Figure 9.7, we called the `parseFloat` function before performing a computation on the text box's contents. Like input returned by the `prompt` function, a value read in from a text box is initially represented as a string. Therefore, you must use `parseFloat` to explicitly convert text-box values before treating them as numbers.

In this example, forgetting to `parseFloat` the value from the text box would not affect the behavior of the page, because applying the subtraction operator would automatically convert the text-box value to a number. However, in cases where a text-box value is added to another value, the browser would interpret the `'+'` operator as specifying concatenation involving the string value. To avoid problems such as this, you should always call `parseFloat` whenever you plan to treat the value in a text box as a number.

EXERCISE 9.3

Enter the revised `convert.html` text from Figure 9.7 into a new Web page, then load the page in the browser to verify that it behaves as described.

In Exercise 7.2 of Chapter 7, you expanded your temperature conversion page so that it could convert in both directions. Make similar modifications to the page from Figure 9.7, using text boxes for input and output. The page should include your `FahrToCelsius` and `CelsiusToFahr` functions, as well as two text boxes, one for Fahrenheit and one for Celsius. If users enter a temperature in the Fahrenheit box and click a button labeled "`Fahr → Celsius`", then the corresponding temperature should appear in the Celsius box. Likewise, if they enter a temperature in the Celsius box and click the button labeled "`Fahr ← Celsius`", the corresponding temperature should appear in the Fahrenheit box. Your page should look similar to the one depicted in Figure 9.9.

Figure 9.9   Sample appearance of temperature conversion page.

Designer Secrets

It is important to recognize that the programming skills you learned in previous chapters are applicable to developing event-driven pages. Most of the pages you wrote involved the same basic steps: (1) obtain inputs from the user *via prompts*, (2) perform some computation on those inputs, then (3) display the results *using write statements*. You placed the code for carrying out these steps within SCRIPT tags in the body of the page, and the browser executed the code when the page loaded.

In an event-driven page, the interface between the user and the code is different—the user enters inputs directly into text boxes, and code executes when the user clicks a button. However, the underlying algorithm for solving problems remains the same: (1) obtain inputs from the user *by accessing text boxes*, (2) perform some computation on those inputs, then (3) display the results *by assigning to text boxes*.

If you compare the code from Chapter 7's `convert.html` page (Figure 7.2) with the event-driven version in Figure 9.7, you will see that the two pages are very similar. Although the event-driven page uses text boxes to handle input and output, the function triggered by the button performs the same tasks that the code from the BODY of the original page does.

EXERCISE 9.4

Reimplement your `grades.html` page from Chapter 5 (Exercise 5.6) using text boxes and a button. Your new page should include text boxes in which the user can enter each individual grade (homework average, lab average, midterm, and final exam), as well as a single button to compute the course average. When the user clicks the button, the program should call a function to determine the average and display it in another text box.

Hint: This page should look a lot like the `convert.html` page from Figure 9.7, except that `grades.html` will contain four text boxes for inputs. Instead of converting a specified temperature from Fahrenheit to Celsius, your button will trigger the calculation of a weighted average. Once the function executes, the result will be displayed in a separate text box.

Text Boxes for Handling Both Input and Output

It is not uncommon for a particular sequence of JavaScript statements to employ the same variable in multiple ways. For example, a program might use a variable initially to store a user input, then later assign the result of some computation to that same variable. If we extend our analogy of text boxes as similar to variables, it follows that the same text box can be used both to obtain user input and to display the result of a computation.

Consider, for example, the JavaScript function in Figure 9.10. Assuming a text box named `number` appears in the page (inside a form named `NumForm`), this function will access the number in the text box, multiply that number by two, and assign the result back to the box. Thus, every time the function is called, the current value of the text box will be doubled. A user can enter any number in the text box, then click the button repeatedly to update the value displayed in the box.

```
function DoubleIt()
// Assumes: document.NumForm.number contains a number
// Results: the number in the box is doubled
{
    var num;
    num = parseFloat(document.NumForm.number.value);
    document.NumForm.number.value = 2 * num;
}
```

Figure 9.10 JavaScript function that doubles the contents of a text box.

EXERCISE 9.5

Create a Web page named `double.html` whose HEAD includes the `DoubleIt` function. The page should contain a text box with an initial value of 1 and a button labeled `"Double It"`. When the user clicks the button, the `DoubleIt` function should be called to double the contents of the text box.

If you start with a value of 1 in the text box, how many times must you click the button before the displayed value exceeds 500? How many times to exceed 1,000?

Input/Output via Text Areas

Although text boxes provide a convenient method of reading in and displaying values in Web pages, the fact that text boxes can contain only one line of text often limits their usefulness. An alternative is a **text area**, which is similar to a text box but can contain any number of text lines. The following represents a generalized text area element:

```
<textarea name="TEXTAREA_NAME" rows=NUM_ROWS cols=NUM_COLS wrap="virtual">
INITIAL_TEXT
</textarea>
```

A text area's NAME attribute specifies the name used to identify that area. The numbers of rows (horizontal lines that can contain text) and of columns (maximum characters per line) in the text area are defined by the attributes ROWS and COLS, respectively. The attribute assignment wrap="virtual" ensures that text will wrap from one line to the next as needed, instead of running off the edge of the text area. The initial text that appears in the text area (if any) is enclosed between the <textarea> and </textarea> tags.

The Web page in Figure 9.11 contains two text boxes, each 15 characters wide, and a text area consisting of four rows of 40 characters. The page asks users to enter their first and last names in the text boxes. Once a user enters the names and clicks the button, the program accesses the contents of

```
1.  <html>
2.  <!-- greetbox.html                                        Dave Reed   -->
3.  <!-- This page displays a personalized greeting in a text area. -->
4.  <!------------------------------------------------------------>
5.
6.  <head>
7.    <title> Long Greeting </title>
8.    <script type="text/javascript">
9.      function Greet()
10.     // Assumes: document.NameForm.firstName and
11.     //          document.NameForm.lastName contain names
12.     // Results: writes a message with those names in document.NameForm.message
13.     {
14.        var firstName, lastName, greeting;
15.
16.        firstName = document.AreaForm.firstName.value;
17.        lastName = document.AreaForm.lastName.value;
18.
19.        greeting = "Hello " + firstName + " " + lastName +
20.                   ", or may I just call you " + firstName +
21.                   "?  You wouldn't be related to the " + lastName +
22.                   "s of Park Avenue, would you?";
23.
24.        document.AreaForm.message.value = greeting;
25.     }
26.   </script>
27. </head>
28.
29. <body>
30.   <form name="NameForm">
31.     Enter your first name: <input type="text" size=15 name="firstName" />
32.     <br />
33.     Enter your last name: <input type="text" size=15 name="lastName" />
34.     <br /><br />
35.     <input type="button" value="Click for Greeting" onClick="Greet();" />
36.     <br /><br />
37.     <textarea name="message" rows=4 cols=40 wrap="virtual"></textarea>
38.   </form>
39. </body>
40. </html>
```

Figure 9.11   Web page that uses a text area for output.

the text boxes and incorporates the names in a greeting, which displays in the text area. Note that there is no text between the opening and closing TEXTAREA tags (line 37), so the text area initially appears empty. The rendered page is shown in Figure 9.12.

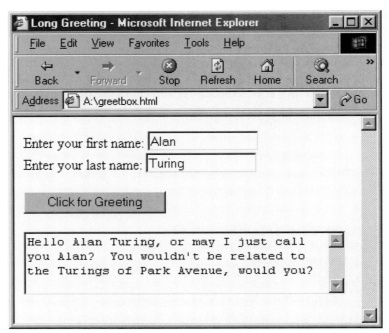

Figure 9.12 `greetbox.html` rendered in a Web browser.

 ## Common errors to avoid...

As we saw in Chapter 2, browsers interpret HTML tags as a page loads, displaying the appropriate formatting and/or elements in the rendered page. Since the contents of a text box or text area can be updated repeatedly after a page loads, the browser does not process text contained in these elements. Therefore, HTML tags cannot be used to format text in a text box or text area. If you mistakenly include HTML tags in the contents of a text box or a text area, the tags will be treated like any other sequence of characters and will be displayed exactly as typed. If you enter extra spaces in the text, they also will appear exactly as you typed them.

If you want to force a line break within a text area, you can include the character sequence \n within the text. Inserting this special sequence causes subsequent text to begin on a new line, producing the same effect that <br /> does in HTML. Similarly, you can include the character sequence \t for a tab.

EXERCISE 9.6

Enter the `greetbox.html` text from Figure 9.11 into a new Web page, then load the page in the browser to verify that it behaves as described.

Once you have done this, modify the page so that it acts as an event-driven version of your `story.html` page from Chapter 4. The page should incorporate text boxes in which the user can enter the story's missing words, and each text box should be accompanied by a label (such as `color:` or `noun:`) to identify the type of word expected. Include a button that, when clicked, incorporates the user's words into the story and displays the story in the text area.

EXERCISE 9.7

Reimplement your Magic 8-Ball page, `magic.html`, from Chapter 7 (Exercise 7.9). The new version should contain a text area in which the user can enter a question, as well as a button for submitting that question. When the user clicks the button, the program should generate a random response (as before) and display this response in a text box.

Note: This page is unique in that it completely ignores the input it receives from the user. Of course, users may not realize this—some may think that the Magic 8-Ball has considered their questions carefully before responding!

Dynamic Images

In Chapter 2, you learned how to insert images in Web pages using the IMG element. For example, suppose that `happy.gif` is an image file containing a picture of a happy face. The following tag, when embedded in a Web page, would cause the `happy.gif` image to appear in the page:

```
<img name="photo" src="happy.gif" alt="Happy Face" />
```

This chapter has already demonstrated that user-initiated events can cause the contents of text boxes and text areas to change. However, you can also use events to access and modify IMG elements within a Web page. This ability enables you to design a page that displays different images when the user clicks a button or enters a value in a text box. In such cases, the event triggers JavaScript statements that assign a new file to the IMG element's SRC attribute. For example, if a Web page contained the IMG tag listed above, the following assignment would replace `happy.gif` with an image stored in the file `sad.gif`:

```
document.images.photo.src = "sad.gif";
```

Note that this assignment to the IMG element is similar to earlier assignments to text boxes and text areas. There are two notable distinctions, however. First, images do not need to be embedded in forms. Instead, all images in a Web page are specified via the group name `images`, which appears in the assignment immediately after the word `document` to identify the element as an image. Second, images do not contain values in the way that text boxes and text areas do. Instead, an IMG element is associated with a source file, so the assignment is made to the SRC attribute of the image (as opposed to a VALUE attribute of a text box or text area).

The Web page in Figure 9.13 contains a single IMG element, which is initially assigned the source file `happy.gif` (assumed to reside in the same directory as the page). When the user clicks the button labeled `"I feel sad"`, the source file assigned to the image is changed to `sad.gif`, which displays a sad face. Likewise, when the user clicks the button labeled `"I feel happy"`, the source is reset back to `happy.gif`, which displays a happy face. See Figure 9.14 for the rendered page.

EXERCISE 9.8

Enter the `pics.html` text from Figure 9.13 into a new Web page and modify the page so that it contains at least three buttons. Each button should assign a new file to the SRC attribute of the IMG. You may choose any images you wish, but remember that you must either download the images to your local directory or list the images' full Web URLs. Make sure that the labels on the buttons accurately describe the images they control.

EXERCISE 9.9

Create a Web page named `newpics.html` that is similar to `pics.html`, but contains only one button controlling the image. When a user clicks this button, a function (with no inputs) should be called to randomly select from among several images.

For example, the following JavaScript statement, when executed, would randomly choose from among four image file names (`happy.gif`, `sad.gif`, `scared.gif`, and `bored.gif`) and assign the chosen file name to the SRC attribute of an image named `face`:

```
document.images.face.src = RandomOneOf(["happy.gif", "sad.gif",
                                        "scared.gif", "bored.gif"]);
```

```
 1.  <html>
 2.  <!-- pics.html                                        Dave Reed -->
 3.  <!-- This page allows the user to select from among two images. -->
 4.  <!------------------------------------------------------------->
 5.
 6.  <head>
 7.    <title> Picture Fun </title>
 8.    <script type="text/javascript">
 9.      function ChangeImage(picFile)
10.      // Assumes: picFile is the name of an image file
11.      // Results: changes the source of pic to picFile
12.      {
13.         document.images.face.src = picFile;
14.      }
15.    </script>
16.  </head>
17.
18.  <body>
19.    <div style="text-align:center">
20.      <h2>How do you feel today?</h2>
21.
22.      <img name="face" src="happy.gif" alt="face image" />
23.      <br /><br />
24.      <form name="PicForm">
25.        <input type="button" value="I feel happy"
26.               onClick="ChangeImage('happy.gif');" />
27.          
28.        <input type="button" value="I feel sad"
29.               onClick="ChangeImage('sad.gif');" />
30.      </form>
31.    </div>
32.  </body>
33.  </html>
```

Figure 9.13 Web page that demonstrates dynamic images.

 # Common errors to avoid...

If you are using an older version of Netscape Navigator (i.e., version 4.7 or earlier), you might notice something odd when you load the previous example. Early versions of the Netscape browser associate an IMG element with specific dimensions when the page loads. Any subsequent assignment will resize the new image to fit the old source's dimensions, which may in turn warp the image.

Internet Explorer and later versions of Netscape Navigator automatically adjust the image dimensions to fit the new source.

Looking Ahead...

In this chapter, you were introduced to a new method of enabling user interaction in your Web pages. By incorporating buttons, text boxes, and text areas, you were able to develop pages in which users could enter information easily and control the occurrence of specific actions. Unlike the pages you wrote in earlier chapters, this chapter's pages reacted to events initiated by the user. Instead of simply viewing output from JavaScript code that executed when the page loaded, the user was able to control when code executed by clicking buttons and changing text-box values.

Figure 9.14 `pics.html` rendered in a Web browser.

These capabilities enabled you to create Web pages that not only look more professional, but also are easier to use. In subsequent chapters, you will utilize this event-driven style of programming more extensively.

Before we move on to more advanced programming skills, however, Chapter 10 pauses at the text's midway point to reflect upon computer science as a discipline. In earlier chapters, you have learned about the hardware and software components of computer systems, the history of computers and the Internet, and the role of algorithms in solving problems. You have also learned fundamental programming concepts as you developed interactive Web pages using JavaScript. The next chapter provides a general overview of computer science, including the basic themes and approaches that unite such disparate topics into a cohesive discipline.

Chapter Summary

- Many Web pages are event-driven, meaning that they react to user-initiated events such as mouse clicks or keyboard entries. Programmers can use JavaScript code to specify the way in which Web pages handle various events.

- A button is the simplest type of event handler that you can insert in a Web page. When a user moves the mouse pointer over a button and clicks, this event triggers a specific action. The following represents a generalized button element:

  ```
  <input type="button" value="BUTTON_LABEL" onClick="JAVASCRIPT_CODE" />
  ```

- Buttons and other event handlers must be enclosed in form elements, which are specified via the tags `<form name="FORM_NAME">` and `</form>`.

- A text box is a form element included in Web pages for accepting user input and displaying output. The following represents a generalized text-box element:

  ```
  <input type="text" name="TEXTBOX_NAME" size=NUM_CHARS value="INITIAL_TEXT" />
  ```

- You can access the contents of a text box by using the text box's full name: document.FORM_NAME.TEXTBOX_NAME.value. Similarly, you can display a value in a text box by assigning the value to that text box's VALUE attribute, such as in the assignment:

  ```
  document.EventForm.firstName.value = "Alan";
  ```

- Like the return value of a prompt function, the contents of a text box are read in as a string but can be converted to a number using parseFloat if desired.

- Whereas a text box is limited to a single line of text, a text area can contain any number of lines. The following represents a generalized text-area element:

  ```
  <textarea name="TEXTAREA_NAME" rows=NUM_ROWS cols=NUM_COLS wrap="virtual">
  INITIAL_TEXT
  </textarea>
  ```

- Images—unlike buttons, text boxes, and text areas—do not have to be embedded in HTML forms.

- An event can be used to access and modify the SRC attribute associated with an IMG element, such as in the assignment:

  ```
  document.images.pic.src="sad.gif";
  ```

Supplemental Material and Exercises

More Practice with Form Elements

The pages that you wrote using prompts and write statements, while functional, left much to be desired in terms of user interaction. Users had to enter each new value via a separate prompt window and, after inputting data, could not review or edit previous entries. By contrast, event-driven form elements such as buttons, text boxes, and text areas enable you to develop simpler, more intuitive user interfaces. In the following exercises, you will reimplement certain pages from previous programming exercises, adding form elements to improve the pages' ease of use.

EXERCISE 9.10

Reimplement your years.html page from Chapter 7 (Exercise 7.7) using buttons and text boxes. You should include a text box in which the user can enter a number of years and a button labeled "Convert to Seconds". When the user clicks the button, the number of years in the box should be converted to seconds and displayed in a separate box in the page. Remember to accompany each text box with a label that describes its purpose.

EXERCISE 9.11

Reimplement your pickem.html page from Chapter 7 (Exercise 7.8) using buttons and text boxes. Recall that this page tested a person's ESP by generating a random number between one and four, then prompting the user to guess which number had been picked. For this exercise, modify the page so that it contains four buttons, labeled "1", "2", "3", and "4". The user should submit a guess by clicking the appropriate button. Once the user has guessed, JavaScript code should generate the random number and display it in a text box or text area.

EXERCISE 9.12

Modify your double.html page from this chapter (Exercise 9.5) so that it includes three additional buttons, labeled "Halve", "Increment", and "Decrement". When the "Halve" button is clicked, the number in the text box should be divided by 2. Similarly, the "Increment" button should add 1 to the value in the box, and "Decrement" should subtract 1 from the value.

Note: The page should contain only one text box, and all four buttons should perform computations on the value in that box. You will probably want to define separate functions to control each of the three new buttons.

EXERCISE 9.13

Write an interactive Web page named swap.html that contains two text boxes and a button. When the user clicks the button, the contents of the two text boxes should be swapped. The text boxes should appear on the same line, centered in the page, and the button should be centered below. Appropriate labels should accompany all elements.

The ONCHANGE Attribute

In most of the event-driven pages we have examined so far, users must trigger each event by clicking a button. However, programmers can also define events to occur when a user changes the contents of a text box. The text box element's optional ONCHANGE attribute, which is similar to the ONCLICK attribute for buttons, specifies JavaScript code that executes when a user enters a new value in a text box and then clicks the mouse pointer outside the box. For example, the Web page in Figure 9.15 contains two text boxes, named box1 and box2. The ONCHANGE attribute for each box is assigned code specifying that the box's contents are to be copied to the other box whenever a user alters the box's value. The effect produced by these two ONCHANGE events is that the two boxes always mirror each other, no matter which is changed. See Figure 9.16 for the rendered page.

```
1.  <html>
2.  <!- copybox.html                                              Dave Reed -->
3.  <!- This page copies the contents of one text box to another when changed. -->
4.  <!------------------------------------------------------------------------>
5.
6.  <head>
7.    <title> Click and Copy </title>
8.  </head>
9.
10. <body>
11.   <h2>Click to copy either value</h2>
12.
13.   <form name="BoxForm">
14.    <input type="text" name="box1" size=10 value=""
15.       onChange="document.BoxForm.box2.value = document.BoxForm.box1.value;" />
16.      <tt><----></tt>  
17.    <input type="text" name="box2" size=10 value=""
18.       onChange="document.BoxForm.box1.value = document.BoxForm.box2.value;" />
19.   </form>
20. </body>
21. </html>
```

Figure 9.15 Web page that demonstrates the ONCHANGE attribute.

Figure 9.16 copybox.html rendered in a Web browser.

EXERCISE 9.14

Enter the copybox.html text from Figure 9.15 into a new Web page, then load the page in the browser to verify that it behaves as described.

EXERCISE 9.15

Modify your convert.html page (Exercise 7.2) so that a button click is no longer required to initiate temperature conversions. Instead, each text box should have an ONCHANGE attribute specifying the action to be taken when a user inputs a number. When the user enters a number in the Fahrenheit box, that value should be accessed, converted to Celsius, and displayed in the Celsius box. Entering a number in the Celsius box should activate the opposite conversion. Thus, your new page should provide the same functionality as the old version but should eliminate the need for a button to trigger the events.

EXERCISE 9.16

Exercise 7.15 involved extending the convert.html page to enable various measurement conversions (e.g., inches ↔ centimeters, feet ↔ meters, and miles ↔ kilometers). If you previously completed this exercise, reimplement your expanded convert.html page using text boxes. Design the page so that it contains six text boxes on three lines; the text boxes representing inches and centimeters should appear on the first line, followed by feet and meters on the second, then miles and kilometers on the third. When a user enters a measurement in one box, the value should be converted to its equivalent in the other system and displayed in the corresponding box. For example, if the user enters 2 in the box labeled "inches:", then 5.08 should automatically appear in the box labeled "centimeters:". Likewise, entering 1 in the box labeled "kilometers:" should cause 0.6213712 to display in the box labeled "miles:".

The ONFOCUS Attribute

Another attribute associated with text boxes and text areas is the ONFOCUS attribute. Similar to the ONCLICK and ONCHANGE attributes, ONFOCUS specifies code that executes as soon as the user focuses attention on the text box or text area, either by clicking the mouse inside it or by using the tab key.

The ONFOCUS attribute is especially useful when you want to designate a text box or text area for output only. For example, suppose you want to create a Web page that computes sales tax on various transactions. The page could allow users to enter a sales amount in a text box, click a button, and view the total price including tax in another box. For security reasons, you would like to prohibit the user from modifying the contents of the total sale box—only the JavaScript code that computes the tax should be able to change the box's value. To prevent users from inputting values in the total sale box, you can specify an ONFOCUS attribute for the box. Any time a user clicks the text box, this event will call the predefined JavaScript function `blur`, which disables the user's ability to enter text in the box. The Web page in Figure 9.17 demonstrates the ONFOCUS attribute and the `blur` function (line 28), and the rendered page is shown in Figure 9.18.

```
1.  <html>
2.  <!-- sales.html                                    Dave Reed -->
3.  <!-- This page computes sales tax and demonstrates blur. -->
4.  <!------------------------------------------------------------>
5.
6.  <head>
7.    <title> Sales Tax  </title>
8.
9.    <script type="text/javascript">
10.      function TotalSale()
11.      // Assumes: document.TaxForm.total contains a sales amount
12.      // Returns: document.TaxForm.total gets amount + 6% sales tax
13.      {
14.        var sales, total;
15.
16.        sales = parseFloat(document.TaxForm.sales.value);
17.        total = sales * 1.06;
18.        document.TaxForm.total.value = total;
19.      }
20.    </script>
21.  </head>
22.
23.  <body>
24.    <h2>Sales tax calculator</h2>
25.    <form name="TaxForm">
26.      Sales amount: $<input type="text" name="sales" size=10 value=0 />
27.      <input type="button" value="Total with 6% tax --->" onClick="TotalSale();" />
28.      <input type="text" name="total" size=10 value="" onFocus="blur();" />
29.    </form>
30.  </body>
31.  </html>
```

Figure 9.17   Web page that demonstrates the ONFOCUS attribute.

EXERCISE 9.17

Enter the `sales.html` text from Figure 9.17 into a new Web page, then load the page in the browser to verify that it behaves as described.

Once you have done this, modify the page so that users can control the sales-tax rate. First, add a text box to the page that accepts a tax rate as input. Then, define the `TotalSale` function so that, when a user clicks the button, JavaScript code accesses the rate box's value and uses it to compute the total sales amount.

Figure 9.18 `sales.html` rendered in a Web browser.

EXERCISE 9.18

Modify your `sales.html` page so that fractional monetary values are rounded up to the next cent. For example, the amount $21.1894 should be rounded up to $21.19. Using the following steps, you can round up a number so that only two digits appear to the right of the decimal place:

1. Multiply the number by 100 (e.g., 21.1894 → 2118.94).
2. Round the value up using the `Math.ceil` function (e.g., 2118.94 → 2119).
3. Divide the number by 100 (e.g., 2119 → 21.19).

Encapsulate this computation in a separate function, then redesign your page so that it uses this function to round up the total sales amount.

Aligning Form Elements with Tables

The supplemental material for Chapter 2 described how tables could be used to align text within a page. Programmers often employ tables in conjunction with text boxes to align boxes and their associated labels. For example, suppose that you wanted a page to include two text boxes, each accompanied by a label to its left. By default, the text boxes would immediately follow the labels, leading to a ragged appearance (Figure 9.19).

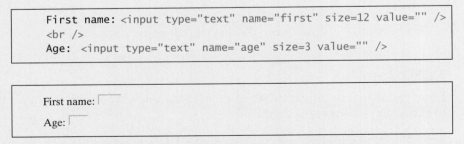

```
First name: <input type="text" name="first" size=12 value="" />
<br />
Age: <input type="text" name="age" size=3 value="" />
```

First name: ☐
Age: ☐

Figure 9.19 Default alignment of text boxes with labels.

By placing the form elements in a table and designating one column for labels and another for text boxes, you can align the elements and improve their appearance (Figure 9.20).

```
<table>
  <tr><td>First name:</td>
    <td><input type="text" size=12 value="" /></td>
  </tr>
  <tr><td>Age:</td>
    <td><input type="text" size=3 value="" /></td>
  </tr>
</table>
```

First name: [   ]

Age: [   ]

Figure 9.20   Aligning the text boxes using a table.

EXERCISE 9.19

Modify your grades.html page (Exercise 9.4) so that the labels and text boxes for the student's grades align in columns.

EXERCISE 9.20

Modify your story.html page (Exercise 9.6) so that the labels and text boxes for the user's words align in columns.

10 Chapter

Computer Science as a Discipline

This chapter uses narrative, illustrations, and review questions to introduce computer science and technology concepts.

Having surveyed the relationships of computer science with other disciplines, it remains to answer the basic questions: What is the central core of the subject? What is it that distinguishes it from the separate subjects with which it is related? What is the linking thread which gathers these disparate branches into a single discipline? My answer to these questions is simple—it is the art of programming a computer. It is the art of designing efficient and elegant methods of getting a computer to solve problems, theoretical or practical, small or large, simple or complex. It is the art of translating this design into an effective and accurate computer program.

C.A.R. Hoare
Essays in Computing Science

Computer Science is the first engineering discipline in which the complexity of the objects created is limited solely by the skill of the creator, and not by the strength of raw materials.

Brian K. Reid
Communications of the ACM, October 1987

In theory, there is no difference between theory and practice. But, in practice, there is.

Jan van de Snepscheut

Most traditional sciences, such as biology and chemistry, trace their origins back hundreds or even thousands of years. Since electronic computers were not introduced until the 1940s, computer science is clearly a much newer field of study. Nonetheless, computers and related technology have made an astounding impact on our society in this short period of time.

This chapter presents an overview of computer science as a discipline, emphasizing its common themes (hardware, software, and theory) as well as its diversity. As you will learn, computer science comprises much more than just the study of computers. It encompasses all aspects of computation, from the design and analysis of algorithms to the construction of computers for carrying out those algorithms. The jobs performed by computer scientists are as varied as computer science itself, and this chapter examines the roles played by computational theorists, programmers, systems architects, and microchip designers, among others. To further your understanding of this diverse field, we delve into specific computer science subfields, providing details on topics such as systems architecture, operating systems, networks, and artificial intelligence. We conclude with a discussion of ethical conduct within the computing profession.

Computer "Science"

Although government and industry began embracing computer technology as early as the 1940s, the scientific community was slower to acknowledge computer science's importance. Most colleges and universities did not even recognize computer science as a separate field of study until the 1970s or 80s. Many people still argue that computer science is not a science in the same sense that biology and chemistry are. In fact, computer science has a lot in common with the natural sciences, but it is also closely related to other fields, such as engineering and mathematics. This interdisciplinary nature has made computer science a difficult field to classify. Biology can be neatly described as the study of life, whereas chemistry can be defined as the study of chemicals and their interactions. Is computer science, as its name suggests, simply the study of computers?

Although computers are the most visible feature of computer science, it would be inaccurate to characterize the field as dealing only with machinery. A more inclusive definition would be that computer science is the study of **computation**. The term computation denotes more than just machinery—it encompasses all aspects of problem solving. This includes the design and analysis algorithms, the formalization of algorithms as programs, and the development of computational devices for executing those programs. The computer science field also addresses more theoretical questions, such as those surrounding the power and limitations of algorithms and computational models.

Whether this combination of problem solving, engineering, and theory constitutes a "science" is a matter of interpretation. Some define "science" as a rigorous approach to understanding complex phenomena and solving problems. The process developed by the scientific community for examining observations and events, commonly referred to as the *scientific method*, can be summarized as an algorithm (Figure 10.1).

The Scientific Method:

1. Formulate a hypothesis that explains an observed behavior.
2. Design an experiment to test your hypothesis.
3. Conduct the experiment.
4. Analyze the results of the experiment — if the results do not support the hypothesis, revise and repeat.

Figure 10.1   The scientific method for understanding phenomena.

Using this definition, we can classify many activities performed by computer scientists as "science." The design and analysis of algorithms for solving problems involves a rigorous approach that is based on the scientific method. In particular, verifying the behavior of an algorithm requires forming hypotheses, testing those hypotheses (either through experimentation or mathematical analysis), and then revising the algorithm in response to the results. For example, to design an effective algorithm for accessing records in a large database, you would need to form hypotheses regarding the database's behavior under various conditions. Then, you would test those hypotheses, either by implementing the algorithm as a computer program and executing it on actual data or by performing rigorous mathematical analysis. Finally, if the result failed to validate your hypotheses, you would modify the algorithm and retest. The development of complex hardware and software systems adheres to this same rigorous, experimental approach—when applied to projects involving millions of transistors or thousands of lines of code, the scientific method is simply implemented on a much larger scale.

Artificial Science

What sets computer science apart from the natural sciences is the type of items being studied. All natural sciences, as well as many social sciences, are concerned with examining complex, naturally occurring phenomena. These sciences work within the confines of innate laws that define the way matter behaves, the way chemicals react, the way life evolves, and even the way people interact. Experiments in physics, chemistry, biology, and psychology strive to understand natural occurrences and extract the underlying laws that control behavior. By contrast, the systems that computer scientists investigate are largely artificial. Programs, computers, and computational models are designed and constructed by people. When a computer scientist analyzes the behavior of a program executing on a particular computer, the phenomena being studied are defined within the artificial world of that machine. Likewise, by devising new computers or other computational models, computer scientists can create their own artificial laws to govern how systems behave. This distinction was effectively summarized by artificial intelligence pioneer Herbert Simon (1916–2001), who coined the phrase "artificial science" to distinguish computer science from the "natural sciences."

European institutions often bypass the question of whether computer science is a science by calling the field "Informatics" or "Information Systems." However, these names are limiting in that they denote an emphasis on information processing, rather than on the machinery used to process that information. Donald Knuth (1938–), a noted computer scientist and author of *The Art of Computer Programming*, has proposed the alternative name "Algorithmics," which highlights the central role of algorithms in computation. The name "Algorithmics" also suggests a mathematical approach to computing, reflecting the fact that many early researchers in what would eventually be called computer science were mathematicians.

It should be noted that computer science is linked to several other disciplines, each of which approaches computing from a slightly different perspective. For instance, computer engineering is an offshoot of electrical engineering focused on applying scientific theory and engineering principles to the development of new computing technology. The fields of information technology and information systems management approach computing from a business perspective, concentrating on the effective use of information and computer technology in supporting government and commercial organizations. Although the historical backgrounds of these fields are very different, the divisions between the disciplines are not always distinct. A computer scientist conducting research in circuit design might use methods similar to those of a computer engineer, and an information technology manager organizing a network might use methods similar to those of a computer scientist.

Computer Science Themes

Since computation encompasses so many different types of activities, the research conducted by computer scientists is often difficult to classify. However, there are three recurring themes that define the discipline: hardware, software, and theory (Figure 10.2). Some computer scientists focus on hardware,

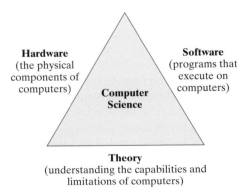

Figure 10.2   Main themes of computer science.

designing and building computers and related infrastructure. Others concern themselves with the process of composing software and encoding algorithms that can be executed on computers. Still others attack computation from a theoretical standpoint, striving to understand the foundations of the discipline. Although it is possible to find computer scientists whose expertise is exclusive to one of these areas, most activities involve a combination of all three.

Hardware

As we saw in Chapter 1, the term *hardware* refers to the physical components of a computer and its supporting devices. The design of most modern computers is based on the von Neumann architecture, which consists of a central processing unit (CPU), memory, and input/output devices (see Chapter 6 for additional information regarding the von Neumann architecture). In combination, these three components form a general-purpose machine that can store and execute programs for accomplishing various tasks.

Although most computers are built according to this basic architecture, ongoing research-and-development projects aim to improve the design and organization of hardware. For example, computer scientists involved in circuit design and microchip manufacturing must draw on expertise from chemistry, particle physics, and mechanical engineering to squeeze millions of transistors onto dime-sized microchips. Systems architects, on the other hand, study different ways of connecting components to increase computational **throughput** (i.e., the amount of work that can be completed in a given time). One subfield of systems architecture is **parallel processing**, in which a computer's computational burden is split across multiple CPUs. As the Internet has grown in popularity, many hardware specialists have turned their attention to networking, creating new ways for separate computers to share information and work together.

Software

Whereas hardware consists of machinery for performing computations, software refers to the programs that execute on computers. Most people in the computer industry work on the software side, holding positions such as programmer, systems analyst, or software engineer. In fact, despite the recent economic recession, the software industry remains one of the fastest growing facets of the U.S. economy.

Software can be divided into three basic categories according to each application's purpose and intended audience. **Systems software** includes programs that directly control the execution of hardware components. For example, an operating system includes systems software for managing files and directories, linking programs with hardware devices such as printers and scanners, and processing user inputs such as keystrokes and mouse clicks. The term **development software** refers to programs that are used as tools in the development of other programs. Microsoft .NET and Metrowerks CodeWarrior are examples of development environments for creating, testing, and executing programs using a variety of languages (such as C++ and Java). The **applications software** category encompasses all other programs, which perform a wide variety of complex tasks. Examples include Web browsers such as Internet Explorer and Netscape Navigator, word processors such as Word and WordPerfect, presentation tools such as PowerPoint and FrameMaker, editors such as NotePad and emacs, and games such as Solitaire and Doom.

Many diverse jobs in computer science are related to the design, development, testing, and maintenance of software. Some software experts' work is more theoretical, focusing on the formulation and analysis of algorithms. While examining general approaches to problems, these computer scientists strive to understand the complexity of those problems and their solutions. Such "software people" may never write a program in their lives! Another subcategory of the software industry involves developing and extending programming languages so that problems can be solved more easily and efficiently. But perhaps the most common type of software expert is the programmer, who designs algorithms and encodes them into a particular programming language for execution on a computer.

Theory

Just as certain computer scientists study algorithms but never write a program, other experts may never even touch a computer. This is because computer science is concerned with the study of computational methods, in addition to the more practical fields of hardware and software. Theoretical computer scientists, whose work is closely related to mathematics and formal logic, examine different models of computation and strive to understand the capabilities of algorithms and computers. It may surprise you to learn that some of computer science's key theories were formulated years before the development of electronic computers. For example, in 1930, Alan Turing (1912–1954) (Figure 10.3) designed an abstract computational machine now known as a *Turing machine*.

Figure 10.3   Alan Turing.

A Turing machine is a very simple processing unit that can read and write data on a potentially infinite tape. The tape, which we can think of as being divided into cells, serves as the Turing machine's memory. The processor has the ability to read the data at a particular cell on the tape, write new data to that cell, move in either direction, and distinguish between a finite number of states (distinct situations that alter the behavior of the machine). A Turing machine is programmable in that you can specify a finite set of rules describing the processor's behavior. However, these rules are limited by the machine's capabilities (reading, writing, and moving right or left) and are specific to the data stored on the tape. For instance, the example Turing machine in Figure 10.4 is programmed to recognize an even number of "a"s written on the tape. If the tape contains an even number of "a"s, the machine writes the value "Y" to the final cell, but if the tape contains an odd number of "a"s, the machine writes "N" to that cell.

1. Initially, the processor is positioned at the left end of the sequence in state 0.
2. Following the processor instructions, the processor moves right, alternating between state 0 (on odd-numbered cells) and state 1 (on even-numbered cells).
3. If the processor reaches the end of the sequence (marked by a space) in state 0, then there were an even number of a's — write "Y" in the cell and HALT.
4. If the processor reaches the end of the sequence (marked by a space) in state 1, then there were an odd number of a's — write "N" in the cell and HALT.

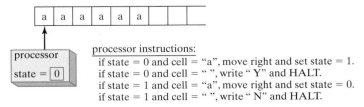

Figure 10.4   Turing machine to recognize an even number of a's on the tape.

Although Turing machines might seem simplistic, analysis has proven them to be as powerful as today's computers. That is, any computation that can be programmed and performed using a modern computer can also be programmed and performed using a Turing machine. Of course, the equivalent Turing machine program might be much more complex and involve a much larger number of steps; however, the Turing machine would eventually complete the task. The advantage of a simple model such as the Turing machine is that it provides a manageable tool for studying computation. In fact, Turing was able to use the Turing machine model of computation to prove a rather astounding result: there exist problems whose solutions cannot be computed. In other words, he was able to verify that certain problems are not solvable using algorithms or any computing device. The most famous example is referred to as the Halting Problem, which Turing demonstrated to be noncomputable in 1930. In programming terminology, the Halting Problem states that you can't write a program that determines in all cases whether another program will terminate. As you will see in Chapter 13, conditional repetition refers to code that executes repeatedly as long as some condition holds. For example, the JavaScript code below will prompt the user for her age, then will keep prompting until she enters a positive number.

```
age = prompt("Please enter your age", "");
age = parseFloat(age);

while (age < 0) {
    age = prompt("You can't have a negative age!  Try again:", "");
    age = parseFloat(age);
}
```

The ability to include conditional repetition in programs is a powerful algorithmic tool, and most real-world algorithms involve some form of repetition. However, when you introduce conditional repetition into a program, it is possible that the condition will hold indefinitely, resulting in a program that never terminates. This phenomenon is called an **infinite loop**. Using the Turing machine as his model of computation, Turing was able to prove the impossibility of writing a program (algorithm) that is guaranteed to recognize every program (algorithm) containing an infinite loop. In general, theoretical computer science attempts to understand computation at a level that is independent of any particular machine architecture. This enables the discipline to provide a strong foundation for developing new algorithms and computers.

Subfields of Computer Science

In his classic description of the field, *Computer Science: The Discipline,* Peter J. Denning identifies 12 major subfields of computer science (Figure 10.5). Each subfield constitutes a unique viewpoint and approach to computation, many of which have close ties to other disciplines, such as physics, psychology, and biology. However, the common themes of computer science—hardware, software, and theory—influence every subfield.

The following sections examine computer science's five most visible subfields: algorithms and data structures, architecture, operating systems and networks, software engineering, and artificial intelligence and robotics. Although it is impossible to include a complete description of these subfields in such a short space, these sections summarize the key ideas that define the disciplines and provide a representative example from each.

Algorithms and Data Structures

The subfield of algorithms and data structures involves developing, analyzing, and implementing algorithms for solving problems. Since algorithms are fundamental to all computer science (see Chapter 8), researchers in this subfield can approach the topic from various perspectives. A theoretical computer scientist might be concerned with analyzing the characteristics, efficiency, and limitations of various algorithms. This type of work is relevant, because examining which types of algorithms are best suited to certain tasks can lead to more effective problem solving. Since programs are simply implementations of

Subfields of Computer Science[1]	
Algorithms and Data Structures	The study of methods for solving problems, designing and analyzing algorithms, and effectively using data structures in software systems.
Architecture	The design and implementation of computing technology, including the integration of effective hardware systems and the development of new manufacturing methods.
Operating Systems and Networks	The design and development of software and hardware systems for managing the components of a computer or network of communicating computers.
Software Engineering	The development and application of methodologies for designing, implementing, testing, and maintaining software systems.
Artificial Intelligence and Robotics	The study and development of software and hardware systems that solve complex problems through seemingly "intelligent" behavior.
Programming Languages	The design and implementation of languages that allow programmers to express algorithms so that they are executable on computers.
Databases and Information Retrieval	The organization and efficient management of large collections of data, including the development of methods for searching and recognizing patterns in the data.
Graphics	The design of software and hardware systems for representing physical and conceptual objects visually, such as with images, video, or three-dimensional holograms.
Human–Computer Interaction	The design, implementation, and testing of interfaces that allow users to interact more effectively with computing technology.
Computational Science	Explorations in science and engineering that utilize high-performance computing, such as modeling complex systems or simulating experimental conditions.
Organizational Informatics	The development and study of management processes and information systems that support technology workers and organizations.
Bioinformatics	The application of computing methodologies and information structures to biological research, such as the characterization and analysis of the human genome.

Figure 10.5 Subfields of computer science.

algorithms, software development is driven by an understanding and mastery of algorithms. In order to develop software, a programmer must be familiar with common algorithmic approaches and the data structures they manipulate. And since programs must ultimately be executed by computers, the connection between algorithms and underlying hardware must also be understood.

One application area in which the design of new algorithms has had great impact is encryption. **Encryption** is the process of encoding a message so that it is decipherable only by its intended recipient—i.e., anyone intercepting the message would be unable to interpret its contents. Since the time of Julius Caesar (100–44 B.C.), people have developed various algorithms for encoding secret messages to ensure military, political, and even commercial security. For example, Caesar is known to have used an algorithm that involved replacing each letter in a message with the letter three positions later in the alphabet. Thus, the Latin phrase "ET TU BRUTE" would be encoded as "HW WX EUXWH", since "H" is three positions after "E", "W" is three positions after "T", and so on. Of course, in order for the message to be decoded, the recipient must understand the encoding method and perform the reverse translation.

Caesar's algorithm is categorized as a **private-key encryption** algorithm, since it relies on the sender and recipient sharing a secret key (in this case, the knowledge that letters are shifted three positions). While Caesar's algorithm is not very secure by modern standards, we now possess more complex secret-key algorithms, enabling parties to transmit sensitive information across networks without fear that their data will be compromised. The Digital Encryption Standard (DES), for example, uses a specific 56-bit number as the key. Decoding a DES-encrypted message without knowing the key is virtually impossible, since this process would involve performing trial-and-error tests on $2^{56} \approx 72$ quadrillion (72×10^{15}) possible keys. The steps required to encode, send, and decode a message using private-key encryption are illustrated in Figure 10.6.

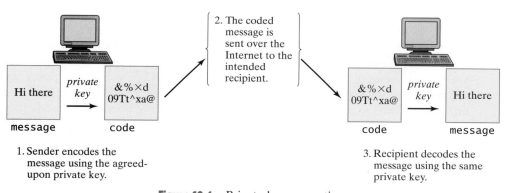

Figure 10.6   Private-key encryption.

Private-key encryption algorithms rely on the assumption that the sender and recipient have agreed upon the secret key ahead of time. However, the exchange of keys for private-key encryption introduces additional security concerns, because anyone who intercepts the key will be able to decode subsequent messages. In situations that require extreme security—for example, the transfer of sensitive government documents—the involved parties might go to great lengths to ensure a safe exchange of keys, such as by arranging a face-to-face meeting. Unfortunately, these sorts of measures are clearly not feasible for other types of communications, such as the exchange of messages or credit information over the Internet.

In 1976, Whitfield Diffie (1944–) and Martin Hellman (1946–) proposed a new class of encryption algorithms, which they called **public-key encryption**. The idea behind public-key encryption is to assign each party a pair of associated keys, one of which is public and the other private. A message encoded with a public key requires the corresponding private key for decoding, and vice versa. Thus, if you know a party's public key, you can encode a message that can be decoded only via that party's private key. The result is that you can send a secure message to someone without having to share any secret keys—each party maintains and protects its own private key.

Another benefit of public-key encryption is that a message recipient can verify the identity of the sender. Because both sender and recipient know each other's public key, it is possible for senders to encode messages using both their own private key and the recipient's public key. If a message is encrypted with both keys, then the recipient must decode the message using the sender's public key, in addition to the recipient's own private key. This enables the recipient to confirm that the indicated sender is actually the one who transmitted the message. Figure 10.7 depicts this double-encryption process, through which both security and identity verification can be achieved. The RSA algorithm, invented in 1977 by Ron Rivest, Adi Shamir, and Len Adleman at MIT, was the first practical implementation of a public-key encryption algorithm and provides the basis for almost all secure communications occurring over the Internet.

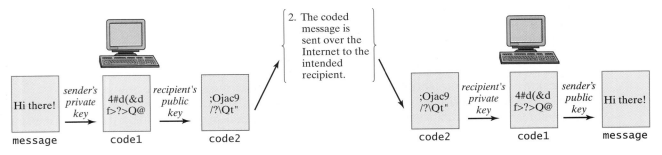

Figure 10.7 Public-key encryption.

Architecture

The architecture subfield is concerned with methods of organizing hardware components into efficient, reliable systems. As we have discussed, the design of most computer systems is based on the von Neumann architecture. However, within this model, new technologies and techniques are constantly being developed to improve system performance and capabilities. For example, Chapter 6 outlined the historical evolution of computers, explaining how new technologies for switching electrical signals (e.g., relays, vacuum tubes, transistors, and finally integrated circuits) facilitated the introduction of smaller, cheaper, and more accessible computers. Other improvements in areas such as microchip manufacturing (see Chapter 16), memory storage and access, and input/output methods have also contributed to the construction of more powerful and usable systems (Figure 10.8).

Figure 10.8 Computer-controlled robots are used to manufacture microchips on a miniscule scale. Here, metal pins are being connected to the circuitry on the microchip by a robotic arm.

In recent years, computer architectures that deviate from the von Neumann model have been developed and used effectively in certain application areas. ***Parallel processing***, as its name suggests, is an approach that employs multiple processors working in parallel to share a computational load. Ideally, if you doubled the number of processors in a system, your program would accomplish its task in half the time, since the various processors can handle subtasks simultaneously. In practice, however, additional computation is required to divide up the work, and not all tasks are well suited for parallel processing. For example, if each step in an algorithm is dependent on the results from the previous step, then the steps must be executed one at a time in the specified order, and additional processors will be of little help. Even when a task can be broken up, there are costs associated with coordinating the processors and enabling them to share information.

Evaluating how and when parallel processing can be effectively applied to solve problems is a complex process. For example, an architect who works on parallel-computing systems must understand theory (in order to divide the algorithmic steps among the processors) and software methods (in order to specify control information within programs), as well as the design and implementation of hardware. Web servers are a common application of parallel-computing technology. Recall that a Web server manages Web pages and other resources, such as images and sound files; when a computer communicates a request to a server, the server must respond by sending the appropriate resources back to that computer. Since a Web server may be called upon to service multiple independent requests during a short period of time, many Web servers distribute their computational loads among multiple processors. Thus, numerous page requests might be served simultaneously by different processors within the Web server.

A more extreme implementation of parallel processing can be seen in Deep Blue, the chess-playing computer developed at IBM. Deep Blue contains 32 general-purpose processors and 512 special-purpose chess processors, each of which can work in parallel to evaluate potential chess moves. Together, these processors can consider an average of 200 million possible chess moves per second! In 1997, Deep Blue became the first computer to beat a world champion in a chess tournament, defeating Gary Kasparov in six games (Figure 10.9).

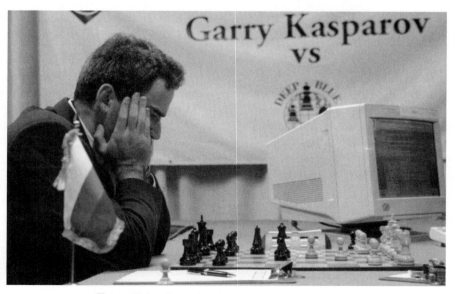

Figure 10.9   Gary Kasparov vs. Deep Blue (1997).

Operating Systems and Networks

The subfield of operating systems and networks examines mechanisms that control the hardware and software components of computer systems. As we saw in Chapter 1, an operating system is the collection of programs that coordinates the hardware and software associated with a single computer. When operating systems were introduced in the 1950s, they were relatively simple, allowing other pieces of software to manage system resources such as printers or external memory devices. In the 1960s, operating systems with *time-sharing* capabilities were introduced, permitting multiple users to share one machine's computing power (Figure 10.10). Recall that, at this time, computers were still relatively expensive, so it was desirable for multiple users to employ the same computer. With a time-sharing computer, multiple users could interact with the same machine from separate physical locations. A portion of the computer's processor was allocated to each user, allowing the processor to rotate among tasks—this rotation occurred so rapidly that human observers could not tell that the applications were not executing simultaneously.

Figure 10.10   DEC PDP-1, the first commercial time-sharing computer. Note that there are different stations in the room where users can interact with the computer simultaneously.

In the 1970s, the idea of time sharing was extended to *multitasking*, through which a single user could have multiple programs executing simultaneously. For example, the user might have three different applications running, with each application allocated a portion of the processor. In addition to these features, modern operating systems such as Windows XP, Mac OS X, and Linux provide intuitive graphical user interfaces (GUIs), enabling users to interact with programs and hardware devices through windows, icons, and menus.

Although an operating system is sufficient to control the software and hardware components of a single machine, today's computers are rarely isolated. Instead, computers are connected in networks, allowing them to communicate with each other and share resources. Every computer network is classified as either a *wide area network (WAN)* or *local area network (LAN)*. A WAN connects computers over long distances, so it must include built-in controls for routing messages and adapting to the failures that will inevitably occur. The most obvious example of a WAN is the Internet, which utilizes a distributed architecture and packet-switching technology to form an effective, robust network (see Chapter 3). By contrast, LANs are used to link computers over short distances, such as within the same room or building. In this type of network, the mechanisms for controlling messages can be much simpler.

The most popular technology used to build LANs is known as *Ethernet*. In an Ethernet network, all the computers that need to communicate with one another are connected to a common communications line, known as the *Ethernet bus* (Figure 10.11). The computers share the Ethernet bus and must take turns transmitting messages over it. Since the network is small, it does not require an elaborate mechanism for routing messages to their intended recipients. Instead, each message is broadcast to all computers on the network via the Ethernet bus, and the individual machines are expected to recognize which messages are directed to them and which can be ignored. Because of their simplicity,

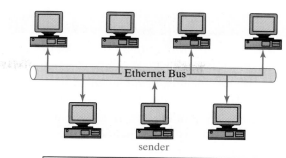

1. All computers connected to the Ethernet bus must constantly monitor its status.
2. If a computer wants to send a message, it first checks to make sure the bus is free (not currently transmitting a message).
3. If the bus is free, the sender labels the message to identify the desired recipient.
4. The labeled message is broadcast over the bus, reaching all connected computers.
5. Upon receipt, each computer checks the label to see if it is the intended recipient. If so, the message is read and processed. If not, the message is ignored.

Figure 10.11 Transmitting messages over an Ethernet network.

Ethernet networks are able to provide impressive communication speeds—information can usually be transmitted at either 10M bits per second, 100M bits per second, or 1,000M bits per second, depending on the type of bus used and the distances covered.

Software Engineering

Software engineering is the subfield of computer science concerned with creating effective software systems. The development and support of computer software has become a major factor in the global, information-based economy of the 21st century. According to the research firm International Data Corp. (IDC), worldwide sales of packaged software grew during the 1990s at an average of 12% per year. Although this growth tapered off during the subsequent economic downturn, IDC still estimates that worldwide software sales will total $183 billion in 2003, up 6% from the $172 billion registered in 2002. Approximately 70% of that software is developed in the United States.[2]

Developing large, reliable, cost-effective software systems can be extremely difficult, as it presents both technical and management challenges. Large software projects can encompass millions of lines of code, requiring extensive teams of programmers and analysts. For example, the Windows XP operating system, released in 2001, contains over 45 million lines of code.[3] When teams of programmers are working together on the same project, software must be carefully designed so that components can be developed and tested independently, then integrated into the whole. A variety of tools are used to facilitate this, including design formalisms (such as the Unified Modeling Language, or UML) that clearly define the intended behavior of software components, and version control systems (such as the Concurrent Versions System, or CVS) that allow multiple programmers to share files and integrate changes. In addition, the efforts of the individual developer must be coordinated to ensure that work is not being duplicated and that the individual components being developed will fit together as a whole. As the software components are developed, they must be tested in isolation and again as part of the overall project to ensure that they are correct and reliable. While different software companies might use different tools or personnel management policies, effective software engineering requires an overall development methodology that addresses all aspects of the software life cycle (Figure 10.12).

As the demand for software continues to grow, increases in programmer productivity threaten to lag behind. It would be nice if there were a software-related equivalent to Moore's Law, which states that the number of transistors that can be placed on a computer chip doubles every 12 to 18 months.

Stages in the Software Life Cycle

1. *Requirement analysis and specification:* Initially, the needs of the customer must be assessed and the intended behavior of the software specified in detail.

2. *Design:* Next, the software system must be designed, including its breakdown into manageable pieces, and the underlying algorithms and data structures to be used.

3. *Implementation:* After completion of the design documents, the code must be written. For large software projects, teams may work independently on separate modules and then integrate those modules to complete the system.

4. *Testing:* The software must be systematically tested, both as independent modules and as a whole. As testing reveals errors or unforeseen conditions, reimplementation and even re-design may need to take place.

5. *Operation and maintenance:* Once the software system is complete, it must be installed and support-ed. It is estimated that maintenance, which involves fixing errors and updating code to meet changing customer needs, accounts for as much as half of a software project's total develop-ment budget.

Figure 10.12   The software life cycle.

However, it is not reasonable to expect programmers to double their output every year. In addition, increased productivity cannot always be obtained just by assigning more programmers to a project, since personnel management and coordination become increasingly complex as project size grows. Fortunately, new development tools and methodologies (such as those mentioned above) are con-stantly being introduced and refined to assist the software developer in managing complexity. In re-cent years, object-oriented programming languages such as Java and C++ have been widely adopted due to their support for code reuse. These languages provide large libraries of software components and enable programmers to easily build upon existing components. Often it is possible to utilize code that has already been developed and tested, as opposed to developing new code from scratch. Thus, the overall complexity of the project can be reduced.

Artificial Intelligence and Robotics

One of the best-known subfields of computer science is artificial intelligence, which aims to design computers that exhibit more humanlike characteristics—i.e., the ability to see, hear, speak, and even reason and think. In his 1950 paper, *Computing Machinery and Intelligence*, Alan Turing predicted that, by the end of the 20th century, the intelligence exhibited by programmed machines would rival that of humans (Figure 10.13).

The Turing Test

In his 1950 paper, *Computing Machinery and Intelligence,* Alan Turing proposed what is still considered the ultimate test for artificial intelligenc The Turing Test is based on the observation that we, as humans, make assumptions about intelligence and self-awareness in other humans by monitoring and interacting with them. Turing proposed that if the behavio of a machine were indistinguishable from a human's behavior, then we ought to give the machine the same credit for being intelligent that we giv people.

The Turing Test involves a human judge and two contestants, one being th computer to be tested and the second being a human control subject. The job of the judge is to converse with the two contestants via computer terminals, without knowing which contestant is which. If, after a sufficientl long period of conversation, the judge is unable to identify the computer, then the computer is said to have passed the test and must be considered to possess human-like intelligence.

Figure 10.13   The Turing Test for artificial intelligence.

While we are still many years away from reaching Turing's goal of artificially intelligent machines, much progress has been made in areas such as robotics, machine vision, and speech recognition. Robots are used extensively in manufacturing (Figure 10.14), and some robotic products (such as the self-powered vacuum cleaner shown in Figure 10.15) are being introduced into private homes. ***Expert systems***—programs that encapsulate the knowledge and reasoning of experts in specific domains, such as medical diagnosis—have been implemented with impressive success. Research on topics such as machine learning and knowledge representation has not only produced practical results, but has also helped further our understanding of how humans reason and learn. ***Neural computing***, the design of computer architectures that mimic the human brain, is an especially promising area of research, both for its technical applications and for its potential to help us understand our own physiology.

Figure 10.14   Manufacturing robots welding automobile parts on an assembly line.

Figure 10.15   The Roomba intelligent floor vacuum from iRobot is able to sense obstacles and move freely around the floor as it vacuums.

The Ethics of Computing

Despite the diverse approaches taken by the various computer science subfields, computing professionals have much in common. All perform work relating to the three themes (theory, software, and hardware), and all contribute to computing's overall impact on society. Careers in this field continue to be attractive and challenging, with demand for computer professionals far exceeding supply and with salaries that are among the highest of any discipline.

In an effort to unite computing professionals into a cohesive community, professional organizations supervise the orchestration of industrywide resources. This includes publishing journals relevant to the field, organizing conferences, providing career resources, and representing technology workers' interests to government and society. The oldest and largest professional organization is the Association for Computing Machinery (ACM), founded in 1947. However, the industry supports numerous similar groups, such as the IEEE Computer Society, which also originated in the 1940s and is especially popular among computing professionals with engineering backgrounds.

In 1992, the ACM responded to society's increasing reliance on technology and technology workers by adopting a Code of Ethics and Professional Conduct for computing professionals. This code outlines computer professionals' responsibilities for ensuring that hardware and software are used safely, fairly, and effectively. Excerpts from this code are listed in Figure 10.16. The moral

---

ACM Code of Ethics and Professional Conduct[4]
Copyright © 1997, Association for Computing Machinery, Inc.

General Moral Imperatives. *As an ACM member I will . . .*

1.1 Contribute to society and human well-being.
1.2 Avoid harm to others.
1.3 Be honest and trustworthy.
1.4 Be fair and take action not to discriminate.
1.5 Honor property rights including copyrights and patent.
1.6 Give proper credit for intellectual property.
1.7 Respect the privacy of others.
1.8 Honor confidentiality.

More Specific Professional Responsibilities. *As an ACM computing professional I will . . .*

2.1 Strive to achieve the highest quality, effectiveness and dignity in both the process and products of professional work.
2.2 Acquire and maintain professional competence.
2.3 Know and respect existing laws pertaining to professional work.
2.4 Accept and provide appropriate professional review.
2.5 Give comprehensive and thorough evaluations of computer systems and their impacts, including analysis of possible risks.
2.6 Honor contracts, agreements, and assigned responsibilities.
2.7 Improve public understanding of computing and its consequences.
2.8 Access computing and communication resources only when authorized to do so.

Figure 10.16 Excerpts from the ACM Code of Ethics.

---

imperatives provided in section 1 of the code represent general guidelines relevant to any professional field. For example, all ethical citizens are expected to behave fairly to all (imperative 1.4) and honor others' property and intellectual rights (imperatives 1.5 and 1.6). Section 2 of the code relates specifically to computing and the need to protect technology users from incompetence and unethical practices in the computing industry. For example, imperative 2.5 recognizes that computer technology plays a role in critical systems, such as those in which human life (e.g., medical monitoring systems) and wealth (e.g., banking systems) are at risk. This part of the code indicates that computer professionals must understand the potential impact of their work and strive to minimize risks. A related section, Imperative 2.7, implies that computer professionals are obligated to publicize the societal impacts of computing, including the inherent risks associated with our technological dependence.

Looking Ahead...

In this chapter, you reviewed the fundamental concepts and research methods that define the computer science field. Computer science is the study of computation, which encompasses all aspects of problem solving. The three themes that span all computer-related research are hardware (the physical manifestation of computation), software (the logical manifestation of computation), and theory (an understanding of computation and its limits). Although these themes recur throughout the discipline, computer science has been divided into subfields that focus on particular aspects of computation, such as the design and analysis of algorithms, methods of engineering software, and the quest for artificial intelligence.

After reading this chapter, you should have greater insight into what computer science is and what computer scientists do. If you are considering a career in any computer-related field, the information that we have presented can help you determine where your particular interests fit in the range of computer science subfields and positions. However, even if you have no interest in continuing your computer science education beyond this course, your newly acquired understanding of the discipline will strengthen your problem-solving skills and will provide additional context for the more advanced programming topics covered in future chapters. The next chapter, Chapter 11, returns to programming by introducing the concept of conditional execution, a programming skill that can greatly expand the expressive power of your algorithms. Conditional execution refers to a program's ability to decide between alternative actions on the basis of some condition. For example, you might write a program that simulates a coin flip and then reacts differently depending on the result of the flip. In JavaScript, conditional execution is implemented using if statements, which will be fully explained in Chapter 11.

Chapter Summary

- Computer science is the study of computation, encompassing all facets of problem solving including the design and analysis algorithms, the formalization of algorithms as programs, and the development of computational devices for executing those programs.

- Computer science shares common elements with natural sciences, including a rigorous approach to understanding complex phenomena and solving problems. However, computer science has been classified by some as an "artificial science," since the systems studied by computer sciences are largely designed and constructed by people.

- The three recurring themes that define the discipline of computer science are hardware (the physical components of computers), software (the programs that execute on computers), and theory (an understanding of the capabilities and limitations of computers).

- A Turing machine is an abstract model of computation designed by Alan Turing in 1930. Using this model, Turing was able to demonstrate that there exist problems whose solutions cannot be computed.

- The discipline of computer science encompasses many subfields, including algorithms and data structures, architecture, operating systems and networks, software engineering, and artificial intelligence and robotics.

- The subfield of algorithms and data structures involves developing, analyzing, and implementing algorithms for solving problems. For example, the development of new algorithms for encrypting data and messages (e.g., public-key and private-key encryption) has had significant impact on electronic commerce and security.

- The architecture subfield of computer science is concerned with methods of organizing hardware components into efficient, reliable systems. For example, new architectures in which multiple processors work in parallel to share a computational load have produced powerful results (e.g., the Deep Blue computer that beat a world champion in chess).

- The subfield of operating systems and networks examines mechanisms that control the hardware and software components of computer systems. For example, Ethernet technology has been developed as a simple yet effective means of networking computers over short distances.

- Software engineering is the subfield of computer science concerned with creating effective software systems. Stages in the development and maintenance of software projects include requirement analysis and specification, design, implementation, testing, operation and maintenance.

- One of the most well known subfields of computer science is artificial intelligence, which aims to design computers that exhibit more human-like characteristics. Commercial successes in this area of research include expert systems and manufacturing robotics.

- In 1992, the Association for Computing Machinery adopted a Code of Ethics and Professional Conduct for computing professionals that identifies general moral imperatives and specific responsibilities of professionals in information technology fields.

Review Questions

1. TRUE or FALSE? The discipline of computer science is concerned solely with the design and development of computational machines.

2. TRUE or FALSE? Unlike in the natural sciences (such as physics and biology), the systems that computer scientists investigate are largely artificial (e.g., programs, computers, computation models).

3. TRUE or FALSE? The three recurring themes that define the discipline of computer science are hardware, software, and theory.

4. TRUE or FALSE? Theoretical computer scientists have proven that any problem that can be stated clearly is solvable via an algorithm.

5. TRUE or FALSE? Private-key encryption algorithms require the sender and recipient of a message to agree upon a secret key (or password) for encoding and decoding the message.

6. TRUE or FALSE? In a time-sharing computer, the processor executes user programs in sequence, completing the execution of one program before beginning the next one.

7. TRUE or FALSE? On an Ethernet network, computer A can send a message directly to computer B, without any other computer on the network receiving that message.

8. TRUE or FALSE? When developing large software projects, it generally takes more time to develop the code than it does to test and maintain it.

9. TRUE or FALSE? The Turing Test was proposed by Alan Turing as a means of determining whether an artificially intelligent machine has been constructed.

10. TRUE or FALSE? According to the Code of Ethics proposed by the Association for Computing Machinery (ACM), a computer professional is responsible for understanding the potential impact of his or her work and for striving to minimize risks to the public.

11. Describe at least two similarities between computer science and natural sciences such as physics, biology, and chemistry. Describe at least two differences.

12. Alan Turing is considered one of computer science's founding fathers. Describe two of his contributions to the discipline, and explain the importance of those contributions.

13. Encrypt the message "Beware the Ides of March" using the Caesar encryption algorithm. Recall that the Caesar algorithm encodes each individual letter by replacing it with the letter three positions later in the alphabet.

14. The following encoded text was created using Caesar's encryption algorithm: "Brx jrw lw". Decode this message by performing the reverse translation, replacing each letter in the code with the letter three positions earlier.

15. Using public-key encryption, the sender and recipient of a message do not need to agree on a shared secret key before initiating secure communications. How is this possible? That is, how can the sender, using publicly available information, encode a message that can be decoded only by the intended recipient?

16. Describe the fundamentals of parallel processing and explain how they are implemented in Deep Blue, the first computer to defeat a world chess champion in a tournament setting.

17. What does it mean for an operating system to support multitasking? How is multitasking different from time sharing?

18. Although Ethernet technology is effective for local area networks (LANs), it is not conducive to wide area networks (WANs). Describe why this is the case.

19. Describe the individual steps that make up the software life cycle. What is the life cycle's significance in relation to the software engineering process?

20. Imagine that you are serving as the judge in a Turing Test. Describe the strategy you would use to identify the computer. That is, what kinds of questions would you ask the contestants, and how would the answers you received help you differentiate between the computer and human?

21. Software piracy, the unauthorized copying of software without payment to the legal owner, is a growing problem worldwide. Suppose that you were offered a chance to copy a friend's disk containing copyrighted software. What portions of the ACM Code of Ethics would address this situation? According to the code, how should a computer professional respond to such an offer?

22. Imagine that you are working for a software company, writing a program that will control air traffic at major airports. Management is pressuring you to complete the program on schedule, but you know that remaining bugs in the software might cause the program to fail under certain circumstances. What portions of the ACM Code of Ethics would address this situation? According to the code, how should you react to the situation?

Endnotes

1. Denning, Peter. *Computer Science: The Discipline*. In *Encyclopedia of Computer Science*, 4th ed., A. Ralston, E. Reilly, and D. Hemmendinger, editors. New York: Nature Publishing Group, 2000. Online at `http://cne.gmu.edu/pjd/PUBS/cs99.pdf`.

2. The Software & Information Industry Association. "Packaged Software Industry Revenue and Growth." July 2003. Online at `http://www.siia.net/divisions/research/growth.asp`.

3. Salkever, Alex. "Windows XP: A Firewall for All." *BusinessWeek Online*, June 12, 2001. Online at `http://www.businessweek.com/bwdaily/dnflash/jun2001/nf20010612_227.htm`.

4. ACM Ethics Task Force. "ACM Code of Ethics and Professional Conduct." *Communications of the ACM*, 35(5), 1992. Online at `http://www.acm.org/constitution/code.html`.

References

Brooks, Frederick P., Jr. *The Mythical Man-Month: Essays on Software Engineering, Anniversary Edition*. Reading, MA: Addison-Wesley, 1995.

IBM Research. "Deep Blue." July 2003. Online at `http://www.research.ibm.com/deepblue/`.

Hodges, Andrew. *Alan Turing: The Enigma.* New York: Walker and Company, 2000.

Joint IEEE Computer Society/ACM Task Force for CC2001. "Computing Curricula 2001 (Dec 15, 2001)." *ACM Journal of Educational Resources in Computing*, 1(3), 2001. Online at `http://www.acm.org/sigcse/cc2001/`.

Knuth, Donald. *The Art of Computer Programming*, Vol. 1, *Fundamental Algorithms*, 3d ed. Reading, MA: Addison-Wesley, 1997.

Simon, Herbert. *The Sciences of the Artificial*, 3d ed. Cambridge, MA: MIT Press, 1996.

Stallings, William. *Cryptography and Network Security: Principles and Practice*, 2d ed. Upper Saddle River, NJ: Prentice Hall, 1999.

Stewart, N.F. "Science and Computer Science." *ACM Computing Surveys*, 27(1), 1995. Extended version online at `http://www.iro.umontreal.ca/~stewart/science_computerscience.pdf`.

Turing, Alan. "Computing Machinery and Intelligence." *Mind*, LIX(236), 1950.

Conditional Execution

This chapter uses narrative, examples, and hands-on exercises to introduce programming concepts and Web development skills.

Destiny is no matter of chance. It is a matter of choice. It is not a thing to be waited for, it is a thing to be achieved.

William Jennings Bryan

"Contrariwise," continued Tweedledee, "if it was so, it might be; and if it were so, it would be; but as it isn't, it ain't. That's logic."

Lewis Carroll
Through the Looking Glass

So far, all the JavaScript code that you have written has been executed unconditionally. This means that the browser carried out statements in a set order, one after another. Given different inputs, your program might produce different results, but it always went through the same steps and produced output of the same form. Event-driven pages provided some variety, because users could initiate specific code sequences by interacting with buttons and boxes. However, once an event was triggered, the JavaScript associated with the event executed unconditionally.

Many programming tasks, however, require code that reacts differently under varying circumstances or conditions. This capability is called ***conditional execution***. For example, consider a program that converts a student's numerical average to a letter grade. Depending upon the particular student's average, the program would need to assign a different letter grade (90 to 100 would be an A, 80 to 89 a B, and so on). Similarly, you might want to design a page that generates a random number to represent a die roll and uses it to determine which of several images to display. In this chapter, you will be introduced to the ***if statement***, which is used to incorporate conditional execution into JavaScript programs. After determining whether some condition is met, an if statement can choose among alternative sequences of code to execute—or can even choose to execute no code at all. This chapter describes the behavior of if statements, including the Boolean tests that control them.

If Statements

Conditional execution refers to a program's ability to execute a statement or sequence of statements only if some condition holds true. The simplest form of conditional statement involves only one possible action. For example, if your program employs a variable to represent a student's grade on a test, you might want to include code that recognizes a failing grade and warns the student. However, conditional execution can also involve alternative JavaScript sequences triggered by related conditions. That is, a program can take one action if some condition is true, but take a different action if the condition is not true (the code that executes in the latter instance is called the ***else case***). For example, you might want your program to display one message for a failing grade and another message for a passing grade. JavaScript if statements enable you to specify both these types of conditional execution.

The general form of an if statement is as follows, where the else case is optional:

```
if (BOOLEAN_TEST) {
    STATEMENTS_EXECUTED_IF_TRUE
}
else {
    STATEMENTS_EXECUTED_IF_FALSE
}
```

Boolean Tests

After encountering a JavaScript if statement, the browser's first action is to evaluate the test that appears in parentheses in the first line. The test can be any ***Boolean expression***—that is, any expression that evaluates to either `true` or `false`. In JavaScript, Boolean tests are formed using ***relational operators***, so named because they test the relationships between values (Figure 11.1). For example, the `==` operator tests for equality, so the Boolean expression (x == 5) would evaluate to `true` if the variable x stored the value 5. Similarly, the Boolean expression (y < 100) would evaluate to `true` if y stored a number less than 100.

Relational Operator	Comparison Defined by the Operator
==	equal to
!=	not equal to
<	less than
<=	less than or equal to
>	greater than
>=	greater than or equal to

Figure 11.1   Relational operators in JavaScript.

The Boolean test at the beginning of an if statement determines which (if any) code will be executed. If the test succeeds (evaluates to `true`), then the code inside the subsequent curly braces is executed. If the test fails (evaluates to `false`) and there is an else case, then the code inside the curly braces following the else is executed. Note that if the test fails and there is no else case, then no statements are executed, and the program moves on to the statement directly after the if.

Figure 11.2 depicts three different if statements that print messages in response to student grades. When executing the first if statement, the browser evaluates the test to see whether the value of variable `grade` is less than 60. If so, the browser calls the `alert` function to display the warning, "You failed! Time to hit the books." However, if `grade` is greater than or equal to 60, then the statement inside the curly braces is skipped over. The second example demonstrates that an if statement can control the execution of entire sequences of statements. If the test succeeds (`grade` is less than 60), then the statements inside the curly braces are executed in order. In this case, the statements compute the difference (stored in variable `diff`) between a passing grade (60) and the grade earned

```
if (grade < 60) {                                      ⎤  code executed if
    alert("You failed!  Time to hit the books.");      ⎬  grade < 60
}                                                      ⎦
```

```
if (grade < 60) {                                      ⎤
    diff = 60 - grade;                                 ⎪  code executed if
    alert("You failed!  If only you could have " +     ⎬  grade < 60
          "earned " + diff + " more points.");         ⎪
}                                                      ⎦
```

```
if (grade < 60) {                                      ⎤
    diff = 60 - grade;                                 ⎪  code executed if
    alert("You failed!  If only you could have " +     ⎬  grade < 60
          "earned " + diff + " more points.")          ⎪
}                                                      ⎦
else {                                                 ⎤  code executed otherwise
    alert("Congratulations, you passed.");             ⎬  (grade >= 60)
}                                                      ⎦
```

Figure 11.2 Example if statements.

(grade), then incorporate the value in an alert message. The third example adds an else case to the if statement, ensuring that a message is generated regardless of grade's value. If the grade is less than 60, the browser will compute and display the difference between a passing grade and the earned grade, as before. If not, then the message, "Congratulations, you passed." is displayed.

Common errors to avoid...

Web browsers ignore indentation and spacing when executing JavaScript code, so such formatting is irrelevant from the browser's perspective. However, from the programmer's perspective, indentation and spacing are vitally important. When you write an if statement, it is important to lay out the code so that its structure is apparent. Otherwise, another programmer modifying your code might introduce errors by misinterpreting which statements are controlled by the if and which are not. For example, in Figure 11.2, the closing curly brace of each if statement is aligned with the beginning if, whereas all statements inside the curly braces are indented. This arrangement emphasizes where each if statement begins and ends, enabling others to read and understand the code more easily.

Technically speaking, the curly braces in an if statement are optional when there is only one statement to be executed conditionally. However, we *strongly* recommend that you include curly braces in every if statement you write. When all if statements look the same, it is easier for you to code them correctly. The consistent use of curly braces also helps prevent subtle errors when code is modified.

The page in Figure 11.3 contains a text box in which to enter a grade and a button for initiating the function ShowMessage. ShowMessage, which displays an alert if the user entered a grade that is less than 60, incorporates the first if statement from Figure 11.2. The resulting Web page is shown in Figure 11.4.

EXERCISE 11.1

Enter the ifdemo.html text from Figure 11.3 into a new Web page. Load this page, then describe how it behaves when you enter various grades in the text box.

Once you have done this, modify the page by replacing the if statement in the ShowMessage function with the third if statement example from Figure 11.2. Load this modified page and describe how it behaves when you enter various grades.

```
1.  <html>
2.  <!-- ifdemo.html                              Dave Reed -->
3.  <!-- This program warns a student of a failing grade -->
4.  <!------------------------------------------------------>
5.
6.  <head>
7.    <title> If Demo page </title>
8.    <script type="text/javascript">
9.      function ShowMessage()
10.     // Assumes: document.IfForm.gradeBox contains a grade
11.     // Results: displays a warning in response to a failing grade
12.     {
13.         var grade;
14.
15.         grade = document.IfForm.gradeBox.value;
16.         grade = parseFloat (grade);
17.
18.         if (grade < 60) {
19.             alert ("you failed!  Time to hit the books.");
20.         }
21.     }
22.   </script>
23.  </head>
24.
25.  <body>
26.    <form name="IfForm">
27.    Your grade: <input type="text" name="gradeBox" size=10 value="" />
28.    <br /><br />
29.    <input type="button" value="Click for Message" onclick="ShowMessage();" />
30.    </form>
31.  </body>
32.  </html>
```

Figure 11.3   Web page that demonstrates an if statement.

EXERCISE 11.2

In the winter, weather reports often refer to the wind-chill factor, a measurement that combines actual temperature and wind speed to estimate the temperature experienced by an exposed human being. If the wind speed is 3 miles per hour or less, then the wind is not considered a factor in the experienced temperature—i.e., the wind chill is the same as the actual temperature. If the wind speed exceeds 3 miles per hour, however, meteorologists use a complex formula to compute the wind chill. Assuming that `temperature` stores the actual temperature (in degrees Fahrenheit) and `windSpeed` stores the wind speed (in miles per hour), we can calculate the wind-chill factor using the following formula:

$$windChill = \begin{cases} temperature & \text{if } windSpeed \leq 3 \\ 35.74 + 0.6215*temperature + \\ (0.4275*temperature - 35.75)*windSpeed^{0.16} & \text{otherwise} \end{cases}$$

When translated into JavaScript, the formula for calculating wind chill can be written using the following if statement:

```
if (windSpeed <= 3) {
  windChill = temperature;
}
```

```
else {
  windChill = 35.74 + 0.6215*temperature +
      (0.4275*temperature - 35.75)*Math.pow(windSpeed, 0.16);
}
```

Create a Web page named `chill.html` that computes the wind-chill factor for a given temperature and wind speed. The user should be able to enter a temperature and wind speed via text boxes, then click a button to view the corresponding wind-chill factor in a separate text box. As part of your page, you should define a function named `WindChill` that accepts the temperature and wind speed as inputs and returns the wind-chill factor.

Once you have completed your page, use it to determine the wind-chill factors for the following weather conditions:

```
wind = 2     temp = 30
wind = 5     temp = 18
wind = 12    temp = 45
wind = 30    temp = 10
```

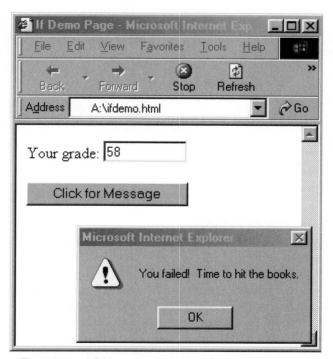

Figure 11.4 `ifdemo.html` rendered in a Web browser.

EXERCISE 11.3

In Chapter 9, you created a `magic.html` page that simulated the behavior of a Magic 8-Ball (Exercise 9.7). As written, your page completely ignores the user's question while randomly selecting from a list of possible responses. In this exercise, modify `magic.html` so that it is less obvious that the entered questions are irrelevant to the program's execution. Add an if statement to your JavaScript code that determines whether the user entered a question. If not (i.e., the value returned from the text area is the empty string), then the browser should open an alert box reminding the user to enter a question. However, if the user did enter a question (i.e., the text area is not empty), the page should proceed as before and display a randomly chosen answer.

Common errors to avoid...

Recall from Chapter 9 that values entered via text boxes or text areas are always returned as strings. If you wish to treat a value obtained from a text box or text area as a number, you must use the parseFloat function to convert the string to its numeric equivalent. As we have established, forgetting to parseFloat such values can introduce subtle errors; this holds true when referencing the contents of text boxes and text areas in if statements. For example, consider the following if statement, which is intended to display a message indicating whether a person is old enough to vote (i.e., whether an age entered in a text box is greater than or equal to 18):

```
if (document.AgeForm.age.value >= 18) {
    alert("You are old enough to vote.");
}
else {
    alert("Sorry.  You are too young to vote.");
}
```

When certain ages are entered in the text box, this code may appear to behave correctly. However, if you test the code using numerous inputs, you can obtain surprising results. For example, a 9-year-old will be considered old enough to vote, but a 100-year-old will not!

The problem is that, without a call to parseFloat, the browser treats the contents of the text box as a string. Thus, when the if test is evaluated, the Boolean expression is comparing a string value (the age from the text box) with a number value (18). In situations where a test must compare values of mixed data types, the browser automatically converts the number value into a string and then performs string comparison. Since strings are compared character by character, "9" is considered to be greater than "18" ("9" > "1"), and "100" is considered to be less than "18" (the first characters are identical, so the comparison moves to the second character, where "0" < "8").

To avoid this type of error, always parseFloat the contents of a text box or text area if you intend to treat the value as a number.

Nested If Statements

Often, programming tasks require code that responds to more than one condition. If you want to attach multiple conditions to the same set of JavaScript statements, you can do so by nesting one if statement inside another. In fact, nesting if statements can be a highly effective way of structuring complex code.

For example, consider the wind-chill calculation you implemented in Exercise 11.2. Technically, the formula for computing wind chill is defined only for temperatures at or below 50 degrees Fahrenheit. When the temperature is above 50 degrees, wind chill is not considered a valid measurement. If we decide to handle this condition in the WindChill function, we can do so by nesting the existing code inside an if statement that determines whether the temperature is one for which wind chill can be computed. If the temperature is less than or equal to 50, then the code for calculating the wind chill should be executed as before. If not, then an alert box notifying the user of the error should be displayed, and the wind chill should be set to NaN, signifying that it is not defined. Figure 11.5 depicts an example of nested if statements that accomplish this task. Note that the inner if statement is reached only in the case where the outer if test succeeds—that is, the wind speed becomes relevant only if it is first determined that the temperature is less than or equal to 50.

EXERCISE 11.4

Modify your chill.html page so that it uses the nested if statements from Figure 11.5. When the input temperature is greater than 50, your WindChill function should return NaN, in addition to displaying a warning in an alert box.

```
if (temp <= 50) {
  if (windSpeed <= 3) {
    windChill = temperature;
  }
  else {
    windChill = 35.74 + 0.6215*temperature +
                (0.4275*temperature - 35.75)*Math.pow(windSpeed, 0.16);
  }
}
else {
  alert("Wind-chill is defined only if temperature <= 50.");
  windChill = NaN;
}
```

Figure 11.5 Generalized code for computing wind chill only on valid temperatures.

Cascading If-Else Statements

In its simplest form, an if statement determines whether or not to execute a sequence of statements. For instance, the first if statement example in Figure 11.2 displayed a message in cases where the value stored in variable `grade` was less than 60, but did nothing otherwise. When an if statement includes an else case, the statement decides between executing two alternative sections of code; this was demonstrated in the third example from Figure 11.2, which displayed different messages for passing and failing grades. By nesting if statements inside each other, it becomes possible to select from among more than two alternatives. For example, your modified wind-chill page recognized three different possibilities and executed separate code in response to each: (1) the temperature was greater than 50, (2) the temperature was less than or equal to 50 and the wind speed was less than or equal to 3, and (3) the temperature was less than or equal to 50 and the wind speed was greater than 3.

Now, let us examine a slightly different type of nested if statement. Imagine that you wanted to extend the grades examples from Figure 11.2 so that the code could differentiate among three classes of grades: failing grades, passing grades less than 90, and grades greater than or equal to 90. The nested if statements in Figure 11.6 would accomplish this task.

```
if (grade < 60) {                                    executed if
  alert("You failed!  Time to hit the books.");      grade < 60
}
else {
  if (grade < 90) {                                  executed if
    alert("You passed, but could do better.");       grade < 90
  }                                                                    executed if
  else {                                                               grade >= 60
    alert("Congratulations!  You got an A.");        executed if
  }                                                  grade >= 90
}
```

Figure 11.6 Nested if statements for differentiating three classes of grades.

Nested if-else structures such as the one in Figure 11.6 are known as ***cascading if-else statements***, because control cascades down the statement like water down a waterfall. The topmost test is evaluated first—in this case: (`grade < 60`). If this test succeeds, then the corresponding statements are executed, and program control moves to the next statement following the cascading if. If the test fails, then control cascades down to the next if test—in this case: (`grade < 90`). In general, control cascades down the statement from one test to another until one succeeds or the end of the statement is reached. If (as in Figure 11.6) the final case is an unconditional else, then this final case will execute if none of the preceding conditional tests succeed. However, if the final case is conditional (i.e., another if statement), it is possible that none of the conditions will be met and that no code controlled by the cascading if-else statements will be executed.

When it is necessary to handle a large number of alternatives, cascading if-else statements can become cumbersome and unwieldy. This is because each nested if-else statement introduces another level of indentation and curly braces, causing the code to look cluttered. Fortunately, programmers can write more concise, clearer cascading if-else statements by adopting a slightly different notation. The left-hand side of Figure 11.7 depicts a set of nested if-else statements that determine a student's letter grade using a traditional grading system. On the right is an equivalent section of code that is much more readable. This cleaner notation omits some redundant curly braces (technically, curly braces can be omitted if the case consists of only one statement) and indents each case an equal amount. Using this notation, it is easier to discern that there are five alternatives, each assigning a letter grade on the basis of grade's value.

```
if (grade < 60) {                    if (grade < 60) {
   letterGrade = "F";                   letterGrade = "F";
}                                    }
else {                               else if (grade < 70) {
   if (grade < 70) {                    letterGrade = "D";
      letterGrade = "D";            }
   }                                else if (grade < 80) {
   else {                              letterGrade = "C";
      if (grade < 80) {             }
         letterGrade = "C";         else if (grade < 90) {
      }                                letterGrade = "B";
      else {                        }
         if (grade < 90) {          else {
            letterGrade = "B";         letterGrade = "A";
         }                          }
         else {
            letterGrade = "A";
         }
      }
   }
}
```

Figure 11.7 Examples of equivalent cascading if-else statements.

EXERCISE 11.5

Augment your grades.html page from Chapter 9 by inserting a cascading if-else statement similar to the one on the right-hand side of Figure 11.7. The modified page should display the student's class average in one text box and the corresponding letter grade in another. For example, if the student's average was calculated to be 85.5, then the corresponding text boxes might resemble the following:

Your average is: 85.5

You are guaranteed at least a: B

Example: Counting Dice Rolls

The Web page in Figure 11.8 is shown rendered in a Web browser in Figure 11.9. It contains a button and an image of a single die (the initial image file depicts a die with one dot on its face). When a user clicks the button, the Roll function is called to simulate the rolling of a six-sided die. Roll uses the RandomInt function from the random.js library to obtain a random integer value between one and six, which represents the result of a random die roll. The function then replaces the die image on the page with the one corresponding to that roll. A cascading if-else statement is used to select the appropriate image—for example, the image file http://www.prenhall.com/reed/Images/die4.gif corresponds to a roll of 4.

```
1.    <html>
2.    <!-- dice.html                                    Dave Reed -->
3.    <!-- This page simulates and displays the roll of a die. -->
4.    <!------------------------------------------------------->
5.
6.    <head>
7.      <title> Die Rolls </title>
8.      <script type="text/javascript"
9.              src="http://www.prenhall.com/reed/random.js">
10.     </script>
11.
12.     <script type="text/javascript">
13.       function Roll()
14.       // Assumes: die images are in www.prenhall.com/reed/Images
15.       // Results: displays a randomly selected image of a 6-sided die
16.       {
17.         var roll;
18.
19.         roll = RandomInt(1, 6);
20.
21.         if (roll == 1) {
22.           document.images.die.src =
23.               http://www.prenhall.com/reed/Images/die1.gif";
24.         }
25.         else if (roll == 2) {
26.           document.images.die.src =
27.               "http://www.prenhall.com/reed/Images/die2.gif";
28.         }
29.         else if (roll == 3) {
30.           document.images.die.src =
31.               "http://www.prenhall.com/reed/Images/die3.gif";
32.         }
33.         else if (roll == 4) {
34.           document.images.die.src =
35.               "http://www.prenhall.com/reed/Images/die4.gif";
36.         }
37.         else if (roll == 5) {
38.           document.images.die.src =
39.               "http://www.prenhall.com/reed/Images/die5.gif";
40.         }
41.         else {
42.           document.images.die.src =
43.               "http://www.prenhall.com/reed/Images/die6.gif";
44.         }
45.       }
46.     </script>
47.   </head>
48.
49.   <body>
50.     <div style="text-align:center">
51.       <img name="die" alt="die image"
52.           src="http://www.prenhall.com/reed/Images/die1.gif" />
53.       <br /><br />
54.       <form name="DiceForm">
55.         <input type="button" value="Click to Roll" onclick="Roll();" />
56.       </form>
57.     </div>
58.   </body>
59.   </html>
```

Figure 11.8   Web page that uses a cascading if-else to control an image.

Figure 11.9 `dice.html` rendered in a Web browser.

Designer Secrets

An if statement is different from other JavaScript statements we have studied in that it does not perform a particular task in and of itself. Instead, it is known as a ***control statement***, since its purpose is to control the execution of other statements. When solving problems, most programmers find it fairly easy to determine when an if statement is required. If the program needs to make any choices during execution—i.e., the code should react differently under different circumstances—then you should include some version of an if statement.

- If the choice involves only one alternative—i.e., the code should carry out some action if a condition holds and do nothing if the condition does not hold—then a simple if statement is needed.
- If the choice involves two alternatives—i.e., the code should carry out some action if a condition holds and do something else if it does not hold—then an if statement with an else case is needed.
- If the choice involves more than two alternatives—i.e., the code should carry out one of three or more actions on the basis of various conditions—then nested or cascading if-else statements are needed.

EXERCISE 11.6

Enter the `dice.html` text from Figure 11.8 into a new Web page. Load this page and click the button repeatedly to verify that all six die faces are obtainable.

You may notice a slight delay the first time a particular die face appears in the page. This is because the image file is stored on a remote Web server and must be downloaded to your computer before it is displayed. Once downloaded, the image file is cached by the browser (stored locally in fast memory) and can be accessed almost instantaneously.

EXERCISE 11.7

Although the cascading if-else statement in `dice.html` is effective, it is also repetitive and tedious. In each case, the IMG element is assigned a new source file corresponding to the value of the die roll.

Since each assignment is identical, aside from the number that appears in the file name, the assignment of the image source could actually be accomplished without an if statement. For example, you could replace the cascading if-else statement with the following code, which assigns the appropriate file name on the basis of the `roll` variable's value.

```
document.images.die.src =
    "http://www.prenhall.com/reed/Images/die" + roll + ".gif";
```

Replace the entire cascading if-else statement with this single assignment and verify that the page behaves as before.

EXERCISE 11.8

Add a second die image to your `dice.html` page so that the two dice appear side by side. When the user clicks the button, both die images should be randomly selected and displayed in the page.

Note: You will need to insert a second IMG tag into the BODY of the page, then add code to the `Roll` function so that the second IMG is also assigned a random SRC file.

Common errors to avoid...

Despite the apparent similarity of = and ==, it is important to distinguish between the two. As you saw in Chapter 4, = is the assignment operator, which programmers use to assign values to variables, text boxes, and text areas. By contrast, == is a comparison operator for testing equality. When you write a Boolean expression that compares two values, always make sure that you type the proper operator (==).

Most of the time, if you accidentally type = rather than == in a Boolean expression, the browser will display an error message. Unfortunately, there are instances in which this mistake will not generate an immediate error, but will instead cause your code to behave in unexpected ways. In particular, if the mistyped expression can be interpreted as an assignment, then the browser will execute the assignment, causing the Boolean test to succeed or fail based upon the assignment's result. In cases where a Boolean test consists of an assignment statement, the test will fail if the value assigned is `false`, 0, or an empty string. However, any other assigned value will cause the if test to succeed.

For example, the if test on the left will succeed, whereas the if test on the right will fail.

```
if (x = 5) {                    if (x = "") {
    THIS WILL BE EXECUTED           THIS WILL NOT
}                               }
```

To avoid such odd behavior, always use the == operator when an equality test is intended.

Counters

In software applications, if statements are often used to count occurrences of conditional or user-initiated events. To understand the relevance of recording such data, consider that many research experiments in the natural sciences involve observing phenomena and keeping track of how many times certain actions occur. For example, a particle physicist might want to count the number of atomic collisions that take place within a certain time period, whereas a biologist might want to count the number of encounters between animals at an oasis over the course of a day. Certain computer programs provide a similar ability to record the number of times a certain action is taken within an application. In computer science terminology, any variable that is used to record occurrences of an event is known as a **_counter_**. Before a counter begins tallying, it must have an initial value of zero. Then, each time the specified event occurs, the value of the counter is incremented (increased by one). At the end of the observation period, the value stored in the counter represents the number of times that the desired event took place.

For example, suppose that your `dice.html` page contained a text box named `numRolls` within the `DiceForm` form. You could treat this text box as a counter by setting its initial value to be 0, then incrementing the value in the box each time the dice are rolled. To ensure that the counter is incremented after every dice roll, you should include the following assignment within the `Roll` function:

```
document.DiceForm.numRolls.value =
    parseFloat(document.DiceForm.numRolls.value) + 1;
```

EXERCISE 11.9

Below the button in your `dice.html` page, add a text box that serves as a counter, keeping track of the number of times the user has rolled the dice. Be sure to set the counter variable's initial value to zero and to accompany the text box with an appropriate text label, such as "Number of dice rolls:". Within the `Roll` function, you should add an assignment similar to the one above that accesses the counter value and increments it each time the function is called.

Counters can be combined with if statements to count conditional events, or events which occur only under certain circumstances. For example, in addition to counting the total number of dice rolls, you might also want your `dice.html` page to record how many times doubles occur (i.e., how many times two identical die faces are displayed concurrently in the page). This will require conditional execution, since the counter corresponding to doubles should be incremented only on the condition that the two dice rolls are the same.

EXERCISE 11.10

Add an additional text box to your `dice.html` page that serves as a conditional counter, keeping track of the number of times the user rolls doubles. The new text box should appear below the counter you added in Exercise 11.9 and should be accompanied by an appropriate label. Within the `Roll` function, add an if statement that checks whether the rolls are identical and, if so, increments the doubles counter in the text box.

Note: Statistically speaking, users should obtain doubles on one-sixth of their rolls. This is due to the fact that six out of the 36 possible dice combinations are doubles. After a *reasonable* number of rolls, is your doubles count roughly one-sixth of the total number of rolls?

EXERCISE 11.11

Imagine that users of your `dice.html` page would like to perform repeated experiments with the dice simulator. It would greatly help these users if they were able to reset the roll and doubles counts within the page. You may note that simply refreshing the page does not suffice—the values in the text boxes are retained when you click "Reload" in the browser. It is possible to reset the counters by completely reloading the page—i.e., by clicking in the browser's Address box and hitting enter. However, this is a rather tedious process, especially if users wish to perform numerous experiments using the counters. A better solution would be to add another button to the page labeled "Reset counters". When the user clicks this button, the values in the two text boxes should be reset to 0. Add such a button to your page and verify that it behaves appropriately.

Boolean Expressions

So far, all the if statements you have written have involved simple tests. This means that each test contained a single comparison using one of the Boolean operators: == (equal to), != (not equal to), < (less than), > (greater than), <= (less than or equal to), and >= (greater than or equal to). For example, the simple test in the if statement below involves evaluating the sum of two variables, `roll1` and `roll2`. If the sum is eight, then the Boolean expression (roll1 + roll2 == 8) will evaluate to true, and the code inside the if statement will be executed.

```
if (roll1 + roll2 == 8) {
    // code to be executed if sum is 8
}
```

In more complex applications, however, simple comparisons between two values may not be adequate to express the conditions under which code should execute. Suppose, for example, that you wanted to count the number of times that both die faces in dice.html display four dots (we call this a 4-4 combination). Simply testing the sum of the two die faces would not suffice, since this would not distinguish between 4-4 and other combinations that total eight, such as 3-5 and 2-6. Instead, the values of both die faces must be tested to determine that they are both 4s.

One option for creating this type of two-part test is to nest one if statement inside another. Since the browser evaluates the nested if statement only if the outer test succeeds, the code inside the nested if statement is executed on the condition that both tests succeed. The following example contains nested if statements that form a two-part test:

```
if (roll1 == 4) {
    if (roll2 == 4) {
        // code for incrementing the 4-4 counter
    }
}
```

Fortunately, JavaScript provides a more natural and compact alternative for expressing multipart tests. The && operator, when placed between two Boolean tests, represents the conjunction of those tests. This operator is referred to as *logical AND*, because the Boolean expression (TEST1 && TEST2) will evaluate to true if TEST1 is true *and* TEST2 is true. Consider the following example:

```
if (roll1 == 4 && roll2 == 4) {
    // code for incrementing the 4-4 counter
}
```

Since && represents conjunction, the Boolean expression (roll1 == 4 && roll2 == 4) will evaluate to true only if both (roll1 == 4) and (roll2 == 4) evaluate to true. That is, the test will succeed if both values are 4s.

Similarly, a disjunction of tests is accomplished in JavaScript using the || operator. This operator is referred to as *logical OR*, because the Boolean expression (TEST1 || TEST2) will evaluate to true if either TEST1 is true *or* TEST2 is true. For example, the Boolean expression (roll1 == 4 || roll2 == 4) will evaluate to true if *either* (roll1 == 4) or (roll2 == 4) evaluates to true. That is, the test will succeed if either of the rolls is a 4.

Finally, the negation of a test is accomplished in JavaScript using the ! operator. This operator is referred to as *logical NOT*, because the Boolean expression (!TEST) will evaluate to true if TEST is not true. For example, the Boolean expression (!(roll1 == 4 && roll2 == 4)) will evaluate to true if (roll1 == 4 && roll2 == 4) is false. That is, the test will succeed as long as double 4s are not obtained.

The &&, ||, and ! operators are known as *logical connectives*, since programmers use them to build complex logical expressions by combining simpler logical expressions.

EXERCISE 11.12

In gambling circles, certain dice combinations are given colorful names. For example, the 1-1 combination is called *snake eyes* (since the single dots suggest eyes), and the 6-6 combination is called *boxcars* (since the parallel rows of dots suggest train tracks). Similarly, the combination of a 3 and 4 (in either order) is known as a *natural 7*.

Add two additional text boxes to your `dice.html` page, one that keeps track of the combined number of snake eyes and boxcars and another that keeps track of the number of natural 7s. [*Hint:* You will most likely want to use logical connectives in order to test for these combinations.]

Since snake eyes and boxcars can each be obtained via a single dice combination, you would expect the combined count for snake eyes and boxcars to be (1/36 + 1/36) = 1/18th of the total number of rolls. According to the same logic, the number of naturals should be 1/18th of the total tally, since there are two combinations (3-4 and 4-3) out of 36 that yield natural 7s. After a *reasonable* number of rolls, is the combined count for snake eyes and boxcars roughly equal to the count of natural 7s? Is each of these counts roughly 1/18th of the total number of rolls?

Common errors to avoid...

Note that logical connectives can be applied only to two complete Boolean expressions. For example, imagine that you want to test whether the first die in `dice.html` displays either a 3 or a 4. A common beginner's mistake would be to write partial expressions using the logical OR operator, such as (`roll1 == 3 || 4`). However, in order to test this condition correctly, full comparisons must appear on each side of the logical connective: (`roll1 == 3 || roll1 == 4`).

Looking Ahead...

In this chapter, you were introduced to the if statement, which specifies conditional execution in JavaScript code. An if statement is known as a control statement, since its purpose is to control the execution of other JavaScript statements. In it simplest form, an if statement allows the browser to skip over a section of code if some condition (expressed as a Boolean test) fails to hold. When an else case is included, an if statement can decide between two alternative sections of code, executing one or the other depending on the result of the Boolean test. If more than two alternatives must be considered, programmers can nest multiple if statements to create a cascading if-else structure. When the browser encounters a cascading if-else structure, the Boolean tests are evaluated in succession, and the corresponding code is executed as soon as a test succeeds. As the examples in the chapter demonstrated, the ability to write code that makes choices can greatly enhance a programmer's expressive power. Using if statements, you can write code that reacts to user input, displays different images on the basis of random dice rolls, and even counts the number of doubles obtained during a series of repeated dice rolls.

Up to this point, you have used the data types provided by JavaScript (number, string, and Boolean) as abstractions. For example, you thought of a number as representing a value (in decimal notation) and a string as representing a sequence of characters (enclosed in quotes). You learned to store and manipulate such values, without worrying about how the various data types were actually implemented. In the next chapter, Chapter 12, you will look more closely at the representation of data—including numbers, strings, and Booleans—inside computers. In particular, you will learn that computers store and process all data values as binary signals. When numbers are represented in binary, the mappings are relatively straightforward. By contrast, the mapping of string and Boolean values to their binary equivalents is a matter of convention, rather than inherent logic. To represent other kinds of data, such as sound and images, computers must apply complex algorithms that compress the data or make it easier to store in binary form. Understanding how data is represented inside the computer should prove useful in later programming chapters as you approach more complex tasks, including counter-controlled repetition and structured data (e.g., strings and arrays).

Chapter Summary

- Conditional execution refers to a program's ability to execute a statement or sequence of statements only if some condition holds. In JavaScript, conditional execution is performed using if statements.

- The general form of an if statement is as follows, where the else case is optional:

```
if (BOOLEAN_TEST) {
    STATEMENTS_EXECUTED_IF_TRUE
}
else {
    STATEMENTS_EXECUTED_IF_FALSE
}
```

  If the Boolean test succeeds (evaluates to `true`), then the browser executes the code inside the subsequent curly braces. If the test fails (evaluates to `false`) and there is an else case, then the code inside the curly braces following the else is executed.

- The following relational operators can be used to build simple Boolean expressions: == (equal to), != (not equal to), < (less than), <= (less than or equal to), > (greater than), and >= (greater than or equal to).

- Programmers can write code that chooses among an arbitrary number of alternative cases by using a cascading if-else statement, which is really nothing more than a series of nested if statements. The general form of a cascading if-else statement is as follows:

```
if (TEST1) {
    STATEMENTS_EXECUTED_IF_TEST1_SUCCEEDS
}
else if (TEST_2) {
    STATEMENTS_EXECUTED_IF_TEST2_SUCCEEDS
}
else if (TEST_3) {
    STATEMENTS_EXECUTED_IF_TEST3_SUCCEEDS
}
  .
  .
  .
else {
    STATEMENTS_IF_ELSE
}
```

- A variable that records the number of occurrences of some event is known as a counter. In order to function properly, a counter must be initialized to zero, then incremented (increased by one) each time the desired event occurs.

- The conjunction (&&) disjunction (||), and negation (!) operators are known as logical connectives, since they are used to build complex logical expressions by combining simpler logical expressions.

- A Boolean expression involving conjunction (&&) will evaluate to true if all its components evaluate to true—e.g., (`true && true`) evaluates to `true`.

- A Boolean expression involving disjunction (||) will evaluate to true if any of its components evaluate to true—e.g., (`true || false`) evaluates to `true`.

- A Boolean expression involving negation (!) will evaluate to true if the expression following the negation operator is not true—e.g., (`! false`) evaluates to `true`.

Supplemental Material and Exercises

More Practice with Nested Ifs

If statements, especially when they are nested or involve logical connectives, can be tricky to follow. Additional exercises may prove beneficial.

EXERCISE 11.13

Consider the following code segment containing a nested if-else statement:

```
if (x >= y) {
    if (x*10 < 100) {
        document.write("ONE<br />");
    }
    else {
        document.write("TWO<br />");
    }
}
else {
    document.write("THREE<br />");

}
```

Given the following assignments, predict the output sequences that the above code would produce:

```
x = 0;     y = 5;
x = 0;     y = -5;
x = 9;     y = 9;
x = 22;    y = 21;
```

EXERCISE 11.14

Consider the following code segment containing a cascading if-else statement:

```
if (x > y) {
    document.write("GREATER<br />");
    y = x;
}
else if (x == y) {
    document.write("EQUAL<br />");
    x = 100;
}
document.write("x = " + x + ", y = " + y);
```

Given the following assignments, predict the output sequences that the above code would produce:

```
x = 0;     y = 5;
x = 0;     y = -5;
x = 9;     y = 9;
x = 22;    y = 21;
```

EXERCISE 11.15

Create a Web page named `classify.html` that reads in a number entered by the user and then determines whether that number is positive, negative, or zero. The page should contain a text box in which the user can enter the number and a button for initiating the analysis. When the user inputs the desired number and clicks the button, a function should be called to identify the number's type and display the result in an alert box. Be sure to `parseFloat` the contents of the text box before testing the value. Load your page and verify that it correctly identifies positive, negative, and zero values.

EXERCISE 11.16

Imagine that variables `roll1`, `roll2`, and `roll3` represent three die rolls (each storing a value between 1 and 6). Examine the following Boolean expressions, then describe in English the condition that each represents.

```
(roll1 == 1 && roll2 == 1)
((roll1 + roll2 == 11) || (roll1 + roll2 == 12))
(roll1 > 2 && roll1 < 5)
(roll3 < 3 || roll3 > 4)
(roll1 == roll2 && roll2 == roll3)
(roll1 == 1 && roll2 == 1 && roll3 == 1)
```

Does the following expression correctly represent the condition that all three die rolls are different? That is, does this expression evaluate to true if all three variables have unique values, but evaluate to false in all other cases? If you believe that the expression accurately represents this condition, justify your claim. If not, provide a correct expression that performs the task.

```
(roll1 != roll2 && roll2 != roll3)
```

Example: Designing an ESP Test

Although no scientific evidence supports the existence of extrasensory perception (ESP), many people believe in its legitimacy. A standard test for determining whether someone has ESP involves a deck of cards with various shapes on them. The test subject is shown the backs of cards and asked to guess the shapes on the reverse sides. If the subject is able to guess the correct shape more frequently than would be expected, then a claim of ESP might be made.

For example, suppose that each card in the deck displayed one of four different shapes. Guessing at random, a person could be expected to pick the correct shape 25% of the time. If the subject were able to consistently guess correctly more than 25% of the time, then some people might view this as evidence of ESP.

In Chapter 7 (Exercise 7.8), you wrote a Web page that performed a rudimentary version of this ESP test. Your program selected a random number between one and four, prompted the user for a guess, then displayed the number along with the guess. Now that you know how to write an if statement, you can write a more advanced program that actually compares the user's guess with the selected number and determines whether the guess was correct. Your new program can also include a counter to keep track of how many times the user is right during a sequence of guesses.

EXERCISE 11.17

Design and implement a Web page named `esp.html` that allows the user to conduct an ESP test. Your page should look something like the one in Figure 11.10. The rectangle containing a question mark represents the back of a card that is associated with a particular shape. After contemplating which shape appears on the front of the card, the user clicks the button corresponding to the shape he or she believes is on the card (here, four possibilities are assumed). After each guess, the question mark should be replaced by a randomly selected shape, and an alert box should notify the user as to whether the guess was correct. Statistics concerning the number and percentage of correct guesses should be maintained in text boxes. After the statistics have been updated and the alert box has been closed, the page should restore the question-mark image, enabling the user to enter another guess.

Figure 11.10 Sample appearance of the enhanced ESP-test page.

Although you can create your own images for the cards, you can also use the images provided for you in the www.prenhall.com/reed/Images directory. This directory contains images of four shapes—square.gif, triangle.gif, circle.gif, and star.gif—as well as mystery.gif, which displays the question mark.

EXERCISE 11.18

Using your esp.html page, test yourself for ESP. After 10 guesses, what is your percentage of correct guesses? After 20 guesses? After 50 guesses? How compelling do you find these percentages to be in deciding whether you have ESP? Justify your answer.

Example: Designing a Dot Race

A recent trend at sporting events is the running of dot races on the scoreboard. In a dot race, dots of different colors speed around a track, and members of the crowd are encouraged to cheer for different dots. Every few seconds, each dot moves forward a different random amount; the dot that reaches the finish line first is the winner.

Figure 11.11 Sample appearance of dot race page

EXERCISE 11.19

Design and implement a Web page named `dotrace.html` that allows the user to simulate a race between two dots. Your page should look something like the one in Figure 11.11. The positions of the two dots (initially 0) should be displayed in text boxes, and a separate text box should indicate the length of the race (i.e., the goal distance). Each time the user clicks the button labeled "Take a Step", each dot should move forward a random amount (either one, two, or three units). When one of the dots crosses the finish line—meaning that its current position is greater than or equal to the goal distance—an alert box should appear to identify the winner. Note that it is possible for the dots to tie if both cross the finish line on the same step. Thus, your code must be able to recognize a tied race and display an appropriate message in the alert box.

EXERCISE 11.20

Augment your `dotrace.html` page so that users can initiate repeated races without having to reload the page. You can accomplish this by adding a button labeled "New Race"; when a user clicks this button, the positions of the dots should be reset to 0. If the user clicks the "Take a Step" button after the current race is complete, an alert box should appear directing the user to click the "New Race" button and begin a new race.

12 Chapter

Data Representation

This chapter uses narrative, illustrations, hands-on experimentation, and review questions to introduce computer science and technology concepts.

> *Drama is life with the dull bits cut out.*
>
> Alfred Hitchcock
>
> *The photographic image ... is a message without a code.*
>
> Roland Barthes
>
> *There are only 10 different kinds of people in the world: those who know binary and those who don't.*
>
> Anonymous

I n Chapter 1, we defined a computer as a device that receives, stores, and processes information. This chapter returns to the concepts of data and storage, detailing how data is represented inside a computer. Most computers store data as digital signals (i.e., sequences of 0s and 1s), but the technology used to retain these signals varies greatly, depending on the storage device and type of data. For example, we explained in Chapter 1 that RAM memory stores data as electrical currents in circuitry, whereas CD-ROMs store data as sequences of pits burned into the disk. However, despite differences among storage technologies, most employ the same sets of rules for converting data into 1s and 0s. For example, nearly all programs utilize the same coding standard for specifying text characters as 8-bit patterns. Similar conventions exist for representing other data types, including numbers, sound, images, and video.

This chapter describes common formats and standards that computers use to maintain data. After covering the basics of digital representation, we explain how specific data types such as integers, real numbers, and text are stored on computers. Since most data representations involve binary numbers, a review of binary-number systems is also provided. The chapter concludes by describing common techniques for storing complex data, including sound and images.

Analog vs. Digital

Data can be stored electronically in two ways, either as ***analog*** or ***digital*** signals. Analog signals represent data in a way that is *analog*ous to real life, in that such signals can vary across an infinite range of values. By contrast, digital signals utilize only a discrete (finite) set of values.

For example, radio signals are inherently analog, since their frequencies are measured on a continuous scale. AM radio stations broadcast at frequencies ranging from 535 to 1,700 kilohertz, whereas FM radio stations broadcast at frequencies ranging from 88 to 108 megahertz. Older radio devices, such as the one pictured on the left in Figure 12.1, imitated radio's analog nature by representing frequency as a position on a dial. The user tuned the radio receiver by turning the dial, whose position could specify any value on a continuum. By contrast, most modern radios represent selected frequencies as discrete values, which appear as numbers on a display panel (as in the radio to the right in Figure 12.1). For example, users of most digital radios can select FM frequencies in increments of 0.1 megahertz, such as 106.7 and 106.8, and AM frequencies in increments of 10 kilohertz, such as 1480 and 1490. Frequencies between these increments are not representable on the radio and thus cannot be selected.

Figure 12.1　Two radios with different frequency displays. On the old-fashioned radio to the left, the dial allows the user to select the frequency on a continuous scale. On the modern Bose® Wave® radio to the right, a digital display allows the user to select the frequency in predetermined increments.

Like radio frequencies, many other types of data can be represented alternatively as analog or digital signals, depending on the particular device or technology involved. An analog thermometer, for instance, contains a column of liquid, such as alcohol or mercury, and specifies different temperatures as the height of the column changes. A digital thermometer is different in that it represents the temperature as a discrete number, usually measured in increments of 0.1 degrees. Similarly, an analog clock consists of hands that circle a numbered dial, where the hands' positions indicate the current time. By contrast, a digital clock displays the time as a series of discrete numbers specifying the hour, minutes, and possibly seconds. More complex data can also be represented in either analog or digital form. Later in this chapter, you will learn that audio cassettes store sound as analog signals on a magnetic tape, whereas compact disks (CDs) store sound as digital signals on the surface of a disk.

The primary tradeoff between analog and digital data representation is variability versus reproducibility. Since an analog system encompasses a continuous range of values, a much greater number of unique signals can be represented. For example, the dial on an analog radio receiver allows you to find the exact frequency corresponding to the best possible reception for a particular station. However, this dial setting may be difficult to reproduce. If you switched to another station for a while and then wanted to return to the previous one, relocating the perfect frequency setting would involve fine-tuning the dial all over again. With a digital radio receiver, you might need to round the optimal frequency (such as 106.899) to the nearest represented alternative (106.9). However, a digital setting such as 106.9 megahertz can be remembered and reselected easily.

In general, analog representations are sufficient for storing data that is highly variable but does not have to be reproduced exactly. Analog radios are functional because station frequencies do not need to be precise—you can listen to a station repeatedly without specifying the perfect optimal frequency every time. Likewise, analog thermometers and clocks are adequate for most purposes, since a person rarely needs to reproduce the exact temperature or time—rough estimates based on looking at the devices usually suffice. However, the disadvantages of analog representation can cause problems under certain circumstances. For example, a radio astronomer might require a precise record of a frequency, or a scientist conducting an experiment might need to reproduce an exact temperature.

When it comes to storing data on a computer, reproducibility is paramount. If even a single bit is changed in a file, the meaning of the data can be drastically altered. Thus, modern computers are digital devices that save and manipulate data as discrete values. The specific means of storage depends on the technology used. For example, an electrical wire might carry voltage or no voltage, a switch might be open or closed, a capacitor might be charged or not charged, a location on a magnetic disk might be magnetized or not magnetized, and a location on a CD-ROM might be reflective or nonreflective. What all these technologies have in common is that they distinguish between only two possibilities. The simplest and most effective digital storage systems include two distinct (binary) states, typically referred to as 0 and 1. Thus, a voltage-carrying wire or a magnetized spot on a floppy disk can be thought of as a 1, whereas a wire with no voltage or a nonmagnetized spot can be thought of as a 0. Because these 1s and 0s—called binary digits, or bits—are central to computer data representation, the next section provides an overview of binary number systems.

Binary Numbers

As humans, we are used to thinking of numbers in their decimal (base 10) form, in which individual digits correspond to escalating powers of ten. When dealing with decimal integers, the rightmost digit is the 1s place ($10^0 = 1$), the next digit is the 10s place ($10^1 = 10$), the next is the 100s place ($10^2 = 100$), and so on. Our use of the decimal number system can be seen as a natural result of evolution, since humans first learned to count on ten fingers. Evolutionary bias aside, however, numbers can be represented using any base, including binary (base 2). In the binary number system, all values are represented using only the two binary digits, 0 and 1; these digits are called *bits*. As with decimal numbers, different digits in a binary number correspond to different powers—however, the digits specify ascending powers of 2, instead of 10. This means that the rightmost bit is the 1s place ($2^0 = 1$), the next bit is the 2s place ($2^1 = 2$), the next the 4s place ($2^2 = 4$), and so on. To distinguish binary numbers from their decimal counterparts, people typically add a subscript identifying the base. For example, 1101_2 would represent the binary number that is equivalent to 13 in decimal (Figure 12.2).

Figure 12.2 Bit positions in a binary number.

Converting a binary number to its decimal equivalent is easy: simply multiply each bit (either 1 or 0) by its corresponding power of 2 and then sum the results. The examples in Figure 12.3 illustrate the process of converting a number from binary (base 2) to decimal (base 10).

The opposite conversion—from decimal to binary—is a little trickier, but still relatively straightforward. The following algorithm describes the conversion of positive decimal numbers to binary. Since the algorithm is worded using computer terminology, it could be translated easily into a programming language.

Binary Number	Decimal Equivalent
11_2 →	$1*2 + 1*1 = 3$
1101_2 →	$1*8 + 1*4 + 1*2 + 1*1 = 13$
10011_2 →	$1*16 + 0*8 + 0*4 + 1*2 + 1*1 = 19$
100110_2 →	$1*32 + 0*16 + 0*8 + 1*4 + 1*2 + 0*1 = 38$

Figure 12.3 Converting from binary (base 2) to decimal (base 10).

Algorithm for converting positive decimal number D to binary number B:

1. Initialize B to be empty.
2. As long as D is nonzero, repeatedly:
   a. If D is even, add 0 to the left of B.
   b. If D is odd, add 1 to the left of B.
   c. Divide D by 2 and round down (i.e., D = Math.floor(D/2))

As an example, Figure 12.4 shows the steps required to convert the decimal values 19 and 116 into binary (10011_2 and 1110100_2, respectively).

Converting 19 to binary:

```
19 is odd   → B =      1,   D = Math.floor(19/2) = 9
 9 is odd   → B =     11,   D = Math.floor(9/2)  = 4
 4 is even  → B =    011,   D = Math.floor(4/2)  = 2
 2 is even  → B =   0011,   D = Math.floor(2/2)  = 1
 1 is odd   → B =  10011,   D = Math.floor(1/2)  = 0
```

Converting 116 to binary:

```
116 is even  → B =       0,   D = Math.floor(116/2) = 58
 58 is even  → B =      00,   D = Math.floor(58/2)  = 29
 29 is odd   → B =     100,   D = Math.floor(29/2)  = 14
 14 is even  → B =    0100,   D = Math.floor(14/2)  = 7
  7 is odd   → B =   10100,   D = Math.floor(7/2)   = 3
  3 is odd   → B =  110100,   D = Math.floor(3/2)   = 1
  1 is odd   → B = 1110100,   D = Math.floor(1/2)   = 0
```

Figure 12.4 Converting from decimal (base 10) to binary (base 2).

Representing Integers

Since computers retain all information as bits (0 or 1), binary numbers provide a natural means of storing integer values. When an integer value must be saved in a computer, its binary equivalent can be encoded as a bit pattern and stored using the appropriate digital technology. Thus, the integer 19 can be stored as the bit pattern 10011, whereas 116 can be stored as 1110100. However, since binary numbers contain varying numbers of bits, it can be difficult for a computer to determine where one value in memory ends and another begins. Most computers and programs avoid this problem by employing fixed-width integers. That is, each integer is represented using the same number of bits (usually 32 bits). Leading 0s are placed in front of each binary number to fill the 32 bits. Thus, a computer would represent 19 as:

00000000000000000000000000010011

Given that each integer is 32 bits long, $2^{32} = 4,294,967,296$ different bit patterns can be represented. By convention, the patterns are divided as evenly as possible between positive and negative integers. Thus, programs that use 32-bit integers can store $2^{32}/2 = 2^{31} = 2,147,483,648$ nonnegative numbers (including 0) and $2^{32}/2 = 2^{31} = 2,147,483,648$ negative numbers. The mapping between integers and bit patterns is summarized in Figure 12.5.

Bit Pattern	Decimal Value
10000000000000000000000000000000	$(-2^{31}$ $= -2,147,483,648)$
10000000000000000000000000000001	$(-2^{31}-1 = -2,147,483,647)$
10000000000000000000000000000010	$(-2^{31}-2 = -2,147,483,646)$
.	
.	
.	
11111111111111111111111111111101	(-3)
11111111111111111111111111111110	(-2)
11111111111111111111111111111111	(-1)
00000000000000000000000000000000	$(\ 0)$
00000000000000000000000000000001	$(\ 1)$
00000000000000000000000000000010	$(\ 2)$
00000000000000000000000000000011	$(\ 3)$
.	
.	
.	
01111111111111111111111111111101	$(2^{31}-3 = 2,147,483,645)$
01111111111111111111111111111110	$(2^{31}-2 = 2,147,483,646)$
01111111111111111111111111111111	$(2^{31}-1 = 2,147,483,647)$

Figure 12.5 Representing integers as bit patterns.

While examining the integer representations in Figure 12.5, you may have noticed that the bit patterns starting with a 1 correspond to negative values, while those starting with a 0 bit correspond to nonnegative values. Thus, the initial bit in each pattern acts as the ***sign bit*** for the integer. When the sign bit is 0, then the remaining bits are consistent with the binary representation of that integer. For example, the bit pattern corresponding to 3 begins with 0 (the sign bit) and ends with the 31-bit binary representation of 3: 0000000000000000000000000000011. Similarly, the bit pattern corresponding to 100 consists of a 0 followed by the 31-bit representation of 100: 0000000000000000000000001100100. If we wanted to encode negative integers using this method, we could write each as a 1 followed by the binary representation of the negative integer's absolute value. However, there are several drawbacks to such a representation. First, this system would identify the pattern 10000000000000000000000000000000 as representing negative zero. Since actual number systems contain only one zero, which is neither positive nor negative, the inclusion of two zeros would be unnecessary and confusing. Second, the process of adding binary values would become unnecessarily complicated (see Chapter 14 for details).

To avert these difficulties, computers assign bit patterns to negative numbers in the exact opposite order. This means that the negative integer with the largest absolute value (2^{-31}) corresponds to the smallest bit pattern (10000000000000000000000000000000), whereas the negative integer with the smallest absolute value (-1) corresponds to the largest bit pattern (11111111111111111111111111111111). In addition to avoiding a negative zero, this notation, known as ***two's-complement*** notation, greatly simplifies binary addition. As you will learn in Chapter 14, adding binary numbers is a relatively simple generalization of adding decimal numbers, and this generalization holds with negative binary numbers as well, as long as they are represented in two's-complement notation.

Representing Real Numbers

Since digital computers store all data as binary values, the correlation between integers and their binary counterparts is relatively intuitive. Real (i.e., noninteger) values can also be stored in binary, but the mapping is not quite so direct. Recall that, in JavaScript, a real number can be specified in either decimal or scientific notation. For instance, the real number 1234.56 can be equivalently represented as 1.23456e3 (1.23456 $\times$ 103). When real numbers are written in scientific notation, their representation is normalized so that only one digit appears to the left of the decimal place. The following examples review the conversion of real numbers from decimal to scientific notation.

1234.56	→	1.23456×10^3
-50.0	→	-5.0×10^1
0.00099	→	9.9×10^{-4}

Any real value can be uniquely identified by the two components of this normalized form: the fractional part (the digits surrounding the decimal place) and the exponent (the power of 10). Furthermore, because the decimal point is always between the first and second digits of the fractional part, it is possible to ignore the decimal point when representing the number. Thus, each component of a real number in scientific notation can be treated as an integer value. For example, the real value 1234×56, which normalizes to 1.23456×10^3, could be represented by the integer pair (123456, 3). Similarly, −50.0, which normalizes to -5.0×101, could be represented by the pair (−5, 1); and 0.00099, which normalizes to $9.9 \times 10-4$, could be represented by the pair (99, −4). Real numbers stored in this format are known as *floating-point numbers*, since the normalization process shifts (or floats) the decimal point until only one digit appears to the left.

In 1985, the Institute of Electrical and Electronics Engineers (IEEE) established a standard format for storing floating-point values that has since been adopted by virtually all computer and software manufacturers. According to the IEEE standard, a floating-point value can be represented using either 32 bits (4 bytes) or 64 bits (8 bytes). The 32-bit representation, known as *single precision*, allots 24 bits to store the fractional part (including the sign bit) and 8 bits to store the exponent, producing a range of potential values that spans from approximately $-1.75494351 \times 10^{-38}$ to $3.402823466 \times 10^{38}$. By contrast, the 64-bit representation, known as *double precision*, allots 53 bits for the fractional part (including the sign bit) and 11 bits for the exponent, yielding a much larger range of potential values (from approximately $-2.2250738585072014 \times 10^{-308}$ to $1.7976931348623158 \times 10^{308}$). (See Figure 12.6.)

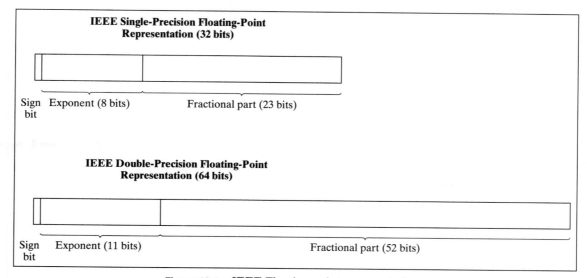

IEEE Single-Precision Floating-Point Representation (32 bits)

Sign bit   Exponent (8 bits)   Fractional part (23 bits)

IEEE Double-Precision Floating-Point Representation (64 bits)

Sign bit   Exponent (11 bits)   Fractional part (52 bits)

Figure 12.6   IEEE Floating-point representations.

Many details of the IEEE single-precision and double-precision formats are beyond the scope of this text. For our purposes, what is important is to recognize that a real value can be converted into a pair of integer values (a fraction and an exponent) that are combined to form a representative binary pattern. It is interesting to note, however, that certain bit patterns are reserved for special values, such as the NaN (Not a Number) value we have encountered in JavaScript.

Since there are an infinite number of real values and only a finite number of 32- or 64-bit patterns, it is not surprising that computers are incapable of representing all real values, even among those that fall within the allotted range. When the result of a calculation yields a real value that cannot be represented exactly, the computer will round off the value to the pattern with the closest corresponding value. In a single-precision floating-point number, roughly 7 decimal digits of precision are obtainable. That is, the computer will round off any real value containing more than 7 significant digits. Using double precision, approximately 16 decimal digits of precision are obtainable. The fact that JavaScript uses double precision to represent numbers explains why 0.9999999999999999 (with 16 9s to the right of the decimal) is represented exactly, whereas 0.99999999999999999 (with 17 9s) is rounded up to the value 1.

Most programming languages differentiate between integer and real values, using 32-bit patterns for storing integers and a floating-point format for storing real numbers. However, JavaScript simplifies number representation by providing only a single number type, which encompasses both integers and reals. Thus, all numbers in JavaScript are stored using the IEEE's double-precision floating-point format.

Representing Characters and Strings

Unlike integers and real values, characters have no natural correspondence to binary numbers. Thus, computer scientists must devise arbitrary systems for representing characters as bit patterns. The standard code for representing characters, known as ASCII (American Standard Code for Information Interchange), maps each character to a specific 8-bit pattern. The ASCII codes for the most common characters are listed in Figure 12.7.

Note that the three character subsets—digits, upper-case letters, and lower-case letters—are each represented using consecutive binary numbers. The digits are assigned the binary numbers with decimal values 48 through 57, the upper-case letters are assigned values 65 through 90, and the lower-case letters are assigned values 97 through 122. These orderings are important, because they enable programs to perform comparisons of character values. For example, the JavaScript expression:

    "a" < "b"

evaluates to true, since the ASCII code for the character "a" is smaller than the ASCII code for "b". It is also clear from this system that upper-case letters have lower values than lower-case letters do. Thus, the JavaScript expression:

    "A" < "a"

evaluates to true.

Since strings are just sequences of characters, a string can be represented as a sequence of bytes, in which each byte corresponds to the ASCII code for a specific character. For example, the string "foobar" is specified using the bit pattern listed in Figure 12.8. The first byte (8 bits) in this pattern is the ASCII code for "f", the second byte is the code for "o", and so on. This representation explains why, when Chapter 11 introduced JavaScript string comparison, it stated that the two strings are compared character by character, with the string that comes first in alphabetical order evaluating to "less than" the other string.

It should be noted that, although 8-bit ASCII codes are sufficient for representing English text, they are far too small to accommodate certain non-Roman alphabets. The Chinese language, for example, encompasses thousands of characters, and it would be impossible to differentiate between all of them using one byte of memory. As computing becomes more and more international, ASCII is being replaced by Unicode, a 16-bit encoding system capable of supporting most foreign-language character sets. To simplify the transition to Unicode, the designers of the new system made it backward compatible with ASCII; this means that the Unicode for an English-language character is equivalent to its ASCII code, preceded by eight leading 0s. Thus, 'f' is 01100110 in ASCII and 0000000001100110 in Unicode.

ASCII Character Codes					
code	char	code	char	code	char
00100000	space	01000000	@	01100000	'
00100001	!	01000001	A	01100001	a
00100010	"	01000010	B	01100010	b
00100011	#	01000011	C	01100011	c
00100100	$	01000100	D	01100100	d
00100101	%	01000101	E	01100101	e
00100110	&	01000110	F	01100110	f
00100111	'	01000111	G	01100111	g
00101000	(	01001000	H	01101000	h
00101001	)	01001001	I	01101001	i
00101010	*	01001010	J	01101010	j
00101011	+	01001011	K	01101011	k
00101100	'	01001100	L	01101100	l
00101101	–	01001101	M	01101101	m
00101110	.	01001110	N	01101110	n
00101111	/	01001111	O	01101111	o
00110000	0	01010000	P	01110000	p
00110001	1	01010001	Q	01110001	q
00110010	2	01010010	R	01110010	r
00110011	3	01010011	S	01110011	s
00110100	4	01010100	T	01110100	t
00110101	5	01010101	U	01110101	u
00110110	6	01010110	V	01110110	v
00110111	7	01010111	W	01110111	w
00111000	8	01011000	X	01111000	x
00111001	9	01011001	Y	01111001	y
00111010	:	01011010	Z	01111010	z
00111011	;	01011011	[	01111011	{
00111100	<	01011100	\	01111100		
00111101	=	01011101	]	01111101	}
00111110	>	01011110	∧	01111110	~
00111111	?	01011111		01111111	delete

Figure 12.7   The ASCII character set.

Figure 12.8   Representing a string as a sequence of ASCII codes.

Representing Other Types of Data

So far, we have explained how basic data values—including integers, real numbers, characters, and strings—are stored as binary-number patterns inside a computer. When programs store and manipulate values of these types, they employ the representations we have described, along with some special-purpose variations. For example, word processing programs will store text using ASCII codes, but will insert special character symbols to denote formatting information. This technique is analogous to the process of inserting HTML tags within text to specify content and formatting information for the browser.

As you know, computers are capable of representing much more than numbers and characters. However, to store and manipulate complex data efficiently, computers require additional techniques and algorithms. Some of these algorithms allow the computer to convert data into binary, whereas others are used to compress the data, shortening its binary representation. The following sections describe commonly used methods of storing sound and images in computers.

Sounds

Sounds are inherently analog signals. Each particular sound produces a pressure wave with a unique amplitude (height, usually measured in pascals) and frequency (duration over time). For example, Figure 12.9 portrays an *oscilloscope*, a device that records sounds and displays their corresponding

Figure 12.9 The sound produced by a tuning fork is displayed as an analog waveform on an oscilloscope.

waveforms on a screen. In this picture, the sound produced by a tuning fork is illustrated as a waveform on the oscilloscope screen. To demonstrate that different sounds produce different waveforms, Figure 12.10 compares the analog waveforms generated by a tuning fork, a violin, a flute, and a gong. When sound waves such as these reach your ear, they cause your eardrum to vibrate; your brain then interprets that vibration as sound.

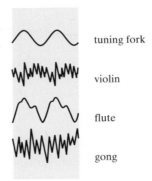

Figure 12.10 Waveforms corresponding to a tuning fork, a violin, a flute, and a gong.

The practice of using analog signals to store and manipulate sounds began with the invention of the telephone by Alexander Graham Bell (1875), which was followed almost immediately by Thomas Edison's phonograph (1877). Telephones translate a waveform into electrical signals of varying strengths, which are then sent over a wire and converted back to sound. By contrast, phonographs reproduce sounds by interpreting waveforms stored as grooves of varying depth and width on the surface of a disk. Audio-cassette technology employs a similar method of storing sounds as analog signals: each waveform is translated into signals of varying strengths and then saved as magnetized spots on a tape.

In most cases, the fact that the analog signal stored on a tape cannot always be reproduced exactly is not a major concern. This is because the human ear is unlikely to notice small inconsistencies in a sound recording. However, if a recording is duplicated repeatedly, then small errors can propagate. You may have noticed this if you have ever made a recording of a recording of a recording of a tape. Sound quality deteriorates as errors pile up during repeated recording. By contrast, digital recordings can be reproduced exactly, so a CD can be copied over and over without any deterioration in sound quality.

Before a sound can be stored digitally, its analog waveform must be converted to a sequence of discrete values. This is accomplished via *digital sampling*, in which the amplitude of the wave is measured at regular intervals and then stored as a sequence of discrete measurements (Figure 12.11).

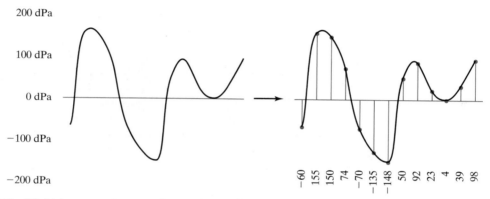

Figure 12.11 Digitizing an analog sound wave. At regular intervals, the amplitude of the waveform (here, measured in decipascals above or below normal air pressure) is recorded as an integer value.

In order to reproduce sounds accurately, frequent measurements must be taken—as many as 44,100 readings per second are needed to achieve CD-quality sound. As a result, even short recordings can require massive amounts of storage. Various techniques have been developed to reduce the size of digital sound files, such as filtering out sounds that are beyond the range of human hearing, or recognizing when one sound will drown out another and filtering out the weaker sound. The MP3 format, for example, utilizes techniques such as these to reduce sound-file sizes by a factor of 10 or more without any noticeable reduction in sound quality. Because it enables sound files to be stored in a compact form, MP3 is extremely popular for portable music players and also for online music distribution (where smaller files allow for faster downloading).

Images

Like sounds, images are stored using a variety of formats and compression techniques. The simplest format for representing images on a computer is known as a *bitmap*. A bitmap partitions an image into a grid of dots, called *pixels* (short for picture elements), and then converts each pixel into a bit pattern. In the case of black-and-white pictures, each pixel can be represented as a single bit: 0 for a black pixel and 1 for a white pixel. For example, Figure 12.12 shows how a simple black-and-white image can be partitioned into 64 pixels and then stored using 64 bits. It should be noted that the partitions in this example are fairly large, resulting in some pixels that are part white and part black. When this occurs, the pixel is usually assigned a bit value corresponding to the majority color, so a partition that is mostly black will be represented as a 0.

Resolution is a term that refers to the sharpness or clarity of an image. Because each pixel is assigned a distinct color value, bitmaps that are divided into smaller pixels will yield higher-resolution

1. To generate a bitmap, the image is first partitioned into a grid of pixels, here 8 × 8.	**2.** For a black-and-white bitmap, a black pixel is represented with a 0 bit, a white pixel with a 1 bit.

Figure 12.12 Generating a bitmap for a black-and-white image.

images. However, every additional pixel increases the necessary storage by one bit. Figure 12.13 illustrates this by comparing the same picture at two different levels of resolution. When stored using 96 pixels per square inch, as shown on the left, the image looks sharp. If the number of pixels is reduced to 48 per square inch, as shown on the right, the image appears blocky, but the storage requirements are cut in half.

Figure 12.13 An image stored using 96 pixels per square inch vs. 48 pixels per square inch.

When creating a bitmap of a color image, more than one bit is required to represent each pixel. The most common system translates each pixel into a 24-bit code, known as that pixel's **_RGB value_**. The term RGB refers to the fact that the pixel's color is decomposed into the different intensities of red, green, and blue. Eight bits are allotted to each of the component colors, allowing for intensities ranging from 0 to 255 (with 0 representing a complete lack of that color and 255 representing maximum intensity). Figure 12.14 lists the RGB values for some common HTML colors. Note that differ-

Common HTML colors					
color	(R, G, B)	color	(R, G, B)	color	(R, G, B)
red	(255, 0, 0)	green	(0, 128, 0)	blue	(0, 0, 255)
darkred	(139, 0, 0)	darkgreen	(0, 100, 0)	darkblue	(0, 0, 139)
maroon	(128, 0, 0)	forestgreen	(34, 139, 34)	royalblue	(65, 105, 225)
crimson	(220, 20, 60)	olive	(128, 128, 0)	lightblue	(173, 216, 230)
pink	(255, 192, 203)	lightgreen	(144, 238, 144)	purple	(128, 0, 128)
violet	(238, 130, 238)	brown	(165, 42, 42)	gray	(128, 128, 128)
orange	(255, 165, 0)	white	(255, 255, 255)	black	(0, 0, 0)

Figure 12.14 Common HTML colors and their (R, G, B) representations.

ent shades of red, such as darkred and maroon, are achieved by adjusting the intensity of the red component. Other colors, such as crimson and pink, require a mixture of the three component colors. Since each color component is associated with 256 possible intensities, $256^3 = 16,777,216$ different color combinations can be represented. Of course, color bitmaps require 24 times more storage than black-and-white bitmaps do, since each pixel requires 24 bits, instead of just one.

If you are familiar with the workings of the Microsoft Windows operating system, you have probably encountered bitmaps before. In Windows, bitmaps are commonly used to represent icons and background images, identified by the extension BMP. Although bitmaps are simple to describe and comprehend, they require a lot of memory to store complex images. The two most common image formats on the Web, GIF (Graphics Interchange Format) and JPEG (Joint Photographic Experts Group), start with a bitmap representation and then employ different methods of compressing the image. Such compression involves applying algorithms that shorten an image's bit-pattern representation, thus conserving memory and reducing the time it takes to transmit the image over the Internet. The GIF format utilizes techniques that identify repetitive patterns in an image and store those patterns efficiently. For example, the sample image in Figure 12.12 includes three entire lines of pixels that are all white. Using the GIF format, this pattern might be stored only once, with a special marker entered in place of each occurrence. By storing frequently occurring patterns only once, the size of the final representation can be reduced.

GIF is known as a *lossless* format, since no information is lost during the compression. This means that the original image can be extracted exactly. Conversely, JPEG is a *lossy* format, since it employs compression techniques that are not fully reversible. For example, JPEG often compresses several neighboring pixels by storing their average color value. In a color photograph, where color changes tend to be gradual, this approach can greatly reduce the necessary storage for an image without noticeably degrading the image's quality. In practice, the GIF format is typically used for line drawings and other images with discrete boundaries (where precision is imperative); the JPEG format, on the other hand, is most commonly used for photographs (where precision can be sacrificed for the sake of compression).

How Computers Distinguish among Data Types

The obvious question you may be asking yourself at this point is: how does the computer know what type of value is stored in a particular piece of memory? If the bit pattern 01100110 is encountered, how can the computer determine whether it represents the integer 97, the character "a", the exponent for a real number, or even a fragment of an image? The answer is that, without some context, it can't! If a program stores a piece of data in memory, it is up to that program to remember what type of data the particular bit pattern represents. For example, suppose you wrote JavaScript code that assigned the character "a" to a variable. In addition to storing the corresponding bit pattern (01100110) in memory, the JavaScript interpreter embedded in the browser must accompany this pattern with information about its type, perhaps using additional bits to distinguish among the possible types. When the variable is accessed later in the program's execution, the bit pattern in memory is retrieved along with the additional bits, enabling the interpreter to recognize the data as a character.

The Web page `data.html` (accessible at `http://www.prenhall.com/reed`) illustrates how a computer can interpret the same bit pattern as representing different values, depending upon context. The user can enter up to 32 bits in the text box, then click to see how that bit pattern would be interpreted as a decimal integer, a single-precision floating-point value, and a sequence of four ASCII characters. Figure 12.15 shows the page converting a sample 32-bit pattern into its corresponding integer, real, and text values.

Looking Ahead...

In this chapter, you studied various methods of representing data inside a computer. Since the data operated on by computers must be accessed and reproduced exactly, computers store data as digital signals, which are represented as binary values—patterns of 1s and 0s. Since any numeric value can be represented in binary notation using 1s and 0s, there is a natural correspondence between numbers (both integers and reals) and the standard bit patterns used to identify them. The mapping of text to binary patterns is more arbitrary, but conventions such as the ASCII standard and Unicode ensure that character representations are consistent across machines. More complex data such as sound and images can also be stored as binary patterns, but advanced algorithms must be applied to such data in order to reduce the representation size.

Figure 12.15   A 32-bit number can represent an integer, a real number, or four ASCII characters.

Understanding how data is represented inside the computer can prove useful as you continue to program and develop Web pages. For example, knowing how characters are represented helps to explain the behavior of string comparisons in JavaScript. Likewise, knowing that not all numbers can be represented exactly inside the computer may help to explain potential errors that may occur in code due to rounding. And recognizing the tradeoffs between lossy and lossless image formats can assist you in choosing the best format for images in a Web page.

Data representation will be revisited in Chapter 14, when we consider the internal workings of computers and the ways in which data and instructions are stored. But first, we will return to JavaScript programming and problem solving. Chapter 13 introduces an additional JavaScript control statement, the while loop, which will enable you to write programs involving repetition. A while loop is similar to an if statement in that it uses the result of a Boolean test to determine whether other statements are executed. Unlike an if statement, however, a while loop specifies that the statements in the loop are to be executed repeatedly, as long as the test succeeds. Thus, tasks that involve repeating an action over and over can be completed using while loops.

Chapter Summary

- Data can be stored electronically in two ways, either as analog signals (which can vary across an infinite range of values) or as digital signals (which utilize only a discrete set of values).

- The primary tradeoff between analog and digital data representation is variability versus reproducibility—analog representations are sufficient for storing data that is highly variable but does not have to be reproduced exactly.

- Since each bit of information on a computer is significant, modern computers are digital devices that store data as discrete, reproducible values. The simplest and most effective digital storage systems include two distinct (binary) states, typically referred to as 0 and 1.

- Any integer value can be stored as a binary number—a sequence of bits (0s and 1s), each corresponding to a power of 2.

- Most computers and programs employ a fixed-width integer representation, utilizing a set number of bits (usually 32 bits) for each integer value. Using the two's-complement notation, bit patterns that begin with a 1 are interpreted as negative values.

- Using the IEEE floating-point standard, a real value is represented as a bit pattern that includes fractional and exponent components.

- ASCII (American Standard Code for Information Interchange) is a standard code for representing characters as 8-bit patterns. As computing becomes more and more international, ASCII is being replaced by Unicode, a 16-bit encoding system capable of supporting most foreign-language character sets.

- Before a sound can be stored digitally, its analog waveform must be converted to a sequence of discrete values via digital sampling.

- The MP3 format reduces the size of sound files by using a variety of techniques, such as filtering out sounds that are beyond the range of human hearing or are drowned out by other, louder sounds.

- The simplest digital format for representing images is a bitmap, in which a picture is broken down into a grid of picture elements, or pixels, and the color or intensity of each pixel is represented as a bit pattern.

- The two most common image formats on the Web, GIF (Graphics Interchange Format) and JPEG (Joint Photography Experts Group), start with a bitmap representation and then employ different methods of compressing the image.

- GIF is known as a lossless format, since no information is lost during the compression. Conversely, JPEG is a lossy format, since it employs compression techniques that are not fully reversible.

- Since all types of data are stored digitally as bit patterns, any program that stores a piece of data in memory must remember its type in order to subsequently access and correctly interpret its meaning.

Review Questions

1. TRUE or FALSE? In contrast to digital signals, analog signals utilize only a discrete (finite) set of values for storing data.

2. TRUE or FALSE? The binary value 1101_2 represents the decimal number 27.

3. TRUE or FALSE? The decimal number 100 is represented as the binary value 110100_2.

4. TRUE or FALSE? Using the two's complement notation for representing integers, any bit pattern starting with a 1 must represent a negative number.

5. TRUE or FALSE? Since the IEEE double-precision format utilizes more bits than the single-precision format does, it allows for a wider range of real values to be represented.

6. TRUE or FALSE? ASCII code is a program written to convert binary numbers to their decimal equivalents.

7. TRUE or FALSE? Digital sampling is the process of converting an analog sound wave into digital values.

8. TRUE or FALSE? GIF and JPEG are examples of formats for representing and storing sounds.

9. TRUE or FALSE? In a bitmap, the number of pixels used to represent an image affects both how sharp the image appears and the amount of memory it requires.

10. TRUE or FALSE? If the bit pattern 001001100 appears at multiple places in a computer's memory, the pattern is guaranteed to refer to the same value each time.

11. Describe two advantages of storing data digitally, rather than in analog format.

12. In addition to the examples given in this chapter, describe a real-world device that can utilize either an analog or digital representation of data.

13. What decimal value is represented by the binary number 01101001_2? Show the steps involved in the conversion, then use the Data Representation Page to verify your answer.

14. What is the binary representation of the decimal value 92? Show the steps involved in the conversion, then use the Data Representation Page to verify your answer.

15. Using 32 bits to represent integers, the largest positive value that can be represented is $2^{31} - 1$, whereas the smallest negative value is 2^{31}. Why aren't these ranges symmetric? That is, why is there one more negative integer than there are positive integers?

16. It was mentioned in the chapter that having two representations of zero, both a positive zero and a negative zero, would be both wasteful and potentially confusing. How might the inclusion of both zeros cause confusion or errors within programs?

17. The IEEE floating-point format reserves several bit patterns for representing special values. For example, a 32-bit pattern that begins with 011111111 has a special meaning. Using the Data Representation Page, determine what 011111111 followed by all zeros represents. What if a pattern other than all zeros follows 011111111?

18. Assuming that a string is stored as a sequence of ASCII codes corresponding to individual characters, how would the string "CU#1" be represented?

19. Assuming that a string is stored as a sequence of ASCII codes corresponding to its individual characters, what string would be represented by the bit pattern 01001110110110111011000001110011?

20. Suppose that a library has a taped recording of a historically significant speech. What advantages would there be to converting the speech to digital format?

21. A grayscale image is one in which each pixel can be white, or black, or various shades of gray in between. Assuming that there are 256 discernible shades of gray, how many bits would a bitmap require to represent a pixel in a grayscale image? How does this number compare to those for black-and-white and color bitmaps?

22. What is the difference between a lossless format and a lossy format for storing digital images? For what type of images might one or the other be preferable?

References

Brain, Marshall. "How MP3 Files Work." January 2003. Online at http://computer.howstuffworks.com/mp3.htm.

Capron, H.L. *Computers: Tools for an Information Age*, 6th ed. Upper Saddle River, NJ: Prentice Hall, 2000.

Comer, Douglas E. *The Internet Book: Everything you need to know about computer networking and how the Internet works*, 3d ed. Upper Saddle River, NJ: Prentice Hall, 2000.

Dale, Nell, and John Lewis. *Computer Science Illuminated*. Sudbury, MA: Jones and Bartlett, 2002.

Harris, Tom. "How File Compression Works." January 2003. Online at http://computer.howstuffworks.com/file-compression.htm

Petzold, Charles. *Code: The Hidden Language of Computer Hardware and Software*. Redmond, WA: Microsoft Press, 1999.

Conditional Repetition

Chapter 13

This chapter uses narrative, examples, and hands-on exercises to introduce programming concepts and Web development skills.

It is not true that life is one damn thing after another. It's one damn thing over and over.

Edna St. Vincent Millay

We cannot always control our thoughts, but we can control our words, and repetition impresses the subconscious, and we are then master of the situation.

Florence Scovel Shinn

In Chapter 11, you were introduced to conditional execution in the form of the JavaScript if statement. Known as a ***control statement***, an if statement is used to control the execution of other JavaScript statements. A simple if statement evaluates a condition and, on the basis of the result, determines whether a program will execute a particular statement or sequence of statements. When an else case is included, the if statement instead selects from among alternative sequences of statements. If statements are useful in solving problems that involve choices—for example, deciding what letter grade a student has earned or whether or not dice doubles have been rolled.

Closely related to the concept of conditional execution is that of conditional repetition. Many problems involve repeating some task over and over until a specific condition is met. For example, you might wish to roll dice repeatedly until you get doubles or halve a number repeatedly until it is reduced to zero. The JavaScript control statement that enables conditional repetition is called the ***while loop***. A while loop is similar to an if statement in that it uses a condition (i.e., a Boolean expression) to control the execution of a statement or sequence of statements. Unlike an if statement, however, a while loop repeatedly executes the statement or statements it controls as long as the condition holds true.

In this chapter, you will learn how while loops work and how they can be incorporated into Web pages. The first while loops that you will encounter repeat their tasks a varying number of times, depending on the data being processed and its effect on the Boolean condition controlling the loop. After mastering the design of these simple loops, you will move on to loops that iterate a predetermined number of times (such loops are commonly referred to as counter driven). In the final section, you will be asked to combine while loops and counters in a page that experiments with the hailstone sequence, an interesting numerical phenomenon that has puzzled mathematicians for years.

While Loops

In Chapter 11, you created a Web page that allowed the user to simulate random dice rolls by clicking a button. This page is sufficient for obtaining a few dice combinations, but using it becomes very tedious if a large number of rolls are required. For example, one exercise in Chapter 11 involved rolling dice until doubles were obtained. Although a counter freed you from tallying the total number of rolls, you were forced to click the button over and over again until two matching die faces were displayed in the page. If you wanted to use the page to determine the likelihood of rolling doubles, you would need to repeat this experiment many times and then average the results—which would require an extremely large number of clicks.

Fortunately, JavaScript provides an additional control statement for specifying that a task should be performed repeatedly. A *while loop* resembles an if statement in that its behavior is dependent on a Boolean condition. However, the statements inside a while loop's curly braces are executed repeatedly as long as the condition remains true. The general form for a while loop is as follows:

```
while (BOOLEAN_TEST) {
        STATEMENTS_EXECUTED_AS_LONG_AS_TRUE
}
```

The statements inside the curly braces are known as the *loop body*, since these statements are controlled by the loop. When the browser encounters a while loop, it first evaluates the Boolean test. If that test succeeds (i.e., evaluates to true), then the statements inside the loop are executed in order, just as if they were enclosed in an if statement. Unlike an if statement, however, a while loop does not stop there. Once all the statements in the loop body have been executed, program control returns to the beginning of the loop. That is, the loop test is evaluated again and, if it succeeds, the statements inside the loop body are executed a second time. This process repeats until the Boolean test fails (i.e., evaluates to false).

For example, Figure 13.1 depicts JavaScript code that rolls two dice repeatedly until doubles are obtained. When executing this code, the browser begins by simulating the initial dice rolls, storing their values

```
roll1 = RandomInt(1, 6);          // simulate the dice rolls,
roll2 = RandomInt(1, 6);          // store in variables, and display
document.write("You rolled: " + roll1 + " " +roll2 + "<br />");

while (roll1 != roll2) {          // as long as you don't have doubles,
    roll1 = RandomInt(1, 6);      // roll again and display the rolls
    roll2 = RandomInt(1, 6);
    document.write("You rolled: " + roll1 + " " +roll2 + "<br />");
}
document.write("DOUBLES!");       // display the fact that you have doubles
```

Figure 13.1 A while loop to roll dice until doubles are obtained.

in variables roll1 and roll2, and displaying the results. Upon reaching the while loop, the browser first evaluates the loop test to determine whether the two rolls are different. If so, then the loop test succeeds (evaluates to true), and the statements inside the loop body are executed. After completing an iteration of the loop body, the browser evaluates the loop test again to determine whether the new dice values are different. As long as the rolls do not equal each other, the browser will repeatedly execute the loop body, rolling the dice and displaying their values. Eventually, the dice combination will be doubles, causing the loop test to fail (evaluate to false) and the loop to terminate. When this finally occurs, the browser will reach the last statement, which displays the message "DOUBLES!" (Figure 13.2).

```
You rolled: 6 4
You rolled: 4 1
You rolled: 2 4
You rolled: 6 3
You rolled: 5 2
You rolled: 1 5
You rolled: 5 2
You rolled: 6 5
You rolled: 1 2
You rolled: 5 5
DOUBLES!
```

Figure 13.2   Example output from the code in Figure 13.1.

Common errors to avoid...

Beginning students often confuse if statements and while loops. This mistake is somewhat understandable, since the two control statements look so much alike. *Don't be thrown by this apparent similarity*—if statements and while loops are very different. Depending on the result of an if statement's Boolean test, the corresponding statements are executed either once or not at all. By contrast, a while loop implies repetition. The statements in the loop body are executed repeatedly as long as the loop test succeeds.

Technically, the curly braces in a while loop are optional if the loop body contains only one statement to be executed. As was the case with if statements, however, we *strongly* recommend that you include curly braces in every while loop you write. This practice maintains consistency and prevents you from introducing errors if you modify the code later on. We also suggest that you indent the statements inside each loop to emphasize the structure of the code.

Figure 13.3 depicts an event-driven page that incorporates the while loop from Figure 13.1. By clicking the "Roll until doubles" button, the user initiates function RollUntil, which simulates rolling two dice until doubles are obtained. We have modified the code from Figure 13.1 so that, instead of using write statements, the page displays the result of each roll in a text area. This enables the user to perform repeated experiments without reloading the page. Figure 13.4 shows the roll.html page rendered in a Web browser.

EXERCISE 13.1

Enter the roll.html text from Figure 13.3 into a new Web page. After loading this page, click the button to verify that the code repeatedly simulates and displays dice rolls until doubles are obtained.

One troublesome feature of the code in roll.html is redundancy. Before the while test can be evaluated the first time, the page must roll the dice and display the result. Then, the same code for simulating and displaying dice rolls must be placed inside the loop. In programming, redundancy is not just annoying—it's dangerous. Imagine that, after writing the code in Figure 13.3, you wanted to modify its behavior—for example, by switching from six-sided to eight-sided dice. To successfully implement the new version, you would need to change the code at multiple locations (first altering the initial roll1 and roll2 assignments, then making the same adjustments to the assignments inside the loop body). In this particular example, accommodating the redundant code might seem trivial. However, as you begin to work on larger applications, it becomes increasingly difficult to ensure that

```
1.   <html>
2.   <!-- roll.html                                      Dave Reed -->
3.   <!-- This page simulates dice rolls until doubles are obtained. -->
4.   <!------------------------------------------------------------>
5.
6.   <head>
7.     <title> Dice Stats </title>
8.     <script type="text/javascript"
9.             src="http://www.prenhall.com/reed/random.js">
10.    </script>
11.    <script type="text/javascript">
12.        function RollUntilDoubles()
13.        // Assumes: document.DiceForm.Output is available for output
14.        // Results: rolls and displays dice until doubles are obtained
15.        {
16.          var roll1, roll2;
17.
18.          roll1 = RandomInt(1, 6);              // roll and display dice
19.          roll2 = RandomInt(1, 6);
20.          document.DiceForm.Output.value =
21.            "You rolled: " + roll1 + " " + roll2 + "\n";
22.
23.          while (roll1 != roll2) {              // while not doubles,
24.            roll1 = RandomInt(1, 6);            //    roll again and display
25.            roll2 = RandomInt(1, 6);
26.            document.DiceForm.Output.value =
27.              document.DiceForm.Output.value +
28.              "You rolled: " + roll1 + " " + roll2 + "\n";
29.          }
30.          document.DiceForm.Output.value =
31.            document.DiceForm.Output.value + "DOUBLES!";
32.        }
33.    </script>
34.  </head>
35.
36.  <body>
37.    <div style="text-align:center">
38.      <form name="DiceForm">
39.        <input type="button" value="Roll until doubles"
40.               onClick="RollUntilDoubles();" />
41.        <br /><br />
42.        <textarea name=Output rows=20 cols=20 wrap="virtual"></textarea>
43.      </form>
44.    </div>
45.  </body>
46.  </html>
```

Figure 13.3 Event-driven page for rolling dice until doubles are obtained.

you've updated every copy of a particular code sequence. To avoid such consistency problems, it is always desirable to remove redundancy from code.

Clearly, code for rolling the dice must appear inside the loop, since this is where the repeated rolls occur. However, it is possible to omit the initial dice-rolling code that appears before the loop. The variables roll1 and roll2 must be initialized to some values before the loop test can be evaluated, but these values do not need to be actual dice rolls. As long as the variables are assigned values that cause the loop test to succeed, the page will execute the loop body and begin rolling the dice. Assigning explicit values to variables so that a loop test initially succeeds is known as "priming the loop."

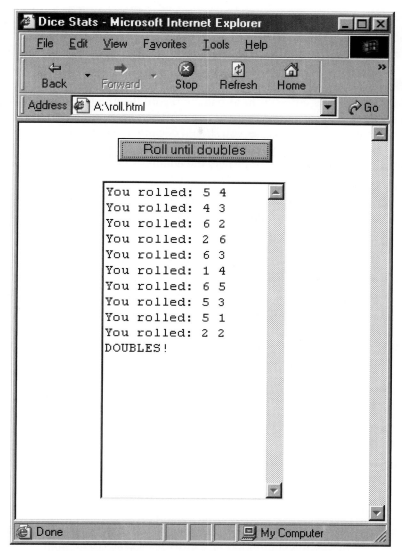

Figure 13.4 `roll.html` rendered in a Web browser.

Figure 13.5 contains a modified version of the while loop from Figure 13.1 that omits the redundant code. Here, the loop is primed by assigning `roll1` and `roll2` different values: −1 and −2, respectively. The choice of negative numbers in the assignments makes it obvious to the user that these are not "real" rolls, but simply initial values for priming the loop. Since these numbers do not equal each other, the loop test will succeed, and the first "real" roll will occur and be displayed inside the loop.

```
roll1 = -1;                    // prime the loop by assigning
roll2 = -2;                    // initial values to variables

while (roll1 != roll2) {       // as long as the roll is not doubles,
    roll1 = RandomInt(1, 6);   // roll again and display the result
    roll2 = RandomInt(1, 6);
    document.write("You rolled: " + roll1 + " " +roll2 + "<br />");
}
```

Figure 13.5 Primed while loop for rolling dice until doubles are obtained.

EXERCISE 13.2

Modify your `roll.html` page so that it incorporates the technique of "priming the loop" shown in Figure 13.5. Then, load the page and verify that the code behaves as before.

EXERCISE 13.3

Add a counter to your `roll.html` page to record the number of rolls that occur before doubles are obtained. Recall that a counter consists of a variable that is initialized to zero and incremented every time some event occurs. In this case, you should declare and initialize the counter variable in the `RollUntil` function, then add code to increment the counter each time the dice are rolled. When doubles are finally obtained, your page should display the counter's current value in an appropriately labeled text box.

As we mentioned earlier, there is a 1-in-6 chance of obtaining doubles when you roll two dice simultaneously. This suggests that, if you rolled a pair of dice many times, roughly one-sixth of those rolls would be doubles. It also implies that, on average, it should take your page six rolls to produce doubles. Of course, there may be times when doubles come up very quickly—for example, in one or two rolls. However, these lucky instances will be offset by unlucky ones, in which your page requires more than six rolls to achieve doubles. Use your page to conduct 20 different experiments, counting how many times it takes to obtain doubles each time. Are your results consistent with the universal odds of rolling doubles?

The while loop in your `roll.html` page causes the dice to be rolled repeatedly until doubles are obtained. However, by modifying the loop test, you could use the same code to roll for any dice combination. For example, changing the loop test to (`roll1 + roll2 != 7`) would cause the code to loop as long as the sum of the dice is not 7. This means that the page would continue rolling until a combination totaling 7 appeared.

EXERCISE 13.4

Modify your `roll.html` page so that it rolls the dice until their combined sum equals 7. Then, use this new page to conduct 20 different experiments, counting how many rolls it takes to obtain a 7 each time. Report your results. On average, a 7 should appear after six rolls. Do your results support this claim? Explain.

Make a similar modification to your page, causing it to roll the dice until their combined sum equals 2. Use your page to conduct 20 different experiments, counting how many rolls it takes to obtain a 2 each time. Report your results. On average, a 2 should appear after 36 rolls. Do your results support this claim? Explain.

Finally, modify your page so that it rolls the dice until both faces equal 4. Use your page to conduct 20 different experiments, counting how many rolls it takes to obtain double 4s each time. Report your results. On average, double 4s should appear after 36 rolls. Do your results support this claim? Explain.

EXERCISE 13.5

Lotteries have been described as "a tax on the gullible." In general, the odds of winning a lottery are so infinitesimal that the cost of the lottery ticket far exceeds the expected payoff. For example, consider a PICK-4 game in which players must select four digits in a specific order. Since any number between 0000 and 9999 might appear, the likelihood that any particular four-digit sequence will be drawn is 1 in 10,000. If the payoff the winner receives is less than $10,000 on a $1 ticket, then the odds are not in the player's favor.

Create a Web page named `lottery.html` that repeatedly simulates PICK-4 lottery drawings until a specific sequence is obtained. The user should be able to enter the desired sequence in a series of four text boxes, then click a button to see how many drawings the page had to perform before their sequence came up. The appearance of your page should resemble that of Figure 13.6.

A common misconception about lotteries is that a distinctive sequence, such as 0-0-0-0, is less likely to occur than a random-looking sequence, such as 3-7-5-2. In reality, each number sequence has the same probability of appearing. It just so happens that there are many more "random-looking" sequences than there are distinctive sequences.

Use your page to conduct 20 different experiments, each time counting how many drawings it takes to obtain 0-0-0-0. Report your results.

Next, pick your favorite four-digit combination and conduct an additional 20 experiments. Report your results. On average, did it require a smaller number of picks to acquire this sequence than were needed to obtain 0-0-0-0? Should it?

 Common errors to avoid...

In English, descriptions of repetitive tasks usually focus on the stopping condition for the loop—an activity recurs *until something happens*. Conversely, the loop test in a while loop specifies the condition under which the loop continues—an activity recurs *as long as something does not happen*. Thus, when you define a test for conditional repetition, the condition you specify should be the exact opposite of the condition as you would state it in English. For example, the task of rolling dice until doubles are obtained requires a while loop whose test is (roll1 != roll2), which tells the page to keep rolling as long as you *don't* have doubles. Likewise, the task of rolling until a 7 is obtained requires the loop test (roll1 + roll2 != 7)—i.e., keep rolling as long as the dice values *don't* total 7.

Deriving the appropriate loop test can be especially tricky if the stopping condition involves logical connectives. For example, consider the task of rolling dice until either a 7 or 11 is obtained. The loop test must specify the condition under which neither total has occurred:

    (roll1+roll2 != 7 && roll1+roll2 != 11)

Note that we employ the && operator here, representing AND. As long as both conditions hold (the total is not 7 and also not 11), the loop should continue to execute.

Figure 13.6 Sample appearance of lottery.html page.

Counter-Driven Loops

While loops facilitate conditional repetition within a program, allowing you to specify a sequence of statements that you want repeatedly executed as long as some condition holds. Since a while loop is controlled by a condition, it is usually impossible to predict the number of repetitions that will occur. As an example, consider your roll.html page that simulated rolling dice until doubles were obtained. In some instances, the first dice roll might produce doubles, causing the loop to terminate after one iteration. On the other hand, it might take tens or even hundreds of rolls to obtain doubles.

Although this kind of unpredictable repetition is ideal for some problems, others involve a predetermined number of loop iterations. In these cases, some action must be carried out a certain number of times in order to complete a task. For example, instead of rolling dice until you obtain doubles, you might want to roll the dice a specific number of times and record the number of doubles that appear. If you rolled the dice 1,000 times, you would expect to obtain roughly 167 doubles (one out of every six rolls). Alternatively, you could roll the dice 1000 times and compare the number of rolls that equaled 7 to the number of rolls that equaled 2. Since six times as many combinations yield 7 as yield 2, you would expect your 2s count to be roughly one-sixth of your 7s count.

If you want to perform a task involving a specific number of repetitions, you can implement a **counter-driven loop**—i.e., a while loop whose test is based on a counter. The counter associated with a counter-driven loop is designed to record the number of times the loop has executed, so we can think of it as a repetition counter. The loop test should be tied to the counter, stopping the loop once the counter's value equals the desired number of repetitions. In general, the following loop structure can be used to execute a sequence of statements some predefined number of times:

```
repCount = 0;
while (repCount < DESIRED_NUMBER_OF_REPETITIONS) {
    STATEMENTS_FOR_CARRYING_OUT_DESIRED_TASK
    repCount = repCount + 1;
}
```

Note that the repetition counter is initialized to 0 before the loop begins and then incremented at the end of the loop body. Thus, the counter will keep track of how many times the statements in the loop body have been executed. When the number of repetitions reaches the number indicated in the condition, the loop test will fail, and the loop will terminate.

Figure 13.7 provides two examples of counter-driven while loops. In the first example, the statements in the loop body are executed 100 times, displaying the word "HOWDY!" on a separate line

```
repCount = 0;                          // initialize the repetition counter
while (repCount < 100) {               // as long as < 100 repetitions
    document.write("HOWDY!<br />");    //   write "HOWDY!"

    repCount = repCount + 1;           // increase the repetition counter
}

-----------------------------------------------------------------------

repCount = 0;                          // initialize the repetition counter
while (repCount < 1000) {              // as long as < 1000 repetitions
    roll1 = randomInt(1, 6);           // simulate and display the rolls
    roll2 = randomInt(1, 6);
    document.write("You rolled: " + roll1 + " " +roll2 + "<br />");

    repCount = repCount + 1;           // increase the repetition counter
}
```

Figure 13.7 Examples of counter-driven loops.

each time. In the second example, the statements in the loop body are executed 1,000 times, simulating a dice roll and displaying the result each time.

The Web page in Figure 13.8 incorporates a counter-driven loop similar to the second example in Figure 13.7. To initiate the loop code, the user enters a desired number of dice rolls in a text box and then clicks a button. This event invokes function RollRepeatedly, which simulates the specified number of rolls. The if statement inside the loop body tests the result of each roll and, if doubles are obtained, increments a separate counter. After performing the desired number of rolls, the loop terminates, and the value of the doubles counter is displayed in a separate text box. The resulting Web page is shown in Figure 13.9.

EXERCISE 13.6

Enter the stats.html text from Figure 13.8 into a new Web page. After loading this page, click the button to verify that the code behaves as described.

Use your page to count the number of doubles that occur during 60 dice rolls. Conduct this experiment 10 times and report the results. Are the counts from the 10 different experiments fairly consistent? Is each result close to the expected number of doubles ($60*1/6 = 10$)?

Increase the number of rolls from 60 to 600 and then perform 10 more experiments. Are the counts more consistent than those you obtained from 60 rolls? Are they closer to the expected number of doubles ($600*1/6 = 100$)? Should they be? Explain.

Increase the number of rolls from 600 to 6,000 and then perform 10 more experiments. Are the counts more consistent than those you obtained from 600 rolls? Are they closer to the expected number of doubles ($6,000*1/6 = 1000$)? Should they be? Explain.

EXERCISE 13.7

Modify your stats.html page so that, in addition to recording the number of doubles, it also counts the number of 7s and the number of 2s obtained. This will require adding two counters to the RollRepeatedly function, as well as two text boxes for displaying the new counts.

If you roll the dice a large number of times, roughly one-sixth of the rolls should equal 7 and 1/36th of the rolls should equal 2. Conduct several experiments with your page to verify this outcome. Are the counts more consistent as you increase the number of rolls?

Variables and Repetition

As we demonstrated in the previous section, you can design a while loop that iterates a specific number of times by using a counter variable to control the loop test. However, this represents only one option for creating while loops with predictable executions. In fact, any variable can be employed to control the number of loop repetitions, and the variable can be updated in various ways. For example, consider the while loop in Figure 13.10, which displays a simple countdown in a Web page. The while loop is controlled by the test (count > 0). As long as this test evaluates to true, the code in the loop body will be executed repeatedly. Imagine that the user entered 10 at the prompt. Since count's initial value is 10, the loop test succeeds and the loop body is executed: the statements inside the loop display 10 in the page and then decrement the value of count. After the loop body completes, the loop test is evaluated again using the current value of count (i.e., 9). Since the test still succeeds, the code inside the loop is executed: 9 is displayed and the value of count is decremented. This process repeats until the tenth iteration through the loop, when the value 1 is displayed and count is decremented to become 0. At this point, the loop test fails and the while loop terminates. The browser then advances to the statement immediately following the while loop, which displays the message "BLASTOFF!"

```
1.  <html>
2.  <!-- stats.html                                  Dave Reed -->
3.  <!-- This page simulates dice rolls and maintains stats. -->
4.  <!------------------------------------------------------->
5.
6.  <head>
7.    <title> Dice Stats </title>
8.    <script type="text/javascript"
9.            src="http://www.prenhall.com/reed/random.js">
10.   </script>
11.   <script type="text/javascript">
12.       function RollRepeatedly()
13.       // Assumes: document.DiceForm.reps contains a number
14.       // Results: simulates that many dice rolls, displays # of doubles
15.       {
16.         var doubleCount, totalRolls, repCount, roll1, roll2;
17.
18.         doubleCount = 0;                          // initialize the counter
19.         totalRolls = parseFloat(document.DiceForm.reps.value);
20.
21.         repCount = 0;
22.         while (repCount < totalRolls) {           // repeatedly:
23.             roll1 = RandomInt(1, 6);              // simulate the dice rolls
24.             roll2 = RandomInt(1, 6);
25.
26.             if (roll1 == roll2) {                 // if doubles,
27.                 doubleCount = doubleCount + 1;    //   increment the counter
28.             }
29.
30.             repCount = repCount + 1;              // incr. repetition counter
31.         }
32.
33.         document.DiceForm.count.value = doubleCount;  // display # doubles
34.       }
35.   </script>
36. </head>
37.
38. <body>
39.   <div style="text-align:center">
40.       <h2>Dice Stats</h2>
41.
42.     <form name="DiceForm">
43.     Desired number of rolls =
44.     <input type="text" name="reps" size=6 value=1000 />
45.     <br /><br />
46.     <input type="button" value="Click to Roll" onClick="RollRepeatedly();" />
47.     <br /><br />
48.     Number of doubles obtained =
49.     <input type="text" name="count" size=6 value=0 />
50.     </form>
51.   </div>
52. </body>
53. </html>
```

Figure 13.8 Counter-driven loop for rolling dice a specific number of times.

Figure 13.9 `stats.html` rendered in a Web browser.

 ## Common errors to avoid...

As we have explained, the browser will repeatedly execute statements in the body of a while loop as long as the loop test succeeds (evaluates to true). Therefore, it is possible to define a while loop that never terminates. For example, suppose you wrote a counter-driven while loop, but forgot to increment the repetition counter inside the loop.

```
repCount = 0;
while (repCount < 100) {
    document.write("HOWDY!<br />");
}
```

Since the repetition counter is initialized to zero and never incremented, the loop test (`repCount < 100`) will always be true. Such a loop is known as an ***infinite loop*** or, more colorfully, a ***black hole loop***. If you are not familiar with astronomy, a black hole is a collapsed star whose gravitational field is so strong that it pulls matter and even light into it. Once inside the "event horizon" of a black hole, there is no way to escape its gravitational pull. Similarly, after the above while loop's test succeeds, execution becomes trapped in the loop and can never move on. When defining while loops, you must be very careful to avoid infinite loops. In particular, the loop body must contain code that affects the loop test in some way (for example, a counter-driven loop must include statements that modify the repetition counter). Otherwise, an infinite loop is sure to occur.

If you accidentally write a page that contains an infinite loop, clicking the browser's `Stop` button will sometimes break the loop, allowing you to fix the logic error and reload the page. If the `Stop` button doesn't work, you will need to close the browser completely and then restart.

```
count = prompt("Enter the start of the countdown", "10");
count = parseFloat(count);

while (count > 0) {
  document.write(count + "<br />");
  count = count - 1;
}
document.write("BLASTOFF!");
```

```
10
9
8
7
6
5
4
3
2
1
BLASTOFF!
```

Figure 13.10 Counter-driven loop that counts backward.

EXERCISE 13.8

Predict the output sequences that would be produced by each of the following while loops.

```
count = 10;
while (count > 0) {
    document.write(count + "<br />");
    count = count - 2;
}
document.write("DONE WITH FIRST!");

num = 1;
while (num <= 5) {
    document.write(num + "<br />");
    num = num + 1;
}
document.write("DONE WITH SECOND!");

x = 1;
y = 10;
while (x < y) {
    document.write(x + " " + y + "<br />");
    x = x + 1;
    y = y - 2;
}
document.write("DONE WITH THIRD!");
```

The Web page in Figure 13.11 contains a generalized, event-driven version of the countdown loop from Figure 13.10. The user can enter the starting number for the countdown in a text box, then click a button to see the countdown displayed in a text area. Note that in Figure 13.12, the user specified a starting number larger than the number of rows in the text area. In such a case, where the amount of output exceeds the text area size, the browser provides a scroll bar so that the user can scroll through the complete output.

EXERCISE 13.9

Enter the count.html text from Figure 13.11 into a new Web page. After loading this page, experiment with it by changing the contents of the text box and verifying that the code behaves as described.

Once you have done this, modify the page so that, instead of decrementing count by 1, the code halves count's value during each loop iteration (any fractional values should be rounded down). For example, the starting value 10 would be halved to 5, then 2, then 1, and finally 0.

EXERCISE 13.10

Recall that Chapter 8 described the binary search algorithm for finding a particular entry in an ordered list. The idea behind binary search is to begin looking in the exact center of the list. If the

```
1.  <html>
2.  <!-- count.html                                    Dave Reed -->
3.  <!-- This page displays a countdown in a text area.       -->
4.  <!------------------------------------------------------>
5.
6.  <head>
7.    <title> Countdown </title>
8.    <script type="text/javascript">
9.      function Countdown()
10.     // Assumes: document.CountForm.count contains a number
11.     // Results: displays countdown from that number in document.CountForm.Output
12.     {
13.         var count;
14.
15.         count = parseFloat(document.CountForm.count.value); // GET INITIAL VALUE
16.         document.CountForm.Output.value = "";               // CLEAR TEXT AREA
17.
18.         while (count > 0) {                         // WHILE NOT AT 0,
19.             document.CountForm.Output.value =       //    DISPLAY COUNT
20.                 document.CountForm.Output.value + count + "\n";
21.             count = count - 1;                      //    AND DECREMENT
22.         }
23.
24.         document.CountForm.Output.value =
25.             document.CountForm.Output.value + "BLASTOFF!";
26.     }
27.   </script>
28. </head>
29.
30. <body>
31.   <div style="text-align:center">
32.     <form name="CountForm">
33.       Start of the countdown: <input type="text" name="count" size=4 value=10 />
34.       <br /><br />
35.       <input type="button" value="Begin Countdown" onClick="Countdown();" />
36.       <br /><br />
37.       <textarea name="Output" rows=15 cols=40 wrap="virtual"></textarea>
38.     </form>
39.   </div>
40. </body>
41. </html>
```

Figure 13.11 Event-driven page for performing a countdown.

desired entry comes before the middle entry in the list's organizational scheme, then you can eliminate all entries beyond the middle and repeat the process on the remaining half of the list. Similarly, if the desired entry comes after the middle entry, you can eliminate all entries before the middle and repeat the process on the remaining half. Every time you perform a comparison, you reduce the size of the list by one half; eventually, you either locate the desired entry or determine that it isn't in the list.

Now that you understand how the binary search algorithm works, you can use your modified count.html page to determine how many checks are needed to locate an item in a particular ordered list. If you enter a list size in the text box, the sequence of numbers displayed in the text area will represent the remaining size of the list to be searched after each successive inspection. Thus, the number of values in the text area will be one more than the number of checks required to find an entry in the worse case. To more easily identify this necessary number of checks, add a counter to your count.html page that records how many times the value is halved before reaching 0. When the countdown completes, the browser should display the counter's value below the sequence in the text area. For example, if the initial value of count were 10, your page would produce the following output:

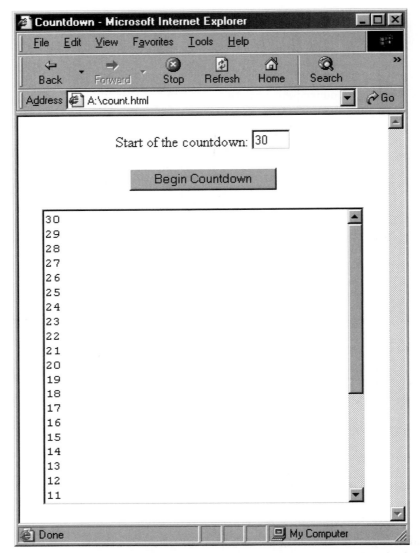

Figure 13.12 `count.html` rendered in a Web browser. Note that the number of lines in the countdown exceeds the size of the text area, so a scroll bar is provided to allow the user to scroll through all of the lines.

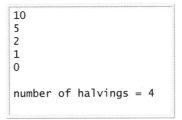

Use your modified `count.html` page to determine how many times the following numbers must be halved (and, if necessary, rounded down) before reaching 0.

     32

     64

    128

6000
281000000
6000000000

The last three numbers in this exercise approximate the size of a small university's student body, the U.S. population, and the world population, respectively. Thus, the results you obtained represent the maximum number of binary search comparisons required to find an entry in listings of these populations.

Designer Secrets

Like if statements, while loops control the execution of other statements. Whenever a program needs to perform some task (potentially) more than once, you should include a while loop. The loop test must specify the logical condition under which the program should keep looping.

If the task involves a specific number of repetitions that can be determined ahead of time, then a counter-driven while loop is needed. To implement a counter-driven loop, you must initialize the counter variable before the loop, compare the counter's value against the desired number of repetitions in the loop test, and increment the counter at the end of the loop.

Example: Generating Hailstone Sequences

An interesting unsolved problem in mathematics concerns what is called the "hailstone sequence." The following algorithm defines this sequence:

1. Start with any positive integer.
2. If that number is odd, then multiply it by three and add one; otherwise, divide it by two.
3. Repeat as many times as desired.

For example, the hailstone sequence starting with 5 is:

5, 16, 8, 4, 2, 1, 4, 2, 1, 4, 2, 1, . . .

Note that the hailstone sequence eventually reaches the pattern 4-2-1, which then loops indefinitely. Similarly, the hailstone sequence starting with 15 is:

15, 46, 23, 70, 35, 106, 53, 160, 80, 40, 20, 10, 5, 16, 8, 4, 2, 1, 4, 2, 1, . . .

It is conjectured that, no matter what positive integer you start with, you will always end up in the 4-2-1 loop. In experimenting with hailstone sequences, mathematicians have demonstrated that this hypothesis holds for all starting values up to 1,200,000,000,000 (and probably higher by the time you read this). However, the conjecture has yet to be proven true for all numbers.

EXERCISE 13.11

Create a Web page named hail.html that computes and displays hailstone sequences. The user should be able to enter a positive integer in a text box and then click a button. When the button is clicked, the hailstone sequence starting with the input number should appear in a separate text area, one number per line. If the sequence gets to 1 (meaning it is stuck in the 4-2-1 loop), then your code should print the word "STUCK!" in the text area and terminate. Include a variable that records and displays the length of the hailstone sequence (up to the point where 1 is reached). For example, the hailstone sequence starting with 5 would be displayed as:

5
16

```
8
4
2
1
STUCK!
Hailstone sequence length: 6
```

[*Hint*: There are many different ways to test whether a number is even or odd. For example, if num/2 is equal to Math.floor(num/2), then num is an even number. Likewise, since the % operator computes the remainder left over after division, the expression (num % 2 == 0), evaluates to true only if num is even.]

EXERCISE 13.12

Using your hail.html page, answer the following questions:

- What is the smallest starting number that generates a hailstone sequence with a length of at least 15?
- Identify a starting number for which the hailstone sequence is at least 30 numbers long. What is the length of the sequence? If you add or subtract 1 from this starting number, how long are the hailstone sequences associated with the new starting numbers?
- What is the length of the hailstone sequence starting at 100? Starting at 200? Starting at 400?
- In general, if the hailstone sequence starting at some number N has length L, how long would the hailstone sequence starting at $2N$ be? Explain your reasoning.

Looking Ahead...

In this chapter, you were introduced to the while loop, which specifies conditional repetition in JavaScript code. Like an if statement, a while loop is a control statement that relies on a Boolean test. However, a while loop is functionally different in that it specifies repetition—the statements in the body of a while loop will be executed repeatedly as long as the loop test evaluates to true. While loops are useful for any situation in which some task must be executed more than once. Often, the number of repetitions that the loop will perform is not known ahead of time, but is instead based on some condition—for example, a loop that rolls dice repeatedly as long as doubles haven't been obtained. Other while loops are designed to repeat a predetermined number of times—for example, a loop that rolls dice 1,000 times and counts doubles. In either case, a while loop can control the repeated execution of the necessary statements.

The next chapter, Chapter 14, returns to the hardware side of computing, focusing on how the physical components of a computer work together to produce the complex behaviors we observe. As we first observed in Chapter 8, repetition plays a central role in this process. The central processing unit (CPU) repeatedly fetches and executes machine-language instructions from memory. Although each instruction represents a simple operation (such as adding two numbers or moving data from one memory location to another), the overall effect of executing millions or even billions of such instructions in a second can be exceedingly complex. In Chapter 14, you will study the internal workings of the computer, focusing on the components defined by the von Neumann architecture (CPU, memory, and input/output devices) and their interactions. Using software simulators that accompany the chapter, you will be able to visualize and experiment with the behavior of the components.

Chapter Summary

- A while loop is a control statement that specifies conditional repetition. A while loop is similar to an if statement in that its behavior is dependent on a Boolean condition. Unlike an if statement, however, a while loop repeatedly executes the statement(s) it controls as long as the condition remains true.

- The general form for a while loop is as follows:

```
while (BOOLEAN_TEST) {
    STATEMENTS_EXECUTED_AS_LONG_AS_TRUE
}
```

The statements inside the curly braces are known as the loop body. If the loop test succeeds (evaluates to true), then the statements in the loop body are executed. After iterating through the loop, the browser returns to the beginning of the while loop and reevaluates the loop test. This process repeats until the loop test fails (evaluates to false).

- Even though they look similar, while loops and if statements are very different control statements—an if statement executes the statement(s) it controls either once or not at all, whereas a while loop can execute its statement(s) repeatedly.

- A counter-driven while loop can be used to repeat some programmatic task a specified number of times. The general form for a counter-driven loop is as follows:

```
repCount = 0;
while (repCount < DESIRED_NUMBER_OF_REPETITIONS) {
    STATEMENTS_FOR_CARRYING_OUT_DESIRED_TASK

    repCount = repCount + 1;
}
```

- Infinite loops (or black hole loops) are while loops that never terminate—i.e., their conditions never evaluate to false. To avoid creating an infinite loop, you must ensure that the loop body contains code that affects the loop test in some way (for example, by incrementing the repetition counter).

Supplemental Material and Exercises

More Practice with Loops

Exercise 13.10 involved experimenting with a while loop that repeatedly halved a value. As you tested various values, you learned that repeatedly halving a number (and rounding down) reduces it to 0 very quickly. For example, a large number such as 1,000 needs to be halved only 10 times before reaching 0. Note that, every time you double the size of the starting number, the number of halvings needed to reach zero increases by one. This means that even extremely large values can be reduced to 0 in a relatively small number of halvings (e.g., 2,000 is reduced to 0 in 11 halvings, 4,000 is reduced to 0 in 12 halvings, …, 10 billion is reduced to 0 in 34 halvings). As the following exercise demonstrates, the opposite principle is also true—if you start with a small number and repeatedly double it, it doesn't take long for that number to get extremely large.

EXERCISE 13.13

Consider a sheet of paper. If you fold the paper in half, then the resulting doubled sheet is twice as thick. Likewise, if you fold the sheet in half again, the thickness is doubled again (and becomes four times greater than that of the original sheet). Starting with a standard sheet of paper, how many folds do you think it would take before the paper's thickness equaled the distance between the earth and the sun (roughly 93 million miles)? Of course, this hypothetical question assumes that the original sheet is large enough and that you are strong enough to keep folding!

Create a Web page named fold.html that determines the number of folds required for a folded paper's thickness to reach from the earth to the sun. You should start with the initial thickness of a piece of paper (assume 0.002 inches) and then repeatedly double that value until it reaches 93 million miles (recall that a mile equals 5,280 feet and a foot equals 12 inches). Declare a counter variable to record the number of folds, and report the final count as your answer.

EXERCISE 13.14

In the spirit of the Old MacDonald page you wrote in Chapter 4, create a Web page named `bottles.html` that displays verses of the song "100 bottles of *root beer* on the wall" (you may insert your favorite beverage). The page should contain a text box in which the user can enter the initial number of bottles. You should also provide a button that, when clicked, calls a function to display (in a text area) the sequence of verses starting with the specified number of bottles. For example, if the user entered the number 100, your page might display:

```
100 bottles of root beer on the wall.
100 bottles of root beer.
Take one down, pass it around.
99 bottles of root beer on the wall.

99 bottles of root beer on the wall.
99 bottles of root beer.
Take one down, pass it around.
98 bottles of root beer on the wall.

. . .

1 bottle of root beer on the wall.
1 bottle of root beer.
Take one down, pass it around.
0 bottles of root beer on the wall.
```

[*Hint:* The variable that drives your loop test should be initialized to the number of bottles entered by the user and then decremented during each iteration of the loop. Within the loop body, include statements that display the verse associated with the variable's current value.]

More Dice Examples

Numerous exercises in this chapter demonstrated that some dice totals are more likely to occur than others. For example, if you rolled a pair of dice repeatedly, you would expect to obtain roughly six times more 7s than 2s. This is because six different dice combinations total to 7, whereas only one combination totals to 2. Figure 13.13 lists every total that can be obtained by rolling two dice, as well as the combinations that yield each total.

The symmetry associated with these combinations suggests that 7, in addition to being the most likely roll, is also the most likely average of multiple rolls. Since there is an equal probability of your combination totaling 2 and 12, 3 and 11, and so on, these numbers balance out. If you rolled the dice many times and averaged the results, you would expect to get 7 (or a value very close to 7).

EXERCISE 13.15

Create a Web page named `avg.html` that simulates a large number of dice rolls and computes the average of the dice totals. The user should be able to enter a number of rolls in a text box and then click a button, which should call a function to simulate the rolls and compute the average. Once calculated, the average should be displayed in a separate text box.

[*Hint:* To compute the average, you must maintain a running sum of the dice rolls. Start by declaring a variable and initializing it to 0 (as you would with a counter). Each time the page simulates a dice roll, add the combined total of the two dice to the variable. Once the loop terminates, divide the sum of all your dice combinations by the number of dice rolls to determine the average roll.]

After implementing your page, use it to answer the following questions. What is the average of 100 dice rolls? 1,000 dice rolls? 10,000 dice rolls? Is there a pattern to the numbers you obtain? Should there be?

Dice Total	Number of Combinations	Possible Combinations
2	1	1-1
3	2	1-2, 2-1
4	3	1-3, 2-2, 3-1
5	4	1-4, 2-3, 3-2, 4-1
6	5	1-5, 2-4, 3-3, 4-2, 5-1
7	6	1-6, 2-5, 3-4, 4-3, 5-2, 6-1
8	5	2-6, 3-5, 4-4, 5-3, 6-2
9	4	3-6, 4-5, 5-4, 6-3
10	3	4-6, 5-5, 6-4
11	2	5-6, 6-5
12	1	6-6

Figure 13.13 Probability of obtaining various dice combinations.

If you have ever been to a casino or watched a gangster movie, you are probably familiar with the game of craps. Craps is a game in which players win or lose depending on the dice combinations they roll. The player's initial roll is known as his point. The point can be an immediate winner (7 or 11) or an immediate loser (2 or 3). If the player's point does not equal one of these game-ending totals, then the player must continue rolling until he either rolls his point again (a winner) or obtains a 7 (a loser).

For example, the following sequence of rolls would cause the player to win.

```
Initial roll:  6   (player's point)
Next roll:    10
Next roll:     4
Next roll:    11
Next roll:     6
WINNER!
```

Generalized code for representing a craps game is provided in Figure 13.14.

EXERCISE 13.16

Create a Web page named `craps.html` that simulates a game of craps. When the user clicks a button, this event should call a function that rolls the dice until the player wins or loses. When implementing this function, use the above generalized code as a guide. The value of each roll should be displayed in a text area, along with a message indicating whether the player won or lost.

For Loops

In this chapter, you examined several examples of counter-driven while loops, in which the following basic form was used to repeat a sequence of code a specific number of times.

```
repCount = 0;
while (repCount < DESIRED_NUMBER_OF_REPETITIONS) {
    STATEMENTS_FOR_CARRYING_OUT_THE_TASK

    repCount = repCount + 1;
}
```

```
myPoint = SUM OF TWO DIE ROLLS
if (myPoint IS 7 OR 11) {
    WINNER!
}
else if (myPoint IS 2 OR 3) {
    LOSER!
}
else {
    while (HAVEN'T ROLLED myPoint OR 7) {
        ROLL THE DICE
    }
    if (ROLLED myPoint) {
        WINNER!
    }
    else {
        LOSER!
    }
}
```

Figure 13.14 Generalized code for determining the outcome of a craps game. Actual JavaScript code must replace descriptive text in the appropriate places before this code could be executed.

By specifying different code in the loop body and a desired number of repetitions, you were able to implement various counter-driven applications. Since this kind of counter-driven loop is common, JavaScript provides a variant of while loops that captures the pattern more succinctly. The following represents the general form of this variant, which is called a *for loop*:

```
for (repCount=0; repCount<DESIRED_NUMBER_OF_REPETITIONS; repCount=repCount+1) {
    STATEMENTS_FOR_CARRYING_OUT_THE_TASK
}
```

A for loop incorporates all the components of a counter-driven loop, but also makes the loop more compact and easier to read. In particular, the steps involving the loop counter—initialization, testing, and incrementing—are isolated on one line, separated by semicolons. Since these statements control the behavior of the loop, listing them together emphasizes the loop's characteristics. In addition, separating the loop control statements from the actual code to be executed in the body (i.e., inside the curly braces) makes it easier for someone reviewing the code to focus on the actions performed by the loop.

Despite these formatting differences, the behavior of a for loop is identical to that of its while loop counterpart. Upon encountering a for loop, the browser executes the first component of the loop header, which initializes the value of the loop counter. Then, the loop test (the loop header's second component) is evaluated; if the test succeeds, then the statements inside the loop body are executed. After iterating through the loop body, the browser increments the loop counter (this action is represented by the loop header's third component). Finally, the loop test is reevaluated, possibly causing the loop body to execute again.

To illustrate the interchangeability of for loops and counter-driven while loops, we designed the for loops in Figure 13.15 to perform tasks identical to those of the counter-driven while loops in Figure 13.7.

EXERCISE 13.17

Reimplement your stats.html page, replacing the while loop with an equivalent for loop. Test the page repeatedly to verify that it behaves identically to the while loop version.

```
for (repCount = 0; repCount < 100; repCount = repCount + 1) {
    document.write("HOWDY!<br />");
}

------------------------------------------------------------------

for (repCount = 0; repCount < 1000; repCount = repCount + 1) {
    roll1 = randomInt(1, 6);
    roll2 = randomInt(1, 6);
    document.write("You rolled: " + roll1 + " " +roll2 + "<br />");
}
```

Figure 13.15 Examples of counter-driven for loops.

EXERCISE 13.18

Reimplement your avg.html page, replacing the while loop with an equivalent for loop. Test the page repeatedly to verify that it behaves identically to the while loop version.

Inside the Computer—The von Neumann Architecture

This chapter uses narrative, illustrations, hands-on experimentation, and review questions to introduce computer science and technology concepts.

Any sufficiently advanced technology is indistinguishable from magic.

Arthur C. Clarke

John von Neumann draws attention to what seemed to him a contrast. He remarked that for simple mechanisms, it is often easier to describe how they work than what they do, while for more complicated mechanisms, it is usually the other way around.

Edsger Dijkstra

As was discussed in Chapter 1, virtually all modern computers have the same basic layout, known as the von Neumann architecture. This layout divides the hardware of a computer into three main components: memory, a central processing unit (CPU), and input/output devices. The first component, memory, provides storage for data and program instructions. The CPU is in charge of fetching instructions and data from memory, executing the instructions, and then storing the resulting values back in memory. Input devices (such as the keyboard, mouse, and microphone) allow a person to interact with the computer by entering information and commands, whereas output devices (such as the screen, speakers, and printer) are used to communicate data, instructions, and the results of computations.

This chapter explores the details of the von Neumann architecture by describing the inner workings of a computer. We develop our explanation incrementally, starting with a simple representation of the CPU datapath and then adding main memory and a control unit. When combined with input and output devices, these components represent an accurate (albeit simplified) model of a modern, programmable computer. Software simulators (originally developed by Grant Braught at Dickinson College) are provided for each model to facilitate experimentation and hands-on learning.

CPU Subunits and Datapath

As we saw in Chapter 1, the CPU acts as the brain of the computer. It is responsible for obtaining data and instructions from memory, carrying out the instructions, and storing the results back in memory. Each computer's CPU can understand and execute a particular set of instructions, known as that computer's ***machine language***. In Chapter 8, we explained that programmers can control a computer by defining instructions for its CPU—this is accomplished either by writing programs directly in machine language, or by writing programs in a high-level language and then translating them into machine language. Even programs that exhibit complex behavior are specified to the CPU as sequences of simple machine-language commands, each performing a task no more complicated than adding two numbers or copying data to a new location. However, the CPU can execute these instructions at such a high speed that complex programmatic behavior is achieved.

CPU Subunits

The CPU itself is comprised of several subunits, each playing a specific role in the processor's overall operation. These subunits are the arithmetic logic unit (ALU), the registers, and the control unit (Figure 14.1).

- The ***arithmetic logic unit (ALU)*** is the collection of circuitry that performs actual operations on data. Basic operations might include addition, subtraction, and bit manipulations (such as shifting or combining bits).
- ***Registers*** are memory locations that are built into the CPU. Since registers are integrated directly into the CPU circuitry, data in registers can be accessed more quickly (as much as 5–10 times faster) than data in main memory. However, due to the limited number of registers in the CPU (commonly 16 or 32), these memory locations are reserved for data that the CPU is currently using. To function efficiently, the computer must constantly copy data back and forth between registers and main memory. These transfers occur across a collection of wires called a ***bus***, which connects the registers to main memory. A separate set of buses connect the registers to the ALU, allowing the ALU to receive data for processing and then store the results of computations back in the registers.
- The *control unit (CU)* can be thought of as "the brain within the brain," in that it oversees the various functions of the CPU. The control unit is the circuitry in charge of fetching data and instructions from main memory, as well as controlling the flow of data from the registers to the ALU and back to the registers.

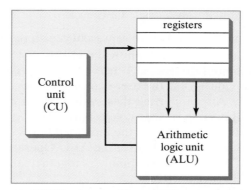

Figure 14.1 Central processing unit (CPU) subunits. Since ALU operations such as addition and subtraction operate on two values, there are two buses connecting the registers to the ALU. The result of the ALU operation is passed back to the registers via a single bus.

CPU Datapath Cycles

The path that data follows within the CPU, traveling along buses from registers to the ALU and then back to registers, is known as the ***CPU datapath***. Every task performed by a computer, from formatting a document to displaying a page in a Web browser, is broken down into sequences of simple operations; the computer executes each individual operation by moving data from the registers to the ALU, performing computations on that data within the ALU, and then storing the result in the registers. A single rotation around the CPU datapath is referred to as a **CPU datapath cycle**, or **CPU cycle**.

Recall that, in Chapter 1, we defined CPU speed as measuring the number of basic instructions that a CPU can carry out in one second. Since each instruction requires a single CPU cycle to execute, we can infer that a CPU's speed will equal the number of CPU cycles that occur per second. For example, an 800-MHz CPU can perform 800 million CPU cycles per second, whereas a 1.4-GHz CPU can perform 1.4 billion CPU cycles per second. However, CPUs cannot be compared solely on the basis of their processor speeds. This is because two machine languages might divide the same task into different sets of instructions, and one set might be more efficient than the other. That is, one CPU might be able to complete a task in a single cycle, whereas another might require several cycles to complete the same task. In order to accurately evaluate a CPU's performance, we must consider the instruction set for that CPU, as well as the number of registers and the size of the buses that carry data between components.

Datapath Simulator

To help you visualize the behavior of the CPU datapath, a simple simulator has been designed to accompany the text. The CPU Datapath Simulator (accessible at `http://www.prenhall.com/reed`) models a simple CPU containing four registers. Using this simulator, you can follow the progress of data as it traverses the CPU datapath, from the registers to the ALU and back to the registers. To keep things simple, we have avoided including an explicit control unit in this simulator. Instead, the user must serve as the control unit, selecting the desired input registers, ALU function, and output register by clicking the knob images. Note that not all features of the simulator will be demonstrated in this chapter. In particular, the ALU has two bit-manipulation operations, & and |, which involve combining individual bits in the two input values. Likewise, there are status boxes within the ALU that identify when an operation results in a negative number, zero, or an overflow (a value too large to be represented). You are free to experiment with these features, but all of the examples in this chapter will involve simple addition and subtraction.

Figures 14.2 through 14.5 demonstrate using the simulator to add two numbers together—a task that can be completed during a single CPU cycle.

- This simulator uses text boxes to represent registers, enabling the user to enter data by typing in the boxes. The knobs, which allow the user to specify how data moves along the CPU datapath and what operations the ALU performs on the data, are images that change when the user clicks them. In Figure 14.2, the user has entered the numbers 43 and −296 in registers R0 and R1, respectively. After inputting these values, the user clicks the A Bus knob so that it selects R0 and the B Bus knob so that it selects R1. This will cause the numbers stored in these two registers to be transferred along the indicated buses to the ALU, which will perform an operation on them. Since the user has set the ALU Operation knob to addition and the C Bus knob to R2, the ALU will add the two numbers together, and the result will travel along the C Bus to be stored back in register R2.

- After entering the desired settings, the user initiates a CPU cycle within the simulator by clicking the button labeled `"Execute"`. Figure 14.3 depicts the state of the CPU as the values in R0 and R1 travel along the A and B buses to the ALU. The arrows that represent the buses blink red, and the numbers being transferred are displayed in text boxes next to the buses.

- Figure 14.4 illustrates the state of the CPU after the ALU has received the numbers and performed the specified operation. Since the user set the ALU Operation knob to addition, the ALU adds the two numbers, 43 and −296. The result, −253, is then sent out along the C Bus.

- Finally, Figure 14.5 shows the end result of the CPU cycle. Since the user set the C Bus knob to R2, the value −253 (which travels along the C Bus) is ultimately stored in register R2.

Figure 14.2 Initial settings of the simulator.

Figure 14.3 Data traveling from registers to the ALU.

Figure 14.4 Data traveling from ALU to registers.

Figure 14.5 Final result of the CPU cycle.

Hands-On Exercises:

Experiment with this simulator until you are familiar with the CPU datapath and the events that occur within a CPU cycle. Then, use the simulator to answer the following questions:

14.1. What would happen if you placed the number 100 in R0, then set the knobs so that A Bus = R0, B Bus = R0, ALU = A−B, and C Bus = R0?

14.2. Describe the settings that would cause the value stored in R2 to be doubled.

14.3. How many cycles are required to add the contents of R0, R1, and R2 and then place the sum in R3? Describe the settings for each cycle.

CPU and Main Memory

Although the CPU datapath describes the way in which a computer manipulates data stored in registers, we have not yet explained how data gets into the registers in the first place, or how the results of ALU operations are accessed outside the CPU. Both these tasks involve connections between the CPU and main memory. Recall from Chapter 1 that all active programs and data are stored in the main memory of a computer. We can think of main memory as a large collection of memory locations, in which each location is accessible via an address. Similar to the way in which a street address (e.g., 27 Maple Drive) allows a mail carrier to find and access a mailbox, a memory address (e.g., memory location 27) allows the CPU to find and access a particular piece of main memory. A bus connects main memory to the CPU, enabling the computer to copy data and instructions to registers and then copy the results of computations back to main memory. Figure 14.6 illustrates the interaction between a computer's main memory and CPU.

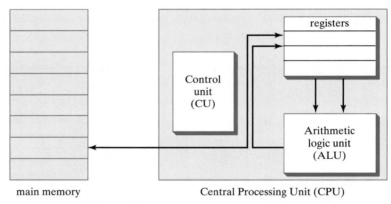

main memory   Central Processing Unit (CPU)

Figure 14.6   A bus connects main memory to the CPU.

Transferring Data to and from Main Memory

As a program is executed, the control unit processes the program instructions and identifies which data values are needed to carry out the specified tasks. The required values are then fetched from main memory along the main memory bus, loaded into registers, and used in ALU operations.

As a concrete example, imagine that you had a file containing 1,000 numbers and needed to compute the sum of those numbers. To begin, the computer would need to load the data from the file into main memory—for example, at memory locations 500 through 1499. Then, the control unit would carry out the following steps to add the numbers and store the resulting sum back in main memory.

1. Initialize one of the registers, say R0, to 0. This register will store the running total of the numbers.
2. For each number stored at memory addresses 500 through 1499:
    a. Copy the number from main memory to another register, say R1.
    b. During one cycle around the CPU datapath, add the contents of R0 and R1 and store the result back in R0.
3. When all the numbers in the file have been processed, the value in R0 will represent their sum. This value can then be copied back to a main memory location.

Note that each number must be transferred into a register before it can be added to the sum. In practice, transferring data between main memory and the CPU takes much longer than executing a single CPU cycle. This is mainly because the electrical signals must travel a greater distance—for example, from a separate RAM chip to the CPU chip. In the time it takes for data to traverse the main memory bus and reach the registers, several CPU cycles may actually occur. Modern processors compensate for this delay with special hardware that allows multiple instructions to be fetched at once. By fetching several instructions ahead, the processor can often identify instructions that are not dependent on the current one, and execute them while the current data transfer is in progress. Thus, the CPU can perform useful computations rather than sitting idle while an instruction waits for data to be copied from main memory to the registers.

Datapath with Memory Simulator

Our next version of the CPU Datapath Simulator has been augmented so that it illustrates the relationship between the CPU and main memory. The main memory incorporated in this extended simulator (accessible at `http://www.prenhall.com/reed`) can store up to 32 16-bit numbers, with addresses 0 through 31. A new bus, labeled "Main Memory Bus", connects the main memory to the CPU, allowing data and computation results to be transferred between the main memory and the registers. As in our previous example, this version of the simulator does not contain an explicit control unit. The user must serve as the control unit, selecting the desired settings on the Main Memory Bus and C Bus to control the data flow. Note that these buses can move data either between main memory and the registers or from the ALU to main memory, depending on how the user sets the switches. The user can open and close these bus switches by clicking them, effectively disconnecting and connecting the buses.

Figures 14.7 through 14.9 demonstrate using the simulator to add two numbers stored in main memory.

Figure 14.7 First, 43 is loaded from memory into R0.

Figure 14.8 Second, −296 is loaded from main memory into R1.

Figure 14.9 Finally, the values are added, and their sum is stored back in main memory.

- When the CPU must add two numbers stored in main memory, the first step is to copy one of the numbers into a register. In Figure 14.7, the user has selected the first number to be added, currently in main memory location 0, by clicking the R/W button next to that location (R/W refers to the fact that the button selects which memory location will be *read from* or *written to*). The user has also configured the arrows surrounding the Main Memory Bus so that they connect main memory to the registers. Once inside the CPU, the Main Memory Bus connects to the C Bus, which loads the number into register R0 (since the C Bus knob is set to R0).
- Figure 14.8 illustrates the next step in our example, which involves copying the second number into a register. Since the user has highlighted the R/W button next to main memory location 1 and set the C Bus knob to R1, the contents of location 1 are fetched and stored in register R1.
- Figure 14.9 depicts the CPU cycle during which the ALU adds the contents of R0 and R1. Note that the A Bus, B Bus, and ALU Operation knob settings are the same as those in Figures 14.3 through 14.6; this is because the two examples portray the same task (i.e., adding the numbers stored in R0 and R1). In Figure 14.9, however, the switches on the Main Memory bus are set so that the result of the addition is sent to main memory, rather than to the registers.

Two interesting observations can be made concerning the behavior of the simulator. First, the simulator requires more time to transfer data between main memory and the CPU than it does to perform a CPU datapath cycle. This delay is meant to simulate the slower access times associated with main memory. In a real computer, as many as 10 CPU cycles might occur in the time it takes to transfer data between the CPU and main memory. The second observation is that, even while data is being fetched from main memory, operations are still performed on the CPU datapath. For example, in Figure 14.8, the number in R0 (43) is sent along both the A and B Buses to the ALU, yielding the sum 86. This might seem wasteful, since the result of the ALU operation is ignored (due to the disconnected C Bus). Surprisingly, this is an accurate reflection of a CPU's internal workings. It is more efficient for the ALU to perform needless computations while data is being transferred to or from main memory than it would be to add extra circuitry to recognize whether the C Bus is connected.

Hands-On Exercises:

Experiment with this simulator until you are familiar with the interactions between main memory and the CPU datapath. Then, use the simulator to answer the following questions:

14.4. What settings would result in the sum of registers R0 and R3 being stored in memory location 4?

14.5. What settings would cause the contents of memory address 4 to be copied into register R0?

14.6. Assuming that data can be copied to and from main memory in a single CPU cycle, how many cycles are required to add the contents of memory addresses 5 and 6 and then store the result in memory address 7? Describe the settings for each cycle.

Stored-Program Computer

Now that we have explored how main memory works, we are ready to focus on the last component of the CPU: a fully functioning, automatic control unit. To understand the role of the control unit, recall the tasks that you performed while using the simulators. When you experimented with the Datapath Simulator (Exercises 14.1–14.3), you defined the computation carried out during a CPU cycle by selecting the registers and ALU operation via knobs. In the datapath and main memory simulator (Exercises 14.4–14.6), you controlled the flow of information between the datapath and main memory via switches on the buses. The key idea behind a stored-program computer is that tasks such as these can be represented as instructions, stored in main memory along with data, and then carried out by the control unit.

Machine Languages

As we explained in Chapter 8, a machine language is a set of binary codes corresponding to the basic tasks that a CPU can perform. In essence, each machine-language instruction specifies how various hardware components must be configured in order for a CPU cycle to perform a particular computation. Thus, we could define machine-language instructions for our simulator by enumerating all the physical settings of the knobs and switches. For example, the settings:

```
A Bus = R0        ALU Switch = closed
B Bus = R1        MMIn Switch = open
ALU = A+B         MMOut Switch = open
C Bus = R2        C Switch = closed
```

would define a configuration in which the contents of R0 and R1 are added and stored back in R2. This notation might suffice to control the behavior of a very simple machine, such as the one represented in our simulator; however, real-world CPUs contain an extremely large number of physical components, and specifying the status of all these parts during every CPU cycle would be impossible. Furthermore, since machine-language instructions are stored in memory along with data, the instructions must ultimately be represented as bit patterns.

Figure 14.10 describes a simple machine language that has been designed for our simulator. Since the main memory locations in our simulator can hold a maximum of 16 bits, our language represents each instruction as a 16-bit pattern. The initial bits indicate the type of task that the CPU must perform, whereas the subsequent bits indicate the registers and/or memory locations involved in the task. Since there are only four registers, two bits suffice to represent a register number; since there are 32 main memory locations, five bits suffice to represent a memory address. For instance, all instructions that involve adding the contents of two registers begin with the bit pattern: 1010000100. The final six

Operation	Machine-Language Instruction	Example
Add contents of two registers, store result in another register e.g., R0 = R1 + R2	1010000100 RR RR RR	1010000100 00 01 10 will add contents of R1 (01) and R2 (10), then store the result in R0 (00)
Subtract contents of two registers, store result in another register e.g., R0 = R1 − R2	1010001000 RR RR RR	1010001000 00 01 10 will take contents of R1 (01), subtract R2 (10), then store the result in R0 (00)
Load contents of memory location into register e.g., R3 = M[5] (11)	100000010 RR MMMMM	100000010 11 00101 will load contents of memory location 5 (00101) into R3
Store contents of register in memory location e.g., M[5] = R3	100000100 RR MMMMM	100000100 11 00101 will store contents of memory location 7 (00101) in R3 (11)
Move contents of one register into another register e.g., R1 = R0	100100010000 RR RR	100100010000 01 00 will move contents of R0 (00) to R1 (01)
Halt the machine	1111111111111111	N/A

Figure 14.10 Machine Language for Computer Simulator.

bits of an addition instruction represent the destination register (i.e., the register where the result will be stored) and the source registers (i.e., the registers whose contents will be added by the ALU), respectively. As an example, suppose that you wanted to add the contents of R0 and R1 and then store the result in R2—i.e., R2 = R0 + R1. The bit patterns for R2 ($2 = 10_2$), R0 ($0 = 00_2$), and

R1 ($1 = 01_2$) would be appended to the initial bit pattern for addition (1010000100), yielding the machine-language instruction: 1010000100**100001**. Similarly, if the intent were R3 $=$ R0 $+$ R1, then the bit pattern for R3 ($3 = 11_2$) would replace that of R2: 1010000100**110001**.

The first two machine-language instructions in Figure 14.10 correspond to tasks that users can perform with the CPU Datapath simulator—i.e., selecting an ALU operation to be executed and the registers to be operated on during a CPU cycle. The next three instructions correspond to tasks that users can perform with the datapath and memory version of the simulator—i.e., controlling the flow of information between the main memory and the datapath. The last instruction, HALT, tells the control unit when a sequence of instructions terminates. Of course, a real CPU would require many more instructions than these. For example, if a CPU executes programs that include conditional statements (such as JavaScript if statements and while loops), its machine language must support branching instructions that allow the CPU to jump from one instruction to another. However, Figure 14.10's limited instruction set is sufficient to demonstrate the workings of a basic CPU and its control unit.

Control Unit

Once a uniform machine language for a particular CPU is established, instructions can be stored in main memory along with data. It is the job of the control unit to obtain each machine-language instruction from memory, interpret its meaning, carry out the specified CPU cycle, and then move on to the next instruction. Since instructions and data are both stored in the same memory, the control unit must be able to recognize where a sequence of instructions begins and ends. In real computers, this task is usually performed by the operating system, which maintains a list of each program in memory and its location. For simplicity, our simulator assumes that the first instruction is stored in memory location 0. The end of the instruction sequence is explicitly identified using the HALT bit pattern.

In order to track the execution of an instruction sequence, the control unit maintains a program counter (PC), which stores the address of the next instruction to be executed. Since we are assuming that all programs start at address 0, the PC's value is initialized to 0 before program execution begins. When the control unit needs to fetch and execute an instruction, it accesses the PC and then obtains the instruction stored in the corresponding memory location. After the control unit fetches the instruction, the PC is incremented so that it identifies the next instruction in the sequence.

The steps carried out by the control unit can be defined as a general algorithm, in which instructions are repeatedly fetched and executed:

Fetch-Execute Algorithm carried out by the control unit:

1. Initialize PC $= 0$.
2. Fetch the instruction stored at memory location PC, and set PC $=$ PC $+$ 1.
3. As long as the current instruction is not the HALT instruction, repeatedly:
   a. Decode the instruction—that is, determine the CPU hardware settings required to carry it out.
   b. Configure the CPU hardware to match the settings indicated in the instruction.
   c. Execute a CPU datapath cycle using those settings.
   d. When the cycle is complete, fetch the next instruction from memory location PC, and set PC $=$ PC $+$ 1.

For example, suppose that main memory contained the program and data shown in Figure 14.11. The first five memory locations (addresses 0 through 4) contain machine-language instructions for adding two numbers and storing their sum back in memory. The numbers to be added are stored in memory locations 5 and 6. To execute this program, the control unit would carry out the following steps:

1. First, the program counter is initialized: PC $= 0$.
2. The instruction at memory location 0 (corresponding to the current value of PC) is fetched, and the PC is incremented: PC $= 0 + 1 = 1$.
3. Since this instruction (1000000100000101) is not a HALT instruction, it is decoded: the CPU hardware is configured so that it will load the contents of memory location 5 into register R0, and a CPU cycle is executed.

```
0: 1000000100000101        // load memory location 5 into R0
1: 1000000100100110        // load memory location 6 into R1
2: 1010000100100001        // add R0 and R1, store result in R2
3: 1000001001000111        // copy R2 to memory location 7
4: 1111111111111111        // halt
5: 0000000000001001        // data to be added: 9
6: 0000000000000001        // data to be added: 1
7: 0000000000000000        // location where sum is to be stored
```

Figure 14.11   Machine-language program for adding two numbers in memory.

4. The next instruction (at memory location 1, corresponding to the current value of PC) is fetched, and the PC is incremented: PC = 1 + 1 = 2.

5. Since this instruction (1000000100100110) is not a HALT instruction, it is decoded: the CPU hardware is configured so that it will load the contents of memory location 6 into register R1, and a CPU cycle is executed.

6. The next instruction (at memory location 2, corresponding to the current value of PC) is fetched, and the PC is incremented: PC = 2 + 1 = 3.

7. Since this instruction (1010000100100001) is not a HALT instruction, it is decoded: the CPU hardware is configured so that it will add the contents of registers R0 and R1 and store the result in register R2, and a CPU cycle is executed.

8. The next instruction (at memory location 3, corresponding to the current value of PC) is fetched, and the PC is incremented: PC = 3 + 1 = 4.

9. Since this instruction (1000001001000111) is not a HALT instruction, it is decoded: the CPU hardware is configured so that it will copy the contents of register R2 to memory location 7, and a CPU cycle is executed.

10. The next instruction (at memory location 4, corresponding to the current value of PC) is fetched, and the PC is incremented: PC = 4 + 1 = 5.

11. Since this instruction (1111111111111111) is a HALT instruction, the control unit recognizes the end of the program and stops executing.

Stored-Program Computer Simulator

The Stored-Program Computer Simulator (accessible at http://www.prenhall.com/reed) models the behavior of a complete, stored-program computer. Instructions and data can be entered into memory, with the first instruction assumed to be at memory location 0. The control unit is responsible for fetching and interpreting the machine-language instructions, as well as carrying out the tasks specified by those instructions.

The simulator contains several display boxes to illustrate the control unit's inner workings. As we described in the previous section, the program counter (PC) lists the address of the next instruction to be executed. In addition to the PC, CPUs also maintain an instruction register (IR), which lists the instruction that the control unit is currently executing. The IR is displayed in the simulator as an additional text box. Above these boxes, the simulator exhibits the actual knob and switch settings defined by the current instruction—this makes the correspondence between the machine-language instruction and the CPU hardware settings more obvious. Knob settings are specified as two-bit binary numbers: 00 represents a knob pointing straight up, 01 represents a knob pointing to the right, 10 represents a knob pointing down, and 11 represents a knob pointing to the left. The four switch settings are represented by a four-bit pattern, with a 1 bit indicating a closed switch and a 0 bit an open switch (the topmost switch in the simulator, the C Bus, corresponds to the first bit, followed by the three remaining switches from left to right).

Figures 14.12 through 14.17 demonstrate using the simulator to execute the example machine-language program from Figure 14.11.

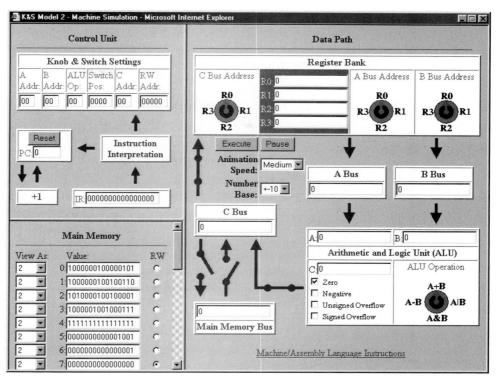

Figure 14.12   Initial state of the simulator, with program stored in main memory.

Figure 14.13   Simulator after the first instruction has been executed (R0 = MM5).

Figure 14.14 Simulator after the second instruction has been executed (R1 = MM6).

Figure 14.15 Simulator after the third instruction has been executed (R2 = R0 + R1).

Figure 14.16 Simulator after the fourth statement has been executed (MM7 = R2).

Figure 14.17 Simulator after the fifth statement has been executed (HALT).

- Figure 14.12 depicts the initial state of the simulator. The machine-language instructions are stored in main memory, starting at address 0. The data required to execute the instructions is also stored in memory, at addresses 5 and 6, immediately following the last instruction. Within the control unit, the program counter (PC) is initialized to 0, so the instruction at address 0 will be the first to be loaded and executed. To assist the user, the page includes a link to a reference page that summarizes all of the machine- and assembly-language instructions, labeled "Machine/Assembly Language Instructions."
- Figure 14.13 portrays the simulator after the first instruction has been executed. Within the control unit, the instruction from address 0 has been loaded into the instruction register and translated into the knob and switch settings required to carry out the specified CPU datapath cycle. Once the control unit determines the correct knob and switch settings, it carries out the corresponding CPU datapath cycle. In this case, the value from memory location 5, the number 9, is loaded into register R0. Note that the PC is automatically incremented when the instruction is executed so the next instruction to be fetched and executed will be the instruction at address 1.
- Figure 14.14 shows the simulator after the next instruction, from memory location 1, has been executed. Here, the value from memory location 6, the number 1, is loaded into register R1.
- Figure 14.15 depicts the result of executing the next instruction, from memory location 2, which adds the contents of registers R0 and R1 and stores the result in register R2.
- Figure 14.16 portrays the result of executing the next instruction, from memory location 3, which copies the result of the addition, stored in R2, into memory location 7.
- Finally, Figure 14.17 shows the computer after the program terminates. Recall that the HALT instruction 1111111111111111 tells the control unit to stop processing. Since no datapath cycle is executed once the HALT instruction is recognized by the control unit, the knob and switch settings within the datapath are not changed from the previous cycle.

The simulator is designed so that the user can enter values in main memory as either decimal or binary numbers. By default, values entered by the user are assumed to be decimal numbers. However, the user can always select 2 from the View As box to the left of a memory location in order to view the contents in binary. Before entering a machine-language instruction in a memory cell, the user must first set the value of the View As box to 2, since machine-language instructions are represented in binary.

Hands-On Exercises:

Experiment with this simulator until you are familiar with its behavior. Then, use the simulator to answer the following questions:

14.7. What task would the following machine-language program perform?

```
0: 1010001000000000
1: 1000001000000011
2: 1111111111111111
```

14.8. What sequence of machine-language instructions would cause the contents of the four registers to be copied into memory locations 7, 8, 9, and 10, respectively?

14.9. What sequence of machine-language instructions would cause the simulator to add the contents of memory locations 10, 11, and 12 and then store the result in memory location 13?

14.10. What do you think would happen if you forgot to place a HALT instruction at the end of a machine-language program? How would the control unit react? Use the simulator to test your prediction, then report the results.

The Role of Input/Output Devices

To complete our description of the stored-program computer, we must at least briefly discuss the role of input and output devices. Input devices such as keyboards, mice, and scanners allow the user to communicate with the computer by entering data and instructions, which are then stored in memory and accessed by the CPU. Likewise, output devices such as display screens, speakers, and printers allow the user to view the current status of the computer and access computation results that are stored in memory.

Computers that are designed to run one program at a time, such as the first programmable computers (introduced in the 1950s) and the first personal computers (introduced in the 1970s), provide relatively straightforward methods of user interaction. The user enters program instructions and data directly into main memory locations via input devices such as keyboards or tape readers. Then, by flipping a switch or entering a specific command, the user instructs the CPU to fetch the program instructions from memory and execute them in sequential order. Once a particular computation has been completed, the user can view its result by sending the contents of memory to a printer or display screen. This process is closely modeled by our simulator, in which the user enters instructions and data by typing them in main memory boxes, then initiates execution by clicking a button. In the case of the simulator, however, the final step of sending results to an output device is not necessary—the contents of the registers and main memory are already visible.

As we discussed in Chapters 6 and 10, most modern computers allow for multitasking, meaning that multiple programs can be loaded in main memory and be active simultaneously. When multiple programs are to be executed, user interactions and the computations that result from those interactions become more complex. In particular, the instructions and data associated with each program must be loaded into separate portions of main memory. When the user switches from one program to another (say by clicking on a different window in the graphical user interface), the CPU must save the state of the current program and be able to locate the portion of memory associated with the new program. These tasks, and many others involving the coordination of programs and CPU processing, are managed by the operating system.

Machine vs. Assembly Languages

It is important to note that the machine language and hardware configurations associated with our simulator are much simpler than those of any actual computer. A real machine language might encompass tens or hundreds of instructions, and a real CPU might contain hundreds or thousands of configurable components. However, our model is sufficient to demonstrate computer behavior at its lowest level.

The simulator is also useful in representing the difficulty and tedium of programming in a machine language. As you learned in Chapter 8, writing, debugging, and understanding bit-sequence instructions can be mind-numbing work. Over the past fifty years, computer programming has advanced significantly, and most modern programmers are able to avoid direct machine-language programming. Some of the earliest programmer tools were assembly languages, which substitute words for bit patterns, allowing the programmer to write:

```
ADD R0 R1 R2
```

instead of the machine-language instruction:

```
1010000100000110
```

It is much easier for programmers to remember and understand assembly-language instructions than patterns of 0s and 1s. Furthermore, most assembly languages support the use of variable names, enabling programmers to specify memory locations by descriptive names, rather than by numerical addresses. This greatly simplifies the programmer's task, since she no longer needs to worry about the physical location of data and how locations might shift as new instructions are inserted into memory. Figure 14.18 lists one possible set of assembly-language instructions that correspond to the machine-language instructions from Figure 14.11.

Within the Stored Program Computer Simulator, the user may enter assembly-language instructions directly in memory. The default mode for displaying the contents of memory locations, labeled "Auto" in the View As box, will automatically recognize assembly-language instructions and will display them as text (changing the label to "Inst" to acknowledge that they are instructions). After inputting the instructions, the user can switch between viewing the instruction in assembly- or

Operation	Machine-Language Instruction	Assembly-Language Instruction
Add contents of two registers, then store result in another register e.g., R0 = R1 + R2	1010000100 RR RR RR e.g., 1010000100 00 01 10	ADD [REG] [REG] [REG] e.g., ADD R0 R1 R2
Subtract contents of two registers, then store result in another register e.g., R0 = R1 − R2	1010001000 RR RR RR e.g., 1010001000 00 01 10	SUB [REG] [REG] [REG] e.g., SUB R0 R1 R2
Load contents of memory location into register e.g., R3 = MM5	100000010 RR MMM e.g., 100000010 11 00101	LOAD [REG] [MEM] e.g., LOAD R3 5
Store contents of register into memory location e.g., MM5 = R3	100000100 RR MMMMM e.g., 100000100 11 00101	STORE [MEM] [REG] e.g., STORE 5 R3
Move contents of one register into another register e.g., R1 = R0	100100010000 RR RR e.g., 100100010000 01 00	MOVE [REG] [REG] e.g., MOVE R1 R0
Halt the machine	1111111111111111	HALT

Figure 14.18   Assembly-language instructions.

machine-language form by selecting `Inst` (for assembly-language instructions) or `2` (for machine-language instructions in binary form) in the `View As` box to the left of the instruction. For example, Figure 14.19 depicts the same program that is pictured in Figure 14.12, but here the instructions are formatted as `Inst`.

Hands-On Exercises:

Experiment with the simulator until you are comfortable with the correspondence between machine-language and assembly-language instructions. Then, use the simulator to answer the following questions:

14.11. What sequence of assembly-language instructions corresponds to the machine-language instruction set from Exercise 14.7?

14.12. What sequence of assembly-language instructions corresponds to the machine-language instruction set you wrote in Exercise 14.9?

14.13. Write a sequence of assembly-language instructions that multiplies the contents of memory location 10 by four. For example, if the number 10 were stored in memory location 10, executing your instructions would cause the simulator to store 40 there. *Note*: Although the ALU Operation knob does not provide a multiplication setting, a number can be multiplied via repeated additions (e.g., 10*4 = 10 + 10 + 10 + 10).

Looking Ahead...

In this chapter, you studied the internal workings of computers, focusing on the CPU, main memory, and their interactions. By experimenting with the various simulators, you saw how the CPU breaks up even the most complex computing tasks into sequences of very simple instructions, each of which can be executed during a single CPU datapath cycle. Although buses that connect the CPU to main

Figure 14.19   Assembly-language program displayed in computer simulator.

memory enable the manipulation of large amounts of data, the computer must transfer each data value into a CPU register, perform operations on the value within the ALU, and then store the result of the computation back in main memory. The combination of a control unit and main memory allows computers to process stored programs. This behavior was modeled by our most sophisticated simulator, in which programs consisting of machine-language instruction sequences were stored in memory, fetched and decoded by the control unit, then executed in a series of CPU datapath cycles.

Building upon your general understanding of computer components and their organization, Chapter 16 will delve deeper into the details of their design and construction. In particular, you will study the construction and behavior of transistors and integrated circuits. However, before you consider how these technologies are used to build the hardware components of computer, Chapter 15 will describe a general methodology for designing and implementing software components. The object-oriented approach to software development attempts to simplify the task of designing and testing software systems by focusing on programming structures that model real-world objects. For example, a JavaScript string is an object that models a word or phrase, with useful operations on a string (such as capitalizing it or extracting a substring) provided as part of the language. Chapter 15 will describe the JavaScript string type, and explore applications that involve storing and manipulating text.

Chapter Summary

- Virtually all modern computers use the von Neumann architecture, which divides the hardware into three main components: memory, a central processing unit (CPU), and input/output devices.
- The CPU is responsible for obtaining data and instructions from memory, carrying out the instructions, and storing the results back in memory.

- The CPU is comprised of the arithmetic logic unit (ALU), registers, and the control unit. The ALU is the collection of circuitry that performs actual operations on data. Registers are memory locations that are built into the CPU and used to store data for fast access. The control unit is the circuitry in charge of fetching data and instructions from main memory, as well as controlling the flow of data from the registers to the ALU and back to the registers.

- The path that data follows within the CPU, traveling along buses from registers to the ALU and then back to registers, is known as the CPU datapath. A single rotation around the CPU datapath is referred to as a CPU datapath cycle, or CPU cycle.

- A bus connects main memory to the CPU, enabling the computer to copy data and instructions to registers and then copy the results of computations back to main memory.

- As a program is executed, the control unit processes the program instructions, identifies which data values are needed to carry out the specified tasks, and loads those values from main memory into registers.

- In practice, transferring data between main memory and the CPU takes much longer than executing a single CPU cycle.

- A machine language is a set of binary codes corresponding to the basic tasks that a CPU can perform.

- In order to execute a program stored in memory, the control unit must repeatedly fetch the next machine-language instruction from memory, interpret its meaning, carry out the specified CPU cycle, and then move on to the next instruction.

- In order to track the execution of an instruction sequence, the control unit maintains a program counter (PC), which stores the address of the next instruction to be executed.

- Computers that are designed to run one program at a time provide relatively straightforward methods of user interaction, such as having the user enter instructions and data directly into main memory locations via a keyboard and viewing the results of computations on a screen.

- Computers that support multitasking—the ability to load and execute multiple programs simultaneously—require support from the operating system to coordinate programs and manage shared resources.

- Since assembly languages substitute words for the bit patterns used in machine languages, they make it much easier for the programmer to write, understand, and debug code.

Review Questions

1. TRUE or FALSE? Any piece of memory that is used to store the sum of numeric values is known as a register.

2. TRUE or FALSE? The path that data follows within the CPU, traveling along buses from registers to the ALU and then back to registers, is known as the CPU datapath.

3. TRUE or FALSE? All modern CPUs provide the same set of basic operations that can be executed in a single CPU cycle.

4. TRUE or FALSE? The size of main memory is generally measured in MHz or GHz.

5. TRUE or FALSE? Suppose you wish to add two numbers that are stored in memory. Before the arithmetic logic unit (ALU) can add the numbers, they must first be transferred to registers within the CPU.

6. TRUE or FALSE? In real computers, it takes roughly the same amount of time to transfer data from main memory to registers as it does to add two numbers in registers.

7. TRUE or FALSE? Within the CPU, the control unit is responsible for fetching machine-language instructions from memory, interpreting their meaning, and carrying out the specified CPU cycles.

8. TRUE or FALSE? Suppose a CPU contains eight registers. Within a machine-language instruction, at least 3 bits would be required to uniquely identify one of the registers.

9. TRUE or FALSE? In a multitasking computer, the program counter keeps track of how many programs are currently loaded into main memory.

10. TRUE or FALSE? In a stored-program computer, both machine-language instructions and the data operated on by those instructions can reside in main memory at the same time.

11. Name the three subunits of the CPU, and describe the role of each subunit in carrying out computations.

12. Describe how data values move around the CPU datapath and what actions occur during a single CPU cycle. How does the datapath relate to CPU speed?

13. Consider two computer systems that are identical except for their CPUs. System 1 contains a 1.8GHz Pentium 4, whereas System 2 contains a 1.8GHz PowerPC processor. Will these two systems always require the same amount of time to execute a given program? Justify your answer.

14. Consider the following tasks: (1) adding 100 numbers stored in main memory, and (2) adding a number to itself 100 times. Although both tasks require 100 additions, the second would be executed much more quickly than the first would. Why?

15. Machine languages are machine specific, meaning that each type of computer has its own machine language. Explain why this is the case.

16. Within the control unit, what is the role of the program counter (PC)? That is, how is the PC used in fetching and executing instructions?

17. In a stored-program computer, both instructions and data are stored in main memory. How does the control unit know where the program instructions begin? How does it know where the instructions end?

18. Describe two advantages of assembly languages over machine languages.

References

Brain, Marshall. "How Microprocessors Work." *HowStuffWorks*, January 2003. Online at `http://www.howstuffworks.com/microprocessor.htm`.

Braught, G. "Computer Organization in the Breadth First Course." *Journal of Computing in Small Colleges*, 16(4), 2001.

Braught, Grant, and David Reed. "The Knob & Switch Computer: A Computer Architecture Simulator for Introductory Computer Science." *ACM Journal of Educational Resources in Computing*, 1(4), 2001.

Malone, Michael. *The Microprocessor: A Biography*. New York: Springer-Verlag, 1995.

"The PC Technology Guide—Components/Processors." *PCTechGuide*, December 2002. Online at `http://www.pctechguide.com/02procs.htm`.

Stallings, William. *Computer Organization and Architecture: Designing for Performance*, 6th ed. Upper Saddle River, NJ: Prentice Hall, 2003.

Tanenbaum, Andrew S. *Structured Computer Organization*, 4th ed. Upper Saddle River, NJ: Prentice Hall, 1999.

15 Chapter

JavaScript Strings

This chapter uses narrative, examples, and hands-on exercises to introduce programming concepts and Web development skills.

> *The basic tool for the manipulation of reality is the manipulation of words. If you can control the meaning of words, you can control the people who must use the words.*
>
> Philip K. Dick
> *I Hope I Shall Arrive Soon*
>
> *Words form the thread on which we string our experiences.*
>
> Aldous Huxley
> *Brave New World*

Throughout this book, you have written numerous interactive Web pages that manipulate numbers. These pages have read in numbers entered by the user (via prompt windows or text boxes/areas), performed calculations using mathematical operators and functions, and displayed the results of computations (via write statements or text boxes/areas). You have also written pages that process words and phrases, but your tools for handling string values have been more limited. Although you have learned to read in string values and display them in a page, the only operation that you have performed on strings is concatenation using the '+' operator.

This chapter explores features of the JavaScript string type, including ways to manipulate text within interactive Web pages. You will learn that strings are different from numbers and Booleans in that they are objects, software units that encapsulate both data and operations that can be performed on that data. The techniques introduced in this chapter will allow you to access various components of a string, construct new strings by modifying existing ones, and traverse strings in search of desired sequences or patterns. By the end of this chapter, you will be able to solve numerous complex problems that involve storing and modifying text.

Strings as Objects

As commercial software projects have become larger and more complex, the designers of programming languages have searched for methods of organizing software that would ease the software development process and, at the same time, be intuitive for programmers. In the 1970s and early 1980s, the ***procedural programming*** approach, which was supported by languages such as Pascal and C, encouraged programmers to design programs around actions—the programmer would identify the main actions to be carried out by the program and would then implement functions for each action. While this approach was effective when programs were relatively small (hundreds or perhaps thousands of lines long), it did not always scale well to larger projects involving teams of developers. Today, the predominant approach to software development is ***object-oriented programming***, which is supported by modern languages such as C++ and Java. Object-oriented languages encourage programmers to design programs around software objects—the programmer identifies the real-world objects that are involved, such as a bank account or customer, and models those objects with programming structures. The object-oriented approach has proven to be effective at managing large systems, since individual objects can be assigned to different programming teams and developed independently. The development of self-contained software objects can also cut development costs by supporting code reuse, since the same or similar objects can be combined in different ways to solve different kinds of problems.

To better understand what a software object consists of, consider the analogy of a common real-world object: a doorbell. A thorough description of a doorbell encompasses not only the bell's physical components (a button, a bell, and wires), but also its functionality. When a doorbell is pressed, the noise generated by the bell alerts you that someone is at the door. A software object represents a similar combination of data and behaviors. For example, we have seen that an HTML button, when combined with JavaScript code, serves as a software model of a doorbell. Each button has properties, including a name and a label, and predefined functionality, as defined by the JavaScript code that is executed when a user clicks the button.

Although JavaScript does not provide the full functionality of advanced languages such as C++ and Java, it does support the development and use of simple software objects. In addition to providing the functionality for HTML objects such as buttons, JavaScript provides its own software objects that aid the programmer in developing code. For example, the `Math` object (first introduced in Chapter 5) contains many useful properties (e.g., constants representing `PI` and `E`) as well as functions (e.g., `sqrt` for computing the square root of a number, and `random` for generating a random value). As you will learn in this chapter, a JavaScript string is an object that models words and phrases, encompassing both properties (characteristics of the string, such as its length and the characters that comprise it) and functionality (operations that can be performed on the string value, such as, concatenation and character access).

Properties and Methods

In previous chapters, we defined a string as a sequence of characters enclosed in quotes. However, strings also possess a set of ***properties*** that describe a string and ***operations*** that can be applied to a string to trigger various actions. For example, each string has a `length` property that records the number of characters in the string. To access the length of a string, you specify the name of the variable that stores the string value, followed by a period and `length`, which is the name of the property. Thus, if `word = "foo"`, then the expression `word.length` would evaluate to 3, since there are three characters in `"foo"`. Figure 15.1 depicts another example, in which `str = "Foo 2 You"`, causing `str.length` to evaluate to 9.

In addition, there are numerous operations (i.e., functions) that are predefined for use with JavaScript strings. For example, when the `toUpperCase` function is applied to a string, it returns a copy of that string in which all lower-case letters are converted to upper case. Likewise, the `toLowerCase` function returns an entirely lower-case version of a given string. Unlike other JavaScript functions, which may be called with any type of input, functions such as `toUpperCase` and `toLowerCase` are explicitly associated with strings. In fact, it is natural to think of each string value as having its own copy of these functions, in the same way that each string has its own `length` property.

To differentiate them from stand-alone functions, functions that belong to an object are known as ***methods*** of that object. As was the case with properties, programmers apply the methods associated with an object to that object by specifying the object's name, a period, and then the method (function) call. Figure 15.1 demonstrates the effects of applying the `toUpperCase` and `toLowerCase` methods to

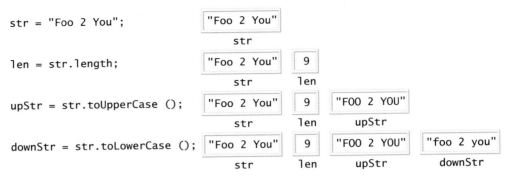

Figure 15.1 Tracing the effects of string manipulations.

the string variable `str`. Note that, instead of modifying the original string value stored in `str`, these method calls simply return new copies of the string in which all letters are upper- or lower case.

The Web page in Figure 15.2 demonstrates accessing a string's `length` property and `toUpperCase` method within a program. The page contains a text box in which the user can enter a string. By clicking the button labeled `"Click to Process"`, the user can view the string length and the string's upper-case equivalent in text boxes.

```
<html>
  <!-- string.html                                              Dave Reed -->
  <!-- This page demonstrates a string property and operation.       -->
  <!------------------------------------------------------------------>
  <head>
    <title> String Fun </title>
    <script type="text/javascript">
      function Process()
      // Assumes: document.StringForm.str contains a string
      // Results: displays the outcome of string operations in other boxes
      {
        var str;
        str = document.StringForm.str.value;
        document.StringForm.strLength.value = str.length;
        document.StringForm.strUpper.value = str.toUpperCase();
      }
    </script>
  </head>
  <body>
    <div style="text-align:center">
      <h2>String Fun</h2>
      <form name="StringForm">
        Enter a string: <input type="text" name="str" size=20 value="" />
        <br /><br />
        <input type="button" value="Click to Process" onClick="Process();" />
        <hr width=50% />
        <br /><br />
        String length = <input type="text" name="strLength" size=3 value=0 />
        <br /><br />
        Uppercase copy = <input type="text" name="strUpper" size=20 value=0 />
      </form>
    </div>
  </body>
</html>
```

Figure 15.2 Web page that demonstrates the `length` property and `toUpperCase` method.

EXERCISE 15.1

Enter the `string.html` text from Figure 15.2 into a new Web page, then load this page to verify that it behaves as described. Figure 15.3 shows the resulting Web page.

After experimenting with `string.html`, augment the page by inserting a text box labeled "Lowercase copy =". Modify the `Process` function so that it displays a lowercase version of the string in the new text box.

Figure 15.3 `string.html` rendered in a Web browser.

Common errors to avoid...

Note that the string methods `toUpperCase` and `toLowerCase` do not in any way change the string value on which they operate. Instead, these methods return a copy of the original string in which all characters are either upper or lower case. As such, a call to one of these methods in a statement by itself serves no real purpose. For example, consider the statement:

```
str.toUpperCase();
```

This call would return a copy of the string value stored in the variable `str`, but with all letters converted to upper case. However, since this returned value is not saved in a variable or otherwise incorporated into a larger expression, the value is lost. To actually modify the value of `str`, making it upper case, you must place the method call on the right-hand side of an assignment to that variable. For example, the following statement would replace `str`'s value with an uppercase version of `str`:

```
str = str.toUpperCase();
```

In general, the only way to change the value of a variable is to write an assignment statement in which that variable appears on the left-hand side.

Common String Manipulation Methods

The toUpperCase and toLowerCase methods described above are only two of many methods defined for strings. For example, other useful methods allow programmers to access and manipulate individual components of a string. Such components are identifiable via indices, or numbers that correspond to the order in which individual characters occur in a string. Indices are assigned in ascending order from left to right, so that the first character in the string is considered to be at index 0, the second character at index 1, and so on. The charAt method takes an index as input and returns the character stored at that particular index of the string. For example, the call str.charAt(0) will return the character at str's index 0 (i.e., the first character in str), and str.charAt(1) will return the character at str's index 1 (i.e., the second character in str). Since string indices start at 0, the last character in a string str can be accessed via the call: str.charAt(str.length - 1).

Whereas the charAt string method enables you to access a single character within a string, the substring method returns a sequence of characters within a string—i.e., a substring. The substring method takes two numbers as inputs, representing the starting (inclusive) and ending (exclusive) indices that delimit the substring. For example, the call str.substring(0, 2) will return the substring consisting of the first two characters in the string str (from indices 0 and 1), and str.substring(1, 4) will return the substring consisting of the second, third, and fourth characters (from indices 1, 2, and 3).

EXERCISE 15.2

Assuming word = "smarmy", predict the values that each of the following method calls would return:

```
word.charAt(0)
word.charAt(5)
word.charAt(word.length-1)
word.substring(0, 5)
word.substring(4, 5)
word.substring(1, word.length)
word.substring(0, word.length-1)
```

Common errors to avoid...

The string methods charAt and substring are very forgiving with respect to invalid indices, and this leeway can lead to undetected logic errors. If you call charAt with an index that is either too small (less than 0) or too big (greater than or equal to the string length), no error occurs. Instead, an empty string is returned. Likewise, if you call substring with indices that extend beyond the valid range for that string, the excess range will be ignored. For example, if word = "smarmy", then word.substring(-1, 2) will return "sm", just as the call word.substring(0,2) would. Similarly, the call word.substring(2, word.length+10) will return "army", just as the call word.substring(2, word.length) would.

Thus, if you are writing code that employs these string methods, you cannot assume that the browser will catch errors related to invalid indices. Check your program's output carefully to ensure that each method call is accessing the intended value(s).

String Concatenation

As we have explained, the charAt and substring methods can be used to break a string into component parts. Conversely, the concatenation ('+') operator, introduced in Chapter 4, can rejoin these parts and reassemble the original string. For example, assuming that the variable word stores a string, the following assignment would leave word's value unchanged:

```
word = word.charAt(0) + word.substring(1, word.length);
```

The method calls to charAt and substring divide the string into two parts, one consisting of the string's first character and the other consisting of the rest of the string. However, the assignment statement concatenates the two parts back together and assigns the result back to word. For example, if word = "smarmy", then the effect of this assignment would be word = "s" + "marmy" = "smarmy".

Although the assignment statement above effectively demonstrates string concatenation, it does not serve any particular purpose, since word's value is not modified. The function defined in Figure 15.4

```
function Capitalize(str)
// Assumes: str is a word
// Returns: str with first letter capitalized, all others lowercase
{
    var firstLetter, restString, cap;
    firstLetter = str.charAt(0);                    // GET FIRST CHAR
    restString = str.substring(1, str.length);      // GET REST OF WORD
    cap = firstLetter.toUpperCase() + restString.toLowerCase();
                                                    // PUT BACK TOGETHER
    return cap;
}
```

Figure 15.4   Function that capitalizes a string.

performs a similar, but more useful task. Function Capitalize takes a string as input and returns a capitalized version of that string. Using the charAt and substring methods, the function divides the string into separate substrings containing the first character and the rest of the string, as before. However, the first character is made upper case (using the toUpperCase method) and the rest of the string is made lower case (using the toLowerCase method) before the function concatenates the two components back together.

EXERCISE 15.3

Insert the Capitalize function definition from Figure 15.4 into the HEAD of your string.html page. Then, augment the page by adding a button labeled "Capitalize" and a text box that will display a capitalized version of the string when the button is clicked.

Once you have done this, test the page using various string inputs to verify that the function produces the desired results. How does the function behave when given a string containing characters other than letters (e.g., digits, spaces, punctuation marks)? Explain your observations.

EXERCISE 15.4

Define a function named RotateLeft that takes a string as input and returns a copy of that string in which all characters are rotated one position to the left. This means that the second character should be shifted from index 1 to index 0, the third character should be shifted from index 2 to index 1, and so on. The first character should be shifted so that it appears at the end of the string. For example, the function call RotateLeft("abcde") should return the string "bcdea". Insert this function definition into the HEAD of your string.html page; then, augment the page by adding a button labeled "Rotate Left" and a text box that will display the rotated string when the button is clicked.

EXERCISE 15.5

Define a similar function named `RotateRight` that shifts all characters in a string one position to the right. For example, the function call `RotateRight("abcde")` should return the string `"eabcd"`. Insert this function definition into the HEAD of your `string.html` page; then, add a button labeled `"Rotate Right"` and a text box that will display the rotated string when the button is clicked.

Searching Strings

The final string method that we will examine is the `search` method, which traverses a string in order to locate a given character or substring. The `search` method takes a character or string as input, then returns the index at which that character or string first occurs in the larger string. For example, if `str` = `"banana"`, then the call `str.search("n")` will return 2, since the character `"n"` first occurs in `str` at index 2. Likewise, the call `str.search("ana")` will return 1, since the first occurrence of the substring `"ana"` begins at index 1. If the desired character or substring does not occur in the string, the `search` method returns −1.

A simple application of the `search` method is to determine whether a string is a single word or a phrase. If the string contains no spaces, the call `str.search(" ")` will return −1, indicating that the string value consists of a single word. However, if `str.search(" ")` returns a nonnegative value, then the presence of spaces signifies a phrase containing multiple words.

EXERCISE 15.6

Define a function named `Classify` that takes a string as input and then determines whether the string is a single word (containing no spaces) or a phrase (containing one or more spaces). The function should return a string value, either `"word"` or `"phrase"`, depending on whether the input string contains any spaces. Once you have developed this function, insert its definition into the HEAD of your `string.html` page. Then, augment the page by adding a button labeled `"Classify"` and a text box that will display the string's classification when the button is clicked.

General Searches

As the above examples demonstrate, the `search` method can be used to locate the first occurrence of a single character (such as a space) within a string. There are times, however, when you might wish to search for a type of character, such as vowels or punctuation marks, rather than a specific value. For example, consider the task of converting a word into Pig Latin. As you may recall from your childhood, Pig Latin is a silly variation on the English language in which words are translated as follows:

- If a word contains no vowels or begins with a vowel, the characters "way" are appended to the end of the word. Thus, the word "nth" is translated as "nthway" in Pig Latin, and "apple" is translated as "appleway".
- If a word begins with a consonant, its initial sequence of consonants is shifted to the end of the word and followed by "ay". Thus, the word "banana" is translated as "ananabay" in Pig Latin, and "cherry" is translated as "errychay".

In order for a program to translate a word into Pig Latin, it must find the first vowel in the word. If the word doesn't contain a vowel or the first vowel is at index 0, then the program should translate the word by concatenating "way" onto the end of the original string. If the first vowel in the word occurs at an index other than 0, then the substring of characters preceding that index should be concatenated onto the substring starting with that index, followed by "ay".

One option for locating the first vowel in a string is to conduct five different searches. That is, you could perform a search to find the first occurrence of an "a" (if any), another search to find the first occurrence of an "e" (if any), and additional searches for "i", "o", and "u". Then, you would have to compare the indices returned by these searches to determine the smallest, which would represent the first occurrence of a vowel. Fortunately, JavaScript provides a simpler means of searching for a class of characters. If you specify a sequence of characters between /[and]/, the search method will traverse the string and find the first occurrence of any character in that sequence. For example, the call:

```
phrase.search(/[aeiou]/)
```

would return the index of the first occurrence of a lowercase vowel in phrase. If phrase contains no vowels, the search method will return −1, as before. Figure 15.5 lists several other search method calls that employ the /[ ]/ notation. Note that a hyphen can be used to more succinctly represent a range of characters, such as all lower-case letters (a–z) or all digits (0–9).

phrase.search(/[aeiou]/)	returns the index of the first occurrence of a lowercase vowel in phrase; returns −1 if not found
phrase.search(/[aeiouAEIOU]/)	returns the index of the first occurrence of a lower- or upper-case vowel in phrase; returns −1 if not found
phrase.search(/[a-z]/)	returns the index of the first occurrence of lower case letter in phrase; returns −1 if not found
phrase.search(/[a-zA-Z]/)	returns the index of the first occurrence of a lower-or upper-case letter in phrase; returns −1 if not found
phrase.search(/[0-9]/)	returns the index of the first occurrence of a digit in phrase; returns −1 if not found
phrase.search(/[!?.,;:-'"]/)	returns the index of the first occurrence of a punctuation mark in phrase; returns −1 if not found

Figure 15.5 search method calls to locate classes of characters.

 # Common errors to avoid...

Although they look similar, the method calls phrase.search("aeiou") and phrase.search(/[aeiou]/) have very different meanings. When given a string (a sequence of characters surrounded by quotes) as input, the search method looks for the first occurrence of that string. When given a class of characters (a sequence of characters surrounded by /[and]/) as input, the search method looks for the first occurrence of any single character from that class.

As you experiment with the search method, make sure that you do not confuse these two types of searches.

EXERCISE 15.7

Create a new Web page named piglatin.html containing a button and a text box in which the user can enter a word. When the user clicks the button, the Pig Latin translation of the input word should appear in another text box.

As part of your page, you should define a function called PigLatin that takes a string as input and returns the Pig Latin translation. For example, the call PigLatin("oops") should return "oopsway", whereas PigLatin("foo") should return "oofay".

Using your page, determine the Pig Latin translation of each of the following words:

```
scheme
3rd
shortstop
abracadabra
```

EXERCISE 15.8

Technically speaking, the Pig Latin rules that we have established apply only to words, not phrases. However, your current `piglatin.html` page does nothing to prevent users from entering a string containing spaces. Thus, a user could enter "foo bar" in the text box and be told that the Pig Latin translation is "oo barfay".

Modify your `PigLatin` function so that, before the string is translated, the function checks whether the input is a single word (i.e., whether it contains any spaces). If there are spaces in the input, the function should return the string "ILLEGAL INPUT".

String Manipulations and Repetition

Although this chapter has introduced multiple string manipulation techniques, none have involved conditional repetition. Capitalizing a word required dividing a string into pieces (using `charAt` and `substring`), modifying the pieces (using `toUpperCase` and `toLowerCase`), and then rejoining them (using the + operator). Likewise, converting a word into Pig Latin required finding a vowel (using `search`), splitting up the word (using `substring`), and putting it back together again (using +). However, certain manipulations, such as reversing a string's character sequence or replacing all the vowels in a string, involve repeatedly performing the same operations. To accomplish such tasks, we can combine while loops (introduced in Chapter 13) with string methods such as `charAt` and `search`.

The JavaScript code segment in Figure 15.6 illustrates how a while loop can be used to access and process each individual character in a string. In this example, the characters that comprise the string `str` are concatenated one-by-one onto another string, resulting in an exact copy. Initially, `str` is `"abcd"` and `copy` is the empty string. During each while-loop iteration, another character from `str` is accessed and concatenated onto the end of `copy`, yielding the strings `"a"`, then `"ab"`, then `"abc"`, and finally `"abcd"`. The variable `i`, which represents the index of the character currently being processed, is initialized to zero, then incremented at the end of the loop body. The table below the code traces the values of `i` and `copy` during each pass through the loop.

```
str = "abcd";
copy = "";                      // INITIALIZE copy TO EMPTY STRING

i = 0;                          // START AT BEGINNING OF str
while (i < str.length) {        // AS LONG AS CHARS LEFT IN str
    copy = copy + str.charAt(i); //    ADD CHAR TO END OF copy
    i = i + 1;                  //    GO TO NEXT CHAR
}

                              copy          i       str.charAt(i)
---------------------------------------------------------------------
before loop                    ""           0          "a"
after 1st loop pass            "a"          1          "b"
after 2nd loop pass            "ab"         2          "c"
after 3rd loop pass            "abc"        3          "d"
after 4th loop pass            "abcd"       4          undefined
```

Figure 15.6 Tracing code that copies a string character by character.

EXERCISE 15.9

Consider a variation on the code in Figure 15.6, in which the string concatenation inside the while loop is reversed:

```
str = "abcd";
copy = "";                    // INITIALIZE copy TO EMPTY STRING
i = 0;                        // START AT BEGINNING OF str
while (i < str.length) {      // AS LONG AS CHARS LEFT IN str
    copy = str.charAt(i) + copy;  //  ADD CHAR TO FRONT OF copy
    i = i + 1;                //   GO TO NEXT CHAR
}
```

Trace the behavior of this modified code in the table below:

	copy	i	str.charAt(i)
before loop	""	0	"a"
after 1st loop pass			
after 2nd loop pass			
after 3rd loop pass			
after 4th loop pass			

EXERCISE 15.10

Define a function named `Reverse` that takes a string as input and returns a copy of that string in reverse order. For example, the function call `Reverse("abcd")` should return the string `"dcba"`. After designing this function, insert its definition into the HEAD of your `string.html` page. Then, augment the page by adding a button labeled `"Reverse"` and a text box that will display the reversed string when the button is clicked.

EXERCISE 15.11

Consider the following code segment, which removes all spaces and punctuation marks from a given phrase. The first statement performs a search to determine whether the phrase contains a space or punctuation mark. If such a character is found, then its index will be stored in the variable `index`, and the loop test will succeed. The while loop removes the character from the phrase by concatenating the pieces of `phrase` that occur before and after that character and then assigning the result back to `phrase`. The last statement inside the loop body searches for an additional space or punctuation mark in the modified `phrase`. If one is found, the loop test will succeed again, and the character will be deleted. This process repeats until all spaces and punctuation marks have been removed.

```
index = phrase.search(/[ !?.,;:-'"]/);  // LOOK FOR SPACE/PUNCT.
while (index != -1) {                    // IF FOUND, REMOVE IT
    phrase = phrase.substring(0,index) +
            phrase.substring(index+1, phrase.length);
    index = phrase.search(/[ !?.,;:-'"]/); // LOOK FOR ANOTHER
}
```

Utilizing this code, define a function named `Strip` that takes a string as input and returns a copy of that string from which all spaces and punctuation marks have been removed. For example, the function call `Strip("Foo 2 You!")` should return `"Foo2You"`.

Insert the `Strip` function definition into your `string.html` page. Then, augment the page by adding a button and a text box that will display the stripped string when the button is clicked.

Example: Recognizing Palindromes

A *palindrome* is a word or phrase that reads the same backward and forward. For example, the words "madam" and "toot" are both palindromes. Generally, any nonletters in a word or phrase are ignored when testing for a palindrome, and case is irrelevant. Thus, the phrase "Madam, I'm Adam" is considered a palindrome. Using the `toUpperCase` method, as well as the `Reverse` and `Strip` functions you wrote earlier, you can design a page that recognizes palindromes.

EXERCISE 15.12

Design and implement a Web page named `pal.html` that tests whether a word or phrase is a palindrome. Your page should allow the user to enter a word or phrase and then display a string indicating whether that word or phrase is a palindrome. The code that evaluates the user's input should be case insensitive and should ignore any nonletters within the string. Thus, the following words and phrases would all be considered palindromes:

```
Bob
Able was I ere I saw Elba.
A man; a plan; a canal: Panama!
```

The choice of page elements (e.g., text boxes, buttons, text areas) and their layout is up to you, but the overall design should be intuitive and user friendly.

Looking Ahead...

In this chapter, you learned that JavaScript represents strings as objects, and that certain properties and operations (methods) are associated with every string value. The properties and methods of strings include the `length` property, which can be accessed to determine the number of characters in a string, and the `charAt` and `substring` methods, which can be used to retrieve individual components of a string. By combining these methods with the concatenation (+) operator, you were able to write pages that manipulate text in complex ways. Toward the end of the chapter, we introduced another string method: `search`. The `search` method's ability to locate a character, substring, or range of characters within a string added to your expressive power when manipulating text.

In Chapter 17, you will study another type of JavaScript object, arrays. Similar to a string object, which encompasses properties and methods for describing and modifying a sequence of characters, an array encapsulates a list of arbitrary items and provides properties and methods for manipulating those items. Before we continue our examination of objects, however, Chapter 16 returns to the study of the computer's internal workings. If you recall, Chapter 14 described the internal workings of the computer at a relatively high level of abstraction. In particular, the components of the CPU, its connections to main memory, and the flow of information between the components were studied. In Chapter 16, you will learn about computer hardware at a more detailed level, starting with transistors and building up to the complex circuitry comprising these key components of modern computer systems.

Chapter Summary

- A software object is a programming structure that models an object in the real world. An object encompasses data (properties) along with the operations (functions) that can be performed on that data.

- To distinguish them from stand-alone functions, functions that belong to an object are known as methods of that object.

- In JavaScript, strings are objects with numerous predefined properties and methods.

    - The `length` property specifies the number of characters in the string.

    - The `toUpperCase` method returns a copy of the string in which all lower-case letters have been replaced with their upper-case equivalents.

    - The `toLowerCase` method returns a copy of the string in which all upper-case letters have been replaced with their lower-case equivalents.

    - The `charAt` method returns the character stored at a particular index of a string.

    - The `substring` method returns a sequence of characters from a string, specified by starting and ending indices.

    - The `search` method returns the index of the first occurrence of a character, substring, or class of characters within a given string.

- Programmers access the properties and methods of an object by placing a period after the object's name and following the period with the desired property name or method call. For example, `str.length` will return the number of characters in `str`, whereas `str.charAt(0)` will return the first character in `str`.

- Using a while loop and the `charAt` method, a string can be traversed and modified/replaced character by character. Similarly, programmers can use a while loop and the `search` method to repeatedly search for characters and modify/replace them.

Supplemental Material and Exercises

More Practice with Strings

This chapter contains several exercises in which you traced code that traversed and manipulated strings. Since string manipulation can be confusing at first, additional exercises may prove beneficial.

EXERCISE 15.13

Consider the following code segment:

```
str = "foobar";
copy = "";

i = 0;
while (i < str.length) {
    copy = copy + str.charAt(i) + "-"
    i = i + 1;
}
```

Trace the behavior of this code by completing the table below:

```
                                copy        i      str.charAt(i)
               ----------------------------------------------------
before loop                      ""         0           "f"
after 1st loop pass
after 2nd loop pass
after 3rd loop pass
after 4th loop pass
after 5th loop pass
after 6th loop pass
```

EXERCISE 15.14

Consider the following code segment:

```
str = "foobar";

i = str.search(/[aeiou]/);
while (i != -1) {
   str = str.substring(0, i) + "*" + str.substring(i+1, str.length);
   i = str.search(/[aeiou]/);
}
```

Trace the behavior of this code by completing the table below:

```
                                        str          i
               ------------------------------------------------
before loop                          "foobar"        1
after 1st loop pass
after 2nd loop pass
after 3rd loop pass
```

EXERCISE 15.15

Advertisers have found that people remember words much more easily than they remember numbers. Thus, we are continually bombarded with phone numbers that are expressed using letters. To help people dial alphabetic phone numbers, most phone buttons list the letters along with their corresponding digits. In case your phone doesn't provide this information, the following list maps letters to their numeric equivalents:

2	ABC	6	MNO
3	DEF	7	PRS
4	GHI	8	TUV
5	JKL	9	WXY

Note that the digits 1 and 0 do not have corresponding letters. Also, the letters Q and Z are not represented.

Design and create a Web page named phoney.html that converts alphabetic phone numbers into entirely numeric ones. Your page should allow the user to enter the number (possibly containing letters) in a text box. When the user clicks a button, the page should call a function to translate the input, generating a version of the phone number in which all letters have been replaced by their corresponding digits. Any nonletters should remain unchanged in the new string. Figure 15.7 depicts an example appearance of the page.

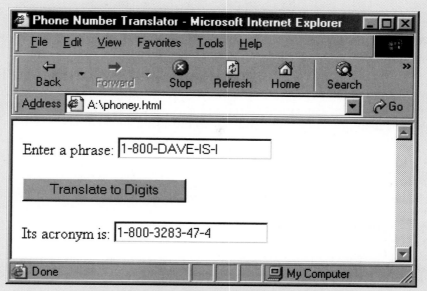

Figure 15.7 Sample appearance of `phoney.html`.

Roman Holiday

The ancient Romans developed a system for representing number values alphabetically. This "Roman numeral" system employed the following letters to symbolize the indicated numeric values:

$$M = 1{,}000 \quad D = 500 \quad C = 100 \quad L = 50 \quad X = 10 \quad V = 5 \quad I = 1$$

To convert an ancient Roman numeral to its numeric equivalent, you must sum up the values represented by each of the letters in the numeral. For example, MCVII represents $1{,}000 + 100 + 5 + 1 + 1 = 1{,}107$, whereas CCIIII represents $100 + 100 + 1 + 1 + 1 + 1 = 204$. By convention, letters are always listed in decreasing order of value.

EXERCISE 15.16

Design and create a Web page named `roman.html` containing a text box in which the user can enter an ancient Roman numeral. When the user clicks a button, the number represented by that Roman numeral should appear in a separate text box.

As part of your page, you should define a function named `RomanToNum` that takes a Roman numeral (a string of letters) as input and returns the value represented by that numeral.

Once you have completed your page, use it to convert the following Roman numerals to numeric values:

    MCLXVI
    XXXX
    MM
    MXXIIII
    LXXXXVIIII

EXERCISE 15.17

Add elements to your `roman.html` page so that the user can perform the opposite conversion, translating a number into an ancient Roman numeral.

[*Hint:* One approach to building the Roman numeral would be to write a series of while loops. As long as the number entered by the user is greater than or equal to 1,000, add the letter "M" to a string representing the Roman numeral and subtract 1,000 from the value. If the resulting number is greater than or equal to 500, add "D" to the string and subtract 500. Then, repeatedly add "C"s and subtract 100 until the number becomes less than 100, and so on.]

EXERCISE 15.18

A more challenging programming exercise would be to modify your `roman.html` page so that it utilizes the modern style of Roman numerals. In this system, I can appear before V and X to represent 4 and 9, respectively; X can appear before L and C to represent 40 and 90, respectively; and C can appear before D and M to represent 400 and 900, respectively.

The Math and document Objects

In this chapter, we have already explained that strings, as well as buttons and other form elements, represent objects. However, you may not remember that you encountered a JavaScript object in Chapter 5, when we introduced mathematical functions such as `Math.sqrt` and `Math.random`. We are now able to recognize `Math` as an object that encapsulates various useful mathematical functions and constants. A set of common mathematical functions, including `Math.sqrt` and `Math.random`, are implemented as methods of the `Math` object. In addition to these methods, the `Math` object encompasses properties that represent standard mathematical constants, such as `Math.PI` for $\pi = 3.14159\ldots$.

EXERCISE 15.19

Whenever you order a pizza, you are faced with the dilemma of which size to order. Is a large pizza a good deal, or would you be better off ordering two mediums?

Create a Web page named `pizza.html` that determines the cost per square inch of any pizza. The page should contain text boxes in which the user can enter the diameter of the pizza (i.e., the number of inches across) and its price. Given this input, the cost per square inch can be computed as:

$$\text{cost per square inch} = \text{cost}/(\pi * (\text{diameter}/2)^2)$$

Using the `Math.PI` property and the `Math.pow` method, your page should compute and display the cost per square inch for any specified pizza.

Once you have completed the page, use it to determine which would be the better deal: a 16-inch pizza for $18.99 or two 12-inch pizzas for $10.99 each.

EXERCISE 15.20

When you computed the cost per square inch of a pizza in Exercise 15.19, you probably encountered results containing many digits of precision. When performing computations that yield dollar amounts, programmers typically limit precision so that only two digits appear to the right of the decimal place, representing the exact number of cents. Thus, a number such as 1.987245 would be rounded to 1.99.

Define a function named RoundDigits that takes a number and rounds it so that a specified number of digits occur to the right of the decimal place. The function should accept two inputs, the first indicating the number to be rounded and the second the number of digits of precision. For example, the call RoundDigits(1.987245, 2) should return 1.99, whereas RoundDigits(10.1234, 3) should return 10.123.

[*Hint:* To round a number so that N digits appear to the right of the decimal place, you can multiply the number by 10^N, round the resulting value to the nearest integer, then divide by 10^N. For example, to round 1.987245 so that two digits follow the decimal, first multiply by $10^2 = 100$ to obtain 198.7245. Then round to the nearest integer, 199. Finally, divide by $10^2 = 100$, yielding 1.99. Use the Math.pow method in implementing the RoundDigits function.

Once you have defined your RoundDigits function, incorporate it into your pizza.html page so that the cost per square inch is displayed as an exact monetary value.

The other object that you have employed in your JavaScript programs is the document object. The document object encapsulates information and operations associated with the Web page itself. For example, the document.write method, which we have used in numerous pages, writes a message in the page as the page is loaded. The document object also provides two useful properties, URL and lastModified. The document.URL property specifies the URL (Web address) of the page, whereas the document.lastModified property specifies the date and time when the page was last modified.

While surfing the Web, you may have noticed Web pages that display their URLs and modification dates at the bottom. This is useful information, in that it reminds users of the page's location and lets them know how up to date its contents are. Although you could include this data as plain text within a page, ensuring the accuracy of the information would require updating the text every time the page was moved or edited. If you display the values by accessing the URL and lastModified properties, however, the information is automatically updated within the page.

EXERCISE 15.21

Add the following code to the bottom of your home page (and any other pages you wish), causing the page to display its URL and modification date:

```
<script type="text/javascript">
    document.write("Page location: " + document.URL + "<br />");
    document.write("Last modified: " + document.lastModified);
</script>
```

Chapter 16

Inside the Computer— Transistors and Integrated Circuits

This chapter uses narrative, illustrations, hands-on experimentation, and review questions to introduce computer science and technology concepts.

> *What we didn't realize then was that the integrated circuit would reduce the cost of electronic functions by a factor of a million to one; nothing had ever done that for anything before.*
>
> Jack Kilby
>
> *Think of it! With VLSI we can pack 100 ENIACS in 1 sq. cm.*
>
> Alan Perlis
>
> *Electricity travels a foot in a nanosecond.*
>
> Grace Murray Hopper

In Chapter 14, you were introduced to the hardware inside a computer at a relatively high level of abstraction. The chapter described components of the von Neumann architecture, such as the central processing unit (CPU) and main memory; the buses that connect these components; and the way in which various pieces are assembled to produce a general-purpose, programmable computer. In this chapter, you will delve further into the workings of computer hardware, focusing on the basic technology used to construct hardware components.

Recall from Chapter 6 that early computing devices, such as Pascal's calculator (1642) and Babbage's Analytical Engine (1833), were purely mechanical. Such devices stored information as different settings on dials and cogs and then processed this information in response to physical actions (e.g., turning a crank to spin interlocking wheels). Modern computers, by contrast, are powered by electricity, using electrical signals to store and manipulate information. This chapter begins by reviewing the fundamental properties of electricity, as well as the importance of electrical switches to computing technology. After covering these basics, the chapter describes transistors, the building blocks of modern computers, and the ways in which transistors can be combined into circuits that store values and perform operations. We end the chapter with a discussion of integrated circuits, microprocessors, and the manufacturing techniques used to create computer chips.

Electricity and Switches

Computers, along with most modern machines, are electrical devices. The components of a computer require electrical power to carry out their assigned tasks. For example, electricity generates the light that shines through a computer screen, illuminating the individual pixels that make up images and letters. Electricity also runs the motor that spins the hard-drive disk, allowing information to be accessed. In addition, the main memory and CPU employ electrical signals to store and manipulate data. For example, numbers are stored in main memory or transferred to the CPU as bit patterns, in which the individual 1s and 0s are represented by the presence or absence of electrical current along a wire. While we are all familiar with electricity in that we use it every day, understanding the details of electrical currents and their properties requires significant knowledge of physics.

Electricity Basics

Simply stated, electricity is a flow of *electrons*—the negatively charged particles in atoms—through a medium. Elements such as copper, silver, and gold are especially good at conducting electricity, meaning that their molecular structure can accommodate the flow of electrons with little resistance. To ensure the efficient delivery of electricity, most power and phone lines are constructed from copper wire (Figure 16.1), whereas computers often use gold for connecting electrical components over small distances. Other elements, especially nonmetals such as carbon and oxygen, are poor conductors of electricity.

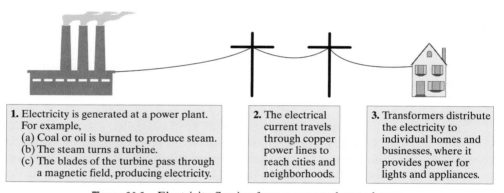

1. Electricity is generated at a power plant. For example,
  (a) Coal or oil is burned to produce steam.
  (b) The steam turns a turbine.
  (c) The blades of the turbine pass through a magnetic field, producing electricity.

2. The electrical current travels through copper power lines to reach cities and neighborhoods.

3. Transformers distribute the electricity to individual homes and businesses, where it provides power for lights and appliances.

Figure 16.1 Electricity flowing from a power plant to homes.

Electricity can be quantified in various ways. An *ampere*, or amp, is a unit that gauges electron flow: 1 amp of current is equal to 6.24 quintillion (6.24×10^{18}) electrons flowing past a given point each second. Another common measure of electricity is *voltage*, which corresponds to the physical force produced by the flow of electrons. In the United States, standard household outlets carry 110 or 120 volts; in Europe, 220-volt outlets are more typical.

Switches

The most basic tool for controlling the flow of electricity is a switch. A *switch* is a device designed to connect or disconnect two wires, thus regulating the flow of electricity between them. For example, a light switch on a wall serves as an intermediary between the power line entering your home and the outlet that operates a lighting fixture. If the switch is in the "on" position, then the wires that link the outlet to the power line are connected, and the lighting fixture receives electricity. However, if the switch is turned off, then the connection is interrupted, and no power reaches the outlet. Figure 16.2 depicts the relationship between a light switch and the electrical connection it regulates. In this and subsequent figures, a blue line symbolizes a wire carrying electrical current, whereas a black line symbolizes a wire carrying no current.

Figure 16.2 A light switch controls the flow of electricity from outside power lines to household appliances.

Transistors

As we have established in previous chapters, computers store and manipulate information as electrical signals. Since switches are integral to controlling electrical flow, it should not be surprising that computer components such as main memory and the CPU incorporate switches. In fact, advances in switching mechanisms have defined the first five generations of computer technology (see Chapter 6 for a detailed analysis of computer history). The first electronic computers (Generation 0) were built in the 1930s using switches called electromagnetic relays. These relays were physical switches whose on/off positions were controlled by voltage to a magnet. In the 1940s, the replacement of relays with vacuum tubes launched computer history's Generation 1. Although a vacuum tube could be turned on and off as if it were a mechanical switch, the tubes' lack of moving parts enabled them to shift between states much more quickly than relays could. However, vacuum tubes had a downside—they generated large amounts of heat and tended to burn out frequently. In 1948, John Bardeen, Walter Brattain, and William Shockley at AT&T Bell Labs invented the transistor, ushering in yet another generation of computer technology (Generation 2). A *transistor*, considered by many to be the most important invention of the 20th century, is a solid piece of metal attached to a wire that serves as a switch by alternatively conducting or resisting electricity (Figure 16.3). Transistors are similar to vacuum tubes in that they contain no moving parts; however, transistors are smaller, more reliable, and more energy efficient than vacuum tubes. Due to these advantages, transistors enabled hardware experts to design smaller, faster machines at a drastically lower cost.

Although the first transistor was made of gold and germanium, modern transistors are constructed from silicon instead of germanium. Both germanium and silicon belong to a category of elements called *semiconductors*, or metals that can be manipulated to be either good or bad conductors of electricity. Through a process known as *doping*, impurities can be added to a slab of germanium or silicon, causing the metal to act as an electrical switch. Today, most transistors are built using metal-oxide semiconductor (MOS) technology. A positively doped metal-oxide semiconductor (PMOS) transistor contains silicon doped with impurities that make it conduct electricity, but it can be made nonconductive by applying current to a separate control wire. Conversely, a negatively doped metal-oxide semiconductor (NMOS) transistor contains silicon doped with impurities that make it nonconductive, but it can be made conductive by applying current

Figure 16.3 A collection of transistors from the 1950s. While packaging varies depending on the manufacturer, each transistor has input and output wires, and at least one control wire for determining whether the transistor will conduct electricity.

to a control wire. When implemented together, PMOS and NMOS transistors are collectively referred to as CMOS (combined metal-oxide semiconductor) technology.

Transistors as Switches

Figures 16.4 and 16.5 are abstractions that illustrate the behavior of PMOS and NMOS transistors. In practice, each transistor acts as a switch that can be opened or closed to control the flow of electricity through a wire. A control wire determines whether the switch is closed, allowing current to move through the connection, or open, halting the flow of electricity. In the case of a PMOS transistor, the switch is closed when there is no current (0 volts) on the control wire, but opens when current (5 volts) is applied. Conversely, the switch on an NMOS transistor is open when there is no current (0 volts) on the control wire, but closes when there is a current (5 volts).

The Web page `logic.html` (accessible at `http://www.prenhall.com/reed`) provides an interactive tool for studying the behavior of PMOS and NMOS transistors. By accessing the pull-down menu to the left of each simulated transistor and selecting the desired voltage for its control wire (0 volts or 5 volts), the user can open and close the switches and observe their behavior.

Figure 16.4 PMOS transistor.

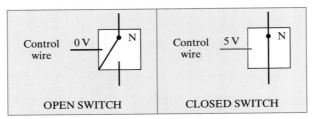

Figure 16.5 NMOS Transistor.

Although transistors were initially more expensive than their vacuum tube counterparts, the benefits that transistors offered in terms of size, power consumption, heat dispersal, and longevity far outweighed the cost disadvantage. The year 1953 marked the launch of the first transistor-powered commercial product, a hearing aid, which was followed by the transistor radio in 1954. A year later, researchers at Bell Labs constructed the first computer built entirely with transistors. As mass production techniques improved throughout the 1950s, the cost of manufacturing transistors dropped steadily, and transistors soon replaced vacuum tubes in virtually all electronic appliances. In addition to commercial success, the invention of the transistor brought scientific recognition to Shockley, Brattain, and Bardeen, earning them the 1956 Nobel Prize in Physics (Figure 16.6).

Figure 16.6 John Bardeen, William Shockley, and Walter Brattain looking at an early transistor through a microscope.

From Transistors to Gates

At first glance, it is not obvious how a transistor—or any electric switch, for that matter—can serve as the building block of modern computers. After all, computers are powerful machines that perform millions of complex mathematical and logical operations per second—how can a simple switch contribute to this impressive behavior? However, as this book has demonstrated, even the most intricate computer functionality is produced by combining sequences of simpler components. For example, Chapter 1 taught you that, while a single bit can differentiate between only two different values, a collection of 8 bits (a byte) can represent any character on a keyboard. Likewise, in Chapter 7, you saw that simple JavaScript statements can be joined to create functions that carry out complex computations. In much the same way, transistors can be combined to form *circuits*, which perform the underlying operations of computers.

A circuit is a collection of transistors (and possibly other electronic devices) wired together to produce a particular behavior. For example, a hardware designer might combine an NMOS transistor and a PMOS transistor to form the circuit shown in Figure 16.7. We can think of the wire on the left as carrying an input signal and the wire on the right as producing a corresponding output signal. A consistent electrical current is supplied to this circuit at the top (labeled 5 V), and the circuit is grounded at the bottom so that any electrical current is carried harmlessly away. Note that the input wire to the left of the circuit serves as the control wire for the two transistors. If no current is applied to the input wire, then the PMOS transistor will close to allow current to travel on the output wire, and the NMOS transistor will open to disconnect the ground (as shown on the left-hand side of Figure 16.7). Likewise, if current is applied to the input wire, then the PMOS transistor will open to disconnect the output wire and the NMOS transistor will close to ground the input (as shown on the right-hand side of Figure 16.7). This example represents the simplest circuit that performs a useful function: producing an output signal that is the opposite of the input signal. A circuit of this type is known as a NOT gate.

Figure 16.7 CMOS circuitry for a NOT gate.

Gates and Binary Logic

The term "gate" suggests a simple circuit that controls the flow of electricity in much the same way that an iron gate might control traffic flow through a fence. In the case of a NOT gate, the flow of electricity is manipulated so that the output signal is always the opposite of the input signal (input voltage → no output voltage, no input voltage → output voltage). Although it is accurate to describe gates' inputs and outputs as voltage levels, we can think of these inputs and outputs more abstractly in terms of binary values: 0 represents no current, and 1 represents current. From this perspective, we can think of a gate as computing a function on binary values. The table on the right-hand side of Figure 16.8 lists each possible input value for a NOT gate, along with its corresponding output value. The left-hand side of the figure depicts a symbol—a large triangle connected to a smaller circle—that is often used to represent a NOT gate; this notation abstracts away all the circuit's underlying details, allowing a designer to draw the circuit simply and easily.

NOT gate

Input ──▷○── Output

input	NOT output
0	1
1	0

Figure 16.8 Behavior of a NOT gate.

You may have noticed a similarity between the NOT gate and the JavaScript logical connective ! from Chapter 11. In fact, the NOT gate inverts voltages in the same way that the NOT (!) operator inverts Boolean values (!true → false, !false → true). If we replaced 0 with false and 1 with true, the table from Figure 16.8 would perfectly describe the behavior of the NOT operator. For this reason, tables that describe the mapping from circuitry inputs to outputs are known as *truth tables*.

In addition to the NOT gate, many other simple circuits can be defined to perform useful tasks. Figure 16.9 shows how two NMOS transistors and two PMOS transistors can be wired together to form an AND gate, which corresponds to the JavaScript connective && (AND). The resulting circuit contains two input wires and produces voltage on its output wire only if both input wires carry voltage. Figure 16.10 depicts the circuitry and behavior of an OR gate, which corresponds to the JavaScript connective || (OR). The output wire of an OR gate carries voltage as long as either input wire carries voltage. Both figures include the symbols used to represent the specified gates, as well as truth tables describing the gates' output.

input1	input2	AND output
0	0	0
0	1	0
1	0	0
1	1	1

Figure 16.9 CMOS circuitry and behavior of an AND gate.

AND, OR, and NOT gates are the simplest circuits that perform well-defined logical operations. By combining these primitive circuits, a hardware designer can construct all the logic required to store and manipulate information within a computer.

To better understand the behavior of each logic gate, both in the abstract and as complex circuits involving NMOS and PMOS transistors, visit the Web page logic.html (accessible at http://www.prenhall.com/reed) and experiment with the simulated gates.

From Gates to Complex Circuits

Throughout this text, we have stressed the centrality of abstraction in the design of software. For example, programmers define functions by combining the basic constructs of a language, such as variables and operators. Once such a function has been defined, a programmer can invoke it without understanding the details of its implementation, since this information was abstracted away when the behavior was encapsulated as a function. Using these abstractions as building blocks, the programmer

OR gate

input1	input2	OR output
0	0	0
0	1	1
1	0	1
1	1	1

Figure 16.10 CMOS circuitry and behavior of an OR gate.

is able to define even more powerful applications, and so on. This same pattern of ever-increasing complexity and abstraction applies to the construction of computer hardware. For instance, transistors are connected to form basic logic gates, which are then combined to build more advanced circuitry.

To demonstrate the process of designing logical circuitry, let us consider the task of adding two numbers. As we saw in Chapter 14, the CPU's arithmetic logic unit (ALU) contains circuitry for adding numbers. Input buses carry numbers as binary signals to the ALU, where the sum of those numbers is calculated and represented as a series of signals on an output bus. Suppose we wished to design circuitry that would perform addition within the ALU. For simplicity, we will initially limit ourselves to the task of adding 4-bit numbers. Figure 16.11 depicts the input and output signals involved in adding 0101 and 1100, which yield the sum 10001 (since $0101_2 + 1100_2 = 10001_2$).

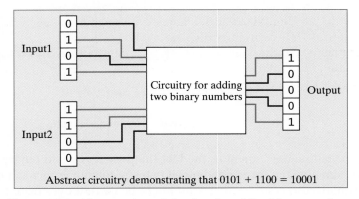

Figure 16.11 Abstract view of circuitry for adding binary numbers.

Before we continue, it might help to quickly review the rules of binary addition. In principle, adding binary (base 2) numbers is no different from adding decimal (base 10) numbers. Recall that, in decimal, corresponding columns of digits are added together, starting from the right. If the sum of any two digits yields a 2-digit number (a number ≥ 10), then the 1 is carried over to the next column. Similarly, in binary, corresponding bits are added together, starting from the right. If the sum of any two bits yields a 2-bit number (a number $\geq 10_2$), then the 1 is carried over to the next column.

For example, Figure 16.12 portrays two different examples of binary addition. In the example on the left, adding the rightmost bits 1 and 1 produces a sum of 10_2 (decimal value two). Thus, a 0 is written in the rightmost column of the result and a 1 is carried over to the next column. The sum of the second set of bits then becomes 10_2 because of the previous carry, causing a second 0 to be written in the result and a 1 to be carried over to the third addition. In the example on the right, a 1 is carried over after adding the leftmost bits. In such an instance, the sum of the numbers will contain one more bit than the largest input value (in the same way that $9 + 9 = 18$, and 18 has one more digit than 9 does).

$$
\begin{array}{r}
{\scriptstyle 1\ 1}\\
1\ 0\ 1\ 1_2\\
+\qquad 1_2\\
\hline
1\ 1\ 0\ 0_2
\end{array}
\qquad\qquad
\begin{array}{r}
{\scriptstyle 1\ 1}\\
1\ 1\ 0\ 0_2\\
+\quad 1\ 0\ 1_2\\
\hline
1\ 0\ 0\ 0\ 1_2
\end{array}
$$

Figure 16.12 Examples of binary addition.

Although binary addition is a relatively straightforward operation, designing a circuit for adding binary numbers is far from trivial. If we attempted to design such a circuit from scratch using transistors, the complexity involved could become overwhelming. However, if we think of circuit design in terms of multitiered complexity, then the underlying layers can establish abstractions that simplify the upper layers. For example, instead of starting at the transistor level, we can use logical gates AND, OR, and NOT as building blocks to create a simple circuit for adding 2 bits. Such a circuit would contain two input lines, representing the bits to be added, and two outputs, representing the sum of the inputs and a possible carry. This functionality can be implemented using only four gates, as illustrated in Figure 16.13. In the pictured configuration, the first input has a value of 1 and the second input has a value of 0, yielding a sum of 1 and a carry of 0. This type of circuit is known as a ***half-adder***.

half-adder demonstrating that 1 + 0 = 01

Figure 16.13 Half-adder circuit.

The term "half-adder" refers to the fact that, when you add binary numbers containing more than one bit, summing the corresponding bit pairs by column is only half the job. As you add up each column, you must also consider that a bit might be carried over from the previous addition. Thus, adding corresponding bits in a number actually requires the ability to add 3 bits: the two input values and a possible carry. Using half-adders and logical gates as building blocks, we can design a circuit that performs this task. Figure 16.14 depicts such a circuit, which is known as a *full-adder* and consists of two half-adders and an OR gate. In the pictured configuration, two of the inputs have values of 1, yielding a sum of 0 and a carry of 1.

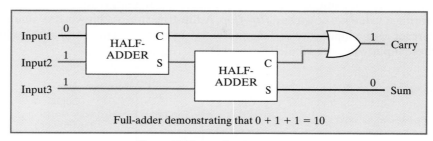

Full-adder demonstrating that 0 + 1 + 1 = 10

Figure 16.14 Full-adder circuit.

Finally, using full-adders as building blocks, we can design a more complex circuit that sums two 4-bit numbers. Since a full adder is required to add each corresponding bit pair together (along with a possible carry from the previous addition), the appropriate circuit will encompass four full-adders wired together (Figure 16.15). In the pictured configuration, the two input numbers are 0101 and 1100, yielding a sum of 10001.

4-bit adder demonstrating that 0101 + 1100 = 10001

Figure 16.15 4-bit adder circuit.

From this basic design, you can see how hardware designers produce circuits that add arbitrarily large binary numbers. For example, to add 8-bit numbers, you could wire eight full-adders together in a similar pattern. You could also achieve this functionality by combining two copies of the 4-bit adder circuit.

To better understand the intricacies of ALU circuitry, you can observe and experiment with the behavior of half-adders, full-adders, and 4-bit adders by visiting the Web page `logic.html` (accessible at `http://www.prenhall.com/reed`).

Example: Designing Memory Circuitry

In addition to performing calculations such as adding numbers, electronic circuitry is also used to implement memory that the CPU can access quickly. For example, both main memory and the registers within the CPU are composed of circuitry. However, the circuitry used to store bits in memory is different from the circuitry that performs operations such as addition. Whereas adders manipulate inputs to produce outputs, memory circuits must maintain values over time. The simplest circuit for storing a value is known as a *flip-flop*. A flip-flop stores a bit whose value can be set to 1 by applying current to one input wire and then reset to 0 by applying current to another input wire. In Figure 16.16, these input wires are labeled Set and Reset, respectively.

Figure 16.16 Flip-flop for storing a bit.

It is important to note that a flip-flop maintains the last value assigned to it, either a 1 if current was most recently applied to the Set wire or a 0 if current was most recently applied to the Reset wire. Thus, setting or resetting a flip-flop requires only a brief current on the appropriate input wire, and once set or reset, the output of the circuit is constant. This behavior is achieved within the circuitry via a feedback loop, which causes the output of the circuit to circle back and refresh the inputs. For example, Figures 16.17 and 16.18 portray a flip-flop that is constructed from two AND gates and four NOT gates. Note that, in each diagram, the outputs of the rightmost NOT gates loop back and serve as inputs for the AND gates. On the left-hand side of Figure 16.17, a current is applied to the Set wire so that the flip-flop stores a 1. On the right-hand side of the figure, the current on the Set wire has stopped flowing, but the flip-flop circuitry retains the output 1. Similarly, Figure 16.18 shows a flip-flop being reset to store a 0 (in the left-hand diagram) and then maintaining that bit value even after the input current has stopped (in the right-hand diagram).

Figure 16.17 Flip-flop being set (storing a 1 bit), then maintaining that value.

Figure 16.18 Flip-flop being reset (storing a 0 bit), then maintaining that value.

In much the same way that full-adders can be wired together to produce the ALU's complex circuitry, flip-flops can be wired together to construct the registers and main-memory cells of a computer. You can observe and experiment with the behavior of flip-flops at the Web page `logic.html` (accessible at `http://www.prenhall.com/reed`).

From Circuits to Microchips

Initially, circuits were built by wiring together individual transistors. If a hardware designer wished to create a new computer component, he or she would assemble a large number of transistors and physically connect them using wire and a soldering iron. In addition to being extremely tedious and error prone, this approach did not lend itself to mass production. Every time a particular circuit was needed, it had to be constructed from scratch out of transistors and wire. Furthermore, there were limitations to the minimum size of circuits built from individual transistors. Since the spacing of transistors within circuits had to accommodate the human hands that inserted and soldered the wires, even simple circuits consisting of tens or hundreds of transistors were quite large.

The Integrated Circuit

In 1958, two researchers independently developed techniques for manufacturing mass-produced, smaller circuitry. Jack Kilby at Texas Instruments and Robert Noyce at Fairchild Semiconductor Corporation both realized that, to enable the mass production of circuits, all the components (including transistors and their connections) would have to be constructed as a single unit. Each researcher proposed a manufacturing process in which circuitry is layered onto a single wafer of silicon, known as a ***microchip***. Because every component of the circuit was integrated onto the same microchip, these circuits became known as ***integrated circuits*** (Figure 16.19).

Figure 16.19   Microscopic photograph of electronic circuitry on the Intel 4004 microchip (1971).

In 1959, both Texas Instruments and Fairchild Semiconductor applied for and were awarded patents on their microchip-manufacturing techniques. After several years of legal battles, the two companies agreed to cross-license their technologies, which marked the beginning of the computer microchip industry. After leaving Fairchild Semiconductor, Noyce went on to cofound Intel, today's dominant microchip producer. Kilby was awarded the 2000 Nobel Prize in Physics in recognition of his contribution to the development of the integrated circuit.

Manufacturing Integrated Circuits

The production of integrated circuits is perhaps the most complex engineering process in the world. The transistors that are manufactured on a microchip can be as small as 0.13 microns (0.13×10^{-6} meters), or roughly 1/750th the width of a human hair. To achieve precision on such a small scale, integrated-circuit manufacturing relies heavily on techniques normally associated with photography. As you may already know, photographic images are created by exploiting chemicals whose physical properties change upon exposure to light. When someone takes a picture, chemicals on the film react to incoming light. These chemical changes are then translated to color intensities when the photograph is developed.

To produce the incredibly small and precise circuitry on microchips, hardware manufacturers use similar light-sensitive chemicals. Initially, the silicon chip is covered with a semiconductor material, then coated with a layer of *photoresist*—a chemical sensitive to ultraviolet light. The pattern of transistors that is to be layered onto the chip is printed on a mask, a transparent surface on which an opaque coating has been applied to form patterns. Ultraviolet light is filtered through the mask, passing through the transparent portions and striking the surface of the chip in the specified pattern. The photoresist that is exposed to ultraviolet light reacts, hardening the layer of semiconductor below it. Once exposure is completed, the photoresist that was not exposed and the soft layer of semiconductor below are etched away, leaving only the desired pattern of semiconductor material on the surface of the chip (Figure 16.20). This process may be repeated 20 or 30 times, depositing layer upon layer of semiconductor material to form the circuit's transistors and their connections. Even the "wires" that connect the transistors are formed by depositing conductive material on the surface of the chip.

Photoresist
Semiconductor
Silicon disc

Mask (black segments are transparent to UV)

1. The surface of the silicon chip is coated with a semiconductor material, followed by a layer of photoresist.

2. Ultraviolet radiation is sent through a mask, reacting with the photoresist where it passes through the mask to strike the chip.

3. The photoresist and unexposed semiconductor material are etched away, leaving the desired pattern on the chip.

Figure 16.20   Adding a single layer of circuitry to a silicon chip.

Not surprisingly, manufacturing microchips requires extreme care and cleanliness. A single human hair or fleck of skin could damage thousands of transistors if it came in contact with the circuit. To prevent such problems, microchip production takes place in "clean rooms," where sealed ventilation systems remove airborne contaminants and workers wear protective suits that contain loose hair and skin cells (Figure 16.21).

Figure 16.21 Workers use specialized equipment to produce and inspect the circuitry on microchips. Note that protective clothing is worn not for the benefit of the worker, but to protect the microchip circuitry from contaminants such as skin cells and loose hairs.

Packaging Microchips

Since a silicon chip containing an integrated circuit is fragile, it is encased in plastic for protection (Figure 16.22). Metal pins are then inserted on both sides of the packaging, facilitating easy connections to other microchips.

Figure 16.22 An early microchip, with circuitry visible in the cutaway portion of the plastic case. Two rows of metal pins are used connect the circuitry to other components of the computer.

It is safe to say that the microchip has revolutionized the way in which computers are designed and built. Useful circuits are implemented and mass produced as microchips. Since microchips can be manufactured in bulk, their invention has drastically lowered the cost of constructing circuitry. Furthermore, the tiny circuits on microchips are much closer to one another, which increases the speed of operations by shortening the distances over which electrical signals must travel. Today, the designers of computer systems do not even need to consider the low-level details of transistors and other electrical devices. Instead, they can simply select prebuilt microchips that contain the needed circuitry and wire those microchips together.

Improvements in manufacturing techniques and technologies are constantly reducing the scale of integrated circuits. In the early 1960s, a microchip one inch across might have contained the circuitry for five to ten logic gates. By the early 1970s, the space required to hold circuitry had shrunk to the point where a complete CPU could be manufactured on a single microchip, known as a microprocessor. The first CPU contained entirely on a microchip was the Intel 4004. Released in 1971, the 4004 consisted of roughly 2,300 transistors and their connections. By the early 1980s, the era of very large scale integration (VLSI) was begun, where hundreds of thousands of transistors could fit on a single chip. For example, the Intel 80286, which was released in 1982 and used in many early personal computers, encompassed more than 134,000 transistors. By the 1990s, microprocessors with millions of transistors were manufactured, with the Pentium 4 microprocessor (released in 2000) encompassing more than 42 million transistors. Moore's Law—named after its originator, Intel's Gordon Moore—describes this remarkable evolution of technology and manufacturing. Moore noted as early as 1965 that the number of transistors that can fit on a microchip doubles every 12 to 18 months. As Figure 16.23 demonstrates, this pattern has been maintained over the past 30 years, and industry analysts predict that it will continue to hold for the near future.

Figure 16.23 This graph (with a logarithmic scale) shows how Intel's family of processors has followed Moore's Law, doubling the number of transistors every 12 to 18 months.

Looking Ahead...

In this chapter, you studied the low-level functionality of computer hardware, including various implementations of electrical switches. After describing the behavior of electrical currents, the chapter explained that a transistor is a solid piece of silicon doped with impurities to make it act as a semiconductor. Transistors are designed to either conduct electricity or not, depending on whether an electrical current is applied to an input wire; this functionality allows each transistor to act as an electrical switch. When wired together, transistors can form circuits that perform computational tasks. The simplest such circuits, known as logic gates, process electrical inputs and produce output signals according to logical functions such as AND, OR, and NOT. In turn, logic gates can be wired together to form more complex circuits, eventually building to the circuitry that makes up the ALU, main memory, and other computer components. Modern technology makes it possible to integrate complex circuitry, consisting of millions of transistors and their connections, on a single microchip that can be mass produced.

With this deeper understanding of computer hardware in mind, Chapter 17 completes our coverage of fundamental programming skills by discussing applications that involve storing and manipulating large amounts of data. Arrays, which are explored in Chapter 17, are lists of items that can be stored and accessed efficiently, allowing programmers to process sequences of words or numbers. As you will discover, arrays have many common features with strings, which were studied in Chapter 15. Both are examples of JavaScript objects, with properties and operations (methods) associated with them. Both also represent sequences of items that can be accessed via indeces. However, arrays are much more flexible than strings, in that they are not limited to sequences of characters only—the values stored in an array can be of any type (including numbers, strings, and even other arrays). As such, they prove to be useful in a variety of applications that require storing and processing collections of related information.

Chapter Summary

- Computers are electrical devices, requiring electricity to perform tasks such as illuminating the screen, powering the hard drive, and transferring data as electrical impulses.

- Electricity is a flow of electrons—the negatively charged particles in atoms—through a medium. Gold and copper are especially good at conducting electricity, and so they are often used to connect computer components.

- An electrical switch is a device designed to connect or disconnect two wires, thus regulating the flow of electricity between them. Switches can be implemented using a variety of technologies, including electromagnetic relays, vacuum tubes, and transistors.

- A transistor, considered by many to be the most important invention of the 20th century, is a solid piece of metal attached to a wire that serves as a switch by alternatively conducting or resisting electricity.

- Transistors were invented by John Bardeen, Walter Brattain, and William Shockley at AT&T Bell Labs in 1948.

- Transistors are constructed from semiconductors—metals that can be doped with impurities to make them either good or bad conductors of electricity. The most common semiconductor used in modern transistors is silicon.

- A Negatively-doped Metal-Oxide Semiconductor (NMOS) transistor serves as a switch that is closed when electrical current is applied to its control wire; otherwise, it is open. Conversely, a Positively-doped Metal-Oxide Semiconductor (PMOS) transistor is open when current is applied to its control wire; otherwise, it is closed.

- Since transistors were smaller, lasted longer, and required less power than vacuum tubes, they began replacing vacuum tubes in consumer devices in the 1950s (e.g., transistorized hearing aid in 1953, transistor radio in 1954, Bell Labs transistor computer in 1955).

- A circuit is a collection of transistors (and possibly other electronic devices) wired together to produce a particular behavior. The simplest circuits that perform well-defined logical operations are the NOT gate, AND gate, and OR gate.

- Tables that describe the mapping from circuitry inputs to outputs are known as truth tables.

- Simple circuits can be wired together to form more complex circuits. For example, starting with simple NOT, AND, and OR gates, the complex circuitry of the ALU can be designed and implemented.

- The simplest circuit for storing a value is known as a flip-flop. A flip-flop stores a bit whose value can be set to 1 by applying current to one input wire and then reset to 0 by applying current to another input wire.

- In 1958, Jack Kilby and Robert Noyce independently proposed manufacturing processes in which circuitry is layered onto a single wafer of silicon, known as a microchip. Because every component of the circuit was integrated onto the same microchip, these circuits became known as integrated circuits.

- To produce the incredibly small and precise circuitry on microchips (transistors can be 1/750th the width of a human hair), hardware manufacturers use light-sensitive chemicals to etch circuitry into layers of semiconductor materials.

- To protect the fragile silicon chip containing an integrated circuit, it is encased in plastic and packaged with metal pins to facilitate connections to other microchips.

- Moore's Law predicts that the number of transistors that can fit on a chip will double every 12 to 18 months.

Review Questions

1. TRUE or FALSE? Nonmetals such as carbon and oxygen tend to be good conductors of electricity.

2. TRUE or FALSE? A semiconductor is a metal that can be manipulated to be either a good or a bad conductor of electricity.

3. TRUE or FALSE? A circuit is a collection of transistors (and possibly other electronic devices) wired together to produce a particular behavior.

4. TRUE or FALSE? NMOS and PMOS were two competing companies that manufactured microchips in the early 1960s.

5. TRUE or FALSE? If there is no electrical current on the input wire to a NOT gate, then there will be current on its output wire.

6. TRUE or FALSE? The sum of the binary numbers 101_2 and 1_2 is 110_2.

7. TRUE or FALSE? A flip-flop is a circuit that serves to store a single bit.

8. TRUE or FALSE? Jack Kilby and Robert Noyce are credited with independently inventing the integrated circuit.

9. TRUE or FALSE? The main reason that workers wear protective clothing when manufacturing integrated circuits is to protect them from exposure to dangerous chemicals.

10. TRUE or FALSE? Moore's Law dictates that integrated circuitry must be manufactured out of silicon, as opposed to other semiconductors such as germanium.

11. Name three different technologies that, over the years, have served as electrical switches in computers. How were these technologies similar, and how were they different? What advantages or disadvantages did each provide?

12. Electricians commonly wear rubber shoes and gloves to protect themselves when working with live wiring. Would this suggest that rubber is an efficient or inefficient conductor of electricity? Explain your answer.

13. Describe the difference between an NMOS transistor and a PMOS transistor.

14. It is possible to develop truth tables for logic circuits, just as we did for individual gates. For example, the logic circuit shown here combines an AND gate and an OR gate. Complete the corresponding truth table by calculating the output value for each set of inputs. [*Hint*: Figure out the output of the AND gate in each case and then use the result to determine the overall output.]

A	B	C	Output
0	0	0	
0	0	1	
0	1	0	
0	1	1	
1	0	0	
1	0	1	
1	1	0	
1	1	1	

15. The logic circuit shown here is similar to the one in Question 14, except that the AND and OR gates are in reversed positions. Complete the corresponding truth table by calculating the output value for each set of inputs.

A	B	C	Output
0	0	0	
0	0	1	
0	1	0	
0	1	1	
1	0	0	
1	0	1	
1	1	0	
1	1	1	

16. What is the sum of the binary numbers 100101_2 and 1011_2? Show the steps you used to calculate your answer.

17. Explain why the circuitry for adding two 4-bit numbers must be constructed by combining full-adders, rather than half-adders.

18. What is the total number of gates required to build a 4-bit adder? Assuming two transistors per NOT gate (as in Figure 16.8) and four transistors per AND and OR gate (as in Figures 16.9 and 16.10, respectively), what is the total number of transistors in the circuitry of the 4-bit adder?

19. Describe how a flip-flop is able to retain the last bit value assigned to it.

20. Does it make any sense for both of a flip-flop's input wires to carry current at the same time? What would happen within the circuit if this were to happen?

21. In what way is integrated-circuit manufacturing similar to photography?

22. Can Moore's Law continue to hold forever? That is, can technology continue to advance at its current rate indefinitely, causing the number of transistors that fit on a microchip to double every 12 to 18 months? Explain.

References

Augenbraun, Eliene, and P. W. Hammer, Executive Producers. *Transistorized!: The History of the Invention of the Transistor.* ScienCentral, Inc., and the American Institute of Physics, 1999. Online at `http://www.pbs.org/transistor/`.

Brain, Marshall. "How Semiconductors Work." *How Stuff Works*, January 2003. Online at `http://electronics.howstuffworks.com/diode.htm`.

Malone, Michael S. *The Microprocessor: A Biography.* New York: Springer-Verlag, 1995.

Mano, M. Morris, and Charles R. Kime. *Logic and Computer Design Fundamentals*, 2d ed. Upper Saddle River, NJ: Prentice Hall, 2000.

Petzold, Charles. *Code: The Hidden Language of Computer Hardware and Software.* Redmond, WA: Microsoft Press, 1999.

Chapter 17

JavaScript Arrays

This chapter uses narrative, examples, and hands-on exercises to introduce programming concepts and Web development skills.

Why can't somebody give us a list of things that everybody thinks and nobody says, and another list of things that everybody says and nobody thinks.

Oliver Wendell Holmes, Sr.
The Professor at the Breakfast-Table

Creativity is a lot like looking at the world through a kaleidoscope. You look at a set of elements, the same ones everyone else sees, but then reassemble those floating bits and pieces into an enticing new possibility. Effective leaders are able to shake up their thinking as though their brains are kaleidoscopes, permitting an array of different patterns out of the same bits of reality.

Rosabeth Moss Kanter

In Chapter 15, you were introduced to the concept of software objects—programming structures that encompass both data (properties) and operations (methods) that can be performed on that data. A string object, for example, has properties that provide information about the string (e.g., the sequence of characters, length), whereas methods can be called to manipulate the string's value (e.g., toUpperCase, charAt). In this chapter, you will learn about another type of JavaScript object, the array. JavaScript uses an array structure to represent a list; each array stores and indexes a sequence of items, allowing users to access individual list items by specifying their corresponding indices. Arrays are useful for handling arbitrarily long user input, as well as for organizing large amounts of data. For example, imagine a program that asks a user to enter a phrase and then displays an acronym consisting of the first letter of every word in that phrase. If the user's input were stored as an array consisting of individual words, the program could process the words individually, copying the first letter of each to form the acronym.

Early exercises in this chapter emphasize a conceptual understanding of arrays, including what they are and how they are stored. While tracing code that assigns values to arrays, you will be asked to draw the memory cells associated with various array values. Eventually, you will apply this knowledge to developing Web pages that process both words and numbers in arrays, including an application in which an array stores a collection of counters for maintaining dice statistics.

Arrays as Objects

In Chapter 7, you created several Web pages that incorporated the RandomOneOf function from the random.js library. This function takes a list of items as input and returns a random item from that list. For example, the call:

```
RandomOneOf(["yes", "no", "maybe"])
```

would return either "yes", "no", or "maybe", each with equal likelihood.

In JavaScript, lists of items that are enclosed in square brackets and separated by commas are known as **arrays**. Like strings, arrays are objects that encapsulate multiple values and their associated properties and methods. However, unlike strings (which store only text characters), the items in an array can be of any data type. Although the above example ["yes", "no", "maybe"] contains three string values, an array can also store numbers, Booleans, nested arrays, or any combination thereof. Since JavaScript places no limitations on arrays' contents or organization, programming with arrays can provide incredible flexibility.

For example, the following statements assign valid array values to variables.

```
responses = ["yes", "no", "maybe"];
nums = [1, 2, 3, 2+1, 7*7, 2*5-1];
misc = [1.234, "foo", 7-5, true, 3, "foo"];
empty = [ ];
```

These examples demonstrate that:

- The items in an array do not have to be of the same type.
- An item can appear in an array more than once.
- An array item can be specified as an expression—in such cases, the array actually stores the expression's equivalent value.
- An array can be empty.

Accessing Items in an Array

Since an array stores a series of values, its associated memory cell is divided into components, each containing an individual value. For example, consider the array assigned to the misc variable in the examples above. Figure 17.1 depicts the organization of misc's memory cell, in which array items are stored in separate components of the cell. Like the characters in a string, array items are assigned sequential indices, allowing programmers to retrieve any item by specifying its corresponding index. Instead of providing a method such as charAt, however, arrays use a bracket notation for allowing access to individual items. Thus, the first item in misc is accessed as misc[0], the second as misc[1], and so on. Similar to strings, arrays have a length property, which identifies the number of items in the array. This means that the last item in the array misc is accessible as misc[misc.length-1]. Note that any expression that evaluates to an integer (such as misc.length-1) can be used to index an array.

Figure 17.1 Memory cell for the misc array.

In addition to being flexible, arrays are especially forgiving data structures. If you specify an index that is beyond the scope of a given array, the array simply returns undefined. For example, misc[6] and misc[100] will both evaluate to undefined.

EXERCISE 17.1

Assume that the following statements have assigned arrays to variables:

```
responses = ["yes", "no", "maybe"];
nums = [1, 2, 3, 2+1, 7*7, 2*5-1];
misc = [1.234, "foo", 7-5, true, 3, "foo"];
empty = [ ];
```

Predict the value that would be accessed by each of the following expressions:

```
responses[0]
responses[responses.length-1]
nums.length
nums[0]
nums[0] + nums[1] + nums[2]
empty.length
empty[0]
misc[ nums[0] ]
```

Now that you know how to create an array and access its values, you can understand the workings of the RandomOneOf function from Chapter 7. The RandomOneOf function (Figure 17.2) utilizes the length property and bracket notation associated with arrays to retrieve a random item from an array. First, RandomOneOf calls the RandomInt function to select a number between 0 and the last index in the array (i.e., the list length minus one). After the random number is returned, the function uses bracket notation to obtain the array item stored at that index.

```
function RandomOneOf(list)
// Given   : list is a nonempty list (array)
// Returns: a random item from the list
{
    var randomIndex;

    randomIndex = RandomInt(0, list.length-1);

    return list[randomIndex];
}
```

Figure 17.2   Function for selecting a random item from an array.

EXERCISE 17.2

Suppose that the assignment to randomIndex in the RandomOneOf function (Figure 17.2) were replaced by the following:

```
 randomIndex = RandomInt(0, list.length);
```

Would this modification cause the function to return an error? Would the function still behave appropriately every time it is called? Explain.

Assigning Items in an Array

In addition to accessing an existing item in an array, bracket notation can also be used to assign a value to an array component. For example, suppose that misc has been assigned the same array value as in the previous examples:

```
misc = [1.234, "foo", 7-5, true, 3, "foo"];
```

The assignment:

```
misc[0] = 1000;
```

would store the value 1000 as the first item in the array misc, overwriting the value that was previously stored there. Figure 17.3 portrays the effect of this assignment on misc's corresponding memory cell.

	misc[0]	misc[1]	misc[2]	misc[3]	misc[4]	misc[5]
misc	1000	"foo"	2	true	3	"foo"

Figure 17.3 Memory cell for the misc array, after assigning misc[0] = 1000.

If the index in an assignment statement is beyond the array's current length, the array will be automatically expanded to accommodate the new item. Any components in between the new item and the original array will be considered undefined. For example, the assignment:

```
misc[8] = "oops";
```

would expand the misc array so that its memory cell resembles Figure 17.4.

	misc[0]	misc[1]	misc[2]	misc[3]	misc[4]	misc[5]	misc[6]	misc[7]	misc[8]
misc	1000	"foo"	2	true	3	"foo"	undefined	undefined	"oops"

Figure 17.4 Memory cell for the misc array, after assigning misc[8] = "oops".

EXERCISE 17.3

For each of the following statements, draw the memory cell associated with the variable after the assignment has been made:

```
vals = [1, 5.3, "house"];
vals[0] = vals[1];
vals[2] = vals[2] + "hold";
blank = [];
blank[0] = "foo";
blank[3] = "bar";
blank[blank.length] = "biz";
blank[blank.length] = "baz";
```

From Strings to Arrays

Throughout this text, you have written interactive Web pages that accept and process user input. For example, in Chapters 4 and 5, you wrote pages that prompted the user to enter a word or number and then displayed that value as part of a message. The pages that you wrote in Chapter 9 also manipulated user inputs, but they incorporated text boxes and text areas for reading in entries and displaying output. However, all of these pages handled any value entered by the user as a single string. If the page needed to treat an input as a number, then the value was converted to the appropriate data type using parseFloat.

The inability to treat user inputs as anything other than single strings or numbers is limiting, since numerous programming tasks involve separately processing an arbitrary number of words or numbers entered by a user. For example, imagine that you need to define a page that generates an acronym for a given phrase by combining the first letter of each word in the phrase. Similarly, you might want to generalize your Pig Latin page (Exercise 15.8) so that it translates entire phrases, instead of just words, into Pig Latin. Accomplishing these tasks would be difficult, if not impossible, using your current set of programming tools.

Common errors to avoid...

As we mentioned earlier, arrays are like strings in that attempts to access invalid array indices do not by themselves cause errors. Instead, the array returns the value `undefined` if you specify an index that is negative or higher than that of the last item in the array. In most cases, however, an error will occur as soon as the code attempts to perform an action using the `undefined` value, such as displaying it or incorporating it into an expression.

For example, suppose that you wanted to add together every value in an array of numbers named `nums`. The following code attempts to accomplish this task, but in fact loops one time too many.

```
sum = 0;
i = 0;
while (i <= nums.length) {
    sum = sum + nums[i];
    i = i + 1;
}
```

Since the while loop test uses `'<='` instead of `'<'`, the last value for which the test succeeds will be `nums[nums.length]`, which is beyond the actual bounds of the array. Although this mistake doesn't generate an immediate error, the code does not behave as desired during the final loop-body iteration. As soon as the code adds the `undefined` value to the sum of the array, the sum becomes NaN, signifying that the result is "Not a Number."

The `split` Method for Strings

Although arrays are useful for organizing and manipulating large amounts of data, no mechanism in JavaScript enables a user to input a series of values directly as an array. As we have seen, JavaScript treats anything entered via a prompt window, text box, or text area as a string. Even if the user enters a sequence of words or numbers, those words or numbers are automatically joined together in a single string. Technically, the individual items could be extracted using string methods such as `search` and `substring`, but such processing would be tedious. Fortunately, JavaScript strings provide a method, `split`, for easily accessing the components of a string.

The only input required by the `split` method is a character or sequence of characters that serves as a delimiter for breaking apart the string. The `split` method separates the string into component substrings at each occurrence of the delimiter and then returns an array consisting of those substrings (the delimiter character or substring is lost during this process). For example, if `user1 = "Grace Murray Hopper"`, then the method call `user1.split(" ")` would break the string every time a space occurs, returning the array `["Grace", "Murray", "Hopper"]`. Likewise, if `user2 = "Hopper, Grace Murray"`, then `user2.split(", ")` would split the string every time that a comma is followed by a space, returning the array `["Hopper", "Grace Murray"]`.

As was the case with the `search` method, `split` will also accept a collection of characters as input, any of which will then act as the delimiter. When the `split` method is given a collection of characters between `/[` and `]/`, the method splits the string every time it encounters a character or sequence of characters from that collection. For example, if `user2 = "Hopper, Grace Murray"`, then `user2.split(/[, ]/)` would split the string at each occurrence of a comma and/or space, returning the array `["Hopper", "Grace", "Murray"]`. Figure 17.5 lists several other `split` method calls and describes the arrays returned by these calls.

EXERCISE 17.4

The first statement below assigns a string to variable `people`, whereas the subsequent three assignments split `people` into various arrays. For each of the following statements, draw the memory cell associated with the variable after the assignment has been made:

```
people = "von Neumann, John 1903\n" + "Turing, Alan 1913";

split1 = people.split(" ");
split2 = people.split(", ");
split3 = people.split(/[ ,\n]/);
```

`phrase.split(" ")`	Breaks the string `phrase` into an array of items, delimited by a single space.
`phrase.split(": ")`	Breaks the string `phrase` into an array of items, delimited by a colon followed by a space.
`phrase.split(/[ ]/)`	Breaks the string `phrase` into an array of items, delimited by any sequence of spaces.
`phrase.split(/[ \t\n,]/)`	Breaks the string `phrase` into an array of items, delimited by any sequence of spaces, tabs (`\t`), newlines (`\n`), and/or commas.

Figure 17.5 Examples of `split` method calls, which divide strings into arrays.

Example: Generating Acronyms

One useful application of the `split` method is to derive acronyms. Although acronyms appear throughout our daily lives, they are especially popular in the computing field. For example, "RAM" is an acronym for "Random Access Memory," "GUI" is an acronym for "Graphical User Interface," and "WWW" is an acronym for "World Wide Web." In addition, many computer companies are known by acronyms, such as IBM (International Business Machines) and SGI (Silicon Graphics, Inc.). The function in Figure 17.6 takes a phrase as input and returns the acronym associated with that phrase.

```
function Acronym(phrase)
// Assumes: phrase is a string of words, separated by whitespace
// Returns: the acronym made up of first letters from the phrase
{
  var words, acronym, index, nextWord;

  words = phrase.split(/\[ \t\n]/);            // CONVERT phrase TO AN ARRAY
  acronym = "";                                // INITIALIZE THE acronym

  index = 0;                                   // START AT FIRST WORD
  while (index < words.length) {               // AS LONG AS WORDS LEFT
    nextWord = words[index];                   //    GET NEXT WORD
    acronym = acronym + nextWord.charAt(0);    //    ADD FIRST CHAR OF WORD
    index = index + 1;                         //    GO ON TO NEXT WORD
    }

  return acronym.toUpperCase();                // RETURN UPPER CASE acronym
}
```

Figure 17.6 Function that returns an acronym for a given phrase.

First, the function calls the `split` method to convert the phrase into an array of words, using spaces, tabs, and newline characters as delimiters. Then a while loop traverses the array, extracting the first letter of each word (via `charAt`) and adding it to a new string named `acronym`. When the loop terminates, the `toUpperCase` method is applied to `acronym`, yielding an entirely upper-case version of `acronym` as the function's return value. For example, the phrase "What you see is what you get" is often represented by the acronym "WYSIWYG." If this phrase were provided as input to the Acronym function, then the variable `words` would be assigned:

```
["What", "you", "see", "is", "what", "you", "get"]
```

Traversing the array, the function would extract each word's first letter and combine them into a new string, as shown in Figure 17.7.

```
                                         nextWord
                    acronym     index   (words[index])  nextWord.charAt(0)
         -----------------------------------------------------------------
before loop            ""         0         "What"            "W"
after 1st pass        "W"         1         "you"             "y"
after 2nd pass        "Wy"        2         "see"             "s"
after 3rd pass        "Wys"       3         "is"              "i"
after 4th pass        "Wysi"      4         "what"            "w"
after 5th pass        "Wysiw"     5         "you"             "y"
after 6th pass        "Wysiwy"    6         "get"             "g"
after 7th pass        "Wysiwyg"   7         undefined         undefined
         -----------------------------------------------------------------
return value:       "WYSIWYG"
```

Figure 17.7 Tracing the behavior of the `Acronym` function.

EXERCISE 17.5

Create a Web page named `acronym.html` that derives an acronym from a given phrase. The page should contain a button and a text box in which the user can enter the phrase. Once the user clicks the button, the page should call the `Acronym` function to construct the appropriate acronym and display it in a separate text box (see Figure 17.8).

Figure 17.8 Sample appearance of `acronym.html` page.

EXERCISE 17.6

Modify your `piglatin.html` page from Chapter 15 (Exercise 15.8) so that the user can translate phrases, instead of just individual words. The page should break the user's input into words, convert each word to Pig Latin, and then combine the Pig Latin words into a new phrase (with a space between each word). Use a separate text box to display the result of the translation (see Figure 17.9).

Figure 17.9 Sample appearance of `piglatin.html` page.

Common errors to avoid...

When using the `split` method to convert user input into an array of values, it is important to recognize that the resulting array might be empty. If the input is the empty string or a string containing only those characters recognized as delimiters, then the `split` method will return an empty array (i.e., an array whose `length` is 0). This means that, when a program uses method `split`, you must make sure that the surrounding code accounts for the possibility of an empty array. For example, code that computed the average of an array of numbers would need to check for an empty array in order to avoid division by zero (yielding NaN). In such a case, an error message might be displayed, or the user might be prompted to reenter the numbers.

When testing and debugging code that involves arrays, it is often useful to view the array as a whole. For testing purposes, you can retrieve the entire contents of an array by calling either the `alert` function or the `document.write` method. Both techniques will display the individual array items in a list, separated by commas. For example, if `nums = [1,4,7]` then the call `alert(nums)` would display `1, 4, 7` in an alert box.

Arrays of Numbers

As demonstrated by your `acronym.html` (Exercise 17.5) and modified `piglatin.html` (Exercise 17.6) pages, certain programming tasks involve treating user input as a sequence of separate words, rather than as one long string. The `split` method is useful in such cases, since this method breaks a string into an array of component substrings. As you might imagine, there are also applications in which user input must be handled as a sequence of separate numbers. For example, Chapter 9 asked you to create a Web page named grades.html that computed a student's grade in a course (Exercise 9.4). Using this page, individuals could enter various averages (for lessons, labs, discussions, etc.) in text boxes and then view their overall average for the course in a separate text box. However, this page was limited, in that it expected the user to provide a precomputed average for each category. A more comprehensive page would accept a list of the user's individual grades for each category (e.g., lesson grades) and then automatically compute the associated category averages.

It is important to note that the split method takes a string as input and returns an array of strings as output. Even if the input string contains numerical digits, split returns each array item as a string. For example, if str = "1 2 3", then str.split(" ") would return the array ["1", "2", "3"]. Of course, it is possible to convert the values in this array to numbers by accessing each one and parseFloating it. However, since processing a sequence of numbers is a fairly common task, it would be useful to define a function that encapsulates the conversion. The ParseArray function (Figure 17.10) takes an array of strings as input and returns a copy of that array in which each item has been converted to a number. The function assumes that each string in the array encompasses a sequence of digits (possibly including a decimal point) that represents a number.

```
function ParseArray(strArray)
// Assumes: strArray is an array of strings representing numbers
// Returns: a copy of array with items converted to numbers
{
  var copyArray, index;

  copyArray = [];                          // CREATE EMPTY ARRAY TO STORE COPY

  index = 0;                               // FOR EACH ITEM IN strArray
  while (index < strArray.length) {        //    CONVERT TO NUM AND COPY
      copyArray[index] = parseFloat(strArray[index]);
      index = index + 1;
  }

  return copyArray;                        // FINALLY, RETURN THE COPY
}
```

Figure 17.10 Function for converting an array of strings into an array of numbers.

The ParseArray function works by traversing an array of strings, applying parseFloat to each array item, and returning a corresponding array of numbers. For example, the call ParseArray(["123", "3.14159", "-99", "0"]) will return the array of numbers [123, 3.14159, -99, 0]. Since ParseArray will prove helpful in many applications, it makes sense to define the function in a separate library file, which can then be accessed by multiple pages. In Exercise 17.7, you will create a library file named array.js in which to store this function definition.

The ParseArray function's usefulness is demonstrated in the accompanying Web page (Figure 17.11), which contains a text box for entering a sequence of numbers. When the user types in the desired number sequence and clicks a button, the page accesses the contents of the text box and calls the split method to break the string into an array (of strings). Once this array has been created, the page calls the ParseArray function to convert the string array into a corresponding array of numbers. The Average function, which is defined within the page, is then called to compute the average of every number in the array (by adding up all of the values in the array and then dividing by the number of values). Finally, the page displays the array values' average in a separate text box. (Figure 17.12 shows the page as rendered in a Web browser.)

```html
<html>
  <!-- average.html                                  Dave Reed -->
  <!-- This page utilizes the ParseArray function to store an -->
  <!--   array of numbers and compute their average.          -->
  <!----------------------------------------------------------->

<head>
  <title> Average Numbers </title>

  <script type="text/javascript" src="array.js"></script>

  <script type="text/javascript">
    function Average(numArray)
    // Assumes: numArray is an array of numbers
    // Returns: average of the numbers in numArray
    {
        var sum, index;

        sum = 0;                            // INITIALIZE sum

        index = 0;                          // START AT FIRST NUMBER
        while (index < numArray.length) {   // AS LONG AS NUMBERS LEFT
            sum = sum + numArray[index];    //   ADD NUMBER TO sum
            index = index + 1;              //   GO ON TO NEXT NUMBER
        }

        return sum/numArray.length;         // RETURN AVERAGE
    }

    function ShowAvg()
    // Assumes: document.AvgForm.nums contains a sequence of numbers
    // Results: writes the average to document.AvgForm.avg
    {
        var str, strArray, numArray;

        str = document.AvgForm.nums.value;  // GET CONTENTS OF BOX
        strArray = str.split(/[ \t\n]/);    // SPLIT INTO AN ARRAY
        numArray = ParseArray(strArray);    // CONVERT ITEMS TO NUMS

        document.AvgForm.avg.value = Average(numArray);  // DISPLAY AVG
    }
  </script>
</head>

<body>
  <form name="AvgForm">
    Enter numbers: <input type="text" name="nums" size=40 value="" />
    <br /><br />
    <input type="button" value="Compute the Average" onclick="ShowAvg();" />
    <br /><br />
    Their average: <input type="text" name="avg" size=8 value="" />
  </form>
</body>
</html>
```

Figure 17.11 Web page that stores numbers in an array and computes their average.

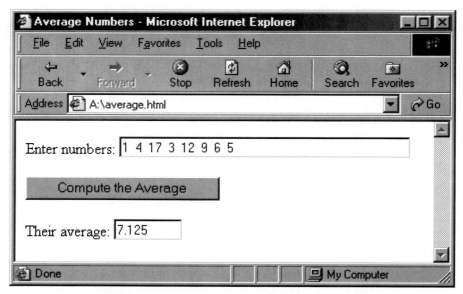

Figure 17.12 `average.html` rendered in a Web browser.

EXERCISE 17.7

Enter the definition of the `ParseArray` function in a file named `array.js`. Once you have done this, enter the `average.html` text into a new Web page and load this page to verify that it behaves as described.

As written, the `Average` function will return NaN if its input is an empty array. This is because the function divides the array items' sum by the number of items in the array, and division by 0 always yields NaN. Modify the `Average` function so that it returns 0, rather than NaN, if its input is empty (i.e., has length 0).

EXERCISE 17.8

Reimplement your `grades.html` page from Chapter 9 (Exercise 9.4). Instead of requiring users to provide precomputed averages, your modified page should provide text boxes in which users can enter a series of grades for each category (e.g., all homework grades obtained by the user could be listed in a text box). *Note:* Your page should include code that determines the category averages by converting each sequence of grades to an array of numbers and then calling the `Average` function on those arrays. Figure 17.13 depicts one possible layout for the page.

Common errors to avoid...

Chapters 5 and 9 demonstrated that, in certain instances, a program will treat a user input as a number, even if you fail to `parseFloat` the value. In particular, the browser will automatically convert a string of digits into a number if a purely numerical operator (such as `'*'` or `'/'`) is applied to the value. However, since the `'+'` operator is compatible with both strings and numbers, string concatenation will be performed whenever `'+'` is applied to string values. To avoid confusion, we strongly recommended that you always call `parseFloat` to explicitly convert numbers before processing them.

For these same reasons, it is strongly suggested that you call `ParseArray` to explicitly convert any array of numbers before attempting to process the numbers. Otherwise, if the `'+'` operator is applied to items from the array, the operator would be interpreted as representing concatenation, rather than addition.

Figure 17.13   Sample appearance of grades.html page.

Example: Maintaining Dice Statistics Using an Array

In Chapter 13, you created a Web page that simulated repeated dice rolls and recorded the number of times that a specific total was obtained (Exercise 13.7). For example, this page allowed you to roll a pair of dice 1,000 times and count the number of 7s obtained. By changing a few numbers in the code, you were able to modify the page to count occurrences of any potential dice total. Statistical analysis predicts that, given a large number of dice rolls, the distribution of totals will mirror the percentages listed in Figure 17.14.

If you were using the page you created in Exercise 13.7, verifying this expected distribution of dice totals would involve performing 11 different experiments—one for each possible total. For example, you could roll the dice 1,000 times, count the number of 2s obtained, and verify that the number was close to 28 (2.8%). Then, you could roll the dice another 1,000 times, count the number of 3s obtained, and verify that the number was close to 55 (5.5%). If you repeated this process for every number up to 12, you would generate a complete set of dice statistics. However, since each experiment involves an independent sequence of 1,000 dice rolls, the total distribution might be skewed. That is, if you added up the counts from each of the 11 experiments, the total might not equal 1,000.

Approach 1: Separate Counters

To obtain a valid distribution of dice totals, you would need to simulate a large number of rolls and simultaneously count the occurrences of every different total. This could be accomplished by defining 11 counters, each corresponding to a particular total (see Figure 17.15).

Dice Total	Likelihood of Obtaining That Total
2	2.8%
3	5.5%
4	8.3%
5	11.1%
6	13.9%
7	16.7%
8	13.9%
9	11.1%
10	8.3%
11	5.5%
12	2.8%

Figure 17.14 Likelihood of possible dice totals.

```
count2 = 0;                          // INITIALIZE EACH
count3 = 0;                          // COUNTER
count4 = 0;                          // (CORRESPONDING TO
.                                    //   THE NUMBER OF 2'S,
.                                    //   3'S, 4'S, … 12'S)
.
count12 = 0;

rep = 0;                             // INITIALIZE rep COUNTER
while (rep < 1000) {                 // AS LONG AS ROLLS REMAIN
    roll = RandomInt(1, 6) + RandomInt(1, 6); // GET NEXT ROLL

    if (roll == 2) {                 //    IF ROLLED 2,
        count2 = count2 + 1;         //    ADD 1 TO 2'S COUNT
    }
    else if (roll == 3) {            //    ELSE IF ROLLED 3,
        count3 = count3 + 1;         //    ADD 1 TO 3'S COUNT
    }
    else if (roll == 4) {            //    ELSE IF ROLLED 4,
        count4 = count4 + 1;         //    ADD 1 TO 4'S COUNT
    }
    .                                //    SIMILAR CASES FOR
    .                                //    ROLLS 5 THROUGH 11
    .
    else if (roll == 12) {           //    ELSE IF ROLLED 12,
        count12 = count12 + 1;       //    ADD 1 TO 12'S COUNT
    }

    rep = rep + 1;                   // GO ON TO NEXT REP
}
```

Figure 17.15 Code that uses 11 counters to keep dice statistics.

This approach would work (assuming that you inserted appropriate code in place of the ' . . . 's), but it is incredibly tedious. After separate assignments initialize each of the 11 counters to 0, a cascading if-else statement containing 11 cases must identify every dice total and increment the corresponding counter. Furthermore, once the counts have been obtained, 11 separate statements would be required to display each counter value.

As if this code were not complex enough, now consider the task of generalizing the page so that it could handle dice with additional sides. Rolling and keeping statistics on 8-sided dice would involve 15 different counters and a cascading if-else with 15 cases. For 12-sided dice, 23 counters and if-else cases would be required. Surely, there must be a better way.

Approach 2: An Array of Counters

After contemplating the use of separate counters to track dice statistics, you can see how arrays would provide an attractive alternative in such cases. Instead of representing each counter as a separate variable, you can define the counters as items in an array. That is, all 11 counters could be stored in a single array and initialized via a single assignment. This approach would also enable each individual counter to be accessed and updated via its corresponding index. Since the smallest possible dice total is two, its counter will be at index 0. The counter for 3s will be at index 1, and each subsequent index will store a counter for a sequentially higher total (up to the 12s counter at index 10). Figure 17.16 depicts an array that keeps dice statistics. Although the code performs the same task as the code in Figure 17.15, this version is much simpler due to the array of counters.

```
count = [0,0,0,0,0,0,0,0,0,0,0];           // INITIALIZE ALL COUNTERS

rep = 0;                                     // INITIALIZE rep COUNTER
while (rep < 1000) {                         // AS LONG AS ROLLS REMAIN
   roll = RandomInt(1, 6) + RandomInt(1, 6); //   GET RANDOM ROLL OF DICE
   count[roll-2] = count[roll-2] + 1;        //   ADD 1 TO COUNTER

   rep = rep + 1;                            //   GO ON TO NEXT REP
}
```

Figure 17.16 Code that uses an array of counters to keep dice statistics.

Note that the assignment statement at the top of the code segment defines an array of 11 counters and initializes all of them to 0. As the loop body is executed, the code accesses the appropriate counter for each `roll` via the statement `count[roll-2]`, since each counter index is two less than the dice total it tracks. Clearly, this approach is much more efficient than using separate counters, and it would be easier to adapt this code for dice with a different number of sides. Furthermore, displaying the counts generated by this code would be less tedious, since a single loop could step through the array and display the count stored at each index (from 0 to 10).

EXERCISE 17.9

Design and create a Web page named `stats.html` that simulates some number of dice rolls and displays statistics on those rolls. The user should be able to specify the number of dice rolls via a text box and then view the resulting counts. In addition, the page should allow users to perform repeated experiments without reloading the page. Figure 17.17 portrays one possible layout for the page.

EXERCISE 17.10

Augment your `stats.html` page so that, in addition to displaying the counts for each dice total, the page also represents the counts as percentages of the total number of rolls. To compute each percentage, you must divide the count by the total number of rolls, then multiply by 100. For example, if 162 out of 1,000 rolls were 2s, then that's 16.2% of the rolls. For our purposes, it is sufficient to round percentages to the nearest integer value, so 162 out of 1000 would be displayed as 16%.

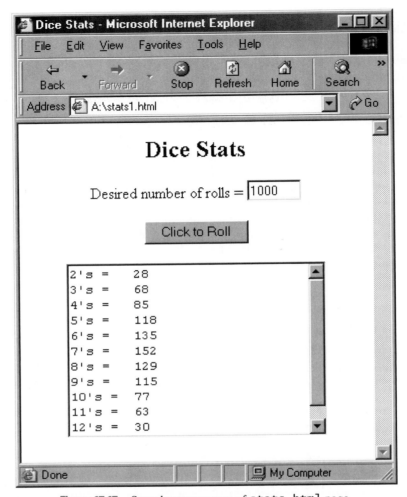

Figure 17.17 Sample appearance of `stats.html` page.

EXERCISE 17.11

Using your `stats.html` page, perform 100 dice rolls and report the results. Are your percentages close to the expected ones listed in Figure 17.14? Should they be?

Now, perform 1,000 dice rolls using your page and report the results. Are the percentages from this experiment closer to the expected percentages? Should they be?

Now, perform 10,000 dice rolls using your page and report the results. Are the percentages from this experiment closer to the expected percentages? Should they be?

Looking Ahead...

In this chapter, you learned how to store and manipulate data in JavaScript arrays. An array is a collection of items in which each item is accessible via an index. For example, the first value in the array `nums` is stored at index 0 and is represented as `nums[0]`. Arrays are especially flexible structures— for example, if you specify an array index that has no corresponding value in the array, the array will return the value `undefined`, rather than an error. Furthermore, if you assign a value to an index outside the current scope of the array, the array will be automatically extended to accommodate the assignment. Arrays are useful for storing and manipulating large amounts of data, particularly if that data represents user input. For example, if a user enters a sequence of words or numbers in a prompt window or text area, then the input can be converted from a string into an array using the string method `split`. Once in array form, the data can be easily traversed and processed, as this chapter's various examples have demonstrated.

This chapter completes the text's coverage of programming concepts. Through the design and implementation of interactive Web pages, you have developed an impressive set of programming and problem-solving skills. Among other tools, you have used variables to store values; prompts, write statements, buttons, text boxes, and text areas to handle input and output; functions to manage and encapsulate complexity; if statements and while loops to control the execution of other statements; and finally strings and arrays to manipulate complex data. In Chapter 18, you will look back on the broader material from this text in order to examine the role of computers in our society.

Chapter Summary

- An array is a list in which individual items are accessible via indices. Arrays are specified in JavaScript by enclosing items in square brackets, separated by commas. For example, `misc = [1, "foo", 3];`

- Like strings, arrays are composite structures, in that multiple values are contained into a single object. Unlike strings, however, the items in an array can be of any type.

- The individual items in an array are accessed by specifying the array name, followed by a bracketed index. For example, the first item in the array `misc` is accessed as `misc[0]`, the second item as `misc[1]`, and so on.

- Similar to strings, all arrays have a `length` property, which identifies the number of items in the array. For example, the last item in the array `misc` would be `misc[misc.length-1]`.

- If you attempt to access an array index that is beyond the length of an array, `undefined` is returned.

- Bracket notation can be used to assign a value to an array component. For example, the assignment `misc[0] = 1000;` will store 1,000 in the first component of the array `misc`, overwriting the value that was previously stored there.

- If you assign a value to a component beyond the current length of the array, the array will be automatically expanded to accommodate the new value. Any components in between the new item and the original array will be considered `undefined`.

- The string method `split` can be used to split a string into an array of individual components. The delimiter, which specifies the character or characters at which `split` breaks the string, is provided as input to the `split` method.

- When a user enters a series of numbers via a text box or text area, this input can be divided into an array (of strings) using the `split` method. In such instances, it is often useful to define a function called `ParseArray` in order to convert the array of strings into a corresponding array of numbers.

- One common use of arrays is to store a collection of counters, each accessible via an index. Since a loop can be used to traverse an array and access each counter by its index, an array of counters is much more concise and flexible than separate counter variables.

Supplemental Material and Exercises

More Practice with Arrays

The following exercises ask you to augment pages that you wrote during this chapter.

EXERCISE 17.12

Define a function named `Minimum` that is similar to the `Average` function from Figure 17.11, but which takes an array of numbers as input and returns the smallest value from that array. For example, the call `Minimum([33, 12, 5, 17, 8])` should return 5. After inserting this function into your `average.html` page, add a text box that displays the array's minimum value when the user clicks an appropriately labeled button.

[*Hint:* To find the minimum value in an array, your function should traverse the array and record the smallest value it encounters. Start by initializing a variable to the first value in the array. Then, compare each subsequent value in the array to the variable, updating the variable whenever a smaller value is found.]

EXERCISE 17.13

When a course has numerous assignments, a kindly instructor may drop a student's lowest grade to allow for one bad day. Modify your `grades.html` page from Exercise 17.8 so that the lowest lesson grade is ignored.

[*Hint:* To compute the average of a collection of grades while dropping the lowest grade, you can use the following formula:]

```
((avg_of_grades * number_of_grades) - minimum_grade)/(number_of_grades - 1)
```

EXERCISE 17.14

Modify your `stats.html` page so that it simulates repeatedly rolling a pair of eight-sided dice and then collects statistics on the dice totals obtained. Because the array of counters provides extreme flexibility, only minimal changes should be required to adapt the page.

Searching an Array

In life, we are constantly searching for things. Looking up a number in the phone book, rifling through a stack of papers to find a particular one, scanning the index of a book for a topic—these are all examples of searching. In computer science, searching is an especially common task. Many problems involve storing, accessing, and updating large collections of data. For example, consider a database program for maintaining a library's inventory of books. In addition to storing an entry for each book, such a program must be able to sort and retrieve these entries by author, title, Library of Congress number, or subject.

As we saw in Chapter 8, the simplest way to search for some item in a list is to scan the list in order, starting at the beginning. If the desired item is not first in the list, then you look at the second item, then the third, and so on until the item is found. This strategy is known as *sequential search*; since it involves searching through list items in sequence. As an example, consider the following array of words:

```
words = ["if", "else", "function", "while", "for", "var", "return"];
```

If we were looking for the word `"function"` in this array, a sequential search would inspect the first component (`"if"`), then the second (`"else"`), and finally the third before finding the desired word.

The SeqSearch function in Figure 17.18 performs a sequential search on a list of items. The two inputs required by this function are the list to be searched (an array) and the desired item. When called on a particular array, the function compares the desired item with each item in the array, starting at the beginning (i.e., at index 0). If the function encounters an item that matches the desired item, it immediately returns the index at which the match was found. If the desired item isn't found by the time the while loop reaches the last index, then the item is not in the list, and −1 will be returned.

```
function SeqSearch(list, desired)
// Assumes: list is an array of items
// Returns: index of list where desired first appears, or -1 if not found
{
    var index;

    index = 0;                          // START AT FIRST ITEM
    while (index < list.length) {       // AS LONG AS ITEMS LEFT
        if (list[index] == desired) {   //     IF NEXT ITEM IS DESIRED ONE,
            return index;               //          THEN RETURN WHERE FOUND
        }
        index = index + 1;              //     GO ON TO NEXT ITEM
    }
    return -1;                          // IF FAILED TO FIND, RETURN -1
}
```

Figure 17.18 Function for sequentially searching an array of items.

EXERCISE 17.15

Create a Web page named seq.html that uses the SeqSearch function in Figure 17.18 to perform sequential searches on user input. The page should contain a text area in which the user can enter a sequence of words separated by white space, as well as a text box in which the user can enter the word to be searched for. When the user clicks a button, SeqSearch should be called to search for the desired word in the sequence and display the result (either the index at which the word was found or else −1) in a separate text box.

EXERCISE 17.16

After experimenting with seq.html's sequential search capabilities, answer the following questions:

- What is the *minimum* number of inspections needed to find an item in an array using sequential search? Where must the desired item occur in the array in order for the page to perform only this minimum number of inspections?
- What is the *maximum* number of inspections required to find an item in an array using sequential search? Where must the desired item occur in the array in order for the page to perform this maximum number of inspections?

Although sequential search is sufficient for searching small lists, the fact that your program might have to examine every list item before completing a search makes this approach infeasible for large lists. As we saw in Chapter 8, however, a list can be searched much more efficiently if the items in the list are ordered. The **binary search** algorithm searches for a particular item in a sorted list by first checking the list's middle entry. The middle entry is compared to the desired item and, if the two are equal, then the search terminates successfully. If the middle entry comes after the desired item in the list's ordering scheme, then all items in the list beyond the middle entry are eliminated from consideration. Likewise, if the middle entry comes before the desired item in the list's ordering scheme, then the items before the middle entry are eliminated. The search then continues by repeatedly checking the middle entry of the remaining half of the list, eventually honing in on the desired entry.

For example, suppose that we were looking for the name "Jack" in the following array of names, which is sorted alphabetically:

```
["Charlie","Dave","Jack","Jerald","Jerroll","Laura","Lois","Winnie"]
```

According to the binary search algorithm, we begin by looking at the middle entry of the array. Since the array indices range from 0 to 7, we will select index 3 as the middle (the average of 0 and 7, rounded down). If the name we are looking for were stored at index 3, then we would be done. Since it is not, we compare the names and find that "Jerald" comes after "Jack". Thus, we know that "Jack" must come before "Jerald" in the list (i.e., our desired item occurs before index 3 in the array). We then repeat the process, this time focusing on the sublist starting at index 0 and ending at index 2. The midpoint in this sublist is at index 1 (the average of 0 and 2), which contains the name "Dave". Since "Dave" comes before "Jack" alphabetically, we know that "Jack" must come after index 1. Finally, the desired name is found at index 2.

To help us better understand binary search, we can define a set of generalized variables to use in our description of the algorithm. In this context, let `left` always refer to the leftmost or lowest possible index at which the desired array item could be located. Likewise, `right` will refer to the rightmost or highest possible index. Before a binary search begins, `left` is 0 and `right` is the last index in the array. During each step of the binary search, the midpoint `mid` between `left` and `right` is inspected. If the item stored at `mid` is the desired item, then the search terminates successfully. If the item at `mid` occurs after the desired item in the ordering scheme, then `right` becomes `mid-1`. Likewise, if the item at `mid` occurs before the desired item, then `left` becomes `mid+1`. Since each step either increases `left` or decreases `right`, the binary search will eventually locate the desired item if it is in the array. If the array doesn't contain a match for the desired item, then the `left` and `right` indices will ultimately cross, indicating that there is no more array to search.

For example, Figure 17.19 traces the steps in the binary search for "Jack" in the array of names listed above. Likewise, Figure 17.20 traces the steps in the binary search for "Sue" in the same array.

name = ["Charlie","Dave","Jack","Jerald","Jerroll","Laura","Lois","Winnie"]

	left	right	mid	names(mid)
1st inspection	0	7	3	"Jerald"
2nd inspection	0	2	1	"Dave"
3rd inspection	2	2	2	"Jack"

On the third inspection, the desired name is found, and the search terminates.

Figure 17.19   Trace of a binary search for the name "Jack."

name = ["Charlie","Dave","Jack","Jerald","Jerroll","Laura","Lois","Winnie"]

	left	right	mid	names(mid)
1st inspection	0	7	3	"Jerald"
2nd inspection	4	7	5	"Laura"
3rd inspection	6	7	6	"Lois"
4th inspection	6	5	–	–

On the fourth inspection, the `right` index becomes smaller than the `left` index, signifying that all indices in the array have been eliminated from consideration. At that point, the binary search can terminate, since the desired name is not present.

Figure 17.20   Trace of a binary search for the name "Sue."

EXERCISE 17.17

Using the array of names from the previous examples (repeated below), perform the following traces:

["Charlie","Dave","Jack","Jerald","Jerroll","Laura","Lois","Winnie"]

a. Trace the binary search for "Dave" in the table below:

	left	right	mid	names(mid)
1st inspection				
2nd inspection				
.				
.				
.				

b. Trace the binary search for "Jerroll" in the table below:

	left	right	mid	names(mid)
1st inspection				
2nd inspection				
.				
.				
.				

c. Trace the binary search for "Zoe" in the table below:

	left	right	mid	names(mid)
1st inspection				
2nd inspection				
.				
.				
.				

EXERCISE 17.18

The sort method, when applied to an array of strings, returns a copy of that array in which the strings appear in alphabetical order. For example, if the variable words stored the array ["foo", "bar", "biz"], then the call words.sort() would return ["bar", "biz", "foo"].

Create a Web page named bin.html that performs binary searches. Like seq.html, this page should contain a text area in which the user can enter a sequence of words and a text box for specifying the word to search for. When the user clicks a button, the page should sort the words in alphabetical order (using the array method sort) and then call a function named BinSearch to perform the search. As in seq.html, the result of the search (either the index at which the word was found or else −1) should be displayed in a separate text box.

EXERCISE 17.19

After experimenting with bin.html's binary search capabilities, answer the following questions:

- What is the *minimum* number of inspections needed to find an item in an array using binary search? Where must the desired item occur in the array in order for the page to perform only this minimum number of inspections?

- What is the *maximum* number of inspections required to find an item in an array using binary search? Where must the desired item occur in the list in order for the page to perform this maximum number of inspections?

Parallel and Nested Arrays

Suppose that you wanted to create a Web page that quizzed the user on state capitals. The page would need to select states at random, ask the user to guess each state's capital, and then compare the user's guesses against the correct answers. To accomplish this, the page must store the names of all 50 states and their capitals. In addition, the page must be able to select a random state and locate the corresponding capital.

Clearly, the easiest way to store state and capital names would be in arrays, as shown in Figure 17.21.

```
STATES =    ["Alabama", "Alaska", "Arizona", "Arkansas", "California",
             "Colorado", "Connecticut", "Delaware", "Florida", "Georgia",
             "Hawaii", "Idaho", "Illinois", "Indiana", "Iowa",
             "Kansas", "Kentucky", "Louisiana", "Maine", "Maryland",
             "Massachusetts", "Michigan", "Minnesota", "Mississippi", "Missouri",
             "Montana", "Nebraska", "Nevada", "New Hampshire", "New Jersey",
             "New Mexico", "New York", "North Carolina", "North Dakota", "Ohio",
             "Oklahoma", "Oregon", "Pennsylvania", "Rhode Island", "South Carolina",
             "South Dakota", "Tennessee", "Texas", "Utah", "Vermont",
             "Virginia", "Washington", "West Virginia", "Wisconsin", "Wyoming"];

CAPITALS =  ["Montgomery", "Juneau", "Phoenix", "Little Rock", "Sacramento",
             "Denver", "Hartford", "Dover", "Tallahassee", "Atlanta",
             "Honolulu", "Boise", "Springfield", "Indianapolis", "Des Moines",
             "Topeka", "Frankfort", "Baton Rouge", "Augusta", "Annapolis",
             "Boston", "Lansing", "St. Paul", "Jackson", "Jefferson City",
             "Helena", "Lincoln", "Carson City", "Concord", "Trenton",
             "Santa Fe", "Albany", "Raleigh", "Bismarck", "Columbus",
             "Oklahoma City", "Salem", "Harrisburg", "Providence", "Columbia",
             "Pierre", "Nashville", "Austin", "Salt Lake City", "Montpelier",
             "Richmond", "Olympia", "Charleston", "Madison", "Cheyenne"];
```

Figure 17.21   Arrays for storing states and capitals.

As you may have noticed, the order in which the states and capitals appear is not random. The states are listed in alphabetical order, and the capitals are listed so that their order mirrors that of their associated states. This means that the city at CAPITALS[0] ("Montgomery") is the capital of STATES[0] ("Alabama"), the city at CAPITALS[1] ("Juneau") is the capital of STATES[1] ("Alaska"), and so on. In general, the city at a particular index of the CAPITALS array corresponds to the state at the same index of the STATES array.

When two separate arrays store related items of data at corresponding indices, they are called **parallel arrays**. You can visualize this concept by drawing the memory cells for the parallel arrays,

Figure 17.22 Memory cells corresponding to the parallel arrays from Figure 17.21.

one above the other (Figure 17.22). When parallel arrays are drawn this way, it is clear that each data entry in one array is related to the corresponding data entry in the other array.

EXERCISE 17.20

Design and create a Web page named `states.html` that quizzes the user on state capitals. The layout of the page is entirely up to you. However, the page should contain a text box in which the user can specify the number of questions on the quiz. After processing this input, the page should repeatedly ask the user to identify the capitals of randomly selected states until the desired number of questions have been posed. Once the quiz is complete, the user's score (number of correct answers and percentage correct) should be displayed in the page.

[*Hint:* Your page should store the states and state capitals in parallel arrays, as shown in Figure 17.19. To select a state for each quiz question, your page will need to generate a random index from 0 to 49 and assign it to a variable (for example, `stateIndex`). Then, the state name can be accessed as `STATES[stateIndex]`. Once the user enters a guess, this input should be checked against the state capital stored at `CAPITALS[stateIndex]`.]

Since arrays can store values of any type, it is possible to nest arrays inside other arrays. This capability can be useful in structuring related data, such as states and state capitals. As an alternative to parallel arrays, we could store each state and its capital together in an array of length 2. All 50 state-capital pairs could then be stored in a single array, as shown in Figure 17.23. The memory cell for this nested structure is depicted in Figure 17.24.

The advantage of using such nested arrays is that you can explicitly group related information together. That is, all the information about a particular state (which could be expanded to include population, state flower, etc.) is stored in one item of the STATE_INFO array. Of course, two levels of access are now required to look at a state name or capital. For example, the assignment

```
state = STATE_INFO[0];
```

assigns the array `["Alabama", "Montgomery"]` to the variable `state`. To access the state name from this pair, the first index must be accessed: `state[0]`. Likewise, the corresponding capital can be accessed at the second index: `state[1]`.

EXERCISE 17.21

Modify your `states.html` page so that it uses the nested array structure STATE_INFO to store the names of the states and their capitals. Then, experiment with the new version to verify that the page behaves as before.

```
STATE_INFO = [["Alabama", "Montgomery"], ["Alaska", "Juneau"], ["Arizona", "Phoenix"],
              ["Arkansas", "Little Rock"], ["California", "Sacramento"],
              ["Colorado", "Denver"], ["Connecticut", "Hartford"],
              ["Delaware", "Dover"], ["Florida", "Tallahassee"],
              ["Georgia", "Atlanta"], ["Hawaii", "Honolulu"], ["Idaho", "Boise"],
              ["Illinois", "Springfield"], ["Indiana", "Indianapolis"],
              ["Iowa", "Des Moines"], ["Kansas", "Topeka"], ["Kentucky", "Frankfort"],
              ["Louisiana", "Baton Rouge"], ["Maine", "Augusta"],
              ["Maryland", "Annapolis"], ["Massachusetts", "Boston"],
              ["Michigan", "Lansing"], ["Minnesota", "St. Paul"],
              ["Mississippi", "Jackson"], ["Missouri", "Jefferson City"],
              ["Montana", "Helena"], ["Nebraska", "Lincoln"],
              ["Nevada", "Carson City"], ["New Hampshire", "Concord"],
              ["New Jersey", "Trenton"], ["New Mexico", "Santa Fe"],
              ["New York", "Albany"], ["North Carolina", "Raleigh"],
              ["North Dakota", "Bismarck"], ["Ohio", "Columbus"],
              ["Oklahoma", "Oklahoma City"], ["Oregon", "Salem"],
              ["Pennsylvania", "Harrisburg"], ["Rhode Island", "Providence"],
              ["South Carolina", "Columbia"], ["South Dakota", "Pierre"],
              ["Tennessee", "Nashville"], ["Texas", "Austin"],
              ["Utah", "Salt Lake City"], ["Vermont", "Montpelier"],
              ["Virginia", "Richmond"], ["Washington", "Olympia"],
              ["West Virginia", "Charleston"], ["Wisconsin", "Madison"],
              ["Wyoming", "Cheyenne"]];
```

Figure 17.23 Nested array structure for storing states and capitals.

Figure 17.24 Memory cell corresponding to the nested arrays from Figure 17.23.

Computers and Society

This chapter uses narrative, illustrations, and review questions to introduce computer science and technology concepts.

Technology is neither good nor bad, nor even neutral. Technology is one part of the complex of relationships that people form with each other and the world around them; it simply cannot be understood outside of that concept.

Samuel Collins

The most likely way for the world to be destroyed, most experts agree, is by accident. That's where we come in; we're computer professionals. We cause accidents.

Nathaniel Borenstein

We are the most unequal of all advanced societies in terms of incomes, benefits, and also wealth. Now why is this happening? It's happening largely because of the two great forces of technology and globalization. It's happening because education and access to learning, that is relevant for this new economy, is so unequal.

Robert Reich
PBS interview, 1999

This chapter explores the effects of technology on the society in which we live. Computers and the Internet have changed the ways in which people carry out daily tasks, access information, communicate with each other, and conduct business. Having completed this book, you are better prepared to place computing in an appropriate historical context and to assess computers' potential for improving quality of life. Of course, the widespread adoption of computer technology also introduces the potential for abuses and unwanted consequences. For example, overreliance on high-tech tools can lead to disaster when complex systems fail. Likewise, as more personal communications and business transactions move online, privacy and security become major concerns. By examining both the positive and potentially negative societal role of computers, this chapter aims to call your attention to computers' wide-ranging influence while helping you become a more knowledgeable technology consumer.

Positive Impact of Technology

In the article "The Greatest Inventions in the Past 1000 Years," historian Larry Gormley ranked technological developments according to their impact on modern life.[1] While any such list leaves room for debate, there is no doubt that the inventions listed by Gormley (Figure 18.1) have influenced the way in which society is structured. For example, the automobile changed the face of America by increasing personal mobility. When people obtained their own affordable mode of transportation, they were able to move away from urban areas and still drive to their jobs, which led to American suburbanization and the rise of today's "commuter culture." The availability of telephone service also contributed to the decentralization of American society, in that phones enabled people to communicate and conduct business over large distances.

	Invention	Year	The Greatest Inventions In the Past 1000 Years[1]	
			Inventor	Notes
1	Printing Press	1450	Johannes Gutenberg	allowed literacy to greatly expand
2	Electric Light	1879	Thomas Edison	powered countless social changes
3	Automobile	1885	Karl Benz	increased personal mobility and freedom
4	Telephone	1876	Alexander Graham Bell	spread communication across wide areas
5	Radio and Television	1895 & 1926	Guglielmo Marconi & John Baird	made the world smaller
6	Vaccination	1796	Edward Jenner	protected people from disease
7	Computer	1939	John Atanasoff, et al.	transformed business world; predecessor to the Internet
8	Airplane	1903	Orville and Wilbur Wright	allowed people and products to quickly move across wide areas
9	Gas powered tractor	1892	John Froelich	started agricultural mechanization
10	Anesthesia	1844	Horace Wells	provided a great leap forward for medicine

Figure 18.1 Greatest inventions, as listed by Larry Gormley.

More than any other invention in Figure 18.1, computer technology is still evolving, which means that it continues to impact society in new ways. As we saw in Chapter 6, the first electronic computers made immediate contributions to world affairs during the 1940s. The COLOSSUS, developed by the British government, was instrumental in breaking the Nazi Enigma code and providing the Allies with an intelligence advantage in World War II. In the United States, the ENIAC and subsequent computers performed the calculations and simulations that enabled American scientists to develop nuclear technology, which precipitated the Japanese surrender and shaped the politics of the subsequent Cold War. More recently, computers have become common in homes and businesses, changing the way in which we communicate and driving today's information-based economy. As computer scientists continue to augment existing technology and develop new applications, the potential for computers to influence daily life appears unlimited.

The sections that follow describe some of the ways in which computers, most notably through the Internet, have improved the quality of modern life.

Computers and Programs for Everyday Tasks

Over the past few years, computer technology has become so pervasive that it is now difficult to imagine life without it. One obvious example is the way in which computers have changed the nature of monetary transactions. When most products and services were bought for cash, people were forced to carry large amounts of money on their person. In addition to being inconvenient, a cash-based society invited crime, since muggings were likely to net thieves large quantities of untraceable funds. Today, many consumers are replacing cash with credit and debit cards, thanks to a computerized banking network that enables the electronic transfer of funds from one banking institution to another. Due to the proliferation of automated teller machines (ATMs) and debit-card scanners, people can access their money around the clock from almost any location, even while traveling (Figure 18.2). As a result, people are no longer dependent on cash reserves to purchase goods. From pay-at-the-pump gas stations to vending machines with credit-card readers, computing technology makes it easier for consumers to make purchases without carrying cash. In addition, the new system discourages traditional theft, since credit-card purchases are traceable. Unfortunately, the electronic era has inspired new forms of illegal activity, including credit-card fraud and identity theft, where a criminal uses false identification to pose as another person in order to make purchases or obtain credit.

Figure 18.2 Debit-card readers provide retail shoppers with direct access to checking-account funds or credit-card accounts.

Although ATMs and debit-card readers serve as visible reminders of our reliance on technology, modern life also depends on thousands of less obvious, hidden computer applications. ***Embedded processors***, computer chips that are built into appliances and machinery to control their workings, account for more than 90% of all computer processors. In 2001, technology author D.P. Samantarai estimated that the average home contained 50 to 100 embedded processors, concealed in devices such as microwave ovens, television remote controls, cordless phones, and automatic thermostats.[2] Similarly, modern automobiles employ embedded processors to control fuel injectors, antilock brakes, and other components (see Figure 18.3).

Microprocessors in Automobiles[3]		
speech technology	high-intensity discharge lamps	lighting system
electronic-memory seat	electric windows	mirror control
premium audio system	door module	climate control
digital radio	transmission control	navigation/GPS
immobilization	alarm systems	trip computer
head-up display	one-way data pager	right-of-cluster display
cruise control	Internet access	integrated cell phone
central body controllers	rain sensor	engine controller
vehicle-to-roadside communications	central locking and remote keyless entry	analog and digital instrumentation

Figure 18.3 Common uses of microprocessors in automobiles, as listed by Warren Webb.

Society has also been affected by the availability of personal computers and easy-to-use software, which enable individuals to accomplish tasks previously reserved for highly trained professionals. For example, word processing and desktop publishing software have made it simple for anyone to produce professional-looking documents, such as business cards and flyers. Similarly, most personal computers now come with video-editing software, which allows users to create, edit, and augment digital video images on their computers. In addition, many software companies market specialized applications that capture human expertise and make it available to users. For example, tax preparation programs such as TaxCut by H&R Block integrate graphics, sound, and video to guide users through the process of completing various tax forms (Figure 18.4). Over the past few years, many of these applications that capture human expertise have become available as Internet-based services. By offering access to such services over the Web on a pay-per-use basis, software companies can drastically reduce the cost to users while ensuring that all included information is regularly updated.

Figure 18.4   TaxCut by H&R Block guides the user in the preparation of his or her income taxes. The program utilizes specialized tax knowledge and even integrates sound and video to provide tax tips.

The Internet and Web as Information Sources

As more people gain access to the Internet, online resources are quickly replacing traditional sources of information. Unlike print media such as newspapers and magazines, Web sites can be updated 24 hours a day, allowing online publishers to report stories as soon as they break. News sites can also integrate text and pictures with other types of media, such as video footage and interactive polls. The immediacy of the online delivery system has been especially appealing during recent crises, such as the September 11 terrorist attacks and the war in Iraq. According to Nielsen/NetRatings, over 10 million users accessed the CNN.com news site (Figure 18.5) from work during the first week of the Iraqi war, constituting a 58% increase in visitors over the previous week.[4] Other online news sources, such as MSNBC.com and Yahoo!® News, experienced similar upsurges in traffic.

In an effort to compete with increasingly popular Internet media, many newspapers and magazines have expanded their offerings to include online versions. For example, *The Washington Post* (www.washingtonpost.com) and *The New York Times* (www.nytimes.com) both publish online editions. In addition, independent media organizations have utilized the Web to present stories and

Figure 18.5 Many traditional media outlets, such as television networks, newspapers, and magazines, now have a presence on the Web. Shown here is the CNN.com homepage from April 27, 2003.

opinions that might not otherwise reach a mainstream audience (Figure 18.6). And since the Internet crosses international borders, it has been instrumental in enabling the citizens of repressive governments to read objective news and communicate with the world.

Traditional media have approached the Internet in a variety of ways—some providing limited services online for free, others providing full services online but at a fee. Responding to the widespread availability of online reference material, the *Encyclopedia Britannica* (www.eb.com) now sells access to its encyclopedia as a subscription service over the Web. In the public sector, the U.S. government has led the campaign to move key data online by posting draft legislation, public service announcements, and various other documents on its network of Web sites.

Although many traditional publications repurpose their content for the Web, the majority of Web pages are unique resources created by individuals and private organizations. As you learned in Chapter 1, anyone with minimal HTML skills and access to a Web server can design pages and make them available to the world. Given the diversity of opinion, perspective, and interests represented by today's online community, it is possible to find Web content on virtually any topic. For example, Web users can locate information about their favorite sports teams (www.cubs.com), directions to a local disc golf course (www.pdga.com), an explanation of how antilock brakes operate (www.iihs.org/safety_facts/qanda/antilock.htm), the complete works of William Shakespeare (the-tech.mit.edu/Shakespeare/), updates on the Kilauea volcanic eruption in Hawaii (hvo.wr.usgs.gov/kilauea/update/main.html), and the schedule for the ferry connecting Hatteras and Ocracoke, NC (www.hatteras-nc.com/ferry/). To help navigate this vast sea of information, search engines such as Google (google.com) and Yahoo!® Search (search.yahoo.com) automatically catalog Web pages and allow users to search for data by topic or keywords. Figure 18.7 depicts the advanced search options available to Google users.

The Internet and Web as Communications Media

As we explained in Chapter 3, the exponential growth of the Internet during the 1970s was fueled in part by a proliferation of communications-based applications. Countless scientists, government

Figure 18.6 In addition to traditional media sources, alternative voices can be expressed on the Web due to its open-access nature. Shown here is the *The Independent Media Center* homepage from June 29, 2003.

workers and college faculty were drawn to the Internet by the availability of electronic mail and newsgroups. When Internet access became more widespread in the 1990s, a broad group of nontechnical users began going online to exchange business and personal information. According to a 2002 survey conducted by Jupiter Research, 93% of all Internet users communicate via email.[5] IDC Research estimates that, during 2002, approximately 31 billion email messages were sent and received each day, with that number expected to reach 60 billion per day by 2006.[6]

Today, it is common for Internet Service Providers (ISPs) to bundle email accounts with other services, making it easy for their customers to use the Internet for both Web access and email communications. One of the most popular email-management programs for Windows-based PCs is Microsoft Outlook, in which individuals send and receive email messages via an intuitive, Web-inspired interface (Figure 18.8). Users who want the ability to check their email from any Internet-enabled computer can take advantage of Web-based email services, such as Microsoft Hotmail (`www.hotmail.com`) and Yahoo!® Mail (`mail.yahoo.com`).

More recently, the Internet has popularized the use of ***instant messaging (IM)*** applications, which enable users to type text messages and view responses immediately in the same window. As a result, people can keep track of friends or business contacts online and can conduct personal conversations or meetings electronically instead of in person or over the phone. According to a Nielsen/NetRatings survey, more than 41 million home users sent instant messages during May 2002, representing 40% of all home Internet users. Likewise, 12.6 million users sent instant messages from work, representing 31% of all office Internet users. As of 2002, AOL Instant Messenger™ was by far the most popular instant messaging service, accounting for 22 million IM users[7] (Figure 18.9).

Figure 18.7   Google's advanced search options allow users to look for any word, exact phrase, or combination of words, and can even limit the scope of the search based on file formats, dates, or location.

The Internet and Web for Commerce

Another popular function of the Web is to facilitate electronic commerce, or *e-commerce*. As the number of Internet users has grown, businesses have recognized the Web's potential as an advertising medium and tool for reaching new customers. Today, almost every company maintains a Web presence, varying from information-based sites—at which the company provides data regarding its mission or products—to transaction-based sites—at which consumers can actually purchase goods.

Online shopping offers numerous benefits to consumers. Instead of searching through the mall and standing in long lines, shoppers can make purchases from the comfort of their homes at any time of day or night. Web-based commerce also makes it easier to comparison shop—i.e., compare the products, features, and prices offered by various companies. Furthermore, online stores provide more detailed product descriptions and reviews than would be available through conventional stores, which helps consumers make more informed purchasing decisions. Many of the largest e-commerce sites are online offshoots of traditional retailers, such as www.bn.com (Barnes & Noble booksellers), www.circuitcity.com (Circuit City electronics stores), and www.sears.com (Sears department stores). In addition, many banks and retailers provide online services such as account tracking and online bill payments for the convenience of their customers.

While companies such as these use the Internet to complement their traditional sales and services, some online companies are strictly Internet ventures. These companies have proven to be a much riskier venture, partly due to their lack of other revenue streams to support startup and development. In fact, many of the companies founded during the e-commerce boom of the late 1990s failed to turn a profit and have since folded. However, the largest e-commerce site in terms of yearly sales, Amazon.com, is a strictly online company that was founded in 1994 (Figure 18.10). According to the U.S. Census Bureau, online sales for the entire e-commerce sector exceeded $45 billion during 2002, an increase of 27% over 2001. Amazon.com by itself generated more than $3.93 billion in sales for 2002.[8]

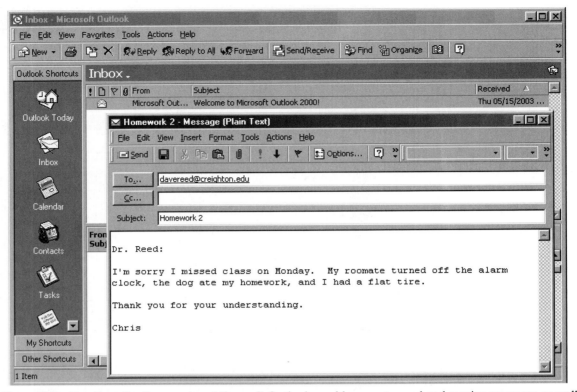

Figure 18.8 Email applications, such as Microsoft Outlook, enable users to send and receive messages, as well as organize contacts and plan their schedules.

Figure 18.9 Instant messenger applications, such as AOL Instant Messenger™, send and receive messages almost instantaneously, allowing for interactive conversations between users.

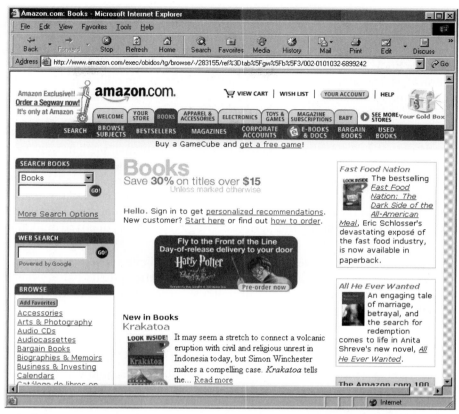

Figure 18.10 Online retail outlets, such as `Amazon.com`, allow consumers to research products as well as purchase them.

The Web has also provided a new advertising channel for businesses and organizations. The most common method of Internet-based advertising involves the owners of popular Web sites charging fees in exchange for hosting advertising banners on their pages. These so-called ***banner ads*** are clickable images that promote a particular company's product or service. For example, the `CNN.com` page in Figure 18.5 contains banner-ads for Netflix® and Land's End. Users who click an ad are typically directed to the company's Web site, where they can make purchases or review additional product-related information. Recently, marketers have turned to more aggressive means of capturing the consumer's attention, such as pop-up ads that pop open a new window that the user must manually close. From a publicity perspective, Internet-based advertising offers potential advantages over other, more traditional channels, since the Web's structure makes targeted marketing easier and allows direct connections between ads and related purchasing interfaces.

In addition to facilitating business-to-consumer (B2C) transactions, the Internet is extensively used for communication and information exchanges within and among businesses. Business-to-business (B2B) transactions allow companies to manage inventory more dynamically, improve efficiency by linking various data channels, and form partnerships based on sharing resources and information.

Potential Dangers of Technology

In conjunction with the benefits we have mentioned, the widespread adoption of technology also introduces the potential for abuses and undesirable consequences. The following sections outline some of the dangers that computers pose for individuals, businesses, and society at large.

Reliance on Complex Systems

As society becomes dependent on complex, computer-based products and services, the effects of computer errors or system failures become far-reaching. Whereas errors in the programs you wrote for this book might cause you frustration or earn you a bad grade, errors in software for air traffic control, electrical power relays, and banking systems can endanger lives and cost companies millions of dollars. The following list describes situations in which computer-system bugs produced dire and unexpected consequences.

- Between 1985 and 1987, six cancer patients received massive radiation overdoses when a Therac-25 radiation therapy machine malfunctioned. These malfunctions were eventually traced to a single coding error in the control mechanism for the machine. Four of the accidents resulted in patient deaths, whereas the other two resulted in patient disfigurement and disability.

- In 1990, AT&T's long-distance telephone network was crippled for nine hours, due to a misplaced statement in the electronic switching software. An estimated 60,000 customers were without long-distance service during this period, costing AT&T more than $60 million in lost revenue and damage to its reputation.

- In 1991, 28 soldiers were killed when a Scud missile struck a U.S. Army barracks near Dharan, Saudi Arabia. It was later determined that a Patriot missile battery failed to track and intercept the incoming Scud missile because of a software error. The control software for the Patriot missiles performed a repeated computation involving the value 1/10, which is a nonterminating number when represented in binary. The resulting round-off error, when compounded over 100 hours of active use, amounted to a .34 second timing error that caused the Patriot missile to miss its target.

- In 1999, NASA's *Mars Climate Orbiter* went off course and was destroyed in the Martian atmosphere. The navigational error that caused the crash was traced to inconsistencies in the software-development process at NASA. Apparently, some development teams on the project designed code using Imperial units (e.g., pounds), whereas other teams used metric units (e.g., kilograms). No one working on the project noticed this inconsistency, and the required measurement conversions were never made. The cost of the Orbiter was $125 million.

To avoid errors such as these, the software industry utilizes design and testing methodologies aimed at minimizing costs while improving the quality of large applications. However, as the size and complexity of software grows, design and testing become significantly more difficult. For example, it might be feasible for an experienced programmer to carefully study a 1,000-line program and ensure that it behaves as expected. However, performing the same type of analysis on a 10,000-line program would require significantly more than 10 times as much work, since each section of code must be tested not only in isolation, but also in relation to the other sections of code. As more software components are added to a system, the number of potential interactions between them grows exponentially. Software bugs are inevitable when the scale of a project renders it too complex for detailed study. For example, when Windows 2000 was released, the operating system was known to contain more than 63,000 bugs in its 35 million lines of code.[9] However, these bugs were not considered critical, since most were extremely unlikely to occur in everyday use and, at worst, required the user to reboot the computer. Clearly, critical systems—such as those that control aircraft or financial networks— necessitate more careful testing and debugging to protect human lives and property.

Information Overload

Although the impressive range of information available online can be viewed as a strength, it is also one of the medium's greatest weaknesses. The fact that individuals can add content to the Web ensures that all ideas and perspectives can be heard. However, the massive volume of data created by the online community isn't particularly organized, which makes finding any single piece of information difficult. As of April 2003, the Google search engine claimed to have cataloged more than three million Web pages. Search engines are useful in narrowing down an Internet search, but users must carefully select their search criteria in order to find specific resources. For example, suppose that a programmer wanted to learn more about the JavaScript prompt function. A search for "JavaScript" produces 11,100,000 matches using Google, whereas a more refined search for "JavaScript prompt function" reduces the number of matching pages to 50,100. In the results of the second search, the first 10 pages include both general-purpose JavaScript tutorials and documentation on the prompt function.

Even after a user locates Web pages related to a desired topic, judging the reliability of those pages is not always easy. Unlike traditional media sources, which have editors and reviewers to ensure at least some degree of accuracy and impartiality, the Web is neither monitored nor censored. Since anyone can be a Web author, there is always a chance that the author is uninformed, misinformed, or biased. Moreover, professional writers are familiar with the idea that complex questions require complex answers, whereas Web authors may settle for short answers that, although not entirely inaccurate, lack context and justification. For example, a Web search on the simple question "What is the capital of Missouri?" returns numerous pages that provide the answer (Jefferson City). However, entering a more complex question such as "Who invented the computer?" produces pages with a variety of answers, including Alan Turing, Konrad Zuse, Charles Babbage, John Atanasoff, and John von Neumann. As you learned in Chapter 6, each of these figures contributed to the development of computing technology in a different way. Responsible researchers would need to explain these answers in context in order to justify them.

Figure 18.11 lists several criteria that can be applied to online content in order to evaluate its credibility.

Author Reputation	Is the author well known or well regarded in his field? If this information is not apparent, try to access biographical information or related works that reference the author in order to determine credibility.
Author Objectivity	Is there reason to believe that the author is objective? If the author has a political agenda or personal history with the topic, there is a greater danger of bias.
Content Review	Has the page been edited or reviewed by other parties? If so, there is more reason to trust its accuracy. Even the reputation of the organization hosting the page can be considered as supporting evidence, since a reputable organization will exert some control over content in order to protect the organization's integrity.
Content Verifiability	Does the author demonstrate scholarship and knowledge of the field by properly referencing other works? If evidence is strictly anecdotal or sources are untraceable, the content may reflect personal opinions that are not supported by the facts.
Content Timeliness	Is the information provided in the material timely? If the sources are old or are not accompanied by explicit dates, then the content may be out of date or contradictory to current practices.

Figure 18.11   Criteria for evaluating online content.

Privacy and Security

When using credit cards or shopping online, consumers must often sacrifice their privacy for the sake of convenience. Most credit-card companies and online retailers maintain detailed records of customer purchases in an effort to identify patterns and predict future sales. While such records can be used to improve customer service, there is significant potential for misuse. By analyzing a person's credit-card records, a company can infer many otherwise private details of the person's life, including hobbies, travel patterns, and personal contacts. Companies commonly sell customer profiles to marketing firms and other retailers, which use the information to contact potential buyers and deliver targeted advertising. However, Web users can limit the exploitation of their personal data by interacting only with reputable online businesses. Most such companies have established privacy policies outlining the way in which they handle customer information, and many explicitly promise not to sell data to third parties (Figure 18.12). To ensure that companies follow their own privacy policies, third-party organizations such as TRUSTe.com have been formed that evaluate companies' privacy procedures and offer accreditation seals.

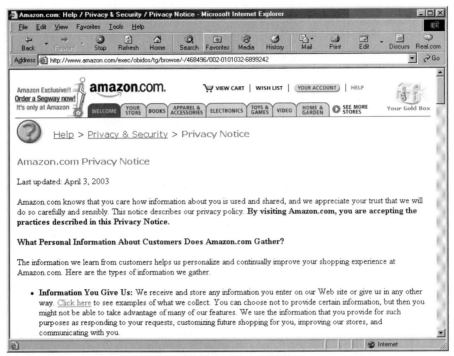

Figure 18.12 Most companies provide an online policy describing the type of information recorded for a customer or site visitor, and the acceptable uses of such information. Shown here is the privacy policy for Amazon.com.

Email also raises privacy concerns in our technology-driven society. When an email message is received, it is commonly stored in a file on the recipient's computer. If that message contains sensitive personal or business information, there is a danger that unauthorized users might get access to that file. Whereas legislation explicitly protects the privacy of letters and packages sent through the U.S. Postal System, there are few laws that apply directly to electronic privacy. Furthermore, courts have overwhelmingly favored employers over employees in invasion-of-privacy suits involving email. Unless a company or organization explicitly states its policy on electronic privacy, it may be assumed that the company has the right to access any content on company-owned machines. This has been ruled to include emails written or received by employees, even if the emails are unrelated to company business.

Privacy is closely linked to the issue of security—i.e., the assurance that Internet transmissions will travel from a verified sender to a verified recipient without being intercepted or corrupted in any way. As email messages travel across the Internet, they pass through numerous routers that direct the messages to their destinations. Each router represents a security risk, because someone could gain access to the router and eavesdrop on messages that are relayed. Although all Internet communications require security, e-commerce is particularly dependent on the ability to conduct secure transactions, since customers must submit credit-card numbers and other vulnerable data. Various security-related technologies have been developed to validate the identities of online customers and to encrypt data that is broadcast over the Internet (see Chapter 10 for details regarding encryption methods). Despite these efforts, however, online fraud is a continuing problem that affects customers and companies alike. Gartner, Inc., a technology research and advisory firm, has estimated that fraudulent online purchases cost companies more than $500 million during the 2002 holiday shopping season alone.[10]

The Digital Divide

An especially troubling aspects of recent technological developments is that the benefits associated with computers are not shared equally by all. According to a 2003 report by the Pew Internet & American Life Project, Americans with minority ancestry, lower incomes, and less education are far less likely to be online than are Americans without these factors (Figure 18.13). As we have outlined in this chapter, Internet access can provide numerous advantages in our society—in addition to helping people become better informed, knowledge of the Web is a prerequisite for jobs in a variety of fields. Many experts worry that discrepancies in Internet access will widen the socio-economic gap between the advantaged and disadvantaged in our society.

How Internet Access Has Changed in America[11] The percentage of each group with Internet access.					
By Gender	**2000**	**2002**	**By Race**	**2000**	**2002**
Men	51%	60%	Whites	50%	60%
Women	46%	56%	Blacks	34%	45%
			Hispanics	43%	54%
By Age	**2000**	**2002**	**By Household Income**	**2000**	**2002**
15–29	69%	74%	less than $30,000	31%	38%
30–49	60%	67%	$30,000–$50,000	52%	65%
50–64	45%	52%	$50,000–$75,000	67%	74%
65 +	14%	18%	$75,000 and above	78%	86%
By Education	**2000**	**2002**	**By Community Size**	**2000**	**2002**
Did not graduate high school	17%	23%	Rural	43%	49%
High school grad	34%	45%	Suburban	54%	63%
Some college	63%	72%	Urban	53%	58%
College +	75%	82%			

Figure 18.13 Statistics on the Digital Divide, from Pew Internet & American Life Project (2003). The Project bears no responsibility for the interpretations presented or conclusions reached based on analysis of the data.

Numerous groups are addressing the digital divide in an effort to ensure that all people can enjoy the benefits of Internet access. During the Clinton administration, the U.S. government made Internet connectivity a priority in public schools. A major part of this campaign was the E-rate program, through which schools received government funding earmarked for computer technology and Internet service. By the fall of 2000, 98% of all public schools in the United States were connected to the Internet, as compared to 35% in 1994. In addition, the number of connected classrooms in public schools has increased dramatically, from only 3% of classrooms in 1994 to 77% in 2000.[12] Following this trend, most public libraries and community centers now provide Internet-enabled computers; in conjunction with nonprofit organizations such as CompuMentor (www.compumentor.org), these organizations have been instrumental in supplying Internet access and technical assistance to minority groups and lower-income individuals. Although the digital divide continues to affect Americans, there is no doubt that the situation has improved over the last decade. Hopefully, public- and private-sector organizations will continue to work together in the quest for universally available Internet access.

It should be noted that the digital divide also exists on a global scale: in particular, America, western Europe, and certain Asian countries having much greater Internet connectivity than other parts of the world. Since high-tech jobs are a major force in the world economy, lack of Internet access places less developed nations at a significant disadvantage and compounds their other economic problems. International organizations such as the United Nations (www.un.org) and World Economic Forum (www.weforum.org) are working to address the global digital divide.

Looking Beyond...

Clearly, computing technology has significantly impacted society over the last 60 years, both positively and negatively. In addition to teaching programming skills, this book has tried to make you a knowledgeable consumer of technology in your personal and professional life. Now that you have studied the structure and behavior of computers, you are better prepared to evaluate and effectively use new technology. Furthermore, your familiarity with computer history should help you recognize and appreciate the impact that new technology can have in your life. Having explored the methodologies employed by programmers and computer professionals, you are equipped with a better understanding of the computer science field and how it relates to other disciplines.

The programming component of this book has also contributed to your development as a student and user of computing technology. In learning to build interactive Web pages using HTML and JavaScript, you have acquired practical Web-development skills that will prove useful for many information-based careers. Through the process of writing JavaScript code, you have mastered fundamental concepts of programming, which can be applied to learning other, more complex programming languages. In a broader context, programming also fosters critical-thinking and problem-solving skills, which pertain to many facets of daily life.

Hopefully, this book has empowered you to be an active participant in a future in which computing technology improves our quality of life.

Chapter Summary

- Computers and the Internet have changed the ways in which people carry out daily tasks, access information, communicate with each other, and conduct business. For example, electronic banking has changed the way people access money, and applications software has enabled individuals to accomplish tasks previously reserved for highly trained professionals.

- Embedded processors, computer chips that are built into appliances and machinery to control their workings, account for more than 90% of all computer processors.

- The Internet and World Wide Web provide alternative sources of news and information that can be updated easily and accessed by people worldwide.

- It has been estimated that 93% of all Internet users communicate via email, and 40% of all home Internet users utilize instant messaging.

- In 2002, online sales for the entire electronic commerce, or e-commerce, sector exceeded $45 billion. Online shopping can be more convenient for consumers, and it makes product research and comparison shopping easier.

- Banner ads are clickable images that promote a particular company's product or service.

- As society becomes dependent on complex, computer-based products and services, the effects of computer errors or system failures become far-reaching (e.g., failure of medical machinery controls can lead to patient deaths, bugs in switching software can lead to telephone network outages).

- As of April 2003, the Google search engine claimed to have cataloged more than three billion Web pages.

- Since the Web is large and there are few controls on the quality of page content, finding desired information on the Web and verifying its authenticity can be difficult.

- Criteria that can be applied to online content in order to evaluate its credibility include author reputation, author objectivity, content review, content verifiability, and content timeliness.

- Privacy and security are concerns, as electronic banking and online shopping provide records of individual activities and preferences. Most reputable companies establish privacy policies outlining the way in which they handle customer information, and also utilize encryption techniques to protect private information as it is transmitted.

- The "digital divide" refers to the fact that the benefits associated with computers are not shared equally by all. Americans with minority ancestry, lower incomes, and less education are far less likely to be online than are other Americans. On a global scale, America, western Europe and certain Asian countries have much greater Internet connectivity than other parts of the world.

Review Questions

1. TRUE or FALSE? Computer technology has greatly impacted the banking industry, to the extent that credit cards and debit cards have reduced consumers' reliance on cash.

2. TRUE or FALSE? Embedded processors are computer chips that are built into appliances and machinery to control their workings.

3. TRUE or FALSE? Instant messaging software allows users to send and receive messages almost instantaneously, allowing for interactive conversations between remote users.

4. TRUE or FALSE? Commercial software systems are thoroughly tested so that all programming errors are identified and fixed before the system is marketed.

5. TRUE or FALSE? Search engines such as Google.com verify the accuracy of information on Web pages before they report those pages.

6. TRUE or FALSE? Amazon.com is the largest e-commerce site in terms of yearly online sales.

7. TRUE or FALSE? Due to budget constraints, public schools are less likely to have Internet access today than they were 10 years ago.

8. TRUE or FALSE? The "digital divide" refers to the fact that the disadvantaged in society (e.g., minorities, poor and uneducated citizens) are less likely to have access to the Internet.

9. Do you think that Gormley's list (Figure 18.1) represents the 10 most important inventions of the last 1,000 years? If not, what inventions do you think are missing from this list? What possible developments in computer technology might increase the relative importance of computers?

10. In addition to the examples listed in this chapter, describe two other aspects of society that have been greatly impacted by computer technology. Within these areas, what specific activities or jobs were most affected? On the whole, has the impact been positive or negative? Justify your answers.

11. Describe two advantages of online newspapers over their print counterparts. Do you think that electronic newspapers will completely replace printed papers in the near future? Why or why not?

12. Perform a Web search on your name. That is, enter your name into a search engine, such as Google or Yahoo!® Search, and then search the Web for occurrences of that name. How many matching pages did the search engine find? If you have your own Web page, did the search engine find it? You may need to include additional search parameters if your name is relatively common.

13. Utilize a search engine to research and answer the following questions. Identify the site at which you obtained your answer, as well as the search parameters you used to locate the page.
    a. Who invented the programming language PHP?
    b. In what year did the Battle of Hastings take place?

c. Who won the Academy Award for best actress in 1996?

d. How many number-one hits did the Beatles have?

Endnotes

1. Gormley, Larry. "The Greatest Inventions in the Past 1000 Years." eHistory.com, 2003. Online at `http://www.ehistory.com/world/articles/ArticleView.cfm?AID=20`.

2. Samantarai, D.P. "The New Era of Embedded Internet." *Cybermedia*, November 2001. Online at `http://www.ciol.com/content/opinion/embedded/101110201.asp`.

3. Webb, Warren. "Embedded Technology Transforms the Automobile." *EDN Magazine*, August 19, 1999. Online at `http://e-insite.net/ednmag/contents/images/46067.pdf`.

4. *Round-The-Clock News Coverage of the War In Iraq Draws Surfers Online.* Nielsen/NetRatings, March 2003. Online at `http://www.nielsen-netratings.com/pr/pr_030327.pdf`.

5. Greenspan, Robyn. "American Surfers Keep it Simple." *CyberAtlas*, September 2002. Online at `http://cyberatlas.internet.com/big_picture/geographics/article/0,,5911_1466661,00.html`.

6. *Email Usage to Exceed 60 Billion by 2006, According to IDC.* IDC Research, September 2002. Online at `http://www.idc.com/getdoc.jhtml?containerId=pr2002_09_23_113035`.

7. *Instant Messaging Used by More Than 41 Million Home Internet Surfers.* Nielsen/NetRatings, June 2002. Online at `http://www.nielsen-netratings.com/pr/pr_020617.pdf`.

8. *United States Department of Commerce News.* February 2003. Online at `http://www.census.gov/mrts/www/data/pdf/20024q.pdf`.

9. Farr, John. "HOW Many Bugs, Did You Say??" Applelinks.com, February 2000. Online at `http://www.applelinks.com/articles/2000/02/20000212012612.shtml`.

10. Haines, Allison. "Gartner Says U.S. E-Tailers Will Lose Nearly $500 Million This Holiday Season to Fraud and Lost Sales." Gartner, Inc., December 2002. Online at `http://www3.gartner.com/5_about/press_releases/2002_12/pr20021211a.jsp`.

11. *The Ever-Shifting Internet Population: A New Look at Internet Access and the Digital Divide.* Pew Research Center, April 2003. Online at `http://www.pewinternet.org/reports/toc.asp?Report=88`.

12. *Internet Access in U.S. Public Schools and Classrooms: 1994–2000.* National Center for Education Statistics, May 2001. Online at `http://nces.ed.gov/pubsearch/pubsinfo.asp?pubid=2001071`.

References

Baase, Sara. *A Gift of Fire: Social, Legal and Ethical Issues in Computing.* Upper Saddle River, NJ: Prentice Hall, 1997.

Cavazos, Edward, and Gavino Morin. *Cyber-space and the Law: Your Rights and Duties in the On-line World.* Cambridge, MA: MIT Press, 1994.

Greenspan, Robyn. "Widespread Use Despite Abuse." *CyberAtlas*, September 2002. Online at `http://cyberatlas.internet.com/big_picture/applications/article/0,,1301_1462941,00.html`.

Huckle, Thomas. "Collection of Software Bugs." July 2002. Online at `http://wwwzenger.informatik.tu-muenchen.de/persons/huckle/bugse.html`.

Norris, Mark, Steve West, and Kevin Gaughan. *eBusiness Essentials: Technology and Network Requirements for the Electronic Marketplace.* New York: John Wiley & Sons, 2000.

Appendix A
Browser Basics

As Chapters 1 and 3 explained, a Web browser is a program for accessing and displaying Web pages. The two most popular Web browsers are Microsoft Internet Explorer and Netscape Navigator, both of which are free. Other freely available browsers are Mozilla, Safari, Opera, AOL, and Konquerer. While any of these suffices for viewing most pages, some subtle differences between them may affect the display of pages, especially with respect to newer features of the Web. The sections that follow describe how to perform common tasks using Internet Explorer and Netscape Navigator. The steps may vary slightly for the other browsers, and you are encouraged to read documentation pertaining to your browser of choice.

Microsoft Internet Explorer

Microsoft Internet Explorer (IE) is the most popular browser in the world today. It is automatically installed on all computers with Microsoft Windows operating systems, and it can also be downloaded for free from Microsoft's site: http://www.microsoft.com. As of January 2004, the latest versions available were Internet Explorer 6 for Windows and Internet Explorer 5 for Mac. Figures A.1 and A.2 show two slightly different appearances for Internet Explorer 6 based on operating system variations—the browser in Figure A.1 is running under Windows 98, whereas the one in Figure A.2 is running under Windows XP.

Starting Up the Browser

Since browsing the Web is a common task, your computer may have an Internet Explorer icon on the desktop or in the taskbar at the bottom of the screen.

If an IE icon appears in the desktop or the taskbar:
1. Double-click on the icon to start up the browser.

If an icon does not appear on the desktop or taskbar, then the browser program must be started through the system menus.

To start IE under the Windows operating system:
1. Click on the Start menu that appears in the bottom-left corner of the screen.
2. Click on the Internet Explorer icon to start up the browser.

To start IE under the Mac OS:
1. Click on the Finder icon in the tool bar at the bottom of the screen.
2. In the window that appears, double-click on the icon for the hard drive (commonly named Macintosh HD).
3. From the menu that appears, select Applications.
4. Click on the Internet Explorer icon to start up the browser.

When the browser window opens, the home page for that computer is automatically loaded. On a new computer, the home page is usually either Microsoft's site or else the Web site for the manufacturer of

Figure A.1   A Web page rendered by Internet Explorer 6 running under the Windows 98 operating system.

Figure A.2   A Web page rendered by Internet Explorer 6 running under the Windows XP operating system.

that computer. However, you can change the home page along with other settings (such as default fonts and colors).

To change the home page under the Windows operating system:

1. Click on the browser's Tools menu.
2. From that menu, select Internet Options.
3. In the Home Page box that appears, enter the desired Web address.
4. Click OK to close the window and save the new settings.

To change the home page under the Mac OS:

1. Click on the browser's Explorer menu.
2. From that menu, select Preferences . . . .
3. In the Home Page box that appears, enter the desired Web address.
4. Click OK to close the window and save the new settings.

Opening a Web Page

To direct the browser to load the page at a particular Web address, the simplest way is to directly enter the Web address in the Address box at the top of the browser window. Alternatively, you may go through the File menu to open a page.

To open a page in the browser (quick method):
1. Type the Web address for that page in the Address box at the top of the browser window.
2. Hit the Enter key, or click on the button labeled Go to load that page.

To open a page in the browser (general method):
1. Click on the browser's `File` menu.
2. From that menu, select `Open`.
3. In the box that appears, enter the desired Web address. If the page is stored locally on the same machine, you may click on the Browse button to select the folder and file name.

When opening a page that is stored on a remote Web server, you can omit the `http://` prefix to the Web address—the browser will automatically add it. Thus, the addresses `http://www.prenhall.com` and `www.prenhall.com` are equivalent.

When opening a page stored on the same computer that the browser is executing on, you must specify the full directory path. For example, if you want to load the file `personal.html` that is stored on a floppy disk (the A: drive), you can enter `A:\personal.html` in the Address box.

Navigating the Web

As you visit pages by entering specific Web addresses or clicking on links in pages, the browser maintains a history of the sites you have visited. The navigation buttons at the top of the browser can be used to move quickly among these recently visited sites.

- Clicking the Back button (left arrow) instructs the browser to move back in the history—that is, to the most recently visited Web page.
- If you have used the Back button to return to previously viewed pages, clicking the Forward button (right arrow) will move forward in the history.
- Clicking the Reload button (curved arrows) will reload the page that is currently in the browser window. This is especially useful when you are developing a Web page, since you can load the page, make changes to it in a separate editor, and then view those changes by clicking the Reload button.
- Clicking the Cancel button (the X) will cause the browser to stop loading the current page.
- Clicking the Home button (the house) will load the home page for the browser.

Viewing the Source of a Web Page

One of the attractive features of the Web, from a developer's standpoint, is its openness. Often you can learn by viewing the source code of other people's Web pages.

To view the HTML source for a Web page:
1. Click on the browser's `View` menu.
2. Select `Source`. The HTML source code for the current page will appear in a separate editor window.

Once the HTML source code for a page appears in the editor window, you are free to study that code, cut and paste sections (if the content is freely available), and even save a copy on your computer.

Downloading/Saving a Web Page

You can also download pages or their elements and save them on your own computer. In doing so, you must be careful not to violate copyrights or otherwise infringe upon the rights of the owner. Unless explicitly stated otherwise, you should assume that any image or page on the Web is private property.

To download a public image under the Windows operating system:
1. Click on the desired image using the right mouse button.
2. From the resulting menu, select `Save Picture As....`
3. A window will then open in which you can browse and select the folder and file name where you want the image stored.

To download a public image under the Mac OS:
1. Hold down the Control key and click on the desired image.
2. From the resulting menu, select `Download Image to Disk`.
3. A window will then open in which you can browse and select the folder and file name where you want the image stored.

Similarly, you can download an entire HTML document and save it on your computer. The simplest way is to download the page and all supporting files (e.g., images that appear in the page) at the same time.

To download a Web page and all supporting files:
1. Click on the browser's `File` menu.
2. From the resulting menu, select `Save As....`
3. A window will then open in which you can browse and select the folder and file name where you want the page stored.

With this sequence of commands, all of the supporting files are stored in a separate folder, and links within the page are adjusted to point to it. If you wish to download only the page itself, with the original links intact, you should instead follow the above instructions to view the source of that page, then save that source code directly from the text editor.

Netscape Navigator

Netscape Navigator was the first commercial Web browser on the market, and it still maintains a loyal following of Web users. It can be downloaded for free from Netscape's site: `http://www.netscape.com`. As of January 2004, the latest version available was Navigator 7 for both the Windows and Mac operating systems. Figure A.3 shows the appearance of Netscape Navigator 7 running under Windows XP.

Starting Up the Browser

Since browsing the Web is a common task, your computer may have a Netscape Navigator icon on the desktop or in the taskbar at the bottom of the screen.

If a Navigator icon appears in the desktop or the taskbar:
1. Double-click on the icon to start up the browser.

If an icon does not appear on the desktop or taskbar, then the browser program must be started through the system menus.

To start Navigator under the Windows operating system:
1. Click on the `Start` menu that appears in the bottom-left corner of the screen.
2. From that menu, select `All Programs`.

Figure A.3 A Web page rendered by Netscape Navigator 7 running under the Windows XP operating system.

3. Then, select Netscape Navigator from the list of programs, and click on the Navigator icon to start up the browser.

To start Navigator under the Mac OS:

1. Click on the `Finder` icon in the tool bar at the bottom of the screen.
2. In the window that appears, double-click on the icon for the hard drive (commonly named `Macintosh HD`).
3. From the menu that appears, select `Applications`.
4. Click on the Navigator icon to start up the browser.

When the browser window opens, the home page for that computer is automatically loaded. On a new computer, the home page is usually either Netscape's site or else the Web site for the manufacturer of that computer. However, you can change the home page along with other settings (such as default fonts and colors).

To change the home page for the browser:

1. Click on the browser's `Edit` menu.
2. From that menu, select `Preferences`.
3. In the Home Page box that appears, enter the desired Web address.
4. Click OK to close the window and save the new settings.

Opening a Web Page

To direct the browser to load the page at a particular Web address, the simplest way is to directly enter the Web address in the Address box at the top of the browser window. Alternatively, you may go through the File menu to open a page.

To open a page in the browser (quick method):

1. Type the Web address for that page in the Address box at the top of the browser window.
2. Hit the Enter key to load that page.

To open a page in the browser (general method):

1. Click on the browser's `File` menu.
2. If the desired page is stored on a remote Web server, select `Open Web Location` and enter the Web address in the box that appears.

3. If the desired page is stored locally on the same machine, select `Open File` and either enter the file name for that page, or else click on Browse in order to select the folder and file location.

When opening a page that is stored on a remote Web server, you can omit the `http://` prefix to the Web address—the browser will automatically add it. Thus, the addresses `http://www.prenhall.com` and `www.prenhall.com` are equivalent.

When opening a page that is stored on the same computer that the browser is executing on, you must specify the full directory path for the file. For example, if you want to load the file `personal.html` that is stored on a floppy disk (the A: drive), you can enter `A:\personal.html` in the Address box.

Navigating the Web

As you visit pages by entering specific Web address or clicking on links in pages, the browser maintains a history of the sites you have visited. The navigation buttons at the top of the browser can be used to move quickly among these recently visited sites.

- Clicking the Back button (left arrow) instructs the browser to move back in the history—that is, to the most recently visited Web page.
- If you have used the Back button to return to previously viewed pages, clicking the Forward button (right arrow) will move forward in the history.
- Clicking the Reload button (curved arrow) will reload the page that is currently in the browser window. This is especially useful when you are developing a Web page, since you can load the page, make changes to it in a separate editor, and then view those changes by clicking the Reload button.
- Clicking the Cancel button (the X) will cause the browser to stop loading the current page.
- Clicking the Home button (the N logo) will load the home page the for browser.

Viewing the Source of a Web Page

One of the attractive features of the Web, from a developer's standpoint, is its openness. Often you can learn by viewing the source code of other people's Web pages.

To view the HTML source for a Web page:
1. Click on the browser's `View` menu.
2. Select `Page Source`. The HTML source code for the current page will appear in a separate editor window.

Once the HTML source code for a page appears in the editor window, you are free to study that code, cut and paste sections (if the content is freely available), and even save a copy on your computer.

Downloading/Saving a Web Page

You can also download pages or their elements and save them or your own computer. In doing so, you must be careful not to violate copyrights or otherwise infringe upon the rights of the owner. Unless explicitly stated otherwise, you should assume that any image or page on the Web is private property.

To download a public image under the Windows operating system:
1. Click on the desired image using the right mouse button.
2. From the resulting menu, select `Save Image As....`
3. A window will then open in which you can browse and select the folder and file name where you want the image stored.

To download a public image under the Mac OS:
1. Hold down the Control key and click on the desired image.
2. From the resulting menu, select `Download Image to Disk`.

3. A window will then open in which you can browse and select the folder and file name where you want the image stored.

Similarly, you can download an entire HTML document and save it on your computer. The simplest way is to download the page and all supporting files (e.g., images that appear in the page) at the same time.

To download a Web page and all supporting files:
1. Click on the browser's File menu.
2. From the resulting menu, select Save Page As....
3. A window will then open in which you can browse and select the folder and file name where you want the page stored.

With this sequence of commands, all of the supporting files are stored in a separate folder, and links within the page are adjusted to point to it. If you wish to download only the page itself, with the original links intact, you should instead follow the above instructions to view the source of that page, then save that source code directly from the text editor.

Appendix B
Common Text Editors

Since a Web page is nothing more than a text file that contains special HTML tags, any text editor that can save documents as plain text files will suffice for developing your own Web pages. Both the Windows and Mac operating systems come with basic, general-purpose text editors: NotePad for Windows and TextEdit for the Mac. This appendix describes the basic operations of creating and editing Web pages using these two editors. However, you are strongly encouraged to obtain and use a special-purpose editor that is customized for Web pages. Web-customized text editors such as MEdit (`www.indus-soft.com`) use different colors and fonts to display HTML and JavaScript elements in a document, and thus make editing and debugging a Web page much simpler. Links to many freely available, Web-customized text editors can be found online at `http://webdevelopersjournal. com/software/html_editors.html`.

NotePad for Windows

NotePad is the basic text editor that comes preinstalled in the Windows operating system. While it lacks many of the advanced features of word processing programs and even Web-customized editors, it is simple to use and sufficient for creating and editing Web pages.

Starting Up NotePad

To start NotePad:
1. Click on the `Start` menu that appears in the bottom-left corner of the screen.
2. From that menu, select `All Programs`.
3. From the menu that appears, select `Accessories`.
4. Select NotePad from the list of accessories to start up the text editor.

Creating a New File

To create a new file:
1. Click on NotePad's `File` menu.
2. From that menu, select `New`.
3. An untitled document will appear in the editor window, and you can start typing in that document.

Opening an Existing File

To open an existing file:
1. Click on NotePad's `File` menu.
2. From that menu, select `Open`.
3. In the window that appears, click on the box labeled `Look in:` to select the directory where the file is stored.
4. Click on the icon for the desired file to select it. The name of that file will appear in the `File name:` box at the bottom of the window.
5. Click the Open button to open that file.

Figure B.1 The NotePad text editor running under the Windows XP operating system.

Saving a File

To save the file currently in the editor:

1. Click on NotePad's File menu.
2. From that menu, select Save. If this is a new file, you will be prompted for a file name. Enter the name in the File name: box. If you want the file stored in a location other than the default directory, click on the Save In: box to select the desired location (e.g., the a:\ drive). When saving a Web page, be sure to specify an extension of .html or .htm, as these extensions are automatically recognized by the browser when loading a page.
3. Click the Save button to save the file.

Copying a File

To save the file currently in the editor under a different name:

1. Click on NotePad's File menu.
2. From that menu, select Save As....
3. In the window that appears, click on the box labeled Save in: to select the directory where the file is be saved.
4. Enter the desired file name in the box labeled File name:. Again, be sure to specify an extension of .html or .htm, as these extensions are automatically recognized by the browser when loading a page.
5. Click the Save button to save the file.

Copy and Paste

When typing text into the editor, you can use the Enter key to move to the next line, and the Backspace key to back up and erase mistyped text. In addition, the arrow keys can be used to move from line to line and subsequently edit text.

For repetitive tasks, it is often useful to be able to copy entire sequences of text and then edit them as desired.

To copy and paste a section of text:
1. Highlight the desired section of text by clicking the mouse at the beginning of the text, holding the mouse button down, and dragging the mouse to the end of the section.
2. Under the Edit menu, select Copy. As a shortcut, you can simply hold down the Ctrl key and type C.
3. Move the mouse to the location in the file where you want the copy to be inserted.
4. Under the Edit menu, select Paste. As a shortcut, you can simply hold down the Ctrl key and type P.

You can undo the last editing action you performed by selecting Undo under the Edit menu. As a shortcut, you can simply hold down the Ctrl key and type U.

TextEdit for the Mac OS

TextEdit is the basic text editor that comes preinstalled in the Mac OS. While this editor lacks many of the advanced features of word processing programs and even Web-customized editors, it is simple to use and sufficient for creating and editing Web pages.

Figure B.2   The TextEdit text editor running under the Mac OS X operating system.

Starting Up TextEdit

To start TextEdit:
1. Click on the Finder icon in the tool bar at the bottom of the screen.
2. In the window that appears, double-click on the icon for the hard drive (commonly named Macintosh HD).
3. From the menu that appears, select Applications.
4. Click on the TextEdit icon to start up the editor.

Configuring TextEdit to Create and Edit Text Files

By default, TextEdit is configured to create files using the Rich Text Format (rtf). In order to create and edit plain text files, which are what you need for Web pages, you must alter the TextEdit Preferences.

To alter TextEdit Preferences for Web development:
1. Click on `TextEdit` menu.
2. From that menu, select `Preferences`.
3. Under the category `New Document Attributes`, click on the button next to `Plain text` so that a dot appears there instead of by `Rich text`.
4. Under the category `Rich text processing`, click on the box next to `Ignore rich text commands in HTML files` so that a check mark appears in the box.
5. Under the category `Saving`, click on the box next to `Append ".txt" extension to plain text files` so that the check mark disappears.

Creating a New File

To create a new file:
1. Click on TextEdit's `File` menu.
2. From that menu, select `New`.
3. An untitled document will appear in the editor window, and you can start typing in that document.

Opening an Existing File

To open an existing file:
1. Click on TextEdit's `File` menu.
2. From that menu, select `Open`.
3. In the window that appears, click on the box labeled `From:` to select the directory where the file is stored.
4. Click on the icon for the desired file to select it. The name of that file should appear in the `Go to:` box at the bottom of the window.
5. Click the Open button to open that file.

Saving a File

To save the file currently in the editor:
1. Click on TextEdit's `File` menu.
2. From that menu, select `Save`. If this is a new file, you will be prompted for a file name. Enter the name in the `Save as:` box. If you want the file stored in a location other than the default directory, click on the `Where:` box to select the desired location (e.g., the `a:\` drive). When saving a Web page, be sure to specify an extension of `.html` or `.htm`, as these extensions are automatically recognized by the browser when loading a page.
3. Click the Save button to save the file.

Copying a File

To save the file currently in the editor under a different name:
1. Click on TextEdit's `File` menu.
2. From that menu, select `Save As...`.
3. In the window that appears, click on the box labeled `Where:` to select the directory where the file is be saved.
4. Enter the desired file name in the box labeled `Save as:`. Again, be sure to specify an extension of `html` or `.htm`, as these extensions are automatically recognized by the browser when loading a page.
5. Click the Save button to save the file.

Copy and Paste

When typing text into the editor, you can use the Enter key to move to the next line, and the Backspace key to back up and erase mistyped text. In addition, the arrow keys can be used to move from line to line and subsequently edit text.

For repetitive tasks, it is often useful to be able to copy entire sequences of text and then edit them as desired.

To copy and paste a section of text:

1. Highlight the desired section of text by clicking the mouse at the beginning of the text, holding the mouse button down, and dragging the mouse to the end of the section.
2. Under the Edit menu, select Copy. As a shortcut, you can simply hold down the ⌘ key and type C.
3. Move the mouse to the location in the file where you want the copy to be inserted.
4. Under the Edit menu, select Paste. As a shortcut, you can simply hold down the ⌘ key and type P.

In addition, you can undo the last editing action you performed by selecting Undo under the Edit menu. As a shortcut, you can simply hold down the ⌘ key and type U.

Appendix C
HTML Reference

Document Structure

`<html> ... </html>`	**HTML:** top-level structure of a Web page.
`<head> ... </head>`	**Head:** section at the top of the document, specifying elements that should be interpreted first when the page loads.

`<body> ... </body>`
 	
optional attributes:
 `bgcolor="COLOR"`
 `background="IMAGE_FILE"`
	Body: section at the bottom of the document, specifying text and other HTML elements that will be rendered in the page. The background color can be set to a color or image using the `bgcolor` or `background` attribute, respectively.

`<title> ... </title>`	**Page Title:** text that will appear in the Title Bar at the top of the browser window.
`<!-- ... -->`	**Comment:** text that is ignored by the browser when rendering the page.

Text Spacing and Formatting

` `	**Break:** a line break that causes subsequent text to begin on the next line in the page.
` `	**Nonbreaking Space:** a space character that is explicitly rendered, overriding the automatic layout of text by the browser.
`<hr />`	**Horizontal Rule:** a line that is displayed across the browser window.
`<b> ... </b>`	**Bold:** text that is to be rendered in bold.
`<i> ... </i>`	**Italics:** text that is to be rendered in italic.
`<u> ... </u>`	**Underline:** text that is to be underlined.

Text Grouping and Headings

`<h1> ... </h1>`
`<h2> ... </h2>`
`...`
`<h6> ... </h6>`
	Headings: section headings that are rendered with blank lines before and after. The smaller the heading number, the larger the font used.

`<p> ... </p>`	**Paragraph:** a grouping of text that is rendered with blank lines before and after.
`<div> ... </div>`	**Page Division:** a grouping of text and/or page elements that can be formatted uniformly. A page division is rendered with blank lines before and after.
`<span> ... </span>`	**Text Span:** a grouping of text and/or HTML elements that can be formatted uniformly. A text span is not separated from surrounding text.

All grouping and heading elements have optional style attributes:
 	
`style="text-align:center"`
`style="text-align:left"`
`style="text-align:right"`
`style="text-align:justify"`
`style="color:COLOR_NAME"`
	The style attribute can be used to align elements in the page (centered, left justified, right justified, or full justified) or to set the color of text.

Hypertext and Multimedia

| `<a href="URL"> ... </a>`

optional attribute:
`target="_blank"` | **Anchor:** a hyperlink to a Web page at the specified URL. If the attribute `target="_blank"` is used, the page will open in a new browser window. |
| `<img src="URL" />`
optional attributes:
`alt="DESCRIPTIVE_TEXT"`
`width=NUMBER_OF_PIXELS`
`height=NUMBER_OF_PIXELS` | **Image:** an image that is stored in the file at the specified URL. Alternative text can be specified using `alt`, and the size of the image can be adjusted using `width` and `height`. |

Tables

`<table> ... </table>`
 	
optional attribute:
`border=WIDTH_IN_PIXELS`
	Table: a collection of text or HTML elements organized into rows and columns. By default, the border between rows and columns is invisible, but it can be made visible by specifying a border width.

`<tr> ... </tr>`	**Table Row:** a sequence of elements that will appear in a row of the table.
`<td> ... </td>`	**Table Data (column):** a data element that will appear in a column of a particular row in the table.

Lists

`<ul> ... </ul>`
 	
optional attribute:
    `style="list-style-type:square"`
	Unordered List: a sequence of items, each preceded by a round bullet (or a square bullet if the style attribute is used).

`<ol> ... </ol>`
optional attributes:
  `style="list-style-type:lower-alpha"`
  `style="list-style-type:upper-alpha"`
  `style="list-style-type:lower-roman"`
  `style="list-style-type:upper-roman"`
	Ordered List: a sequence of numbered items. The style attribute can be used to specify letters or roman numerals instead of numbers.

`<li> ... </li>`	**List Item:** an item that appears within an unordered or ordered list.

Programming and Event Handling

`<script type="text/javascript> ... </script>`	**JavaScript Code:** statements that are to be executed by the browser's built-in JavaScript interpreter.
`<form name="FORM_NAME"> ... </form>`	**Form:** a collection of interactive elements in the page.
`<input type="button" value="BUTTON_LABEL"` `onClick="JAVASCRIPT_CODE" />`	**Button:** a form element that serves as a clickable button. When clicked, the code specified by the onClick attribute is executed.

`<input type="text" name="TEXTBOX_NAME"`
`size=NUM_CHARS value="INITIAL_TEXT" />`
 	
optional attributes:
  `onFocus="JAVASCRIPT_CODE"`
  `onChange="JAVASCRIPT_CODE"`
	Text Box: a form element that displays a single line of text. Attributes can specify actions to take place when the user clicks or types in the box.

`<textarea name="TEXTAREA_NAME"`
`rows=NUM_ROWS cols=NUM_COLS wrap="virtual">`
`INITIAL_TEXT`
`</textarea>`
optional attributes:
  `onFocus="JAVASCRIPT_CODE"`
  `onChange="JAVASCRIPT_CODE"`
	Text Area: a form element that displays multiple lines of text. Attributes can specify actions to take place when the user clicks or types in the area.

Common HTML Colors

aqua	darkgray	green	navy	royalblue	tan
beige	darkgreen	greenyellow	olive	silver	teal
blue	darkred	lightblue	orange	skyblue	violet
black	fuchsia	lightgreen	pink	slateblue	wheat
brown	gold	lightgrey	purple	slategray	yellow
darkblue	gray	mediumblue	red	steelblue	yellowgreen

Appendix D
JavaScript Reference

Variables

`Legal variable name:` consists of letters, digits and underscores, and must begin with a letter

Reserved words that shouldn't be used as variable names because they are already used by JavaScript or the browser.				
abstract	delete	function	null	throw
boolean	do	goto	package	throws
break	double	if	private	transient
byte	else	implements	protected	true
case	enum	import	public	try
catch	export	in	return	typeof
char	extends	instanceof	short	var
class	false	int	static	void
const	final	interface	super	volatile
continue	finally	long	switch	while
debugger	float	native	synchronized	with
default	for	new	this	

Data Types

Data Type	Examples
Number	1 −1024 18.0 3.14159 1.024e3
String	" " "foo" "2 words" 'uses single quotes'
Boolean	true false

Mathematical Operators

Operator	Name	Examples	
+	Addition	2 + 12	evaluates to 14
		4 + 7.432	evaluates to 11.432
−	Subtraction	7 − 2	evaluates to 5
		5 - 3.359	evaluates to 1.641
*	Multiplication	2 * 5	evaluates to 10
		10 * 9.773	evaluates to 97.73
/	Division	10 / 4	evaluates to 2.5
		2.5 / 8	evaluates to 0.3125
%	Remainder	10 % 4	evaluates to 2
		2 % 0.75	evaluates to 0.5

Comparison Operators

Operator	Name	Examples	
==	Equality	3 == 3	evaluates to true
		"foo" == "bar"	evaluates to false
		false == false	evaluates to true
!=	Inequality	12 != 39	evaluates to true
		"foo" != "bar"	evaluates to true
		false != false	evaluates to false
<	Less Than	2 < 3.1415	evaluates to true
		"b" < "a"	evaluates to false*
<=	Less Than or Equal To	17 <= 17	evaluates to true
		"ABD" <= "ABC"	evaluates to false*
>	Greater Than	12 > −4	evaluates to true
		"bar" > "foo"	evaluates to false*
>=	Greater Than or Equal To	3.99 >= 3.98	evaluates to true
		"foo" >= "fool"	evaluates to false*

*Strings follow standard dictionary ordering, i.e.,
"A" < "B" < . . . < "Z" < "a" < "b" . . . < "z"
"a" < "aa" < . . . < "ab" < "aba" < . . . < "b"

Logical (Boolean) Connectives

Operator	Name	Examples	
&&	AND	true && true	evaluates to true
		true && false	evaluates to false
		false && true	evaluates to false
		false && false	evaluates to false
||	OR	true || true	evaluates to true
		true || false	evaluates to true
		false || true	evaluates to true
		false || false	evaluates to false
!	NOT	!true	evaluates to false
		!false	evaluates to true

Statements

Statement	General Form	Examples
Comment	// Comment. . .	// A one-line comment.
	/* Comment. . . */	/* A comment that spans two lines */

Assignment Statement	VARIABLE = VALUE_OR_EXPRESSION;	x = 7.5;
		firstName = "Dave";
		done = false;
		
		y = (x + 1) * 3;
		msg = "Hi " + firstName;

If Statement	if (BOOLEAN_TEST) {
	    STATEMENTS_EXECUTED_IF_TRUE
	}
		if (x < 0) {
		  x = 0 − x;
		}

	if (BOOLEAN_TEST) {
	    STATEMENTS_EXECUTED_IF_TRUE
	}
	else {
	    STATEMENTS_EXECUTED_IF_FALSE
	}
		if (user == "Dave") {
		  found = true;
		}
		else {
		  found = false;
		}

While Loop	while (BOOLEAN_TEST) {
	    STMTS_EXECUTED_AS_LONG_AS_TRUE
	}
		while (x >= 0) {
		  x = x − 5;
		}

|  | | | ```
reps = 1;
while (reps < = 10) {
  document.write("Hi");
  reps = reps + 1;
}
``` |
| For Loop | ```
for (INIT; BOOLEAN_TEST; UPDATE)
    STMTS_EXECUTED_AS_LONG_AS_TRUE
}
``` | | ```
for (r=1; r<=10; r=r+1) {
  document.write("Hi");
}
``` |

Predefined Functions

Function	Description	Input → Output	Examples	
Math.sqrt	Square Root	*Number → Number*	Math.sqrt(9)	returns 3
Math.abs	Absolute Value	*Number → Number*	Math.abs(−23) Math.abs(99)	returns 23 returns 99
Math.max	Maximum Value	*2 Numbers → Number*	Math.max(3, 14)	returns 14
Math.min	Minimum Value	*2 Numbers → Number*	Math.min(3, 14)	returns 3
Math.pow	Raise to a Power	*2 Numbers → Number*	Math.pow(2, 3)	returns 8
Math.floor	Round Down	*Number → Number*	Math.floor(3.14159) Math.floor(4.5623)	returns 3 returns 4
Math.ceil	Round Up	*Number → Number*	Math.ceil(3.14159) Math.ceil(4.5623)	returns 4 returns 5
Math.round	Round to Nearest	*Number → Number*	Math.round(3.14159) Math.round(4.5623)	returns 3 returns 5
parseFloat	Convert to Number	*String → Number*	parseFloat("12.8") parseFloat("ABC")	returns 12.8 returns NaN
alert	Open Alert Window	*String → undefined*	alert("Welcome to my page.") opens a new window with the message Welcome to my page.	
prompt	Open Prompt Window	*2 Strings → String*	prompt("Enter your name", "???") opens a new window with the message Enter your name and a text box. Returns the value entered in the box (??? by default).	
document.write	Write	*String → undefined*	document.write("Howdy") displays Howdy in the page. document.write("foo"+2) displays foo2 in the page (the number 2 is converted to "2").	
```

User-Defined Functions

Action	General Form	Examples

Function Definition	```function FUNC_NAME(PARAM1, PARAM2, ...)```
	```// Assumes: ASSUMPTIONS ABOUT PARAMS```
	```// Returns: VALUE RETURNED BY FUNCTION```
	```{```
	```var VAR1, VAR2, ...; // optional```
	
	```STATEMENTS_TO_BE_EXECUTED```
	
	```return RETURN-VALUE; // optional```
	```}```
		```function Stars(N)```
		```// Assumes: N > = 0```
		```// Returns: string of N stars```
		```{```
		``` var theStr;```
		
		``` theStr = "";```
		``` while (N > 0)```
		``` theStr = theStr + "*";```
		``` N = N - 1;```
		``` }```
		``` return theStr;```
		```}```
		
		```function Greet(name)```
		```// Assumes: name is a string```
		```// Results: displays greeting```
		```{```
		``` document.write ("Hi "+ name);```
		```}```

Function Call	```FUNC_NAME(INPUT1, INPUT2, ...)```	```str = Stars(5);```
		```// Result: str == "*****"```
		
		```Greet("Dave");```
		```// Result: displays Hi Dave```

Strings

Property	Description	Examples (assuming word = "Foo 2";)	
length	Specifies the number of characters in the string.	word.length	evaluates to 5

Methods	Description	Examples (assuming word = "Foo 2";)	
+	Concatenation operator: appends two strings end to end	"ab" + "cd" word + "U"	evaluates to "abcd" evaluates to "Foo 2U"
toUpperCase	Returns a copy of the string with all letters made uppercase	word.toUpperCase()	evaluates to "FOO 2"

toLowerCase	Returns a copy of the string with all letters made lowercase	`word.toLowerCase()`	evaluates to "foo 2"

charAt	Returns the character stored at a particular index	`word.charAt(0)`
		`word.charAt(1)`
		`word.charAt(4)`
		`word.charAt(5)`
			evaluates to "F"
			evaluates to "o"
			evaluates to "2"
			evaluates to " "

substring	Returns a sequence of characters from a string, specified by starting and ending indices	`word.substring(0, 3)`
		`word.charAt(4, 5)`
		`word.charAt(1, 3)`
			evaluates to "Foo"
			evaluates to "2"
			evaluates to "oo"

search	Returns the index of the first occurrence of a character, substring, or class of characters	`word.search("f")`
		`word.search("oo")`
		`word.search(/[0-9]/)`
		`word.search("x")`
			evaluates to 0
			evaluates to 1
			evaluates to 4
			evaluates to −1

split	Splits the string based on the specified delimiter, and returns the substrings in an array	`word.split(" ")` `word.split(/[ \t]/)`	evaluates to ["foo", "2"] evaluates to ["foo", "2"]

Arrays

Property	Description	Examples (assuming `arr = [1, "foo", 3.8];`)	
length	Specifies the number of items in the array	`arr.length`	evaluates to 3
Methods	**Description**	**Examples** (assuming `arr = [1, "foo", 3.8];`)	

[]	Indexing operator: returns the item stored at the specified index	`arr[0]`
		`arr[1]`
		`arr[2]`
		`arr[3]`
			evaluates to 1
			evaluates to "foo"
			evaluates to 3.8
			evaluates to undefined

sort	Returns a copy of the array, with items sorted into increasing order	`arr.sort()`
		
		`nums = [3, 6, 2.7];`
		`nums.sort()`
		`strs.sort()`
			evaluates to [1, 3.8, "foo"]
			
			evaluates to [2.7, 3, 6]
			evaluates to ["a", "ab", "xy"]

Manipulating HTML Form Elements

Action	General Form	Examples

Accessing the contents of a text box (or text area)	`document.FORM_NAME.BOX_NAME.value`
	
	`document.FORM_NAME.AREA_NAME.value`
		`document.Names.First.value = "Alan";`
		`user = document.Names.First.value;`

Accessing the source of an image	`document.images.IMAGE_NAME.src`	`document.images.pic.src = "sad.gif";` `moodFile = document.images.pic.src;`

Appendix E
random.js Library

```
// File:    random.js
// Author: Dave Reed
//
// This file contains several routines for generating random values.
// Source code is available at http://www.prenhall.com/reed
/////////////////////////////////////////////////////////////////////

function RandomNum(low, high)
// Given   : low <= high
// Returns : a random number in the range [low, high)
{
    return Math.random()*(high-low) + low;
}

function RandomInt(low, high)
// Given   : low <= high
// Returns : a random integer in the range [low, high]
{
    return Math.floor(Math.random()*(high-low+1)) + low;
}

function RandomChar(str)
// Given  : str is a nonempty string
// Returns: a random character from the string
{
    return str.charAt(RandomInt(0, str.length-1));
}

function RandomOneOf(list)
// Given  : list is a nonempty list (array)
// Returns: a random item from the list
{
    return list[RandomInt(0, list.length-1)];
}
```

Index

Photo Credits

Cover Image	Digital Vision Ltd.
Chapter Opening Figure	Nicolas Rigg/Digital Vision Ltd.

Chapter 1

Figure 1.1a	David Parker/Science Photo Library. Photo Researchers, Inc.
Figure 1.1b	Dell, Inc.
Figure 1.1c	Fujitsu Siemens Computers
Figure 1.1d	PalmOne, Inc.
Figure 1.9d	palmOne, Zire, Tungsten, Treo, logos, stylizations, and design marks associated with all the preceding and trade dress associated with palmOne, Inc.TM's products, are among the trademarks or registered trademarks owned by or exclusively licensed to palmOne, Inc.
Figure 1.3	Courtesy of International Business Machines Corporation. Unauthorized use not permitted.
Figure 1.5a	Intel Corporation Museum Archives and Collection. Photo courtesy of Intel Corporation.
Figure 1.5b	Intel Corporation Pressroom Photo Archives
Figure 1.8a	Kingston Technology Company
Figure 1.8b	Seagate Technology
Figure 1.8c	PhotoDisc/Getty Images
Figure 1.8d	Dorling Kindersley Media Library
Figure 1.9a	©2004 Dell Inc. All Rights Reserved.
Figure 1.9b	palmOne, Zire, Tungsten, Treo, logos, stylizations, and design marks associated with all the preceding and trade dress associated with palmOne, Inc.^{TM}'s products, are among the trademarks or registered trademarks owned by or exclusively licensed to palmOne, Inc.
Figure 1.10	Screen shots reprinted by permission from Apple Computer.
Figure 1.11	Screen shot reprinted by permission from Microsoft Corporation.
Figure 1.12a	PhotoDisc/Getty Images
Figure 1.12b	©Tom Wagner/CORBIS SABA

Chapter 3

Figure 3.1	Courtesy MIT Museum
Figure 3.2	Dr. Lawrence G. Roberts
Figures 3.3, 3.4, and 3.5	Cybergeography.org
Figure 3.13	Photo Courtesy of CERN
Figure 3.14	AP/Wide World Photos

Chapter 6

Figure 6.2	Science Museum/Science and Society Picture Library
Figure 6.3	Deutsches Museum
Figure 6.4	Corbis/Bettmann
Figure 6.5	Getty Images Inc.–Hulton Archive Photos
Figure 6.6	Grant Braught
Figure 6.7	Paul and Linda Marie Ambrose. Getty Images, Inc.–Taxi
Figure 6.8	Photo Courtesy of The Computer History Museum
Figure 6.9	U.S. Army
Figure 6.10	Courtesy of the Archives of the Institute for Advanced Study. Photographer: Alan Richards.
Figure 6.11	Corbis/Bettmann
Figure 6.12	Astrid and Hans Freider. Photo Researchers, Inc.
Figure 6.13	Photodisc/Getty Images
Figure 6.14	Michael W. Davidson at Florida State University
Figure 6.16	AP/Wide World Photos
Figure 6.17	Reprinted with permission from Microsoft Corporation.

Chapter 8

Figure 8.2	British Museum, London, UK/Bridgeman Art Library
Figure 8.7	Sir Isaac Newton, engraved by W.T. Fry. Library of Congress
Figure 8.12	© Wally McNamee/CORBIS